CliffsAP®

5 Chemistry Practice Exams

CliffsAP®

5 Chemistry Practice Exams

by

Gary S. Thorpe, M.S.

Consultant

Jerry Bobrow, Ph.D.

WILEY

Wiley Publishing, Inc.

About the Author

Gary S. Thorpe has taught AP Chemistry, College Chemistry, and gifted programs for over 30 years. Recipient of numerous awards in teaching. He is currently on staff at Beverly Hills High School, Beverly Hills, California.

Author's Acknowledgments

I would like to thank my wife, Patti, and my two daughters, Kris and Erin, for their patience and understanding while I was writing this book. I would also like to acknowledge Dr. Jerry Bobrow of Bobrow Test Preparation Services and Christopher Bushee for their input, proofreading, and suggestions.

Publisher's Acknowledgments

Editorial

Acquisitions Editor: Greg Tubach

Project Editor: Donna Wright

Technical Editor: Christopher Bushee

Composition

Proofreader: Tricia Liebig

Wiley Publishing, Inc. Composition Services

CliffsAP® 5 Chemistry Practice Exams

Published by:
Wiley Publishing, Inc.
111 River Street
Hoboken, NJ 07030-5774
www.wiley.com

Copyright © 2006 Wiley, Hoboken, NJ

Published by Wiley, Hoboken, NJ
Published simultaneously in Canada

Library of Congress Cataloging-in-Publication Data

Thorpe, Gary S.
  CliffsAP 5 chemistry practice exams / by Gary S. Thorpe.
    p. cm. — (CliffsAP)
  ISBN-13: 978-0-471-77026-8 (pbk.)
  ISBN-10: 0-471-77026-4 (pbk.)
  1. Chemistry—Examinations—Study guides. 2. Advanced placement programs (Education)—Examinations—Study guides. 3. Universities and colleges—United States—Entrance examinations—Study guides. I. Title. II. Title: CliffsAP five chemistry practice exams. III. Series.
  QD42.T493 2006
  540.76—dc22
2006008782

ISBN-13 978-0-471-77026-8

ISBN-10 0-471-77026-4

10 9 8 7 6 5 4 3 2 1

1B/RZ/QV/QW/IN

WILEY

Table of Contents

Introduction

College-level lectures, tests, quizzes, homework problems, and labs are to be evaluated in a 3-hour examination. It's just you and the AP exam. In preparing to do the very best job possible, you have four options:

1. Read your entire textbook again.
2. Do all of your homework problems again.
3. Buy a test preparation guide that has every conceivable type of problem in it. In many cases, it will be thicker than your textbook, and you'll never be able to finish. That test preparation guide **MAY NOT** explain how to do well on the essay portion of the exam and **MAY** not review all of the laboratory experiments required and tested.
4. Use *CliffsAP Chemistry,* 3rd Edition and this book, *CliffsAP 5 Chemistry Practice Exams.*

I'm glad you chose option four. I've taught chemistry for over 30 years. I've put together in this book, what I believe are the most up-to-date type of questions that you will experience on the AP Chemistry Exam. Each question is thoroughly explained, and the format of each practice exam is exactly what you will see when you take the actual exam. With other AP exams to study for and other time commitments, you need a quick set of practice exams that will cover everything you need to know. With *CliffsAP Chemistry,* 3rd Edition to help you cover in more detail the topics covered in the practice exams, you will be absolutely prepared.

The Practice Exams

You will be given five practice AP Chemistry Exams. Each practice exam is formatted exactly to the actual AP exams. Time limits are included. Each multiple-choice question and free-response (essay) question is thoroughly explained.

This book is not a textbook. The last thing you need to study right now is your AP Chemistry textbook. It's too large and doesn't provide you with the type of exam you will be seeing shortly. By taking the five practice exams in this book and reviewing your mistakes, you will ace the AP Chemistry Exam.

Study Guide Checklist

❑ Read the *Advanced Placement Course Description—Chemistry* (also commonly known as the "Acorn Book") produced by Educational Testing Service (ETS) and available from your AP Chemistry teacher, testing office, counseling center, or directly from The College Board.

❑ Read the Introduction to this book including the "Topics Covered by the AP Chemistry Exam," "Questions Commonly Asked About the AP Chemistry Exam," and "Strategies for Taking the AP Chemistry Exam."

❑ Purchase *CliffsAP Chemistry*, 3rd Edition. Use that book along with this book for a more comprehensive review of chemistry topics. *CliffsAP Chemistry* also reviews all labs that you will be tested on. No other book on the market does that.

❑ Take Practice Exam 1. Be careful to follow the time allowed.

❑ Check your answers for Practice Exam 1 and predict your actual score.

❑ Take Practice Exam 2. Be careful to follow the time allowed.

❑ Check your answers for Practice Exam 2 and predict your actual score.

❑ Take Practice Exam 3. Be careful to follow the time allowed.

❑ Check your answers for Practice Exam 3 and predict your actual score.

❑ Take Practice Exam 4. Be careful to follow the time allowed.

❑ Check your answers for Practice Exam 4 and predict your actual score.

❑ Take Practice Exam 5. Be careful to follow the time allowed.

❑ Check your answers for Practice Exam 5 and predict your actual score.

Format of the AP Chemistry Exam

Section I: Multiple-Choice Questions

90 minutes

75 questions   45% of total grade

Periodic table provided; no calculators allowed; no table of equations or constants provided.

Section II: Free-Response (Essay) Questions

Periodic table, a table of standard reduction potentials, and a table containing various equations and constants are provided.

90 minutes

6 questions   55% of total grade

Part A: 40 minutes; calculator allowed (no qwerty keyboards). Any programmable or graphing calculator may be used, and you will not be required to erase the calculator memories before or after the examination. Questions require mathematical computations. It is essential that you show all steps in solving mathematical problems because partial credit is awarded for each problem that shows how the answer was obtained.

Question 1 (Required): 20%   Always on equilibrium: K_{sp}, K_a, K_b, K_c, or K_p

Question 2 or 3 (Choose either one): 20%   Only one of these problems will be scored. If you start both problems, be sure to cross out the one you do not want scored. Both questions require mathematical computations.

Part B: 50 minutes; calculator not allowed. Questions do not require mathematical computations.

Question 4 (Required): 15%   Write the formulas to show the reactants and the products for any five of eight chemical reactions. Each of the reactions occurs in aqueous solution unless otherwise indicated. Represent substances in solution as ions if the substance is extensively ionized. Omit formulas for any ions or molecules that are unchanged by the reaction. In all cases a reaction occurs. You need not balance the equations.

Question 5 (Required): 15%

Question 6 (Required): 15%

Question 7 or 8 (Choose either one): 15%   Only one of the problems will be scored. If you start both problems, be sure to cross out the one you do not want scored.

Format and allotment time may vary slightly from year to year.

Topics Covered by the AP Chemistry Exam

I. Structure of Matter (20%)

   A. Atomic theory and atomic structure

      1. Evidence for the atomic theory

      2. Atomic masses; determination by chemical and physical means

      3. Atomic number and mass number, isotopes

      4. Electron energy levels: atomic spectra, quantum numbers, atomic orbitals

      5. Periodic relationships including, for example, atomic radii, ionization energies, electron affinities, oxidation states

B. Chemical bonding

  1. Binding forces

    a. Types: ionic, covalent, metallic, hydrogen bonding, van der Waals (including London dispersion forces)

    b. Relationships to states, structure, and properties of matter

    c. Polarity of bonds, electronegativities

  2. Molecular models

    a. Lewis structures

    b. Valence bond: hybridization of orbitals, resonance, sigma and pi bonds

    c. VSEPR

  3. Geometry of molecules and ions, structural isomerism of simple organic molecules and coordination complexes, dipole moments of molecules, relation of properties to structure

C. Nuclear chemistry: nuclear equations, half-lives, radioactivity, chemical applications

II. States of Matter (20%)

A. Gases

  1. Laws of ideal gases

    a. Equation of state for an ideal gas

    b. Partial pressures

  2. Kinetic-molecular theory

    a. Interpretation of ideal gas laws on the basis of this theory

    b. Avogadro's hypothesis and the mole concept

    c. Dependence of kinetic energy of molecules on temperature

    d. Deviations from ideal gas laws

B. Liquids and solids

  1. Liquids and solids from the kinetic-molecular viewpoint

  2. Phase diagrams of one-component systems

  3. Changes of state, including critical points and triple points

  4. Structure of solids, lattice energies

C. Solutions

  1. Types of solutions and factors affecting solubility

  2. Methods of expressing concentration (the use of formalities is not tested)

  3. Raoult's Law and colligative properties (nonvolatile solutes); osmosis

  4. Non-ideal behavior (qualitative aspects)

III. Reactions (35–40%)

A. Reaction types

  1. Acid-base reactions; concepts of Arrhenius, Brønsted-Lowry, and Lewis; coordination complexes, amphoterism

  2. Precipitation reactions

    3. Oxidation-reduction reactions

      a. Oxidation number

      b. The role of the electron in oxidation-reduction

      c. Electrochemistry: electrolytic and galvanic cells, Faraday's laws, standard half-cell potentials, Nernst equation, prediction of the direction of redox reactions

B. Stoichiometry

    1. Ionic and molecular species present in chemical systems: net ionic equations

    2. Balancing of equations including those for redox reactions

    3. Mass and volume relations with emphasis on the mole concept, including empirical formulas and limiting reactants

C. Equilibrium

    1. Concept of dynamic equilibrium (physical and chemical), Le Chatelier's principle, equilibrium constants

    2. Quantitative treatment

      a. Equilibrium constants for gaseous reactions: K_p, K_c

      b. Equilibrium constants for reactions in solution

        (1) Constants for acids and bases: pK_a, pK_b, pH

        (2) Solubility product constants and their application to precipitation and the dissolution of slightly soluble compounds

        (3) Common ion effect, buffers, hydrolysis

D. Kinetics

    1. Concept of rate of reaction

    2. Use of experimental data and graphical analysis to determine reactant order, rate constants, and reaction rate laws

    3. Effect of temperature change on rates

    4. Energy of activation, the role of catalysts

    5. The relationship between the rate-determining step and a mechanism

E. Thermodynamics

    1. State functions

    2. First law: change in enthalpy, heat of formation, heat of reaction, Hess's Law, heats of vaporization and fusion, calorimetry

    3. Second law: entropy, free energy of formation, free energy of reaction, dependence of change in free energy on enthalpy and entropy changes

    4. Relationship of change in free energy to equilibrium constants and electrode potentials

IV. Descriptive Chemistry (10–15%)

    1. Chemical reactivity and products of chemical reactions

    2. Relationships in the periodic table: horizontal, vertical, and diagonal with examples from alkali metals, alkaline earth metals, halogens, and the first series of transition elements

    3. Introduction to organic chemistry: hydrocarbons and functional groups (structure, nomenclature, chemical properties)

V. Laboratory (5–10%)

Refer to *CliffsAP Chemistry,* 3rd Edition for a complete review of all 22 labs.

1. Determination of the empirical formula of a compound
2. Determination of the percentage water in a hydrate
3. Determination of molar mass by vapor density
4. Determination of molecular mass by freezing-point depression
5. Determination of the molar volume of a gas
6. Standardization of a solution using a primary standard
7. Determination of concentration by acid-base titration, including a weak acid or weak base
8. Determination of concentration by oxidation-reduction titration
9. Determination of mass and mole relationships in a chemical reaction
10. Determination of the equilibrium constant for a chemical reaction
11. Determination of appropriate indicators for various acid-base titrations, pH determination
12. Determination of the rate of a reaction and its order
13. Determination of enthalpy change associated with a reaction and Hess's Law
14. Separation and qualitative analysis of cations and anions
15. Synthesis of a coordination compound and its chemical analysis
16. Analytical gravimetric determination
17. Colorimetric or spectrophotometric analysis
18. Separation by chromatography
19. Preparation and properties of a buffer solution
20. Determination of electrochemical series
21. Measurement using electrochemical cells and electroplating
22. Synthesis, purification, and analysis of an organic compound

Questions Commonly Asked About the AP Chemistry Exam

Q. **What is the AP Chemistry Exam?**

A. The AP Chemistry Exam is given once a year to high school students to test their knowledge of concepts in first-year college-level chemistry. The student who passes the AP exam may receive 1 year of college credit for taking AP Chemistry in high school. Passing is generally considered to be achieving a score of 3, 4, or 5. The test is administered each May. It has two sections.

- Section I, worth 45% of the total score, is 90 minutes long and consists of 75 multiple-choice questions. The total score for Section I is the number of correct answers minus ¼ for each wrong answer. If you leave a question unanswered, it does not count at all. A student generally needs to answer from 50% to 60% of the multiple-choice questions correctly to obtain a 3 on the exam. The multiple-choice questions fall into three categories:

    Calculations—These questions require you to quickly calculate mathematical solutions. Because you will not be allowed to use a calculator for the multiple-choice questions, the questions requiring calculations have been limited to simple arithmetic so that they can be done quickly, either mentally or with paper and pencil. Also, for some questions, the answer choices differ by several orders of magnitude so that the questions can be answered by estimation.

Conceptual—These questions ask you to consider how theories, laws, or concepts are applied.

Factual—These questions require you to quickly recall important chemical facts.

- Section II, worth 55% of the total score, is 90 minutes long and consists of four parts—one equilibrium problem, one mathematical essay, writing and predicting five chemical equations, and three nonmathematical essays.

Q. What are the advantages of taking AP Chemistry?

A. Students who pass the exam may, at the discretion of the college in which the student enrolls, be given full college credit for taking the class in high school.

- Taking the exam improves your chance of getting into the college of your choice. Studies show that students who successfully participate in AP programs in high school stand a much better chance of being accepted by selective colleges than students who do not.
- Taking the exam reduces the cost of a college education. In the many private colleges that charge upward of $500 a unit, a first-year college chemistry course could cost as much as $3,000. Taking the course during high school saves money.
- Taking the exam may reduce the time needed to earn a college degree.
- If you take the course and the exam while still in high school, you will not be faced with the college course being closed or overcrowded.
- For those of you who are planning on a science career, passing the AP Chemistry Exam may fulfill the laboratory science requirement at the college, thus making more time available for you to take other courses.
- Taking AP Chemistry greatly improves your chances of doing well in college chemistry. You will already have covered most of the topics during your high school AP Chemistry program, and you will find yourself setting the curve in college.

Q. Do all colleges accept AP exam grades for college credit?

A. Almost all of the colleges and universities in the United States and Canada, and many in Europe, take part in the AP program. The vast majority of the 2,900 U.S. colleges and universities that receive AP grades grant credit and/or advanced placement. Even colleges that receive only a few AP candidates and may not have specific AP policies are often willing to accommodate AP students who inquire about advanced placement work.

To find out about a specific policy for the AP exam(s) you plan to take, contact the college's Director of Admissions. You should receive a written reply telling you how much credit and/or advanced placement you will receive for a given grade on an AP exam, including any courses you will be allowed to enter.

The best source of specific and up-to-date information about an individual institution's policy is its catalog or website. Other sources of information include The College Handbook with College Explorer CD-ROM and College-Search. For more information on these and other products, log on to the College Board's online store at http://store.collegeboard.com/enter.do.

Q. How is the AP exam graded and what do the scores mean?

A. The AP exam is graded on a five-point scale:

5: Extremely well qualified. About 15% of the students who take the exam earn this grade.

4: Well qualified. Roughly 18% earn this grade.

3: Qualified. Generally, 23% earn this grade.

2: Possibly qualified. Generally considered "not passing." About 22% of the students who take the exam earn this grade.

1: Not qualified. About 24% earn this grade.

Of the roughly 78,000 students who take the AP Chemistry Exam each year, the average grade is 2.80 with a standard deviation of 1.38. Approximately 1,500 colleges receive AP scores from students who pass the AP Chemistry Exam.

Section I, the multiple-choice section, is machine graded. Each question has five answers to choose from. Remember, there is a penalty for guessing: $\frac{1}{4}$ point is taken off for each wrong answer. A student generally needs to correctly answer 50% to 60% of the multiple-choice questions to obtain a 3 on the exam. Each answer in Section II, the free-response section, is read several times by different chemistry instructors who pay great attention to consistency in grading.

Q. Are there old exams out there that I could look at?

A. Yes. Questions (and answers) from previous exams are available from The College Board. Request an order form by contacting: AP Services, P.O. Box 66721, Princeton, NJ 08541-6671; (609) 771-7300 or (888) 225-5427; Fax (609) 530-0482; TTY (609) 882-4118; http://apcentral.collegeboard.com or e-mail: apexams@ets.org.

Q. What materials should I take to the Exam?

A. Be sure to take your admission ticket, some form of photo and signature identification, your social security number, several sharpened No. 2 pencils, a good eraser, a watch, and a scientific calculator with fresh batteries. You may bring a programmable calculator (it will not be erased or cleared), but it must not have a typewriter-style (qwerty) keyboard. You may use the calculator only in Section II, Part A.

Q. When will I get my score?

A. The exam itself is generally given in the second or third week of May. The scores are usually available during the second or third week of July.

Q. Should I guess on the test?

A. Except in certain cases explained later in this book, you should not guess. There is a penalty for guessing on the multiple-choice section of the exam. As for the free-response section, it simply comes down to whether you know the material or not.

Q. Suppose I do terribly on the test. May I cancel the test and/or scores?

A. You may cancel an AP grade permanently only if the request is received by June 15 of the year in which the exam was taken. There is no fee for this service, but a signature is required to process the cancellation. After a grade is cancelled, it is permanently deleted from the records.

You may also request that one or more of your AP grades are not included in the report sent to colleges. There is a $5 fee for each score not included in the report.

Q. May I write on the test?

A. Yes. Because scratch paper is not provided, you'll need to write in the test booklet. Make your notes in the booklet near the questions so that if you have time at the end, you can go back to your notes to try to answer the question.

Q. How do I register or get more information?

A. For further information contact: AP Services, P.O. Box 66721, Princeton, NJ 08541-6671; (609) 771-7300 or (888) 225-5427; Fax (609) 530-0482; TTY (609) 882-4118; log on to the College Board's website or e-mail: apexams@ets.org.

Strategies for Taking the AP Chemistry Exam

Section I: The Multiple-Choice Section

The "Plus-Minus" System

Many students who take the AP Chemistry Exam do not get their best possible score on Section I because they spend too much time on difficult questions and fail to leave themselves enough time to answer the easy ones. Don't let this happen to you. Because every question within each section is worth the same amount, consider the following guidelines:

1. Note in your test booklet the starting time of Section I. Remember that you have just over 1 minute per question.

2. Go through the entire test and answer all the easy questions first. Generally, the first 25 or so questions are considered by most to be the easiest questions, with the level of difficulty increasing as you move through Section I. Most students correctly answer approximately 60% of the first 25 multiple-choice questions, 50% of the next 25 questions, and only 30% of the last 25 questions. (The fact that most students do not have time to finish the multiple-choice questions is factored into the percentages.)

3. When you come to a question that seems impossible to answer, make a large minus sign (–) next to it in your test booklet. You are penalized for wrong answers, so do not guess at this point. Move on to the next question.

4. When you come to a question that seems solvable but appears too time-consuming, mark a large plus sign (+) next to that question in your test booklet. Do not guess; move on to the next question. A "time-consuming" question is one that you estimate will take you several minutes to answer.

5. Your time allotment is just over 1 minute per question; don't waste time deciding whether a question gets a plus or a minus. Act quickly. The intent of this strategy is to save you valuable time.

   After you have worked all the easy questions, your booklet should look something like this:

   1. C
   +2.
   3. B
   –4.
   5. A

   and so on.

6. After doing all the problems you can do immediately (the easy ones), go back and work on your "+" problems.

7. If you finish working your "+" problems and still have time left, you can do either of two things:

   Attempt the "–" problems, but remember *not* to guess under any circumstance.

   Forget the "–" problems, and go back over your completed work to be sure you didn't make any careless mistakes on the questions you thought were easy to answer.

You do not have to erase the pluses and minuses you made in your test booklet.

The Elimination Strategy

Take advantage of being able to mark in your test booklet. As you go through the "+" questions, eliminate choices from consideration by marking them out in your test booklet. Mark with question marks any choices you wish to consider as possible answers. See the following example:

   A.
   ?B.
   C.
   D.
   ?E.

This technique will help you avoid reconsidering those choices that you have already eliminated and will thus save you time. It will also help you narrow down your possible answers.

If you are able to eliminate all but two possible answers, answers such as **B** and **E** in the previous example, you may want to guess. Under these conditions, you stand a better chance of raising your score by guessing than by leaving the answer sheet blank.

Section II: The Free-Response (Essay) Section

Many students waste valuable time by memorizing information that they feel they should know for the AP Chemistry Exam. Unlike the A.P. U.S. History Exam, for which you need to have memorized hundreds of dates, battles, names, and treaties, the AP Chemistry Exam requires you to have memorized comparatively little. Rather, it is generally testing whether you can *apply* given information to new situations. You will be frequently asked to explain, compare, and predict in the essay questions.

Section II of the AP Chemistry Exam comes with

- a periodic table
- an $E°_{red}$ table
- a table of equations and constants

Method for Writing the Essays

The Restatement

In the second section of the AP Chemistry Exam, you should begin all questions by numbering your answer. You do not need to work the questions in order. However, the graders must be able to identify quickly which question you are answering. You may wish to underline any key words or key concepts in your answer. Do not underline too much, however, because doing so may obscure your reasons for underlining. In free-response questions that require specific calculations or the determination of products, you may also want to underline or draw a box around your final answer(s).

After you have written the problem number, restate the question in as few words as possible, but do not leave out any essential information. Often a diagram will help. By restating the question, you put the question in your own words and allow time for your mind to organize the way you intend to answer it. As a result, you eliminate a great deal of unnecessary language that clutters the basic idea. Even if you do not answer the question, a restatement may be worth one point.

If a question has several parts, such as (a), (b), (c), and (d), do not write all of the restatements together. Instead, write each restatement separately when you begin to answer that part. In these practice exams, you will see many samples of the uses of restatements.

Three Techniques for Answering Free-Response Questions

When you begin Section II, the essays, the last thing you want to do is start writing immediately. Take a minute and scan the questions. Find the questions that you know you will have the most success with, and put a star (*) next to them in your response book.

After you have identified the questions that you will eventually answer, the next step is to decide what format each question lends itself to. Let's do an actual essay question to demonstrate each format.

The Chart Format

In this format, you fill in a chart to answer the question. When you draw the chart, use the edge of your calculator case to make straight lines. Fill in the blanks with symbols, phrases, or incomplete sentences. The grid forces you to record all answers quickly and makes it unlikely that you will forget to give any part of the answer.

Essay 1

---

1. Given the molecules SF_6, XeF_4, PF_5, and ClF_3:

    A. Draw a Lewis structure for each molecule.
    B. Identify the geometry for each molecule.
    C. Describe the hybridization of the central atom for each molecule.
    D. Give the number of unshared pairs of electrons around the central atom.

Answer

1. Restatement: Given SF_6, XeF_4, PF_5, and ClF_3 For each, supply

    A. Lewis structure
    B. geometry
    C. hybridization
    D. unshared pairs

Characteristic	*SF₆*	*XeF₄*	*PF₅*	*ClF₃*
Lewis structure				
Geometry	Octahedral	Square planar	Triangular bipyramidal	T-shaped
Hybridization	sp^3d^2	sp^3d^2	sp^3d	sp^3d
Unshared pairs	0	2	0	2

The Bullet Format

The bullet format is also a very efficient technique because it, like the chart format, does not require complete sentences. In using this format, you essentially provide a list to answer the question. A • is a bullet, and each new concept receives one. Try to add your bullets in a logical sequence and leave room to add more bullets. You may want to come back later and fill them in. Don't get discouraged if you do not have as many bullets as the samples contain—it takes practice. Reviewing the key terms in *CliffsAP Chemistry,* 3rd Edition may suggest additional points that you can incorporate.

Essay 2

---

2. As one examines the periodic table, one discovers that the melting points of the alkali metals increase as one moves from cesium to lithium, whereas the melting points of the halogens increase from fluorine to iodine.

    A. Explain the phenomenon observed in the melting points of the alkali metals.
    B. Explain the phenomenon observed in the melting points of the halogens.
    C. Given the compounds CsI, NaCl, LiF, and KBr, predict the order of their melting points (from high to low) and explain your answer using chemical principles.

Answer

2. Given—melting points: alkali metals increase from $Cs \rightarrow Li$

halogens increase from $F \rightarrow I$

(**a**) Restatement: Explain alkali metal trend.

- Observed melting point order: $Li > Na > K > Rb > Cs$
- All elements are metals
- All elements contain metallic bonds
- Electrons are free to migrate in a "sea"
- As one moves down the group, size (radius) of the atoms increases
- As volume of atom increases, charge density decreases
- Attractive force between atoms is directly proportional to melting point
- Therefore, as attractive forces decrease moving down the group, melting point decreases

(**b**) Restatement: Explain halogen trend.

- Observed melting point order: $I > Br > Cl > F$
- All halogens are nonmetals
- Intramolecular forces = covalent bonding
- Intermolecular forces = dispersion (van der Waals) forces, which exist between molecules
- Dispersion forces result from "temporary" dipoles caused by polarization of electron clouds
- As one moves up the group, the electron clouds become smaller
- Smaller electron clouds result in higher charge density
- As one moves up the group, electron clouds are less readily polarized
- Less readily polarized clouds result in weaker dispersion forces holding molecules to other molecules
- Therefore, attractive forces between molecules decrease as one moves up the group, resulting in lower melting points

(**c**) Restatement: Predict melting point order (high to low) CsI, NaCl, LiF, and KBr and explain.

- $LiF > NaCl > KBr > CsI$
- All compounds contain a metal and a nonmetal ion
- Predicted order has ionic bonds
- Larger ionic radius results in lower charge density
- Lower charge density results in smaller attractive forces
- Smaller attractive forces result in lower melting point

The Outline Format

This technique is similar to the bullet format, but instead of bullets it uses the more traditional outline style that you may have used for years: Roman numerals, letters, and so on. The advantages of this format are that it does not require full sentences and that it progresses in a logical sequence. The disadvantage is that it requires you to spend more time thinking about organization. Leave plenty of room here because you may want to come back later and add more points.

Essay 3

The boiling points and electrical conductivities of six aqueous solutions are as follows:

Solution	Boiling Point	Relative Electrical Conductivity
0.05 m $BaSO_4$	100.025° C	0.03
0.05 m H_3BO_3	100.038° C	0.78
0.05 m NaCl	100.048° C	1.00
0.05 m $MgCl_2$	100.068° C	2.00
0.05 m $FeCl_3$	100.086° C	3.00
0.05 m $C_6H_{12}O_6$	100.025° C	0.01

3. Discuss the relationship among the composition, the boiling point, and the electrical conductivity of each solution.

Answer

3. Given: Boiling point data and electrical conductivities of six aqueous solutions, all at 0.05 m.

Restatement: Discuss any relationships between B.P. and electrical conductivities.

I. $BaSO_4$

    A. $BaSO_4$ is an ionic compound.

    B. According to known solubility rules, $BaSO_4$ is not very soluble.

        1. If $BaSO_4$ were totally soluble, one would expect its B.P. to be very close to that of NaCl because $BaSO_4$ would be expected to ionize into two ions (Ba^{2+} and SO_4^{2-}) just as NaCl would (Na^+ and Cl^-). The substantial difference between the B.P. of the NaCl solution and that of the $BaSO_4$ solution suggests that the dissociation of the latter is negligible.

        2. The electrical conductivity of $BaSO_4$ is closest to that of $C_6H_{12}O_6$, an organic molecule, which does not ionize; this observation further supports the previous evidence of the weak-electrolyte properties of $BaSO_4$.

II. H_3BO_3

    A. H_3BO_3 is a weak acid.

    B. In the equation $\triangle t = i \cdot m \cdot K_b$, where $\triangle t$ is the boiling-point elevation, m is the molality of the solution, and K_b is the boiling-point-elevation constant for water, i (the van't Hoff factor) would be expected to be 4 if H_3BO_3 were completely ionized. According to data provided, (i) is about 1.5. Therefore, H_3BO_3 must have a relatively low K_a.

III. NaCl, $MgCl_2$, and $FeCl_3$

    A. All three compounds are chlorides known to be completely soluble in water, so they are strong electrolytes and would increase electrical conductivities.

    B. The van't Hoff factor (i) would be expected to be 2 for NaCl, 3 for $MgCl_2$, and 4 for $FeCl_3$.

C. Using the equation

$$\frac{\Delta t}{m \cdot K_b} = \frac{\text{B.P. of solution} - 100°\text{C}}{(0.05 \text{ mole solute/kg})(0.512°\text{C kg/mole solute})}$$

we find that the van't Hoff factors for these solutions are

Compound	Calculated i	Expected i
NaCl	1.9	2.0
$MgCl_2$	2.7	3.0
$FeCl_3$	3.4	4.0

which are in agreement.

D. The electrical conductivity data support the rationale just provided: the greater the number of particles, which in this case are ions, the higher the B.P.

IV. $C_6H_{12}O_6$

A. $C_6H_{12}O_6$, glucose, is an organic molecule. It would not be expected to dissociate into ions that conduct electricity. The reported electrical conductivity for glucose supports this.

B. Because $C_6H_{12}O_6$ does not dissociate, i is expected to be close to 1. The equation in III C gives i as exactly 1.

C. The boiling-point-elevation constant of 0.512°C · kg/mole would be expected to raise the B.P 0.026°C for a 0.05m solution when $i = 1$. The data show that the boiling-point elevation is 0.026°C. This agrees with theory. Therefore, $C_6H_{12}O_6$ does not ionize. With few or no ions in solution, poor electrical conductivity is expected. This is supported by the evidence in the table.

Multiple-Choice Answer Sheet for Practice Exam 1

Remove this sheet and use it to mark your answers.
Answer sheets for "Section II: Free-Response Questions" can be found at the end of this book.

Section I
Multiple-Choice Questions

1 Ⓐ Ⓑ Ⓒ Ⓓ Ⓔ	26 Ⓐ Ⓑ Ⓒ Ⓓ Ⓔ	51 Ⓐ Ⓑ Ⓒ Ⓓ Ⓔ
2 Ⓐ Ⓑ Ⓒ Ⓓ Ⓔ	27 Ⓐ Ⓑ Ⓒ Ⓓ Ⓔ	52 Ⓐ Ⓑ Ⓒ Ⓓ Ⓔ
3 Ⓐ Ⓑ Ⓒ Ⓓ Ⓔ	28 Ⓐ Ⓑ Ⓒ Ⓓ Ⓔ	53 Ⓐ Ⓑ Ⓒ Ⓓ Ⓔ
4 Ⓐ Ⓑ Ⓒ Ⓓ Ⓔ	29 Ⓐ Ⓑ Ⓒ Ⓓ Ⓔ	54 Ⓐ Ⓑ Ⓒ Ⓓ Ⓔ
5 Ⓐ Ⓑ Ⓒ Ⓓ Ⓔ	30 Ⓐ Ⓑ Ⓒ Ⓓ Ⓔ	55 Ⓐ Ⓑ Ⓒ Ⓓ Ⓔ
6 Ⓐ Ⓑ Ⓒ Ⓓ Ⓔ	31 Ⓐ Ⓑ Ⓒ Ⓓ Ⓔ	56 Ⓐ Ⓑ Ⓒ Ⓓ Ⓔ
7 Ⓐ Ⓑ Ⓒ Ⓓ Ⓔ	32 Ⓐ Ⓑ Ⓒ Ⓓ Ⓔ	57 Ⓐ Ⓑ Ⓒ Ⓓ Ⓔ
8 Ⓐ Ⓑ Ⓒ Ⓓ Ⓔ	33 Ⓐ Ⓑ Ⓒ Ⓓ Ⓔ	58 Ⓐ Ⓑ Ⓒ Ⓓ Ⓔ
9 Ⓐ Ⓑ Ⓒ Ⓓ Ⓔ	34 Ⓐ Ⓑ Ⓒ Ⓓ Ⓔ	59 Ⓐ Ⓑ Ⓒ Ⓓ Ⓔ
10 Ⓐ Ⓑ Ⓒ Ⓓ Ⓔ	35 Ⓐ Ⓑ Ⓒ Ⓓ Ⓔ	60 Ⓐ Ⓑ Ⓒ Ⓓ Ⓔ
11 Ⓐ Ⓑ Ⓒ Ⓓ Ⓔ	36 Ⓐ Ⓑ Ⓒ Ⓓ Ⓔ	61 Ⓐ Ⓑ Ⓒ Ⓓ Ⓔ
12 Ⓐ Ⓑ Ⓒ Ⓓ Ⓔ	37 Ⓐ Ⓑ Ⓒ Ⓓ Ⓔ	62 Ⓐ Ⓑ Ⓒ Ⓓ Ⓔ
13 Ⓐ Ⓑ Ⓒ Ⓓ Ⓔ	38 Ⓐ Ⓑ Ⓒ Ⓓ Ⓔ	63 Ⓐ Ⓑ Ⓒ Ⓓ Ⓔ
14 Ⓐ Ⓑ Ⓒ Ⓓ Ⓔ	39 Ⓐ Ⓑ Ⓒ Ⓓ Ⓔ	64 Ⓐ Ⓑ Ⓒ Ⓓ Ⓔ
15 Ⓐ Ⓑ Ⓒ Ⓓ Ⓔ	40 Ⓐ Ⓑ Ⓒ Ⓓ Ⓔ	65 Ⓐ Ⓑ Ⓒ Ⓓ Ⓔ
16 Ⓐ Ⓑ Ⓒ Ⓓ Ⓔ	41 Ⓐ Ⓑ Ⓒ Ⓓ Ⓔ	66 Ⓐ Ⓑ Ⓒ Ⓓ Ⓔ
17 Ⓐ Ⓑ Ⓒ Ⓓ Ⓔ	42 Ⓐ Ⓑ Ⓒ Ⓓ Ⓔ	67 Ⓐ Ⓑ Ⓒ Ⓓ Ⓔ
18 Ⓐ Ⓑ Ⓒ Ⓓ Ⓔ	43 Ⓐ Ⓑ Ⓒ Ⓓ Ⓔ	68 Ⓐ Ⓑ Ⓒ Ⓓ Ⓔ
19 Ⓐ Ⓑ Ⓒ Ⓓ Ⓔ	44 Ⓐ Ⓑ Ⓒ Ⓓ Ⓔ	69 Ⓐ Ⓑ Ⓒ Ⓓ Ⓔ
20 Ⓐ Ⓑ Ⓒ Ⓓ Ⓔ	45 Ⓐ Ⓑ Ⓒ Ⓓ Ⓔ	70 Ⓐ Ⓑ Ⓒ Ⓓ Ⓔ
21 Ⓐ Ⓑ Ⓒ Ⓓ Ⓔ	46 Ⓐ Ⓑ Ⓒ Ⓓ Ⓔ	71 Ⓐ Ⓑ Ⓒ Ⓓ Ⓔ
22 Ⓐ Ⓑ Ⓒ Ⓓ Ⓔ	47 Ⓐ Ⓑ Ⓒ Ⓓ Ⓔ	72 Ⓐ Ⓑ Ⓒ Ⓓ Ⓔ
23 Ⓐ Ⓑ Ⓒ Ⓓ Ⓔ	48 Ⓐ Ⓑ Ⓒ Ⓓ Ⓔ	73 Ⓐ Ⓑ Ⓒ Ⓓ Ⓔ
24 Ⓐ Ⓑ Ⓒ Ⓓ Ⓔ	49 Ⓐ Ⓑ Ⓒ Ⓓ Ⓔ	74 Ⓐ Ⓑ Ⓒ Ⓓ Ⓔ
25 Ⓐ Ⓑ Ⓒ Ⓓ Ⓔ	50 Ⓐ Ⓑ Ⓒ Ⓓ Ⓔ	75 Ⓐ Ⓑ Ⓒ Ⓓ Ⓔ

PERIODIC TABLE OF THE ELEMENTS

1 **H** 1.0079																	2 **He** 4.0026
3 **Li** 6.941	4 **Be** 9.012											5 **B** 10.811	6 **C** 12.011	7 **N** 14.007	8 **O** 16.00	9 **F** 19.00	10 **Ne** 20.179
11 **Na** 22.99	12 **Mg** 24.30											13 **Al** 26.98	14 **Si** 28.09	15 **P** 30.974	16 **S** 32.06	17 **Cl** 35.453	18 **Ar** 39.948
19 **K** 39.10	20 **Ca** 40.08	21 **Sc** 44.96	22 **Ti** 47.90	23 **V** 50.94	24 **Cr** 51.00	25 **Mn** 54.93	26 **Fe** 55.85	27 **Co** 58.93	28 **Ni** 58.69	29 **Cu** 63.55	30 **Zn** 65.39	31 **Ga** 69.72	32 **Ge** 72.59	33 **As** 74.92	34 **Se** 78.96	35 **Br** 79.90	36 **Kr** 83.80
37 **Rb** 85.47	38 **Sr** 87.62	39 **Y** 88.91	40 **Zr** 91.22	41 **Nb** 92.91	42 **Mo** 95.94	43 **Tc** (98)	44 **Ru** 101.1	45 **Rh** 102.91	46 **Pd** 105.42	47 **Ag** 107.87	48 **Cd** 112.41	49 **In** 114.82	50 **Sn** 118.71	51 **Sb** 121.75	52 **Te** 127.60	53 **I** 126.91	54 **Xe** 131.29
55 **Cs** 132.91	56 **Ba** 137.33	57 *****La** 138.91	72 **Hf** 178.49	73 **Ta** 180.95	74 **W** 183.85	75 **Re** 186.21	76 **Os** 190.2	77 **Ir** 192.22	78 **Pt** 195.08	79 **Au** 196.97	80 **Hg** 200.59	81 **Ti** 204.38	82 **Pb** 207.2	83 **Bi** 208.98	84 **Po** (209)	85 **At** (210)	86 **Rn** (222)
87 **Fr** (223)	88 **Ra** 226.02	89 †**Ac** 227.03	104 **Rf** (261)	105 **Db** (262)	106 **Sg** (263)	107 **Bh** (262)	108 **Hs** (265)	109 **Mt** (266)	110 **§** (269)	111 **§** (272)	112 **§** (277)						

§ Not yet named

***** Lanthanide Series

58 **Ce** 140.12	59 **Pr** 140.91	60 **Nd** 144.24	61 **Pm** (145)	62 **Sm** 150.4	63 **Eu** 151.97	64 **Gd** 157.25	65 **Tb** 158.93	66 **Dy** 162.50	67 **Ho** 164.93	68 **Er** 167.26	69 **Tm** 168.93	70 **Yb** 173.04	71 **Lu** 174.97
90 **Th** 232.04	91 **Pa** 231.04	92 **U** 238.03	93 **Np** 237.05	94 **Pu** (244)	95 **Am** (243)	96 **Cm** (247)	97 **Bk** (247)	98 **Cf** (251)	99 **Es** (252)	100 **Fm** (257)	101 **Md** (258)	102 **No** (259)	103 **Lr** (260)

† Actinide Series

Practice Exam 1

Section I: Multiple-Choice Questions

Time: 90 minutes

75 questions

45% of total grade

No calculators allowed

This section consists of 75 multiple-choice questions. Mark your answers carefully on the answer sheet.

General Instructions

Do not open this booklet until you are told to do so by the proctor.

Be sure to write your answers for Section I on the separate answer sheet. Use the test booklet for your scratch work or notes, but remember that no credit will be given for work, notes, or answers written only in the test booklet. After you have selected an answer, blacken thoroughly the corresponding circle on the answer sheet. To change an answer, erase your previous mark completely, and then record your new answer. Mark only one answer for each question.

Example   Sample Answer

The Pacific is   Ⓐ Ⓑ ● Ⓓ Ⓔ

    A.   a river
    B.   a lake
    C.   an ocean
    D.   a sea
    E.   a gulf

To discourage haphazard guessing on this section of the exam, a quarter of a point is subtracted for every wrong answer, but no points are subtracted if you leave the answer blank. Even so, if you can eliminate one or more of the choices for a question, it may be to your advantage to guess.

Because it is not expected that all test takers will complete this section, do not spend too much time on difficult questions. Answer first the questions you can answer readily, and then, if you have time, return to the difficult questions later. Don't get stuck on one question. Work quickly but accurately. Use your time effectively. The preceding table is provided for your use in answering questions in Section I.

GO ON TO THE NEXT PAGE

Directions: Each group of lettered answer choices below refers to the numbered statements or questions that immediately follow. For each question or statement, select the one lettered choice that is the best answer and fill in the corresponding circle on the answer sheet. An answer choice may be used once, more than once, or not at all in each set of questions.

Questions 1–3 refer to atoms of the following elements:

    A. carbon
    B. fluorine
    C. hydrogen
    D. nitrogen
    E. aluminum

1. In the ground state, has only 1 electron in a *p* orbital.

2. Has the largest atomic radius.

3. Has the largest value for first ionization energy.

Questions 4–5

    A. CO_2
    B. CH_4
    C. SF_6
    D. H_2O
    E. NH_3

4. Which of the molecules is linear?

5. Which of the molecules can be described as having *sp* hybridization?

6. A buffer is formed by adding 500 mL of 0.20 M $HC_2H_3O_2$ to 500 mL of 0.10 M $NaC_2H_3O_2$. What would be the maximum amount of HCl that could be added to this solution without exceeding the capacity of the buffer?

    A. 0.01 mol
    B. 0.05 mol
    C. 0.10 mol
    D. 0.15 mol
    E. 0.20 mol

Questions 7–11

Directions: Predict the change in entropy using the choices provided.

    A. The change in entropy will be positive.
    B. The change in entropy will be zero.
    C. The change in entropy will be negative.
    D. The change in entropy can be either positive or negative.
    E. The change in entropy cannot be determined from the information given.

7. $Cl_{2(g)} \rightarrow 2Cl_{(g)}$

8. $H_{2(g)}$ at 5.0 atm $\rightarrow H_{2(g)}$ at 1.0 atm

9. Sublimation of solid CO_2

10. $2H_{2\,(g)} + O_{2(g)} \rightarrow 2H_2O_{(g)}$

11. $PCl_{5(g)} \longleftrightarrow PCl_{3(g)} + Cl_{2(g)}$

Questions 12 and 13

    A. KNO_3
    B. CaO
    C. $NaHCO_3$
    D. $MgSO_4$
    E. $Mg(OH)_2$

12. Commonly known as "baking soda."

13. Fertilizer that can also be used to neutralize acid rain in lakes.

14. A molecule exhibits sp^3d^2 hybridization in its bonding structure. The most probable geometric shape of this molecule is

    A. triangular bipyramidal
    B. T-shaped
    C. octahedral
    D. linear
    E. hexagonal

15. A solution has a pH of 11.0. What is the hydrogen ion concentration?

   A. 1.0×10^{-11} M
   B. 1.0×10^{-3} M
   C.   0.0 M
   D. 1.0×10^{3} M
   E. 1.0×10^{11} M

16. A catalyst affects the activation energy by

   A.   increasing the forward rate of reaction.
   B.   changing the enthalpy of the reaction.
   C.   increasing the rate of the reverse reaction.
   D.   changing the reaction mechanism, thus lowering the activation energy.
   E.   catalysts do not affect activation energies.

17. At constant temperature and pressure, the heats of formation of $H_2O_{(g)}$, $CO_{2(g)}$, and $C_2H_{6(g)}$ (in kilojoules per mole) are as follows:

Species	$\triangle H_f$ (kJ/mole)
$H_2O_{(g)}$	−251
$CO_{2(g)}$	−393
$C_2H_{6(g)}$	−84

If $\triangle H$ values are negative for exothermic reactions, what is $\triangle H$ for 1 mole of C_2H_6 gas to oxidize to carbon dioxide gas and water vapor (temperature and pressure are held constant)?

   A.   −8730 kJ/mole
   B.   −2910 kJ/mole
   C.   −1455 kJ/mole
   D.   1455 kJ/mole
   E.   2910 kJ/mole

18. What is the molality of a 10. % (by weight) C_6H_2O (MW = 90.) solution?

   A.   0.012 *m*
   B.   0.12 *m*
   C.   1.2 *m*
   D.   12 *m*
   E.   Not enough information is provided.

19. Excess of $S_{8(s)}$ is heated with a metallic element until the metal reacts completely. All excess sulfur is combusted to a gaseous compound and escapes from the crucible. Given the information that follows, determine the most probable formula for the residue.

mass of crucible, lid, and metal = 55.00 grams

mass of crucible and lid = 41.00 grams

mass of crucible, lid, and residue = 62.00 grams

   A.   CuS
   B. Cu_2S
   C.   FeS
   D. Fe_2S_3
   E.   Not enough information is given to solve the problem.

20. According to Raoult's Law, which statement is false?

   A.   The vapor pressure of a solvent over a solution is less than that of the pure solvent.
   B.   Ionic solids ionize in water, increasing the effects of all colligative properties.
   C.   The vapor pressure of a solvent decreases as its mole fraction increases.
   D.   The solubility of a gas increases as the temperature decreases.
   E.   The solubility of a gas in solution increases as the pressure of the gas increases.

21. When a solid melts, which of the following is true?

   A. $\triangle H > 0$, $\triangle S > 0$
   B. $\triangle H < 0$, $\triangle S < 0$
   C. $\triangle H > 0$, $\triangle S < 0$
   D. $\triangle H < 0$, $\triangle S > 0$
   E.   More information is required before one can specify the signs of $\triangle H$ and $\triangle S$.

22. For the isoelectronic series S^{2-}, Cl^-, Ar, K^+, and Sc^{3+}, which species requires the least energy to remove an outer electron?

   A. S^{2-}
   B. Cl^-
   C.   Ar
   D. K^+
   E. Sc^{3+}

GO ON TO THE NEXT PAGE

23. A test tube containing $CaCO_3$ is heated until the entire compound decomposes. If the test tube plus calcium carbonate originally weighed 30.08 grams and the loss of mass during the experiment was 4.40 grams, what was the approximate mass of the empty test tube?

   A. 20.08 g
   B. 21.00 g
   C. 24.50 g
   D. 25.08 g
   E. 25.68 g

24. When 100 grams of butane gas (C_4H_{10}, MW = 58.4) is burned in excess oxygen gas, the theoretical yield of H_2O (in grams) is:

   A. $\dfrac{54.14 \times 18.02}{100 \times 5}$

   B. $\dfrac{5 \times 58.4}{100 \times 18.02}$

   C. $\dfrac{4 \times 18.02}{\frac{13}{2} \times 100} \times 100\%$

   D. $\dfrac{5 \times 58.14 \times 18.02}{100}$

   E. $\dfrac{100 \times 5 \times 18.02}{58.14}$

25. Given the following heat of reaction and the bond energies listed in the accompanying table (measured under standard conditions), calculate the energy of the C=O bond. All numerical values are in kilojoules per mole, and all substances are in the gas phase.

$$CH_3CHO + H_2 \rightarrow CH_3CH_2OH$$
$$\triangle H° = -71 \text{ kJ/mole}$$

Bond	O–H	C–H	C–C	C–O	H–H
Bond Energy (kJ/mole)	464	414	347	351	435

   A. 180 kJ
   B. 361 kJ
   C. 723 kJ
   D. 1446 kJ
   E. 2892 kJ

26. Given these two standard enthalpies of formation:

Reaction 1:

$$S_{(s)} + O_{2\,(g)} \longleftrightarrow SO_{2\,(g)} \qquad \Delta H° = -295 \text{ kJ/mole}$$

Reaction 2:

$$S_{(s)} + \tfrac{3}{2}O_{2\,(g)} \longleftrightarrow SO_{3\,(g)} \qquad \Delta H° = -395 \text{ kJ/mole}$$

What is the heat of reaction for $2SO_{2\,(g)} + O_{2\,(g)} \longleftrightarrow 2SO_{3\,(g)}$ under the same conditions?

   A. -1380 kJ/mole
   B. $-690.$ kJ/mole
   C. -295 kJ/mole
   D. $-200.$ kJ/mole
   E. $-100.$ kJ/mole

27. When 2.00 grams of a certain volatile liquid is heated, the volume of the resulting vapor is 821 mL at a temperature of 127°C at standard pressure. The molecular mass of this substance is

   A. 20.0 g/mole
   B. 40.0 g/mole
   C. 80.0 g/mole
   D. 120. g/mole
   E. 160. g/mole

28. Given the following:

$$H_2O_{2(aq)} \rightarrow O_{2(g)} + 2H^+_{(aq)} + 2e^- \qquad E°_{ox} = -0.68 \text{ V}$$
$$2H_2O_{(l)} \rightarrow H_2O_{2(aq)} + 2H^+_{(aq)} + 2e^- \qquad E°_{ox} = -1.77 \text{ V}$$

Which of the following is true?

   A. $E° = 1.09$ for the disproportionation of hydrogen peroxide.
   B. $E° = -2.45$ for the synthesis of hydrogen peroxide.
   C. $E° = -1.09$ for the decomposition of hydrogen peroxide.
   D. $E° = +2.45$ for the synthesis of water.
   E. All answers are false.

29. 100 grams of $O_{2(g)}$ and 100 grams of $He_{(g)}$ are in separate containers of equal volume. Both gases are at 100°C. Which one of the following statements is true?

   A. Both gases would have the same pressure.

   B. The average kinetic energy of the O_2 molecules is greater than that of the He molecules.

   C. The average kinetic energy of the He molecules is greater than that of the O_2 molecules.

   D. There are equal numbers of He molecules and O_2 molecules.

   E. The pressure of the $He_{(g)}$ would be greater than that of the $O_{2(g)}$.

30. Which of the following elements most readily shows the photoelectric effect?

   A. noble gases

   B. alkali metals

   C. halogen elements

   D. transition metals

   E. the chalcogens

31. An energy value of 3.313×10^{-19} joules is needed to break a chemical bond. What is the wavelength of energy needed to break the bond? (The speed of light $= 3.00 \times 10^{10}$ cm/sec; Planck's constant $= 6.626 \times 10^{-34}$ J · sec).

   A. 5.00×10^{18} cm

   B. 1.00×10^{15} cm

   C. 2.00×10^{5} cm

   D. 6.00×10^{-5} cm

   E. 1.20×10^{-8} cm

32. Which one of the following does NOT exhibit resonance?

   A. SO_2

   B. SO_3

   C. HI

   D. CO_3^{2-}

   E. NO_3^-

33. As the atomic number of the elements increases down a column

   A. the atomic radius decreases.

   B. the atomic mass decreases.

   C. the elements become less metallic.

   D. ionization energy decreases.

   E. the number of electrons in the outermost energy level increases.

34. What ions would you find in solution if potassium perchlorate was dissolved in water?

   A. KCl, O_2

   B. K^+, Cl^-, O^{2-}

   C. KCl, O^{2-}

   D. K^+, ClO_4^-

   E. K^+, Cl^-, O^{2-}

35. Which of the following statements is true of the critical temperature of a pure substance?

   A. The critical temperature is the temperature above which the liquid phase of a pure substance can exist.

   B. The critical temperature is the temperature above which the liquid phase of a pure substance cannot exist.

   C. The critical temperature is the temperature below which the liquid phase of a pure substance cannot exist.

   D. The critical temperature is the temperature at which all three phases can coexist.

   E. The critical temperature is the temperature at which the pure substance reaches, but cannot go beyond, the critical pressure.

36. A 10.0% sucrose solution has a density of 2.00 g/mL. What is the mass of sucrose dissolved in 1.00 liter of this solution?

   A. 1.00×10^2 g

   B. 2.00×10^2 g

   C. 5.00×10^2 g

   D. 1.00×10^3 g

   E. 1.00×10^4 g

GO ON TO THE NEXT PAGE

37. Which of the following is a correct Lewis structure for glycine (NH_2CH_2COOH)?

A.

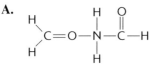

B.

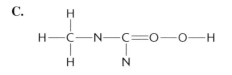

C.

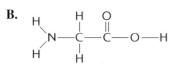

D.

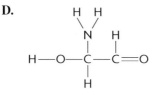

E.

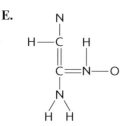

38. Calculate the number of grams of glycerol, $C_3H_5(OH)_3$ (MW = 92.1 g/mol), that must be dissolved in 520. grams of water to raise the boiling point to 102.00°C.

A. 92 g
B. 135 g
C. 184 g
D. 400 g
E. 625 g

39. The rate of the chemical reaction between substances A and B is found to follow the rate law

$$\text{rate} = k[A]^2[B]$$

where k is the rate constant. The concentration of A is reduced to half of its original value. To make the reaction occur at 50% of its original rate, the concentration of B should be

A. decreased by ¼
B. halved
C. kept constant
D. doubled
E. increased by a factor of 4

40. 6.0 moles of chlorine gas are placed in a 3.0-liter flask at 1250 K. At this temperature, the chlorine molecules begin to dissociate into chlorine atoms. What is the value for K_c, if 50.% of the chlorine molecules dissociate when equilibrium has been achieved?

A. 1.0
B. 3.0
C. 4.0
D. 6.0
E. 12.0

41. Given that the first, second, and third dissociation constants for H_3PO_4 are 7.0×10^{-3}, 6.0×10^{-8}, and 5.0×10^{-13} respectively, calculate K for the complete dissociation of H_3PO_4.

A. 2.10×10^{-32}
B. 2.10×10^{-28}
C. 2.10×10^{-22}
D. 2.10×10^{-11}
E. 2.10×10^{22}

42. What is the OH^- concentration (M) of a solution that contains 5.00×10^{-3} mole of H^+ per liter? $K_w = 1.00 \times 10^{-14}$

A. 7.00×10^{-14} M
B. 1.00×10^{-12} M
C. 2.00×10^{-12} M
D. 1.00×10^{-11} M
E. 2.00×10^{-11} M

43. Which of the following salts contains a basic anion?

    A. NaCl
    B. $Ba(HSO_4)_2$
    C. KI
    D. Li_2CO_3
    E. NH_4ClO_4

44. Suppose that 0.500 liter of 0.0200 M HCl is mixed with 0.100 liter of 0.100 M $Ba(OH)_2$. What is the pH in the final solution after neutralization occurred?

    A. 3.00
    B. 5.00
    C. 7.00
    D. 9.00
    E. 12.00

45. Given the balanced equation

$$H_{2\,(g)} + F_{2\,(g)} \longleftrightarrow 2HF_{(g)} \qquad \Delta G° = -546 \text{ kJ/mole}$$

Calculate ΔG if the pressures were changed from the standard 1 atm to the following and the temperature was changed to 500°C.

$$H_{2(g)} = 0.50 \text{ atm} \quad F_{2(g)} = 2.00 \text{ atm}$$
$$HF_{(g)} = 1.00 \text{ atm}$$

    A. -1090 kJ/mole
    B. -546 kJ/mole
    C. -273 kJ/mole
    D. 546 kJ/mole
    E. 1090 kJ/mole

46. Given the following notation for an electrochemical cell:

$$Pt_{(s)} \big| H_{2\,(g)} \big| H^+_{\,(aq)} \big\| Ag^+_{\,(aq)} \big| Ag_{(s)}$$

Which of the following represents the overall balanced (net) cell reaction?

    A. $H_{2(g)} + Ag^+_{\,(aq)} \rightarrow 2H^+_{\,(aq)} + Ag_{(s)}$
    B. $H_{2(g)} + Ag_{(s)} \rightarrow H^+_{\,(aq)} + Ag^+_{\,(aq)}$
    C. $Ag_{(s)} + H^+_{\,(aq)} \rightarrow Ag^+_{\,(aq)} + H_{2(g)}$
    D. $2H^+_{\,(aq)} + Ag_{(s)} \rightarrow H_{2(g)} + Ag^+_{\,(aq)}$
    E. none of the above

47. For the reaction

$$Pb_{(s)} + PbO_{2(s)} + 4H^+_{\,(aq)} + 2SO_4^{2-}_{\,(aq)} \rightarrow$$
$$2PbSO_{4(s)} + 2H_2O_{(l)}$$

which is the overall reaction in a lead storage battery, $\Delta H° = -315.9$ kJ/mole and $\Delta S° = 263.5$ J/(K · mole). What is the proper setup to find $E°$ at 75°C?

    A. $\dfrac{-315.9 - 349\,(0.2635)}{-2\,(96.487)}$

    B. $\dfrac{-348 + 315.9\,(0.2635)}{2\,(96.487)}$

    C. $\dfrac{-348 + 315.9\,(0.2635)}{96.487}$

    D. $\dfrac{-2\,(-348) + 263.5}{96.487 + 315.9}$

    E. $\dfrac{2\,(-315.9) - 263.5}{(96.487)(348)}$

Questions 48–51

    A. alcohol
    B. carboxylic acid
    C. ester
    D. ether
    E. ketone

48. The product of the reaction of an alcohol and a carboxylic acid.

49. The product of the reaction of an alkene and water.

50. The product formed by the oxidation of a secondary alcohol.

51. The product formed by the condensation reaction of alcohols.

52. Which of the following choices correctly describes the decreasing ability of the radiation to penetrate a sheet of lead that is 3 inches thick?

    A. alpha particles > beta particles > gamma rays
    B. gamma rays > alpha particles > beta particles
    C. alpha particles > gamma rays > beta particles
    D. beta particles > alpha particles > gamma rays
    E. gamma rays > beta particles > alpha particles

GO ON TO THE NEXT PAGE

Questions 53–55

A. Wave nature of matter
B. Shielding effect
C. Pauli Exclusion Principle
D. Heisenberg Uncertainty Principle
E. Hund's Rule

53. States that the more precisely the position of an electron is determined, the less precisely the momentum is known at that instant.

54. This principle can be used to determine if an oxygen atom in its ground state is diamagnetic or paramagnetic.

55. States that an atomic orbital cannot hold more than two electrons and that they must spin opposite to each other.

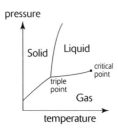

56. At the triple point, which of the following is NOT true?

A. All phases of H_2O can exist.
B. It is possible to change all of the substance to ice, water, or steam by making infinitesimally small changes in pressure and temperature.
C. At a constant pressure higher than the triple point, heating ice changes it to liquid, then to steam.
D. At pressures below the triple point, liquid water cannot exist.
E. At pressures below the triple point, liquid water can exist.

57. Beyond the critical point of H_2O

A. H_2O exists in a state of equilibrium with all phases
B. liquid water can no longer exist
C. only the solid phase can exist
D. H_2O can no longer exist as a molecule
E. only the liquid phase can exist

58. Which of the following molecules does not exhibit sp^3d hybridization?

A. XeF_2
B. ClF_3
C. SCl_4
D. SF_6
E. PCl_5

59. Relatively fast rates of chemical reactions are associated with all of the following EXCEPT:

A. the presence of a catalyst
B. strong bonds in reactant molecules
C. high temperatures
D. high concentration of reactants
E. low activation energy

60. Arrange the following species in order of increasing oxidation number of the sulfur atom

SCl_2 S_8 SO_2 H_2S S_2Cl_2 SO_3

A. H_2S, S_8, S_2Cl_2, SCl_2, SO_2, SO_3
B. SO_3, SO_2, SCl_2, S_2Cl_2, S_8, H_2S
C. H_2S, S_8, SCl_2, S_2Cl_2, SO_3, SO_2
D. SO_2, SO_3, S_2Cl_2, H_2S, SCl_2, S_8
E. S_8, H_2S, SO_3, SCl_2, SO_2, S_2Cl_2

61. Hemoglobin contains ~ 0.33 % of iron by mass. What is the approximate <u>minimum</u> molar mass of hemoglobin?

A. 1.6×10^2 g · mol^{-1}
B. 1.6×10^3 g · mol^{-1}
C. 1.6×10^4 g ·· mol^{-1}
D. 1.6×10^5 g · mol^{-1}
E. 1.6×10^6 g · mol^{-1}

62. Consider diethyl ether and 1-butanol. Which of the following are correct?

A. Diethyl ether will have the higher boiling point.
B. 1-butanol will have the higher boiling point.
C. Because they contain the same number and types of atoms, they will boil at the same temperature.
D. Because they contain the same number of atoms, but different types of atoms, more information is needed in order to determine which one will boil at a higher temperature.
E. Because they contain different numbers of atoms, but the same type of atoms, more information is needed in order to determine which one will boil at a higher temperature.

63. How many asymmetric carbon atoms are present in the following molecule?

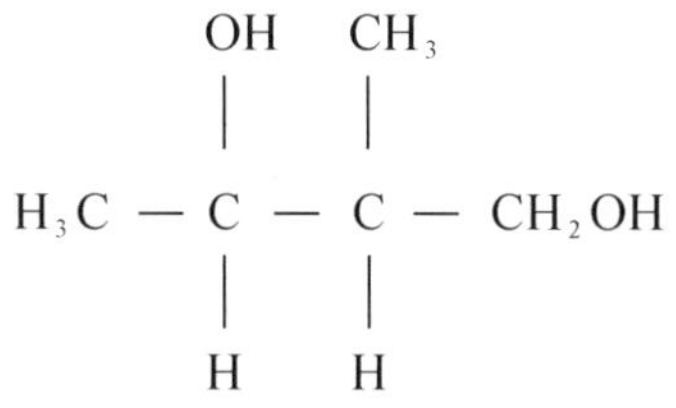

$$H_3C - \underset{\underset{H}{|}}{\overset{\overset{OH}{|}}{C}} - \underset{\underset{H}{|}}{\overset{\overset{CH_3}{|}}{C}} - CH_2OH$$

- **A.** 0
- **B.** 1
- **C.** 2
- **D.** 3
- **E.** 4

64. A lunar expedition brought back some moon rocks. Analysis of the rocks showed them to contain 17% potassium-40 and 83% argon by mass. The half-life of K-40 is 1.2×10^9 years. K-40 decays through positron emission. Ar-40 is the decay product of the reaction. How old was the rock sample (in years)?

- **A.** $0.83 \cdot (1.2 \times 10^9)^{0.693}$
- **B.** $(0.693)^{1/2} \cdot (1.2 \times 10^9)$
- **C.** $\dfrac{0.693}{1.2 \times 10^9} \cdot \ln \dfrac{1.00}{0.17}$
- **D.** $\dfrac{1.2 \times 10^9 \, yr}{0.17} \cdot \ln \dfrac{0.693}{1.00}$
- **E.** $\dfrac{1.2 \times 10^9}{0.693} \cdot \ln \dfrac{1.00}{0.17}$

65. Given $[Cr(NH_3)_6](NO_3)_3$, what is the oxidation number of the Cr?

- **A.** 0
- **B.** +1
- **C.** +2
- **D.** +3
- **E.** +5

66. Which of the following does NOT exist?

- **A.** SF_6
- **B.** OF_6
- **C.** H_3PO_3
- **D.** NH_4NO_2
- **E.** NH_2OH

67. Which of the following unbalanced equation(s) demonstrates aluminum hydroxide's amphoteric properties?

- **(1)** $Al(OH)_{3(s)} + H_2O_{(l)} \longleftrightarrow Al_{(s)} + O_{2(g)} + H_2O_{(l)}$
- **(2)** $Al(OH)_{3(s)} \rightarrow Al_{(s)} + H_2O_{(g)}$
- **(3)** $Al(OH)_{3(s)} + O_{2(g)} \rightarrow Al_{(s)} + H_2O_{(g)}$
- **(4)** $Al(OH)_{3(s)} + NaOH_{(aq)} \rightarrow NaAl(OH)_{4(aq)}$
- **(5)** $Al(OH)_{3(s)} + HCl_{(aq)} \rightarrow AlCl_{3(aq)} + H_2O$

- **A.** 1
- **B.** 2 and 3
- **C.** 3 and 4
- **D.** 4 and 5
- **E.** all

68. A certain reaction is spontaneous at 77°C. If the enthalpy change for the reaction is 35 kJ, what is the minimum value of $\triangle S$ (in J/K) for the reaction?

- **A.** 10 J/K
- **B.** 100 J/K
- **C.** 1,000 J/K
- **D.** 10,000 J/K
- **E.** 100,000 J/K

69. Which of the following cities and times would most favor the following reaction sequences?

$$N_{2(g)} + O_{2(g)} \rightarrow 2NO_{(g)}$$
$$2NO_{(g)} + O_{2(g)} \rightarrow 2NO_{2(g)}$$
$$NO_{2(g)} + h\upsilon \rightarrow NO_{(g)} + O_{(g)}$$
$$O_{(g)} + O_{2(g)} \rightarrow O_{3(g)}$$

- **A.** Los Angeles in December
- **B.** New York in January
- **C.** Mexico City in August
- **D.** Honolulu anytime
- **E.** All would favor the reaction equally.

GO ON TO THE NEXT PAGE

70. A student added a KI solution to a solution of mercury(II) chloride and observed the formation of a precipitate. Which of the following graphs would be consistent with the observation?

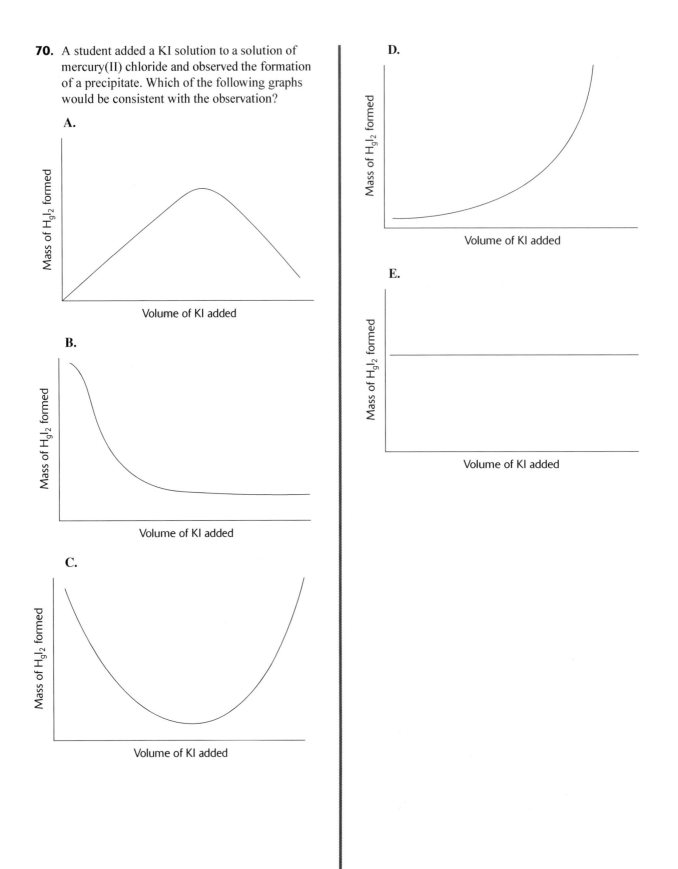

A.

Mass of Hg_{I_2} formed

Volume of KI added

B.

Mass of Hg_{I_2} formed

Volume of KI added

C.

Mass of Hg_{I_2} formed

Volume of KI added

D.

Mass of Hg_{I_2} formed

Volume of KI added

E.

Mass of Hg_{I_2} formed

Volume of KI added

71. Which of the following figures shows the titration curve of a weak acid vs. a strong base?

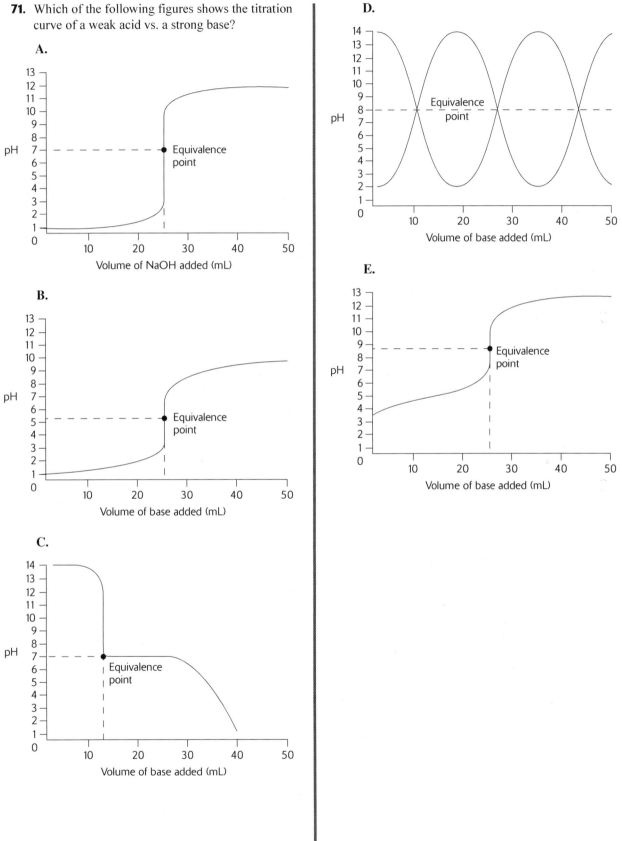

A.

B.

C.

D.

E.

GO ON TO THE NEXT PAGE

72. Which one of the following would be classified as a Lewis acid?

   A. H_2O

   B. I^-

   C. NH_3

   D. OH^-

   E. BCl_3

73. Gas A decomposed according to the following reaction:

$$A_{(g)} \longleftrightarrow B_{(g)} + C_{(g)}$$

A student conducted an experiment and determined that the equilibrium pressure of gas A was $0.20P$, where P was the total pressure of the system. What is the equilibrium constant K_P for this reaction?

   A. $0.10P$

   B. $0.20P$

   C. $0.40P$

   D. $0.80P$

   E. $1.6P$

74.

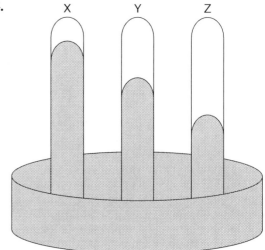

Consider manometers X, Y, and Z pictured. One of the manometers had 2 mL of water placed on top of the mercury, another had 2 mL of a 1 *m* glucose solution placed on top of the mercury, and another had 2 mL of a 1 *m* KCl solution placed on top of the mercury.

   A. Manometer X contained the water, manometer Y contained the glucose solution, and manometer Z contained the KCl solution.

   B. Manometer X contained the water, manometer Y contained the KCl solution, and manometer Z contained the glucose solution.

   C. Manometer X contained the glucose solution, manometer Y contained the water, and manometer Z contained the KCl solution.

   D. Manometer X contained the KCl solution, manometer Y contained the glucose solution, and manometer Z contained the water.

   E. Manometer X contained the glucose solution, manometer Y contained the KCl solution, and manometer Z contained the water.

75. The addition of aqueous ammonia to a solution containing a metallic ion may result in all of these EXCEPT

   A. an increase in the pH

   B. a decrease in the pH

   C. the formation of a precipitate containing OH^-

   D. the formation of a complex ion containing NH_3

   E. All of these effects occur.

IF YOU FINISH BEFORE TIME IS CALLED, CHECK YOUR WORK ON THIS SECTION ONLY. DO NOT WORK ON ANY OTHER SECTION IN THE TEST.

PERIODIC TABLE OF THE ELEMENTS

1 **H** 1.0079																	2 **He** 4.0026
3 **Li** 6.941	4 **Be** 9.012											5 **B** 10.811	6 **C** 12.011	7 **N** 14.007	8 **O** 16.00	9 **F** 19.00	10 **Ne** 20.179
11 **Na** 22.99	12 **Mg** 24.30											13 **Al** 26.98	14 **Si** 28.09	15 **P** 30.974	16 **S** 32.06	17 **Cl** 35.453	18 **Ar** 39.948
19 **K** 39.10	20 **Ca** 40.08	21 **Sc** 44.96	22 **Ti** 47.90	23 **V** 50.94	24 **Cr** 51.00	25 **Mn** 54.93	26 **Fe** 55.85	27 **Co** 58.93	28 **Ni** 58.69	29 **Cu** 63.55	30 **Zn** 65.39	31 **Ga** 69.72	32 **Ge** 72.59	33 **As** 74.92	34 **Se** 78.96	35 **Br** 79.90	36 **Kr** 83.80
37 **Rb** 85.47	38 **Sr** 87.62	39 **Y** 88.91	40 **Zr** 91.22	41 **Nb** 92.91	42 **Mo** 95.94	43 **Tc** (98)	44 **Ru** 101.1	45 **Rh** 102.91	46 **Pd** 105.42	47 **Ag** 107.87	48 **Cd** 112.41	49 **In** 114.82	50 **Sn** 118.71	51 **Sb** 121.75	52 **Te** 127.60	53 **I** 126.91	54 **Xe** 131.29
55 **Cs** 132.91	56 **Ba** 137.33	57 ***La** 138.91	72 **Hf** 178.49	73 **Ta** 180.95	74 **W** 183.85	75 **Re** 186.21	76 **Os** 190.2	77 **Ir** 192.22	78 **Pt** 195.08	79 **Au** 196.97	80 **Hg** 200.59	81 **Ti** 204.38	82 **Pb** 207.2	83 **Bi** 208.98	84 **Po** (209)	85 **At** (210)	86 **Rn** (222)
87 **Fr** (223)	88 **Ra** 226.02	89 **†Ac** 227.03	104 **Rf** (261)	105 **Db** (262)	106 **Sg** (263)	107 **Bh** (262)	108 **Hs** (265)	109 **Mt** (266)	110 **§** (269)	111 **§** (272)	112 **§** (277)						

§ Not yet named

* Lanthanide Series	58 **Ce** 140.12	59 **Pr** 140.91	60 **Nd** 144.24	61 **Pm** (145)	62 **Sm** 150.4	63 **Eu** 151.97	64 **Gd** 157.25	65 **Tb** 158.93	66 **Dy** 162.50	67 **Ho** 164.93	68 **Er** 167.26	69 **Tm** 168.93	70 **Yb** 173.04	71 **Lu** 174.97
† Actinide Series	90 **Th** 232.04	91 **Pa** 231.04	92 **U** 238.03	93 **Np** 237.05	94 **Pu** (244)	95 **Am** (243)	96 **Cm** (247)	97 **Bk** (247)	98 **Cf** (251)	99 **Es** (252)	100 **Fm** (257)	101 **Md** (258)	102 **No** (259)	103 **Lr** (260)

GO ON TO THE NEXT PAGE

STANDARD REDUCTION POTENTIALS IN AQUEOUS SOLUTION AT 25°C

Half-reaction			$E°(V)$
$F_{2\,(g)} + 2\,e^-$	→	$2\,F^-$	2.87
$Co^{3+} + e^-$	→	Co^{2+}	1.82
$Au^{3+} + 3\,e^-$	→	$Au_{(s)}$	1.50
$Cl_{2\,(g)} + 2\,e^-$	→	$2\,Cl^-$	1.36
$O_{2\,(g)} + 4\,H^+ + 4\,e^-$	→	$2\,H_2O_{(l)}$	1.23
$Br_{2\,(l)} + 2\,e^-$	→	$2\,Br^-$	1.07
$2\,Hg^{2+} + 2\,e^-$	→	Hg_2^{2+}	0.92
$Hg^{2+} + 2\,e^-$	→	$Hg_{(l)}$	0.85
$Ag^+ + e^-$	→	$Ag_{(s)}$	0.80
$Hg_2^{2+} + 2\,e^-$	→	$2\,Hg_{(l)}$	0.79
$Fe^{3+} + e^-$	→	Fe^{2+}	0.77
$I_{2\,(s)} + 2\,e^-$	→	$2\,I^-$	0.53
$Cu^+ + e^-$	→	$Cu_{(s)}$	0.52
$Cu^{2+} + 2\,e^-$	→	$Cu_{(s)}$	0.34
$Cu^{2+} + e^-$	→	Cu^+	0.15
$Sn^{4+} + 2\,e^-$	→	Sn^{2+}	0.15
$S_{(s)} + 2\,H^+ + 2\,e^-$	→	$H_2S_{(g)}$	0.14
$2\,H^+ + 2\,e^-$	→	$H_{2(g)}$	0.00
$Pb^{2+} + 2\,e^-$	→	$Pb_{(s)}$	−0.13
$Sn^{2+} + 2\,e^-$	→	$Sn_{(s)}$	−0.14
$Ni^{2+} + 2\,e^-$	→	$Ni_{(s)}$	−0.25
$Co^{2+} + 2\,e^-$	→	$Co_{(s)}$	−0.28
$Cd^{2+} + 2\,e^-$	→	$Cd_{(s)}$	−0.40
$Cr^{3+} + e^-$	→	Cr^{2+}	−0.41
$Fe^{2+} + 2\,e^-$	→	$Fe_{(s)}$	−0.44
$Cr^{3+} + 3\,e^-$	→	$Cr_{(s)}$	−0.74
$Zn^{2+} + 2\,e^-$	→	$Zn_{(s)}$	−0.76
$2\,H_2O_{(l)} + 2\,e^-$	→	$H_{2(g)} + 2\,OH^-$	−0.83
$Mn^{2+} + 2\,e^-$	→	$Mn_{(s)}$	−1.18
$Al^{3+} + 3\,e^-$	→	$Al_{(s)}$	−1.66
$Be^{2+} + 2\,e^-$	→	$Be_{(s)}$	−1.70
$Mg^{2+} + 2\,e^-$	→	$Mg_{(s)}$	−2.37
$Na^+ + e^-$	→	$Na_{(s)}$	−2.71
$Ca^{2+} + 2\,e^-$	→	$Ca_{(s)}$	−2.87
$Sr^{2+} + 2\,e^-$	→	$Sr_{(s)}$	−2.89
$Ba^{2+} + 2\,e^-$	→	$Ba_{(s)}$	−2.90
$Rb^+ + e^-$	→	$Rb_{(s)}$	−2.92
$K^+ + e^-$	→	$K_{(s)}$	−2.92
$Cs^+ + e^-$	→	$Cs_{(s)}$	−2.92
$Li^+ + e^-$	→	$Li_{(s)}$	−3.05

Note: Unless otherwise stated, assume that for all questions involving solutions and/or chemical equations, the system is in water at room temperature.

ADVANCED PLACEMENT CHEMISTRY EQUATIONS AND CONSTANTS

ATOMIC STRUCTURE

$$E = hv \qquad c = \lambda v$$

$$\lambda = \frac{h}{mv} \qquad p = mv$$

$$E_n = \frac{-2.178 \times 10^{-18}}{n^2} \text{ joule}$$

EQUILIBRIUM

$$K_a = \frac{[H^+][A^-]}{[HA]}$$

$$K_b = \frac{[OH^-][HB^+]}{[B]}$$

$$K_w = [OH^-][H^+] = 1.0 \times 10^{-14} \text{ @ } 25°C$$
$$= K_a \times K_b$$

$$pH = -\log[H^+], \quad pOH = -\log[OH^-]$$

$$14 = pH + pOH$$

$$pH = pK_a + \log\frac{[A^-]}{[HA]}$$

$$pOH = pK_b + \log\frac{[HB^+]}{[B]}$$

$$pK_a = -\log K_a, \quad pK_b = -\log K_b$$

$$K_p = K_c(RT)^{\Delta n}$$

where Δn = moles product gas − moles reactant gas

THERMOCHEMISTRY/KINETICS

$$\Delta S° = \Sigma S° \text{ products} - \Sigma S° \text{ reactants}$$

$$\Delta H° = \Sigma \Delta H_f° \text{ products} - \Sigma \Delta H_f° \text{ reactants}$$

$$\Delta G° = \Sigma \Delta G_f° \text{ products} - \Sigma \Delta G_f° \text{ reactants}$$

$$\Delta G° = \Delta H° - T\Delta S°$$
$$= -RT \ln K = -2.303 \, RT \log K$$
$$= -n \, \mathscr{F} \, E°$$

$$\Delta G = \Delta G° + RT \ln Q = \Delta G° + 2.303 \, RT \log Q$$
$$q = mc\Delta T$$
$$C_p = \frac{\Delta H}{\Delta T}$$

$$\ln[A]_t - \ln[A]_0 = -kt$$

$$\frac{1}{[A]_t} - \frac{1}{[A]_0} = kt$$

$$\ln k = \frac{-E_a}{R}\left(\frac{1}{T}\right) + \ln A$$

E = energy $\qquad v$ = velocity
v = frequency $\qquad n$ = principal quantum number
λ = wavelength
p = momentum $\qquad m$ = mass

Speed of light, $c = 3.0 \times 10^8 \text{ m} \cdot \text{s}^{-1}$

Planck's constant, $h = 6.63 \times 10^{-34} \text{ J} \cdot \text{s}$

Boltzmann's constant, $k = 1.38 \times 10^{-23} \text{ J} \cdot \text{K}^{-1}$

Avogadro's number $= 6.022 \times 10^{23} \text{ mol}^{-1}$

Electron charge, $e = -1.602 \times 10^{-19} \text{ coulomb}$

1 electron volt per atom $= 96.5 \text{ kJ} \cdot \text{mol}^{-1}$

Equilibrium Constants
K_a (weak acid)
K_b (weak base)
K_w (water)
K_p (gas pressure)
K_c (molar concentrations)

$S°$ = standard entropy
$H°$ = standard enthalpy
$G°$ = standard free energy
$E°$ = standard reduction potential
T = temperature
n = moles
m = mass
q = heat
c = specific heat capacity
C_p = molar heat capacity at constant pressure
E_a = activation energy
k = rate constant
A = frequency factor

Faraday's constant, $\mathscr{F} = 96,500$ coulombs per mole of electrons

Gas constant, $R = 8.31 \text{ J} \cdot \text{mol}^{-1} \cdot \text{K}^{-1}$
$= 0.0821 \text{ L} \cdot \text{atm} \cdot \text{mol}^{-1} \cdot \text{K}^{-1}$
$= 8.31 \text{ volt} \cdot \text{coulomb} \cdot \text{mol}^{-1} \cdot \text{K}^{-1}$

GO ON TO THE NEXT PAGE

GASES, LIQUIDS, AND SOLUTIONS

$$PV = nRT$$

$$\left(P + \frac{n^2 a}{V^2}\right)(V - nb) = nRT$$

$$P_A = P_{total} \times X_A, \text{ where } X_A = \frac{\text{moles A}}{\text{total moles}}$$

$$P_{total} = P_A + P_B + P_C + \ldots$$

$$n = \frac{m}{M}$$

$$K = {}^\circ C + 273$$

$$\frac{P_1 V_1}{T_1} = \frac{P_2 V_2}{T_2}$$

$$D = \frac{m}{V}$$

$$u_{rms} = \sqrt{\frac{3kT}{m}} = \sqrt{\frac{3RT}{m}}$$

$$KE \text{ per molecule} = \tfrac{1}{2}mv^2$$

$$KE \text{ per mole} = \tfrac{3}{2}RT$$

$$\frac{r_1}{r_2} = \sqrt{\frac{M_2}{M_1}}$$

molarity, M = moles solute per liter solution

molality, m = moles solute per kilogram solvent

$$\Delta T_f = i \cdot K_f \times \text{molality}$$

$$\Delta T_b = i \cdot K_b \times \text{molality}$$

$$\pi = i \cdot M \cdot R \cdot T$$

$$A = a \cdot b \cdot c$$

P = pressure
V = volume
T = temperature
n = number of moles
D = density
m = mass
v = velocity

u_{rms} = root-mean-square speed
KE = kinetic energy
r = rate of effusion
M = molar mass
π = osmotic pressure
i = van't Hoff factor
K_f = molal freezing-point depression constant
K_b = molal boiling-point elevation constant
A = absorbance
a = molar absorptivity
b = path length
c = concentration
Q = reaction quotient
I = current (amperes)
q = charge (coulombs)
t = time (seconds)
E° = standard reduction potential
K = equilibrium constant

OXIDATION-REDUCTION; ELECTROCHEMISTRY

$$Q = \frac{[C]^c [D]^d}{[A]^a [B]^b}, \text{ where } a\,A + b\,B \rightarrow c\,C + d\,D$$

$$I = \frac{q}{t}$$

$$E_{cell} = E^\circ_{cell} - \frac{RT}{n\mathscr{F}} \ln Q = E^\circ_{cell} - \frac{0.0592}{n} \log Q \text{ @ } 25^\circ C$$

$$\log K = \frac{n \cdot E^\circ}{0.0592}$$

Gas constant, R = 8.31 J $\cdot$ mol^{-1} $\cdot$ K^{-1}
= 0.0821 L $\cdot$ atm $\cdot$ mol^{-1} $\cdot$ K^{-1}
= 8.31 volt $\cdot$ coulomb $\cdot$ mol^{-1} $\cdot$ K^{-1}

Boltzmann's constant, k = 1.38 $\times$ 10^{-23} J $\cdot$ K^{-1}

K_f for H_2O = 1.86 K $\cdot$ kg $\cdot$ mol^{-1}

K_b for H_2O = 0.512 K $\cdot$ kg $\cdot$ mol^{-1}

1 atm = 760 mm Hg
= 760 torr

STP = 0.000° C and 1.000 atm

Faraday's constant, $\mathscr{F}$ = 96,500 coulombs per mole of electrons

Section II: Free-Response Questions

CHEMISTRY

Section II

(Total time—90 minutes)

Part A

Time—40 minutes

YOU MAY USE YOUR CALCULATOR FOR PART A

CLEARLY SHOW THE METHOD USED AND STEPS INVOLVED IN ARRIVING AT YOUR ANSWERS. It is to your advantage to do this, because you may obtain partial credit if you do and you will receive little or no credit if you do not. Attention should be paid to significant figures.

Answer Question 1 below. The Section II score weighting for this question is 20%.

$$HOCl_{(aq)} \longleftrightarrow H^+_{(aq)} + OCl^-_{(aq)} \qquad K_a = 2.9 \times 10^{-8}$$

1. Hypochlorous acid, HOCl, is a weak acid that ionizes in water, as shown in the equation above.

    (a) Calculate the $[H^+]$ in a HOCl solution that has a pH of 5.24.

    (b) Write the equilibrium expression for the ionization of HOCl in water, then calculate the concentration of $HOCl_{(aq)}$ in a HOCl solution that has $[H^+]$ equal to 2.4×10^{-5} M.

    (c) A solution of $Ba(OH)_2$ is titrated into a solution of HOCl.

        (i) Calculate the volume of 0.200 M $Ba(OH)_{2(aq)}$ needed to reach the equivalence point when titrated into a 75.0 mL sample of 0.150 M $HOCl_{(aq)}$.

        (ii) Calculate the pH at the equivalence point.

    (d) Calculate the number of moles of $NaOCl_{(s)}$ that would have to be added to 150 mL of 0.150 M HOCl to produce a buffer solution with $[H^+] = 6.00 \times 10^{-9}$ M. Assume that volume change is negligible.

    (e) HOCl is a weaker acid than $HClO_3$. Account for this fact in terms of molecular structure.

Answer EITHER Question 2 or 3 below. Only one of these two questions will be graded. If you start both questions, be sure to cross out the question you do not want graded. The Section II score weighting for the question you choose is 20%.

2. A rigid 9.50 L flask contained a mixture of 3.00 moles of hydrogen gas, 1.00 moles of oxygen gas, and enough neon gas so that the partial pressure of the neon in the flask was 3.00 atm. The temperature was 27°C.

    (a) Calculate the total pressure in the flask.

    (b) Calculate the mole fraction of oxygen in the flask.

    (c) Calculate the density $(g \cdot mL^{-1})$ of the mixture in the flask.

    (d) The gas mixture is ignited by a spark and the reaction below occurs until one of the reactants is totally consumed.

$$O_{2(g)} + 2H_{2(g)} \rightarrow 2H_2O_{(g)}$$

Give the mole fraction of all species present in the flask at the end of the reaction.

GO ON TO THE NEXT PAGE

3. The following question concerns acetylsalicylic acid, the active ingredient in aspirin.

   (a) A manufacturer produced an aspirin tablet that contained 350 mg of acetylsalicylic acid per tablet. Each tablet weighed 2.50 grams. Calculate the mass percent of acetylsalicylic acid in the tablet.

   (b) The structural formula of acetylsalicylic acid, also known as 2–acetoxybenzoic acid is shown below.

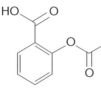

   A scientist combusted 5.000 grams of pure acetylsalicylic acid and produced 2.004 g of water and 6.21 L of dry carbon dioxide, measured at 770. mm Hg and 27°C. Calculate the mass (in grams) of each element in the 5.000 g sample.

   (c) The chemist then dissolved 1.593 grams of pure acetylsalicylic acid in distilled water and titrated the resulting solution to the equivalence point using 44.25 mL of 0.200 M $NaOH_{(aq)}$. Assuming that acetylsalicylic acid has only one ionizable hydrogen, calculate the molar mass of the acid.

   (d) A 3.00×10^{-3} mole sample of pure acetylsalicylic acid was dissolved in 20.00 mL of water and was then titrated with 0.200 M $NaOH_{(aq)}$. The equivalence point was reached after 15.00 mL of the NaOH solution had been added. Using the data from the titration, shown in the table below, determine

   (i) the value of the acid dissociation constant, K_a, for acetylsalicylic acid

   (ii) the pH of the solution after a total volume of 30.00 mL of the NaOH solution had been added (assume that volumes are additive)

Volume of 0.200 M NaOH added (mL)	pH
0.00	2.40
5.00	3.03
7.50	3.56
15.00	4.05
30.00	?

CHEMISTRY

Part B

Time—50 minutes

NO CALCULATORS MAY BE USED FOR PART B

Answer Question 4 below. The Section II score weight for this question is 15%.

4. Write the formulas to show the reactants and the products for any FIVE of the laboratory situations described below. Answers to more than five choices will not be graded. In all cases, a reaction occurs. Assume that solutions are aqueous unless otherwise indicated. Represent substances in solution as ions if the substances are extensively ionized. Omit formulas for any ions or molecules that are unchanged by the reaction. You need not balance the equations.

Example: A strip of magnesium is added to a solution of silver nitrate.

Ex.	$Mg + Ag^+ \longrightarrow Mg^2 + Ag$

   (a) A piece of solid tin is heated in the presence of chlorine gas.

   (b) Ethane is burned completely in air.

   (c) Solid copper shavings are added to a hot, dilute nitric acid solution.

   (d) Dilute sulfuric acid is added to a solution of mercuric nitrate.

   (e) Sulfur trioxide gas is heated in the presence of solid calcium oxide.

   (f) Copper sulfate pentahydrate is strongly heated.

   (g) A strong ammonia solution is added to a suspension of zinc hydroxide.

   (h) Ethane gas is heated in the presence of bromine gas to yield a monobrominated product.

Your responses to the rest of the questions in this part of the examination will be graded on the basis of the accuracy and relevance of the information cited. Explanations should be clear and well organized. Examples and equations may be included in your responses where appropriate. Specific answers are preferable to broad, diffuse responses.

Answer BOTH Question 5 AND Question 6 below. Both of these questions will be graded. The Section II score weighting for these questions is 30% (15% each).

5. Give a brief explanation for each of the following:

   (a) Water can act either as an acid or as a base.

   (b) HF is a weaker acid than HCl.

   (c) For the triprotic acid H_3PO_4, K_{a_1} is 7.5×10^{-3} whereas K_{a_2} is 6.2×10^{-8}.

   (d) Pure HCl is not an acid.

   (e) $HClO_4$ is a stronger acid than $HClO_3$, HSO_3^-, or H_2SO_3.

GO ON TO THE NEXT PAGE

6. Interpret each of the following four examples using modern bonding principles.

    (a) C_2H_2 and C_2H_6 both contain two carbon atoms. However, the bond between the two carbons in C_2H_2 is significantly shorter than that between the two carbons in C_2H_6.

    (b) The bond angle in the hydronium ion, H_3O^+, is less than $109.5°$, the angle of a tetrahedron.

    (c) The lengths of the bonds between the carbon and the oxygens in the carbonate ion, CO_3^{2-}, are all equal and are longer than one might expect to find in the carbon monoxide molecule, CO.

    (d) The CNO^- ion is linear.

Answer EITHER Question 7 or 8 below. Only one of these two questions will be graded. If you start both questions, be sure to cross out the question you do not want graded. The Section II score weighting for the question you choose is 15%.

7. If one completely vaporizes a measured amount of a volatile liquid, the molecular weight of the liquid can be determined by measuring the volume, temperature, and pressure of the resulting gas. When using this procedure, one must use the ideal gas equation and assume that the gas behaves ideally. However, if the temperature of the gas is only slightly above the boiling point of the liquid, the gas deviates from ideal behavior.

    (a) Explain the postulates of the ideal gas equation.

    (b) Explain why, if measured just above the boiling point, the molecular weight deviates from the true value.

    (c) Explain whether the molecular weight of a real gas would be higher or lower than a predicted by the van der Waals equation.

8. Given three compounds PH_3, H_2O, and F_2:

    (a) What factors would influence their boiling points?

    (b) Which compound would have the highest boiling point and explain your reasoning.

    (c) Which compound would have the lowest boiling point and explain your reasoning.

    (d) Which compound would be intermediate between your choices for (b) and (c) and explain your reasoning.

Answer Key for Practice Exam 1

Section I: Multiple-Choice Questions

1. E		**26.** D		**51.** D	
2. E		**27.** C		**52.** E	
3. B		**28.** A		**53.** D	
4. A		**29.** E		**54.** E	
5. A		**30.** B		**55.** C	
6. B		**31.** D		**56.** E	
7. A		**32.** C		**57.** B	
8. A		**33.** D		**58.** D	
9. A		**34.** D		**59.** B	
10. C		**35.** B		**60.** A	
11. B		**36.** B		**61.** C	
12. C		**37.** B		**62.** B	
13. B		**38.** C		**63.** C	
14. C		**39.** D		**64.** E	
15. A		**40.** C		**65.** D	
16. D		**41.** C		**66.** B	
17. C		**42.** C		**67.** D	
18. C		**43.** D		**68.** B	
19. A		**44.** E		**69.** C	
20. C		**45.** B		**70.** A	
21. A		**46.** E		**71.** E	
22. A		**47.** A		**72.** E	
23. A		**48.** C		**73.** D	
24. E		**49.** A		**74.** D	
25. C		**50.** E		**75.** B	

Predicting Your AP Score

The table below shows historical relationships between students' results on the multiple-choice portion (Section I) of the AP Chemistry exam and their overall AP score. The AP score ranges from 1 to 5, with 3, 4, or 5 generally considered to be passing. Over the years, around 60% of the students who take the AP Chemistry Exam receive a 3, 4, or 5.

After you've taken the multiple-choice practice exam under timed conditions, count the number of questions you got correct. From this number, subtract the number of wrong answers times $\frac{1}{4}$. Do NOT count items left blank as wrong. Then refer to this table to find your "probable" overall AP score. For example, if you get 39 questions correct, based on historical statistics, you have a 25% chance of receiving an overall score of 3, a 63% chance of receiving an overall score of 4, and a 12% chance of receiving an overall score of 5. Note that your actual results may be different from the score this table predicts. Also, remember that the free-response section represents 55% of your AP score.

No attempt is made here to combine your specific results on the practice AP Chemistry free-response questions (Section II) with your multiple-choice results (which is beyond the scope of this book and for which no data is available). However, you should have your AP chemistry instructor review your essays before you take the AP Chemistry Exam so that he or she can give you additional pointers.

Number of Multiple-Choice Questions Correct*	*Overall AP Score*				
	1	*2*	*3*	*4*	*5*
47 to 75	0%	0%	1%	21%	78%
37 to 46	0%	0%	25%	63%	12%
24 to 36	0%	19%	69%	12%	0%
13 to 23	15%	70%	15%	0%	0%
0 to 12	86%	14%	0%	0%	0%
% of Test Takers Receiving Score	21%	22%	25%	15%	17%

*Corrected for wrong answers

Answers and Explanations for Practice Exam 1

1. **(E)** The electron configuration for aluminum is $1s^2 2s^2 2p^6 3s^2 3p^1$.

2. **(E)** Atoms get bigger as you go down groups. The reason is that principal energy levels of electrons are being added. Leaving the noble gases out, atoms get smaller as you go across a period.

3. **(B)** As we move from left to right across a period, the ionization energy tends to increase: Z_{eff} is increasing, while 'n' is unchanged. The valence electrons experience greater effective nuclear charge, are closer to the nucleus, and hence are more difficult to remove. As we move down a family, ionization energy decreases. As one increases the charge on a species it becomes more difficult to remove an electron. Again, size can be used as an indicator: small size = hard to remove the valence electron.

4. **(A)** The carbon of carbon dioxide has two double bonds. Because there are no unshared pairs of electrons on the central carbon atom, VSEPR theory predicts a linear molecular geometry (type AX_2).

5. **(A)** Hybridization involves making combination of s and p atomic orbitals to form molecular orbitals that are directed along certain directions. In sp^3 hybridization, the bonds are along the four directions connecting the center of a regular tetrahedron to its four corners. In sp^2 hybridization, the bonds are along the sides of a hexagon and make angles of $120°$ with each other. In sp hybridization, the bonds are directed along a linear chain. Because CO_2 is linear, it has sp hybridization.

6. **(B)** 0.05 moles would be the maximum amount that would react completely with the given amount of the weak base: moles $C_2H_3O_2^- = (0.50 \text{ L}) (0.10 \text{ M}) = 0.050$ moles. Because the acid and base react in a 1:1 mole ratio, 0.050 moles of HCl would use up all of the acetate ion.

7. **(A)** The greater the disorder of the system, the larger the entropy. There is an increase in the number of particles and thus greater disorder.

8. **(A)** Entropy increases upon expansion. The molecules under 1.0 atm of pressure are freer to move around. They are less constricted.

9. **(A)** Sublimation means the change from the ordered solid phase to the random gas phase.

10. **(C)** There are three molecules on the left for every two on the right. The reaction system is becoming more ordered on the right.

11. **(B)** The system is in equilibrium. The rate of the forward reaction equals the rate of the reverse reaction. No one particular side is becoming more (or less) ordered than the other. No additional stress is being placed on the system.

12. **(C)** Baking soda is sodium hydrogen carbonate.

    This is the modern method and is called the Stock system. This name arises from the universal name of "carbonate" given to CO_3^{2-}. The name "sodium bicarbonate" is also accepted; it is an older, historically used name.

13. **(B)** Calcium oxide, also known as 'lime' is a white crystalline solid and is manufactured by heating limestone, coral, sea shells, or chalk, which are mainly $CaCO_3$, to drive off carbon dioxide. This reaction is reversible; calcium oxide will react with carbon dioxide to form calcium carbonate. CaO reacts with H^+ to form Ca^{2+} and H_2O.

14. **(C)**

Number of Atoms Bonded to Central Atom X	Number of Unshared Pairs on X	Hybridization	Geometry	Example
6	0	sp^3d^2	octahedral	SF_6

15. **(A)** Remember, $\log [H^+] = -pH$, so $[H^+] = 10^{-pH}$

16. (D) A catalyst is a substance that increases the rate of a chemical reaction without itself being consumed. The catalyst may react to form an intermediate, but it is regenerated in a subsequent step of the reaction. The catalyst speeds up a reaction by providing a set of elementary steps (reaction mechanisms) with more favorable kinetics than those that existed in its absence. Choices A and C, even though they are true statements, are the results of a lowered activation energy.

17. (C) Begin this problem by balancing the reaction.

$$2C_2H_{6(g)} + 7O_{2(g)} \rightarrow 4CO_{2(g)} + 6H_2O_{(g)}$$

Because $\triangle H° = \Sigma \triangle H°_{f\ products} - \Sigma \triangle H°_{f\ reactants}$, you can substitute at this point (because calculators are NOT allowed, it is best to estimate).

$$\triangle H° = [4(-400) + 6(-250)] - 2(-100) = -1600 - 1500 + 200$$
$$= -2900 \text{ kJ}$$

However, remember that the question calls for the answer per mole of C_2H_2. Thus, because the balanced equation is written for 2 moles of C_2H_6, simply divide -2900 by 2 and you get the approximate answer of -1455 kJ.

18. (C) This problem can be solved using the factor-label method.

100. g solution – 10. g solute = 90 g solvent (H_2O)

$$\frac{10. \text{g } C_6H_2O}{90. \text{g } H_2O} \times \frac{1000 \text{ g } H_2O}{1 \text{ kg } H_2O} \times \frac{1 \text{ mole } C_6H_2O}{90. \text{g } C_6H_2O} = 1.2 \ m$$

This problem can be done faster through estimation:

$$\frac{(10)(1000)}{(90)(90)} = \frac{(10)(10)}{(9)(9)} = \frac{100}{81} \approx 1.2$$

19. (A) Begin by writing as much of an equation as you can:

$$S_{8(s)} + M_{(s)} \rightarrow M_aS_{b(s)}$$

From the information provided, you can determine that the residue, $M_aS_{b(s)}$, weighed 21.00 grams ($62.00 - 41.00$) and that the metal M weighed 14.00 grams ($55.00 - 41.00$). According to the Law of Conservation of Mass, the sulfur that reacted with the metal must have weighed 7.00 grams ($21.00 - 14.00$). You can now set up a proportion that relates the grams of S_8 and M to the respective equivalent weights (molar mass divided by the oxidation number):

$$\frac{7.00 \text{ grams sulfur } (S_8)}{16.0 \text{ grams/equiv. sulfur}} = \frac{14.00 \text{ grams M}}{x \text{ grams/equiv.}}$$

Solving for x, you obtain 32.00 grams/equiv. for metal M. From this information, it would seem reasonable that the unknown metal is copper, forming the compound CuS. Copper, with a +2 valence, has an equivalent weight of 31.78.

20. (C) Raoult's Law states that the partial pressure of a solvent over a solution, P_1, is given by the vapor pressure of the pure solvent, $P_1°$, times the mole fraction of the solvent in the solution, X_1.

$$P_1 = X_1 P_1°$$

21. (A) Heat needs to be absorbed when a solid melts; therefore, the reaction is endothermic, $\triangle H > 0$. When a solid melts and becomes a liquid, it is becoming more disordered, $\triangle S > 0$.

22. (A) Because all choices have 18 electrons in their valence shell, you should pick the species with the fewest protons in the nucleus; this would result in the weakest electrostatic attraction. That species is sulfur.

23. **(A)** Begin by writing a balanced equation. Remember that all Group II carbonates decompose to yield the metallic oxide plus carbon dioxide gas:

$$CaCO_{3(s)} \rightarrow CaO_{(s)} + CO_{2(g)}$$

According to the balanced equation, any loss of mass during the experiment would have to have come from the carbon dioxide gas leaving the test tube. 4.40 grams of CO_2 gas corresponds to ≈ 0.100 mole (4.40 g CO_2 / (44.01 g · mol^{-1}). Because all of the calcium carbonate decomposed, and the calcium carbonate and carbon dioxide gas are in a 1:1 molar ratio, you must originally have had ≈ 0.100 moles of calcium carbonate, or ≈ 10.0 grams (0.100 mole $CaCO_3$ / (100. g · mol^{-1}). The calcium carbonate and test tube weighed 30.08 grams, so if you get rid of the calcium carbonate, you are left with ≈ 20.08 grams for the empty test tube.

24. **(E)** Begin with a balanced equation:

$$C_4H_{10} + {}^{13}\!/_2\, O_2 \rightarrow 4CO_2 + 5H_2O$$

Next, set up the equation in factor-label fashion:

$$\frac{100 \text{ g } C_4H_{10}}{1} \times \frac{1 \text{ mole } C_4H_{10}}{58.14 \text{ g } C_4H_{10}} \times \frac{5 \text{ mole } H_2O}{1 \text{ mole } C_4H_{10}} \times \frac{18.02 \text{ g } H_2O}{1 \text{ mole } H_2O} = \text{ g } H_2O$$

25. **(C)** Draw a structural diagram.

Step 1: Decide which bonds need to be broken on the reactant side of the reaction. Add up all the bond energies for the bonds that are broken. Call this subtotal $\triangle H°_1$. Assign $\triangle H°_1$ a positive value because energy is required when bonds are broken. In this example, a C=O and a H–H bond need to be broken. This becomes $\triangle H_1 =$ x kJ/mole + 435 kJ/mole. **Note:** Because four C–H bonds are broken and then reformed, they do not need to be considered.

Step 2: Decide which bonds need to be formed on the product side of the reaction. Add up all of the bond energies that are formed. Call this subtotal $\triangle H°_2$. Assign $\triangle H°_2$ a negative value because energy is released when bonds are formed. In the example given, a C–H, a C–O, and a O–H bond need to be formed. This becomes 414 kJ/mole + 351 kJ/mole + 464 kJ/mole, or 1229 kJ/mole. Remember to assign a negative sign, which makes $\triangle H°_2 = -1229$ kJ/mole.

Step 3: Apply Hess's Law: $\triangle H° = \triangle H°_1 + \triangle H°_2$. You know that $\triangle H°$ is –71 kJ/mole, so Hess's Law becomes

–71 kJ/mole = 435 kJ/mole + x kJ/mole – 1229 kJ/mole

x = 723 kJ/mole

which represents the bond energy of the C=O bond.

Because the answer choices are fairly far apart, a student who wishes to save time could round the bond energies to the nearest tens:

$$\triangle H°_2 = -(410 + 350 + 460) = -1220$$

$$\triangle H° = \triangle H°_1 + \triangle H°_2$$

$$-70 \text{ kJ/mole} = 440 \text{ kJ/mole} + x \text{ kJ/mole} - 1220 \text{ kJ/mole}$$

$$\approx 710 \text{ kJ/mole}$$

26. (D) Examine the first reaction and realize that $SO_{2(g)}$ needs to be on the reactant side. Reverse the equation and change the sign of $\triangle H°$. When you examine the second reaction, you notice that $SO_{3(g)}$ is on the correct side, so there is no need to reverse this equation. At this point, the two reactions can be added together:

$$SO_{2\,(g)} \rightarrow S_{(s)} + O_{2\,(g)} \qquad \triangle H° = 295 \text{ kJ/mole}$$
$$S_{(s)} + \tfrac{1}{2}O_{2\,(g)} \rightarrow SO_{3\,(g)} \qquad \triangle H° = -395 \text{ kJ/mole}$$
$$\overline{SO_{2\,(g)} + \tfrac{1}{2}O_{2\,(g)} \rightarrow SO_{3\,(g)} \qquad \triangle H° = -100 \text{ kJ/mole}}$$

But before concluding that this is your answer, note that the question asks for $\triangle H°$ in terms of 2 moles of $SO_{2(g)}$. Doubling the $\triangle H°$ gives the answer, –200. kJ/mole.

27. (C) Begin this problem by listing the known facts:

$m = 2.00$ g $\quad V = 0.821$ liter $\qquad T = 127°C + 273 = 400.$ K

$P = 1.00$ atm $\quad MM = ?$

You will need to use the ideal gas law to solve the problem:

$PV = nRT$. Because moles can be calculated by dividing the mass of the sample by its molecular weight, the ideal gas law becomes

$$P \cdot V = \frac{m}{MW} = R \cdot T$$

Solving for MW yields

$$MW = \frac{m \cdot R \cdot T}{P \cdot V} = \frac{(2.00 \text{ g})(0.0821 \text{ liter} \cdot \text{atm})(400. \text{ K})}{(1.00 \text{ atm})(0.0821 \text{ liter}) \cdot \text{mole} \cdot \text{K}}$$
$$= 80.0 \text{ g/mole}$$

28. (A) H_2O_2 is not stable—it disproportionates (it is both oxidized and reduced).

$$H_2O_{2\,(aq)} \rightarrow O_{2\,(g)} + 2H^+_{\,(aq)} + 2e^- \qquad E°_{ax} = -0.68V$$
$$H_2O_{2\,(aq)} + 2H^+_{\,(aq)} + 2e^- \rightarrow 2H_2O_{(l)} \qquad E°_{red} = 1.77V$$
$$\overline{2H_2O_{2\,(aq)} \rightarrow 2H_2O_{(l)} + O_{2\,(g)} \qquad E° = 1.09V}$$

29. (E) Oxygen gas weighs 32 grams per mole, whereas helium gas weighs only 4 grams per mole. One can see that there are roughly 3 moles of oxygen molecules ($100 \text{ g} / (32 \text{ g} \cdot \text{mol}^{-1})$) and 25 moles of helium atoms ($100 \text{ g} / (4 \text{ g} \cdot \text{mol}^{-1})$). Gas pressure is proportional to the number of molecules and temperature, and inversely proportional to the size of the container. Since there are more helium molecules, you would expect a higher pressure in the helium container (with all other variables being held constant). As long as the temperatures of the two containers are the same, the average kinetic energies of the two gases are the same.

30. (B) The photoelectric effect is the emission of electrons from the surface of a metal when light shines on it. Electrons are emitted, however, only when the frequency of that light is greater than a certain threshold value characteristic of the particular metal. The alkali metals, with only one electron in their valence shells, have the lowest threshold values.

31. (D) You need to know two relationships to do this problem. First,

$$\nu = \frac{E}{h} = \frac{3.313 \times 10^{-19} \text{ J}}{6.626 \times 10^{-34} \text{ J} \cdot \text{sec}} = 5.000 \times 10^{14} \text{ sec}^{-1}$$

The second relationship you need to know is

$$\lambda = \frac{c}{\nu} = \frac{3.00 \times 10^{10} \text{ cm} \cdot \text{sec}}{\text{sec} \cdot (5.000 \times 10^{14})} = 6.00 \times 10^{-5} \text{ cm}$$

Radiation of 6.00×10^{-5} cm is equivalent to 600 nm, placing the radiation in the visible spectrum (yellow-orange).

An alternative approach would be to use the relationship

$$\lambda = \frac{h \cdot c}{E} = \frac{6.626 \times 10^{-34} \, \text{J} \cdot \text{sec} \cdot 3.00 \times 10^{10} \, \text{cm} \cdot \text{sec}^{-1}}{3.313 \times 10^{-19} \, \text{J}}$$

32. (C) There are no alternative ways of positioning electrons around the HI molecule. Resonance only occurs in species that contain double and/or triple bonds. If you missed this question, refer to your textbook on the concept of resonance.

33. (D) Because the distance between the electrons and the nucleus is increasing, the electrons are becoming farther away from the nucleus, making it easier to remove them by overcoming the electrostatic force attracting them to the nucleus. Also, there are more electrons in the way, increasing interference (the electron-shielding effect).

34. (D) Potassium is a metal, and the polyatomic anion, ClO_4^- is a nonmetal; therefore, the compound is an ionic solid at room temperature. When the compound is dissolved in water, the ionic bond between the cation K^+ and the polyatomic anion ClO_4^- is broken due to the polarity of the water molecule, resulting in the two aqueous ions, K^+ and ClO_4^-.

35. (B) This is the definition of critical temperature.

36. (B) This problem can be easily solved using the factor-label method:

$$\frac{1.00 \; \text{liter sol'n}}{1} \times \frac{1000 \; \text{mL sol'n}}{1 \; \text{liter sol'n}} \times \frac{2.00 \; \text{g sol'n}}{1 \; \text{mL sol'n}} \times \frac{10.0 \; \text{g sucrose}}{100.0 \; \text{g sol'n}} = 2.00 \times 10^2 \, \text{g sucrose}$$

37. (B) Note that the nonbonding electron pairs have been deleted from oxygen and nitrogen for simplicity.

38. (C) $\triangle T = \text{molality} \cdot k_f$

$\triangle T = 102°C - 100°C = 2°C$

Because molality = mol solute (n) / kg water (m_w)...then $\triangle T = (n/m_w) \cdot k_f$

Finally, because $MM = m_{solute}/n$ . . . then $n = m_{solute}/MM$.

So, $\triangle T = m_{solute} \cdot k_f / (MM \cdot m_w)$

or, $m_{solute} = (\triangle T \cdot MM \cdot m_w)/ k_f$

This problem can now be solved using the factor-label method:

$$\frac{520. \; \text{g H}_2\text{O}}{1} \times \frac{1 \; \text{kg H}_2\text{O}}{1000 \; \text{g H}_2\text{o}} \times \frac{1 \; \text{mole C}_3\text{H}_5(\text{OH})_3}{0.52°C \cdot \text{kg H}_2\text{O}} \times \frac{92.1 \; \text{g C}_3\text{H}_5(\text{OH})_3}{1 \; \text{mole C}_3\text{H}_5(\text{OH})_3} \times \frac{2.00°C}{1} = 184 \, \text{g C}_3\text{H}_5(\text{OH})_3$$

39. (D) Let x be what needs to be done to [B].

$$\frac{\text{rate}_{new}}{\text{rate}_{old}} = \frac{1}{2} = \frac{k\left(\dfrac{[A]}{2}\right)^2 \cdot x[B]}{k[A]^2 \cdot [B]} = \frac{x}{4}$$

$x = 2$

40. (C) Begin by writing the balanced equation at equilibrium.

$Cl_{2(g)} \longleftrightarrow Cl_{(g)}$

Next, write an equilibrium expression.

$$K_c = \frac{[Cl]^2}{[Cl_2]}$$

Then create a chart that outlines the initial and final concentrations for the various species.

Species	Initial Concentration	Final Concentration
Cl_2	$\dfrac{6.0 \text{ moles}}{3.0 \text{ liters}} = 2.0 \text{ M}$	$6.0 \text{ moles} - (0.5)(6.0) = 3.0 \text{ moles}$ $\dfrac{3.0 \text{ moles}}{3.0 \text{ liters}} = 1.0 \text{ M}$
Cl	$\dfrac{0 \text{ moles}}{3.0 \text{ liters}} = 0 \text{ M}$	$\dfrac{3.0 \text{ moles } Cl_2 \text{ dissociated}}{1} \times \dfrac{2 \text{ moles } Cl}{1 \text{ mole } Cl_2}$ $= 6.0 \text{ moles } Cl \text{ at equilibrium}$ $\dfrac{6.0 \text{ moles } Cl}{3.0 \text{ liters}} = 2.0 \text{ M}$

Finally, substitute the concentrations (at equilibrium) into the equilibrium expression.

$$K_c = \frac{[Cl]^2}{[Cl_2]} = \frac{(2.0)^2}{1.0} = 4.0$$

41. **(C)** This problem involves the concept of multiple equilibria. The dissociation constants given in the example are related to the following reactions:

$$H_3PO_{4(aq)} \longleftrightarrow H^+_{(aq)} + H_2PO_4^-_{(aq)} \qquad K_1 = 7.0 \times 10^{-3}$$

$$H_2PO_4^-_{(aq)} \longleftrightarrow H^+_{(aq)} + HPO_4^{2-}_{(aq)} \qquad K_2 = 6.0 \times 10^{-8}$$

$$HPO_4^{2-}_{(aq)} \longleftrightarrow H^+_{(aq)} + PO_4^{3-}_{(aq)} \qquad K_3 = 5.0 \times 10^{-13}$$

For multiple equilibrium dissociation constants (such as polyprotic acids), K for the overall reaction is the product of the equilibrium constants for the individual reactions. Therefore,

$$K = K_1 \times K_2 \times K_3$$

$$= \frac{(H^+)(H_2PO_4^-)}{(H_3PO_4)} \times \frac{(H^+)(HPO_4^{2-})}{(H_2PO_4^-)} \times \frac{(H^+)(PO_4^{3-})}{(HPO_4^{2-})}$$

$$= \frac{(H^+)^3(PO_4^{3-})}{(H_3PO_4)}$$

$$= (7.0 \times 10^{-3}) \times (6.0 \times 10^{-8}) \times (5.0 \times 10^{-13}) = 210 \times 10^{-24}$$

$$= 2.10 \times 10^{-22}$$

which is the equilibrium constant for the sum of three individual reactions:

$$H_3PO_{4(aq)} \longleftrightarrow 3H^+_{(aq)} + PO_4^{3-}_{(aq)}$$

42. **(C)** $[H^+][OH^-] = 10^{-14}$. Substituting gives $(5.00 \times 10^{-3})(x) = 10^{-14}$. Solving for x yields $x = 2.00 \times 10^{-12}$.

43. **(D)** Any anion derived from a weak acid acts as a base in a water solution. The carbonate polyatomic anion, $CO_3^{2-}_{(aq)}$, is derived from carbonic acid, H_2CO_3, a weak acid. There are no common basic cations.

44. **(E)** **Step 1:** Write a balanced equation.

$$2 \text{ HCl} + Ba(OH)_2 \rightarrow BaCl_2 + 2 H_2O$$

Step 2: Calculate the number of moles of H^+.

$$\frac{0.500 \text{ liter}}{1} \times \frac{0.0200 \text{ mole}}{1 \text{ liter}} = 1.00 \times 10^{-2} \text{ mole } H^+$$

Step 3: Calculate the number of moles of OH^-.

There should be twice as many moles of OH^- as moles of $Ba(OH)_2$.

$$\frac{2 \text{ moles } OH^-}{1 \text{ mole } Ba(OH)_2} \times \frac{0.100 \text{ liter}}{1} \times \frac{0.100 \text{ mole } Ba(OH)_2}{1 \text{ liter}}$$

$$= 0.0200 \text{ moles } OH^-$$

Step 4: Write the net ionic equation.

$$H^+ + OH^- \rightarrow H_2O$$

Step 5: Because every mole of H^+ uses 1 mole of OH^-, calculate the number of moles of excess H^+ or OH^-.

$$2.00 \times 10^{-2} \text{ mole } OH^- - 1.00 \times 10^{-2} \text{ mole } H^+$$

$$= 1.00 \times 10^{-2} \text{ mole } OH^- \text{ excess}$$

Step 6: What is the approximate pH in the final solution?

Because 0.6 L of solution is close to 1 L, the number of moles of OH^- and the molarity of OH^- will be fairly close . . . because molarity is defined as the number of moles of solute divided by the volume of solution in liters.

$$pOH = -\log[OH^-] = -\log[1.00 \times 10^{-2}] = 2$$

$$pH = 14.00 - pOH = 14.00 - 2.00 = 12.00$$

Another way to do this step, if you could use a calculator, would be

$$[OH^-] = \frac{1.00 \times 10^{-2} \text{ mole}}{0.600 \text{ liter}} = 0.0167 \text{ M}$$

$$pOH = 1.778$$

$$pH = 14.000 - 1.778 = 12.222$$

45. (B) Realize that you will need to use the equation

$$\triangle G = \triangle G^\circ + RT \ln Q$$

Step 1: Solve for the reaction quotient, Q.

$$Q = \frac{(P_{HF})^2}{(P_{H_2})(P_{F_2})} = \frac{(1.00)^2}{(0.50)(2.00)} = 1.00$$

$$\ln 1.00 = 0$$

Step 2: Substitute into the equation

$$\triangle G = \triangle G^\circ + RT \ln Q$$

$$= -546,000 \text{ J} + (8.3148 \text{ J} \cdot K^{-1} \cdot \text{mole}^{-1}) \cdot 773 \text{ K } (0)$$

$$= -546 \text{ kJ/mole}$$

46. (E) The vertical lines represent phase boundaries. By convention, the anode is written first, at the left of the double vertical lines, followed by the other components of the cell as they would appear in order from the anode to the cathode. The platinum represents the presence of an inert anode. The two half-reactions that occur are

Anode: $H_{2(g)} \rightarrow 2H^+_{(aq)} + 2e^-$ oxidation

OIL (**O**xidation **I**s **L**osing electrons)

AN OX (**AN**ode is where **OX**idation occurs)

Cathode: $Ag^+_{(aq)} + e^- \rightarrow Ag_{(s)}$ reduction

RIG (**R**eduction **I**s **G**aining electrons)

RED CAT (**RED**uction occurs at the **CAT**hode)

In adding the two half-reactions, multiply the reduction half-reaction by 2 so the electrons are in balance, giving the overall reaction:

$$H_{2(g)} + 2Ag^+_{(aq)} \rightarrow 2H^+_{(aq)} + 2\,Ag_{(s)}$$

47. **(A)** Use the relationships

$$\triangle G° = -n\mathscr{F}E° = \triangle H° - T\triangle S°$$

to derive the formula

$$E° = \frac{\triangle H° - T\triangle S°}{-n\,\mathscr{F}}$$

Next, take the given equation and break it down into the oxidation and reduction half-reactions so that you can discover the value for n, the number of moles of electrons either lost or gained.

Anode reaction (oxidation): $Pb_{(s)} + SO_4^{2-}{}_{(aq)} \rightarrow PbSO_{4(s)} + 2e^-$

Cathode reaction (reduction): $\dfrac{PbO_{2\,(s)} + SO_4^{2-}{}_{(aq)} + 4H^+_{(aq)} + 2e^- \rightarrow PbSO_{4\,(s)} + 2H_2O_{(l)}}{Pb_{(s)} + PbO_{2\,(s)} + 4H^+_{(aq)} + 2SO_4^{2-}{}_{(aq)} \rightarrow 2PbSO_{4\,(s)} + 2H_2O_{(l)}}$

Because 1 joule = 1 coulomb × 1 volt, then C = J / V.

$1\,\mathscr{F} = 96{,}487\ C/mol = 96.487\ kJ \cdot V^{-1}$

Now substitute all the known information into the derived equation.

$$E° = \frac{H° - T\triangle S°}{-n\,\mathscr{F}} = \frac{\left(-315.9\ \cancel{kJ}\ /\ \cancel{mole} - 348\ \cancel{K} \cdot 0.2635\ \cancel{kJ}\ /\ \cancel{K} \cdot \cancel{mole}\right)}{-2\left(96.487\ \cancel{kJ}\ /\ V \cdot \cancel{mole}\right)}$$

48. **(C)** An example of esterification is the production of ethyl acetate by the reaction of ethanol with acetic acid.

49. **(A)** An example is the production of ethanol by the addition of water to ethylene.

50. **(E)** A secondary alcohol has the general structure

where the R and R' (which may be the same or different) represent hydrocarbon fragments. An example is the oxidation of isopropyl alcohol to acetone.

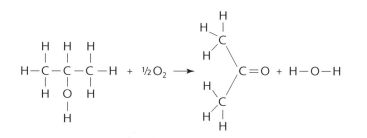

51. (D) A condensation reaction is characterized by the joining of two molecules and the elimination of a water molecule. In the example below, two methyl alcohol molecules react to form dimethyl ether.

52. (E) Gamma rays (γ) have high penetrating power and are not deflected by electronic or magnetic fields. Beta particles (β) have a lower ionizing power and greater penetrating power than alpha particles (α).

53. (D) The Heisenberg Uncertainty Principle says that it is impossible to determine the exact position and momentum of an electron at the same time. It is a fundamental principle of quantum mechanics.

54. (E) Hund's Rule states that every orbital in a sublevel is occupied with one electron before any one orbital is doubly occupied, and all electrons in singly occupied orbitals have the same spin. Diamagnetism is a very weak form of magnetism that is only exhibited in the presence of an external magnetic field. It is the result of changes in the orbital motion of electrons due to the external magnetic field. The induced magnetic moment is very small and in a direction opposite to that of the applied field. When placed between the poles of a strong electromagnet, diamagnetic materials are attracted towards regions where the magnetic field is weak. Diamagnetism is found in elements with paired electrons. Oxygen was once thought to be diamagnetic, but a new revised molecular orbital (MO) model confirmed oxygen's paramagnetic nature.

55. (C) The Pauli Exclusion Principle states that no two electrons in an atom can have identical quantum numbers. The Pauli Exclusion Principle underlies many of the characteristic properties of matter, from the large-scale stability of matter to the existence of the periodic table of the elements.

56. (E) The triple point is the combination of pressure and temperature at which water, ice, and water vapor can coexist in a stable equilibrium. For water this occurs at 0.01°C and a pressure of 611.73 Pascals or 6 millibars. At pressures below the triple point, such as in outer space where the pressure is low, liquid water cannot exist; ice skips the liquid stage and becomes gaseous on heating, in a process known as sublimation.

57. (B) A critical point specifies the conditions (temperature and pressure) at which the liquid state of the matter ceases to exist. As a liquid is heated, its density decreases while the pressure and density of the vapor being formed increases. The liquid and vapor densities become closer and closer to each other until the critical temperature is reached where the two densities are equal and the liquid-gas line or phase boundary disappears. At extremely high temperatures and pressures, the liquid and gaseous phases become indistinguishable. In water, the critical point occurs at around 647K (374°C or 705°F) and 22.064 MPa (3200 PSIA).

58. (D) SF_6 exhibits sp^3d^2 hybridization with 0 unshared pairs of electrons around the sulfur and octahedral geometry.

59. (B) When strong bonds exist in reactant molecules, it takes more energy and is therefore more difficult to break these bonds for a reaction to occur.

60. (A) The charge of S in H_2S is –2; in S_8 it is 0; in S_2Cl_2 it is +1; in SCl_2 it is +2; in SO_2 it is +4 and in SO_3 it is +6.

61. (C) In a 100.0 g sample of hemoglobin, there would be ~ 0.33 grams of iron (55.85 g · mol^{-1}) or

$$\frac{0.33 \text{ g Fe}}{1} \times \frac{1 \text{ mol Fe}}{55.85 \text{ g Fe}} = \sim 0.0060 \text{ mol Fe}$$

$$\frac{100.0 \text{ g hemoglobin}}{0.0060 \text{ mol Fe}} \approx 1.6 \times 10^4 \text{ g hemoglobin / mol Fe}$$

62. (B) First, draw the isomers:

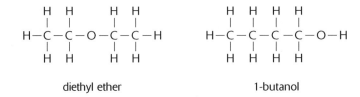

diethyl ether   1-butanol

1-butanol has the higher boiling point because the molecules can form hydrogen bonds with each other. Diethyl ether is not capable of forming hydrogen bonds.

63. (C) A carbon atom is asymmetric if it is bonded to four different atoms or groups. The asymmetric carbons are marked with an asterisk.

OH CH$_3$

$H_3C-C^*-C^*-CH_2OH$

H   H

64. (E) Begin by writing a balanced equation:

$$^{40}_{19}K \rightarrow \ ^{40}_{18}Ar + \ ^{0}_{+1}\beta$$

For first-order decay processes, $t_{1/2} = 0.693/k$

Therefore, $k = 0.693 / t_{1/2}$

$k^{-1} = t_{1/2} \cdot 0.693^{-1}$

$$K = \frac{1}{5} \ln \frac{[A]_0}{[A]} = \frac{1.2 \times 10^9 \text{ yr}}{0.693} \ln \frac{1.00}{0.17}$$

$$\approx 3.0 \times 10^9 \text{ years}$$

65. (D) Each nitrate ion has a charge of -1; therefore, the cation must be $[Cr(NH_3)_6]^{3+}$. NH_3 is neutral, so the oxidation number of Cr is $+3$.

66. (B) To form OF_6 there would have to be six bonds (twelve electrons around the oxygen atom). This would violate the octet rule. O does not have an empty d sublevel into which it can form expanded octets. S has an empty $3d$ sublevel that it uses to form six bonds in SF_6.

67. (D) Amphoterism means the ability to act both as an acid and as a base.

68. (B) For the reaction to be spontaneous, $\triangle G < 0$.

$\triangle G = \triangle H - T \triangle S$

Given that $\triangle H = 35 \text{ kJ} = 35,000 \text{ J}$, then

$\triangle G = 35,000 - (273 \text{ K} + 77 \text{ K}) (\triangle S)$

Solving the equation with the value of $\triangle G = 0$, $\triangle S = 100 \text{ J/K}$

69. **(C)** Recognize that the reactions create photochemical smog. The formation of smog depends on two things: concentration of reactants and light energy ($h\nu$). Los Angeles in December and New York in January would not receive as much solar energy as Mexico City in August. Honolulu would not have the concentration due to population size and trade winds. Mexico City also has a high population density resulting in higher concentrations of reactants.

70. **(A)** Begin by writing the equation for the formation of the first precipitate.

$$Hg^{2+}_{(aq)} + I^-_{(aq)} \rightarrow HgI_{2(s)}$$

When the student added more $I^-_{(aq)}$ to the solution with the addition of KI, a soluble complex $HgI_4^{2-}_{(aq)}$ was formed and the precipitate redissolved.

71. **(E)** (1) Because base is being added to the system, the pH will rise throughout the titration; (2) the weak acid is entirely converted into its conjugate weak base at the equivalence point; and (3) because the weak base is the predominant species present at the equivalence point, the pH will be basic (>7) at this equivalence point.

72. **(E)** A Lewis acid is a substance that can accept a pair of electrons. To be a Lewis acid an atom or molecule must participate in reactions in which an electron pair is accepted from some Lewis base to form a covalent bond.

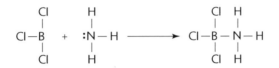

B is the only central atom among the choices that violates the octet rule by having only 6 valence electrons in BCl_3.

73. **(D)** Any gas A that is lost results in equal amounts of gas B and gas C. Therefore,

B + C = P – 0.20P = 0.80P. The pressure of B = C = 0.40P

$$K_P = \frac{P_B P_C}{P_A} = \frac{(0.40P)(0.40P)}{0.20P} = 0.80P$$

74. **(D)** Pure water will create the highest vapor pressure and will therefore force the mercury down the most. Because KCl ionizes into K^+ and Cl^- with a van't Hoff factor of $i = 2$, it will push the mercury down the least when compared to the glucose solution (which does not ionize and therefore $i = 1$). A larger van't Hoff factor means greater lowering of the solvent vapor pressure.

75. **(B)** Ammonia is a weak base. Addition of a base will raise the pH.

Section II: Free-Response Questions

Scoring Guidelines

One point deduction for mathematical error (maximum once per question)

One point deduction for error in significant figures (maximum once per question and the number of significant figures must be correct within +/– one digit)

Part A:

Question 1

$$HOCl_{(aq)} \longleftrightarrow H^+_{(aq)} + OCl^-_{(aq)} \qquad K_a = 2.9 \times 10^{-8}$$

1. Hypochlorous acid, HOCl, is a weak acid that ionizes in water, as shown in the equation above.

   (a) Calculate the $[H^+]$ in an HOCl solution that has a pH of 5.24.

pH = –log [H⁺] $\,$ $[H^+] = 10^{-5.24}$	1 point for correct setup.
$[H^+] = 5.75 \times 10^{-6}$ M	1 point earned for correct calculation.

   (b) Write the equilibrium expression for the ionization of HOCl in water, then calculate the concentration of $HOCl_{(aq)}$ in an HOCl solution that has $[H^+]$ equal to 2.4×10^{-5} M.

$K_a = \dfrac{[H^+][OCl^-]}{[HOCl]}$	1 point earned for correct expression for K_a.
If $[H^+] = 2.4 \times 10^{-5}$ M, then $[OCl^-] = 2.4 \times 10^{-5}$ M.	1 point earned for $[H^+] = [OCl^-]$.
Substituting, $2.9 \times 10^{-8} = \dfrac{[H^+][OCl^-]}{[HOCl]}$ $= \dfrac{(2.4 \times 10^{-5}\,M)(2.4 \times 10^{-5}\,M)}{[HOCl]}$	1 point earned for correct substituted expression for K_a.
$[HOCl] = \dfrac{(2.4 \times 10^{-5}\,M)^2}{2.9 \times 10^{-8}\,M} = 2.0 \times 10^{-2}\,M$	1 point earned for correct [HOCl].

   (c) A solution of $Ba(OH)_2$ is titrated into a solution of HOCl.

   (i) Calculate the volume of 0.200 M $Ba(OH)_{2(aq)}$ needed to reach the equivalence point when titrated into a 75.0 mL sample of 0.150 M $HOCl_{(aq)}$.

$0.0750\,L = \left(\dfrac{0.150\ mol\ \text{HOCl}}{1\ L}\right) \times \left(\dfrac{1\ mol\ Ba(OH)_2}{2\ mol\ \text{HOCl}}\right)$	1 point earned for stoichoiometric ratio.
$\times \left(\dfrac{1\ L}{0.200\ mol\ Ba(OH)_2}\right) = 0.0281\,L$ or 28.1 mL	1 point earned for correct substitution and calculation.

    (ii) Calculate the pH at the equivalence point.

$OCl^- + H_2O \longleftrightarrow HOCl + OH^-$ $K_b(OCl^-) = \left(\dfrac{K_w}{K_a(HOCl)} \right)$ $= \dfrac{1.0 \times 10^{-14}}{2.9 \times 10^{-8}} = 3.4 \times 10^{-7}$	
$K_b = \dfrac{[OH^-][HOCl]}{[OCl^-]}$	
Let $x = [OH^-]$ $3.4 \times 10^{-7} = \dfrac{x^2}{[OCl^-]}$	1 point earned for correct setup.
$[OCl^-] = \dfrac{0.075\,L \times 0.150\,M}{0.0750\,L + 0.0281\,L}$	
$\dfrac{x^2}{0.109} = 3.4 \times 10^{-7}$ $x^2 = 3.71 \times 10^{-8}$ $x = 1.93 \times 10^{-4} = [OH^-]$	
$[H^+] = \dfrac{1 \times 10^{-14}}{1.93 \times 10^{-4}}$ $[H^+] = 5.18 \times 10^{-11}$	
pH = 10.28	1 point for correct pH.

(d) Calculate the number of moles of $NaOCl_{(s)}$ that would have to be added to 150 mL of 0.150 M HOCl to produce a buffer solution with $[H^+] = 6.00 \times 10^{-9}$ M. Assume that volume change is negligible.

$K_a = \dfrac{[H^+][OCl^-]}{[HOCl]}$ $[OCl^-] = \dfrac{[HOCl] \cdot K_a}{[H^+]}$ $= \dfrac{(0.150\,M)(2.9 \times 10^{-8})}{6.00 \times 10^{-9}\,M} = 0.73\,M$	1 point earned for $[OCl^-]$, the setup, and the substitution.
mol NaOCl = 0.150 $\cancel{L}$ $\left(\dfrac{0.73\,mol\,OCl^-}{1\,\cancel{L}} \right)$ $= 1.1 \times 10^{-1}$ mol	1 point earned for correct mol NaOCl.

(e) HOCl is a weaker acid than $HClO_3$. Account for this fact in terms of molecular structure.

The H–O bond is weakened or increasingly polarized by the additional oxygen atoms that are bonded to the central chlorine atom in $HClO_3$.	1 point earned for a correct explanation.

Question 2

2. A rigid 9.50 L flask contained a mixture of 3.00 moles of hydrogen gas, 1.00 moles of oxygen gas, and enough neon gas so that the partial pressure of the neon in the flask was 3.00 atm. The temperature was 27°C.

(a) Calculate the total pressure in the flask.

$P_{H_2} = \dfrac{n_{H_2}RT}{V}$ $T = 27°C + 273 = 300\ K$ $= \dfrac{(3.00\ \text{mol})(0.0821\ L \cdot atm\ /\ mol \cdot K)(300\ K)}{9.50\ L}$ $= 7.78\ atm$	1 point earned for the correct partial pressure of H_2.
$P_{O_2} = \dfrac{n_{O_2}RT}{V}$ $= \dfrac{(1.00\ \text{mol})(0.0821\ L \cdot atm\ /\ mol \cdot K)(300\ K)}{9.50\ L}$ $= 2.59\ atm$ $P_{Ne} = 3.00\ atm$	1 point earned for the correct partial pressure of O_2.
$P_T = P_{H_2} + P_{O_2} + P_{Ne}$ $= 7.78\ atm + 2.59\ atm + 3.00\ atm = 13.4\ atm$	1 point earned for the correct total pressure.

(b) Calculate the mole fraction of oxygen in the flask.

$\text{mol fraction}\ O_2 = \dfrac{\text{mol}\ O_2}{\text{mol}\ H_2 + \text{mol}\ O_2 + \text{mol}\ Ne}$ $\text{mol}\ H_2 = 3.00\ \text{mol}$ $\text{mol}\ O_2 = 1.00\ \text{mol}$ $\text{mol}\ Ne = \dfrac{PV}{RT} = \dfrac{(3.00\ atm)(9.50\ L)}{(0.0821\ L \cdot atm\ /\ mol \cdot K)(300\ K)}$ $= 1.16\ \text{mol}\ Ne$ $\text{total moles} = 3.00 + 1.00 + 1.16 = 5.16\ \text{mol}$	1 point earned for correct mol Ne.
$\text{mol fraction}\ O_2 = \dfrac{\text{mol}\ O_2}{\text{total moles}}$ $= \dfrac{1.00\ \text{mol}\ O_2}{5.16\ \text{total moles}} = 0.194$	1 point earned for correct mol fraction O_2.

(c) Calculate the density $(g \cdot mL^{-1})$ of the mixture in the flask.

$3.00 \text{ mol H}_2 \left(\dfrac{2.016 \text{ g H}_2}{1 \text{ mol H}_2} \right) = 6.05 \text{ g H}_2$	
$1.00 \text{ mol O}_2 \left(\dfrac{32.0 \text{ g O}_2}{1 \text{ mol O}_2} \right) = 32.0 \text{ g O}_2$	1 point earned for correct mass of all species.
$1.16 \text{ mol Ne} \left(\dfrac{20.18 \text{ g Ne}}{1 \text{ mol Ne}} \right) = 23.4 \text{ g Ne}$	
total mass = 6.05 g + 32.0 g + 23.4 g = 61.5 g	
$\text{density} = \dfrac{\text{total mass}}{\text{volume}} = \dfrac{61.5 \text{ g}}{9.50 \text{ L}} \times \dfrac{1 \text{ L}}{10^3 \text{ mL}}$ $= 6.47 \times 10^{-3} \text{ g} \cdot \text{mL}^{-1}$	1 point earned for correct density.

(d) The gas mixture is ignited by a spark and the reaction below occurs until one of the reactants is totally consumed.

$$O_{2(g)} + 2H_{2(g)} \rightarrow 2H_2O_{(g)}$$

Give the mole fraction of all species present in the flask at the end of the reaction.

	$O_{2(g)}$	$+ 2H_{2(g)}$	$\rightarrow 2H_2O_{(g)}$	
I	1.00	3.00	0	1 point earned for 2.00 mol H_2O.
C	−1.00	−2.00	2(+1.00)	
E	0.00	1.00	2.00	
total moles after reaction = mol H_2 + mol H_2O + mol Ne = 1.00 + 2.00 + 1.16 = 4.16 mol total				1 point earned for correct total moles.
mol fraction $H_2 = \dfrac{1.00 \text{ mol H}_2}{4.16 \text{ mol}} = 0.240$				
mol fraction $O_2 = \dfrac{0 \text{ mol O}_2}{4.16 \text{ mol}} = 0$				1 point earned for any two correct mol fractions, excluding O_2.
mol fraction Ne $= \dfrac{1.16 \text{ mol Ne}}{4.16 \text{ mol}} = 0.279$				
mol fraction $H_2O = \dfrac{2.00 \text{ mol H}_2O}{4.16 \text{ mol}} = 0.481$				

Question 3

3. The following question concerns acetylsalilcylic acid (a.a), the active ingredient in aspirin.

(a) A manufacturer produced an aspirin tablet that contained 350 mg of acetylsalicylic acid per tablet. Each tablet weighed 2.50 grams. Calculate the mass percent of acetylsalicylic acid in the tablet.

$\dfrac{350 \text{ mg a.a.}}{1 \text{ tablet}} \times \dfrac{1 \text{ g a.a.}}{10^3 \text{ mg a.a.}} \times \dfrac{1 \text{ tablet}}{2.50 \text{ grams}} \times 100\%$	1 point for proper setup.
$= 14.0\%$	1 point for correct answer.

(b) The structural formula of acetylsalicylic acid, also known as 2-acetoxybenzoic acid is shown below.

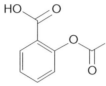

A scientist combusted 5.000 grams of pure acetylsalicylic acid and produced 2.004 g of water and 6.21 L of dry carbon dioxide gas, measured at 770. mm Hg and 27°C. Calculate the mass (in grams) of each element in the 5.000 g sample.

$\dfrac{2.004 \text{ g H}_2\text{O}}{18.02 \text{ g / mol}} = 0.1112 \text{ mol H}_2\text{O}$ $\dfrac{0.1112 \text{ mol H}_2\text{O}}{1} \times \dfrac{2 \text{ mol H}}{\text{mol H}_2\text{O}} \times \dfrac{1.008 \text{ g H}}{1 \text{ mol H}}$ $= 0.2242 \text{ g H}$	1 point for correct mass of H.
$T = 27°C + 273 = 300 \text{ K}$ $n_{CO_2} = \dfrac{PV}{RT} = \dfrac{(770./760)\text{ atm} \times 6.21 \text{ L}}{(0.0821 \text{ L} \cdot \text{atm / mol} \cdot \text{K})(300 \text{ K})}$ $= 0.255 \text{ mol CO}_2$ $\dfrac{0.255 \text{ mol CO}_2}{1} \times \dfrac{1 \text{ mol C}}{1 \text{ mol CO}_2} \times \dfrac{12.0 \text{ g C}}{1 \text{ mol C}}$ $= 3.06 \text{ g C}$	1 point for correct mass of C.
grams of oxygen $= 5.000 \text{ g} - (3.06\text{g} + 0.224 \text{ g})$ $= 1.72 \text{ g O}$	1 point for correct mass of O.

(c) The chemist then dissolved 1.593 grams of pure acetylsalicylic acid in distilled water and titrated the resulting solution to the equivalence point using 44.25 mL of 0.200 M $NaOH_{(aq)}$. Assuming that acetylsalicylic acid has only one ionizable hydrogen, calculate the molar mass of the acid.

$\dfrac{0.04425 \, \text{L}}{1} \times \dfrac{0.200 \, \text{moles OH}^-}{1 \, \text{L}} = 0.00885 \, \text{mol OH}^-$ If 0.00885 mol OH^- was neutralized by 0.00885 mol of H^+, and there is 1 H^+ per molecule acid, there is 0.00885 mol acid.	1 point for correct mol OH^-.
$MM = \dfrac{1.593 \, \text{g acid}}{0.00885 \, \text{mol acid}} = 174 \, \text{g / mol}$	1 point for correct MM of a.a.

(d) A 3.00×10^{-3} mole sample of pure acetylsalicylic acid was dissolved in 20.00 mL of water and was then titrated with 0.200 M $NaOH_{(aq)}$. The equivalence point was reached after 15.00 mL of the NaOH solution had been added. Using the data from the titration, shown in the table below, determine

   (i)   the value of the acid dissociation constant, K_a, for acetylsalicylic acid.

$pK_a = pH$ halfway to the equivalence point. At 7.50 mL of added NaOH, pH = 3.56, therefore $pK_a = 3.56$ $K_a = 10^{-3.56} = 2.75 \times 10^{-4}$	1 point for correct K_a.

   (ii)   the pH of the solution after a total volume of 30.00 mL of the NaOH solution had been added (assume that volumes are additive).

Volume of 0.200 M NaOH Added (mL)	pH
0.00	2.40
5.00	3.03
7.50	3.56
15.00	4.05
30.00	?

Beyond the end point, there is excess OH^-, and the $[OH^-]$ determines the pH.	1 point for recognizing that the pH past the end point is determined by the amount of excess OH^- ions.
Volume of excess OH^-: 0.030 mL − 0.015 mL = 0.015 mL	
Moles of excess $OH^- = (0.015\ \bcancel{L})\ (0.200\ mol/\bcancel{L})$ $= 3.00 \times 10^{-3}\ mol\ OH^-$	
Total volume of solution: 0.0300 L titrant + 0.0200 L of original solution = 0.0500 L	
$[OH^-] = \dfrac{3.00 \times 10^{-3}\ mol\ OH^-}{0.0500\ L}$ $= 6.0 \times 10^{-2}\ M\ OH^-$	
pOH = 1.22	
pH = 14.00 − 1.22 = 12.78	1 point for correct pH.

Part B:

Question 4

(For a complete list of reaction types that you will encounter, refer to *CliffsAP Chemistry,* 3rd Edition.)

4. Students choose five of the eight reactions. Only the answers in the boxes are graded (unless clearly marked otherwise). Each correct answer earns 3 points, 1 point for reactants and 2 points for products. All products must be correct to earn both product points. Equations do not need to be balanced and phases need not be indicated. Any spectator ions on the reactant side nullify the 1 possible reactant point, but if they appear again on the product side, there is no product-point penalty. A fully molecular equation (when it should be ionic) earns a maximum of 1 point. Ion charges must be correct.

(a) A piece of solid tin is heated in the presence of chlorine gas.

| $Sn + Cl_2 \rightarrow SnCl_4$ | 1 point for reactant(s), 2 points for product(s). |
| | Synthesis reaction. Usually pick the higher oxidation state of the metal ion. |

(b) Ethane is burned completely in air.

| $C_2H_6 + O_2 \rightarrow CO_2 + H_2O$ | 1 point for reactant(s), 2 points for product(s). |
| | Al hydrocarbons burn in oxygen gas to produce CO_2 and H_2O. ("Air" almost always means oxygen gas.) Note the use of the word "completely." Unless this word was in the problem, a mixture of CO and CO_2 gases would result. |

(c) Solid copper shavings are added to a hot, dilute nitric acid solution.

| $Cu + H^+ + NO_3^- \rightarrow Cu^{2+} + H_2O + NO$ | 1 point for reactant(s), 2 points for product(s). |
| | This reaction is well known and is covered quite extensively in textbooks. Note how it departs from the rubric. Copper metal does not react directly with H^+ ions because it has a negative standard oxidation voltage. However, it will react with 6 M HNO_3 because the NO_3^- ion is a much stronger oxidizing agent than H^+. The fact that copper metal is difficult to oxidize indicates that it is easily reduced. This fact allows one to qualitatively test for the presence of it by reacting it with dithionite (hydrosulfite) ion ($S_2O_4^{2-}$), as the reducing agent to produce copper: $Cu^{2+}_{(aq)} + S_2O_4^{2-}_{(aq)} + 2H_2O_{(l)} \rightarrow Cu_{(s)} + 2SO_3^{2-}_{(aq)} + 4H^+_{(aq)}$. |

(d) Dilute sulfuric acid is added to a solution of mercuric nitrate.

| $SO_4^{2-} + Hg^{2+} \rightarrow HgSO_4$ | 1 point for reactant(s), 2 points for product(s). |
| | All nitrates are soluble. $HgSO_4$ is not soluble. |

(e) Sulfur trioxide gas is heated in the presence of solid calcium oxide.

$SO_3 + CaO \rightarrow CaSO_4$	1 point for reactant(s), 2 points for product(s).
	Synthesis.

(f) Copper sulfate pentahydrate is strongly heated.

$CuSO_4 \cdot 5H_2O \rightarrow CuSO_4 + 5H_2O$	1 point for reactant(s), 2 points for product(s).
	Thermal decomposition of a hydrate.

(g) A strong ammonia solution is added to a suspension of zinc hydroxide.

$Zn(OH)_2 + NH_3 \rightarrow Zn(NH_3)_4^{2+} + OH^-$	1 point for reactant(s), 2 points for product(s).
	The formation of the complex ion $Zn(NH_3)_4^{+2}$ occurs in a stepwise manner: $Zn^{+2} + NH_3 \longleftrightarrow Zn(NH_3)^{+2}$ $Zn(NH_3)^{+2} + NH_3 \longleftrightarrow Zn(NH_3)_2^{+2}$ $Zn(NH_3)_2^{+2} + NH_3 \longleftrightarrow Zn(NH_3)_3^{+2}$ $Zn(NH_3)_3^{+2} + NH_3 \longleftrightarrow Zn(NH_3)_4^{+2}$

(h) Ethane gas is heated in the presence of bromine gas to yield a monobrominated product.

$C_2H_6 + Br_2 \rightarrow C_2H_5Br + HBr$	1 point for reactant(s), 2 points for product(s).
	Organic substitution.

Question 5

5. Give a brief explanation for each of the following:

(a) Water can act either as an acid or as a base.

Water can provide both H^+ and OH^- $$H_2O \longrightarrow H^+ + OH^-$$ According to Brønsted-Lowry theory, a water molecule can accept a proton, thereby becoming a hydronium ion. In this case, water is acting as a base (proton acceptor). $$H_2O + H^+ \rightarrow H_3O^+$$	1 point given for correct Brønsted-Lowry concept of water being able to accept a proton resulting in a hydronium ion.
When water acts as a Brønsted-Lowry acid, it donates a proton to another species, thereby converting to the hydroxide ion. $$H_2O + H_2O \longrightarrow OH^- + H_3O^+$$ base acid $\longrightarrow$ conjugate conjugate base acid	1 point given for correct Brønsted-Lowry concept of water being able to donate a proton, resulting in a hydroxide ion.
According to Lewis theory, water can act as a Lewis base (electron pair donor). Water contains an unshared pair of electrons that is utilized in accepting a proton to form the hydronium ion. $$\overset{\displaystyle H}{\underset{}{:\overset{\cdot\cdot}{O}:H}} \;+\; H^+ \longrightarrow \left[H:\overset{\displaystyle H}{\underset{\displaystyle H}{\overset{\cdot\cdot}{O}:}} \right]^+$$	1 point given for correct Lewis theory of water acting as an electron pair donor.

(b) HF is a weaker acid than HCl.

F is more electronegative than Cl.	1 point awarded for difference in electronegativity between F and Cl.
The bond between H and F is therefore stronger than the bond between H and Cl.	1 point awarded for correlation between electronegativity and bond strength.
Acid strength is measured in terms of how easy it is for the H to ionize. The stronger the acid, the weaker the bond between the H atom and the rest of the acid molecule; measured as K_a or, if the acid is polyprotic, $K_{a_1}, K_{a_2}, K_{a_3}, \ldots$	1 point awarded for explanation that bond strength and ability to form H^+ determines acid strength.

(c) For the triprotic acid H_3PO_4, K_{a_1} is 7.5×10^{-3} whereas K_{a_2} is 6.2×10^{-8}.

K_{a_1} represents the first hydrogen to depart the H_3PO_4 molecule, leaving the conjugate base, $H_2PO_4^-$.	1 point awarded for correct explanation of how $H_2PO_4^-$ is formed. 1 point awarded for correct identification of conjugate base(s).
The conjugate base, $H_2PO_4^-$, has an overall negative charge. The overall negative charge of the $H_2PO_4^-$ species increases the attraction of its own conjugate base HPO_4^{2-} to the departing proton. This creates a stronger bond, which indicates that it is a weaker acid.	1 point awarded for correctly correlating that the strength of the bond between H^+ and $H_2PO_4^-$ is weaker than the bond between H^+ and HPO_4^{2-} and that it is what determines acid strength.

(d) Pure HCl is not an acid.

An acid is measured by its concentration of H^+ (its pH).	1 point given for correlation between concentration of H^+ and pH.
Pure HCl would not ionize; the sample would remain as molecular HCl (a gas). In order to ionize, a water solution of HCl is required. $HCl_{(ag)} + H_2O_{(l)} \rightarrow H_3O^+_{(ag)} + Cl^-_{(ag)}$	1 point given that HCl requires water in order to ionize.

(e) $HClO_4$ is a stronger acid than $HClO_3$, HSO_3^-, or H_2SO_3.

As the number of lone oxygen atoms (those not bonded to H) increases, the strength of the acid increases. Thus, $HClO_4$ is a stronger acid than $HClO_3$.	1 point given for concept that the number of lone oxygen atoms is correlated to acid strength.
As electronegativity of the central atom increases, the acid strength increases. Thus, Cl is more electronegative than S.	1 point given for correlation of central atom electronegativity and acid strength.
Loss of H^+ by a neutral acid molecule (H_2SO_3) reduces acid strength. Thus, H_2SO_3 is a stronger acid than HSO_3^-.	1 point given for correlation between loss of H^+ and acid strength.
As effective nuclear charge (Z_{eff}) on the central atom increases, acid strength is likewise increased. Thus, a larger nuclear charge draws the electrons closer to the nucleus and binds them more tightly.	1 point given for correlation between Z_{eff} and acid strength.

Question 6

6. Interpret each of the following four examples using modern bonding principles.

    (a) C_2H_2 and C_2H_6 both contain two carbon atoms. However, the bond between the two carbons in C_2H_2 is significantly shorter than that between the two carbons in C_2H_6.

Lewis structure of C_2H_2 $H-C\equiv C-H$ Lewis structure of C_2H_6 $\begin{array}{cc} H & H \\ \vert & \vert \\ H-C-C-H \\ \vert & \vert \\ H & H \end{array}$	1 point awarded for correct Lewis structures.
C_2H_2 has a triple bond, whereas C_2H_6 consists only of single bonds.	1 point awarded for bond differences between C_2H_2 and C_2H_6.
Triple bonds are shorter than single bonds because bond energy is larger for a multiple bond. The extra electron pairs strengthen the bond, making it more difficult to separate the bonded atoms from each other.	1 point for connection between bond length and bond energy. 1 point given for connection between extra electron pairs and strength of bond.

    (b) The bond angle of the hydronium ion, H_3O^+, is less than 109.5°, the angle of a tetrahedron.

Lewis structure of H_3O^+ $\left[\begin{array}{c} H \\ \vert \\ \overset{..}{O} \\ {}_{H} \quad {}^{H} \end{array} \right]^{+}$	1 point for correct Lewis structure.
H_3O^+ is pyramidal in geometry due to a single pair of unshared electrons.	1 point for correct geometry of the hydronium ion.
Angle of a tetrahedron is 109.5°; this exists only if there are no unshared electrons.	1 point for theoretical bond angle of a tetrahedron.
Repulsion between shared pairs of electrons is less than repulsion between an unshared pair and a shared pair. This stronger repulsion found in the shared-unshared pair condition, as seen in H_3O^+, decreases the bond angle of the pure tetrahedron (109.5°).	1 point for correctly identifying relationship between repulsion of shared and unshared pairs of electrons.

(c) The lengths of the bonds between the carbon and the oxygens in the carbonate ion, CO_3^{2-}, are all equal and are longer than one might expect to find in the carbon monoxide molecule, CO.

Lewis structure of CO $:C\equiv O:$	1 point for correct Lewis structure of CO.
Lewis structure of CO_3^{2-} CO_3^{2-} exists in three resonance forms.	1 point for correct Lewis structures of CO_3^{2-}.
CO bond length in the carbonate ion is considered to be the average of the lengths of all single and double bonds. The average bond length for triple bonds is shorter than for either single or double bonds.	1 point that the C–O bond length is the average.

(d) The CNO⁻ ion is linear.

Lewis structure of CNO⁻ $\left[\ddot{C}=N=\ddot{O}\right]^{-}$	1 point for correct Lewis structure of CNO⁻.
There are no unshared pairs of electrons around the central atom N, resulting in a linear molecule.	1 point for recognition that there are no unshared pairs of electrons around N which results in a linear molecule.
The molecule is polar because O is more electronegative than C.	1 point for recognition that the molecule is polar.

Question 7

7. If one completely vaporizes a measured amount of a volatile liquid, the molecular weight of the liquid can be determined by measuring the volume, temperature, and pressure of the resulting gas. When using this procedure, one must use the ideal gas equation and assume that the gas behaves ideally. However, if the temperature of the gas is only slightly above the boiling point of the liquid, the gas deviates from ideal behavior.

(a) Explain the postulates of the ideal gas equation.

The ideal gas equation, $PV = nRT$, stems from three relationships known to be true for gases:	1 point for correctly stating the formula for the ideal gas equation.
(i) the volume is directly proportional to the number of moles: $V \sim n$	
(ii) the volume is directly proportional to the absolute temperature: $V \sim T$	1 point each for stating each of the three postulates.
(iii) the volume is inversely proportional to the pressure: $V \sim 1/P$	

(b) Explain why, if measured just above the boiling point, the molecular weight deviates from the true value.

n, the symbol used for the moles of gas, can be obtained by dividing the mass of the gas by the molecular weight. In effect, $n =$ mass $\cdot$ molecular weight^{-1} ($n = m \cdot MW^{-1}$). Substituting this relationship into the ideal gas law gives $P \cdot V = \dfrac{m \cdot R \cdot T}{MW}$ Solving this equation for the molecular weight yields $MW = \dfrac{m \cdot R \cdot T}{P \cdot V}$	1 point for stating the equation to determine molecular weight of a gas.
Real gas behavior deviates from the values obtained using the ideal gas equation because the ideal equation assumes that: (1) the molecules do not occupy space, and (2) there is no attractive force between the individual molecules. However, at low temperatures (just above the boiling point of the liquid), these two postulates are not true and one must use an alternative equation known as the van der Waals equation, which accounts for these factors.	1 point for concept that ideal gas molecules do not occupy space. 1 point for concept that there are no attractive forces between individual gas molecules in an ideal gas. 1 point for stating that the van der Waals equation accounts for these factors. 1 point for relationship that attraction between molecules increases as temperature is lowered (less kinetic energy).

(c) Explain whether the molecular weight of a real gas would be higher or lower than predicted by the van der Waals equation.

Because the attraction between molecules becomes more significant at lower temperatures due to a decrease in kinetic energy of the molecules, the compressibility of the gas is increased. This causes the product $P \cdot V$ to be smaller than predicted. $P \cdot V$ is found in the denominator in the equation listed above, so the molecular weight tends to be higher than its ideal value.	1 point for stating that gases with lower temperatures have less kinetic energy.
	1 point for correct explanation that the molecular weight of a real gas tends to be higher than that of an ideal gas.

Question 8

8. Given three compounds PH_3, H_2O, and F_2:

(a) What factors would influence their boiling points?

Boiling point (BP) is a result of the strength of intermolecular forces—the forces between molecules.	1 point for mentioning that BP is a result of intermolecular forces.
A direct relationship exists between the strength of intermolecular forces and the BP: the stronger the intermolecular force, the higher the BP.	1 point for relationship that the stronger the intermolecular force, the higher the BP.
Relative strength of intermolecular forces: H bonds > dipole forces > dispersion forces. BP is directly proportional to increasing MW-dispersion forces (van der Waals force). Greater MW results in greater dispersion forces.	1 point for mentioning the intermolecular forces involved: hydrogen bonds, dipole forces, dispersion forces.
Strength of the dispersion force(s) depends on how readily electrons can be polarized.	1 point for mentioning the concept of polarization of molecules and its effect on BP.
Large molecules are easier to polarize than small, compact molecules. Hence, for comparable MW, compact molecules have lower BP.	1 point for mentioning that large molecules are easier to polarize than compact molecules.
Polar compounds have slightly higher BP than nonpolar compounds of comparable MW.	1 point for mentioning that polar compounds have higher BP.
Hydrogen bonds are very strong intermolecular forces, causing very high BP.	1 point for mentioning relationship of hydrogen bonds and BP.

(b) Which compound would have the highest boiling point and explain your reasoning.

Highest BP: H_2O	1 point for predicting that H_2O would have the highest BP.
H_2O is covalently bonded. H_2O is a bent molecule; hence, it is polar.	1 point for mentioning that water is a polar molecule.
Between H_2O molecules there exist hydrogen bonds.	1 point for mentioning that hydrogen bonds exist between water molecules.
Even though H_2O has the lowest MW of all three compounds, the hydrogen bonds outweigh any effects of MW or polarity.	1 point for stating that hydrogen bonds result in very high boiling points.

(c) Which compound would have the lowest boiling point and explain your reasoning.

Lowest BP: F_2	1 point for predicting that F_2 would have the lowest BP.
F_2 is nonpolar; the only intermolecular attraction present is due to dispersion forces.	1 point for stating that F_2 only has dispersion forces between molecules.
Dispersion forces are weakest of all intermolecular forces. F_2 is covalently bonded. F_2 has a MW of 38 g/mole.	1 point for mentioning that dispersion forces are the weakest of all intermolecular forces.

(d) Which compound would be intermediate between your choices for (b) and (c) and explain your reasoning.

Intermediate BP: PH_3	1 point for predicting that PH_3 would be intermediate in BP.
PH_3 is polar; geometry is trigonal pyramidal; presence of lone pair of electrons.	1 point for mentioning that PH_3 would be polar.
PH_3 is primarily covalently bonded; two nonmetals. There are dipole forces present between PH_3 molecules because PH_3 is polar. PH_3 has a MW of 34g/mole (even though PH_3 has a lower MW than F_2 and might be expected to have a lower BP, the effect of the polarity outweighs any effect of MW).	1 point for mentioning that dipole forces would exist between PH_3 molecules because the molecule is polar.

Multiple-Choice Answer Sheet for Practice Exam 2

Remove this sheet and use it to mark your answers.
Answer sheets for "Section II: Free-Response Questions" can be found at the end of this book.

Section I
Multiple-Choice Questions

1 Ⓐ Ⓑ Ⓒ Ⓓ Ⓔ	26 Ⓐ Ⓑ Ⓒ Ⓓ Ⓔ	51 Ⓐ Ⓑ Ⓒ Ⓓ Ⓔ
2 Ⓐ Ⓑ Ⓒ Ⓓ Ⓔ	27 Ⓐ Ⓑ Ⓒ Ⓓ Ⓔ	52 Ⓐ Ⓑ Ⓒ Ⓓ Ⓔ
3 Ⓐ Ⓑ Ⓒ Ⓓ Ⓔ	28 Ⓐ Ⓑ Ⓒ Ⓓ Ⓔ	53 Ⓐ Ⓑ Ⓒ Ⓓ Ⓔ
4 Ⓐ Ⓑ Ⓒ Ⓓ Ⓔ	29 Ⓐ Ⓑ Ⓒ Ⓓ Ⓔ	54 Ⓐ Ⓑ Ⓒ Ⓓ Ⓔ
5 Ⓐ Ⓑ Ⓒ Ⓓ Ⓔ	30 Ⓐ Ⓑ Ⓒ Ⓓ Ⓔ	55 Ⓐ Ⓑ Ⓒ Ⓓ Ⓔ
6 Ⓐ Ⓑ Ⓒ Ⓓ Ⓔ	31 Ⓐ Ⓑ Ⓒ Ⓓ Ⓔ	56 Ⓐ Ⓑ Ⓒ Ⓓ Ⓔ
7 Ⓐ Ⓑ Ⓒ Ⓓ Ⓔ	32 Ⓐ Ⓑ Ⓒ Ⓓ Ⓔ	57 Ⓐ Ⓑ Ⓒ Ⓓ Ⓔ
8 Ⓐ Ⓑ Ⓒ Ⓓ Ⓔ	33 Ⓐ Ⓑ Ⓒ Ⓓ Ⓔ	58 Ⓐ Ⓑ Ⓒ Ⓓ Ⓔ
9 Ⓐ Ⓑ Ⓒ Ⓓ Ⓔ	34 Ⓐ Ⓑ Ⓒ Ⓓ Ⓔ	59 Ⓐ Ⓑ Ⓒ Ⓓ Ⓔ
10 Ⓐ Ⓑ Ⓒ Ⓓ Ⓔ	35 Ⓐ Ⓑ Ⓒ Ⓓ Ⓔ	60 Ⓐ Ⓑ Ⓒ Ⓓ Ⓔ
11 Ⓐ Ⓑ Ⓒ Ⓓ Ⓔ	36 Ⓐ Ⓑ Ⓒ Ⓓ Ⓔ	61 Ⓐ Ⓑ Ⓒ Ⓓ Ⓔ
12 Ⓐ Ⓑ Ⓒ Ⓓ Ⓔ	37 Ⓐ Ⓑ Ⓒ Ⓓ Ⓔ	62 Ⓐ Ⓑ Ⓒ Ⓓ Ⓔ
13 Ⓐ Ⓑ Ⓒ Ⓓ Ⓔ	38 Ⓐ Ⓑ Ⓒ Ⓓ Ⓔ	63 Ⓐ Ⓑ Ⓒ Ⓓ Ⓔ
14 Ⓐ Ⓑ Ⓒ Ⓓ Ⓔ	39 Ⓐ Ⓑ Ⓒ Ⓓ Ⓔ	64 Ⓐ Ⓑ Ⓒ Ⓓ Ⓔ
15 Ⓐ Ⓑ Ⓒ Ⓓ Ⓔ	40 Ⓐ Ⓑ Ⓒ Ⓓ Ⓔ	65 Ⓐ Ⓑ Ⓒ Ⓓ Ⓔ
16 Ⓐ Ⓑ Ⓒ Ⓓ Ⓔ	41 Ⓐ Ⓑ Ⓒ Ⓓ Ⓔ	66 Ⓐ Ⓑ Ⓒ Ⓓ Ⓔ
17 Ⓐ Ⓑ Ⓒ Ⓓ Ⓔ	42 Ⓐ Ⓑ Ⓒ Ⓓ Ⓔ	67 Ⓐ Ⓑ Ⓒ Ⓓ Ⓔ
18 Ⓐ Ⓑ Ⓒ Ⓓ Ⓔ	43 Ⓐ Ⓑ Ⓒ Ⓓ Ⓔ	68 Ⓐ Ⓑ Ⓒ Ⓓ Ⓔ
19 Ⓐ Ⓑ Ⓒ Ⓓ Ⓔ	44 Ⓐ Ⓑ Ⓒ Ⓓ Ⓔ	69 Ⓐ Ⓑ Ⓒ Ⓓ Ⓔ
20 Ⓐ Ⓑ Ⓒ Ⓓ Ⓔ	45 Ⓐ Ⓑ Ⓒ Ⓓ Ⓔ	70 Ⓐ Ⓑ Ⓒ Ⓓ Ⓔ
21 Ⓐ Ⓑ Ⓒ Ⓓ Ⓔ	46 Ⓐ Ⓑ Ⓒ Ⓓ Ⓔ	71 Ⓐ Ⓑ Ⓒ Ⓓ Ⓔ
22 Ⓐ Ⓑ Ⓒ Ⓓ Ⓔ	47 Ⓐ Ⓑ Ⓒ Ⓓ Ⓔ	72 Ⓐ Ⓑ Ⓒ Ⓓ Ⓔ
23 Ⓐ Ⓑ Ⓒ Ⓓ Ⓔ	48 Ⓐ Ⓑ Ⓒ Ⓓ Ⓔ	73 Ⓐ Ⓑ Ⓒ Ⓓ Ⓔ
24 Ⓐ Ⓑ Ⓒ Ⓓ Ⓔ	49 Ⓐ Ⓑ Ⓒ Ⓓ Ⓔ	74 Ⓐ Ⓑ Ⓒ Ⓓ Ⓔ
25 Ⓐ Ⓑ Ⓒ Ⓓ Ⓔ	50 Ⓐ Ⓑ Ⓒ Ⓓ Ⓔ	75 Ⓐ Ⓑ Ⓒ Ⓓ Ⓔ

PERIODIC TABLE OF THE ELEMENTS

1																	2
H 1.0079																	**He** 4.0026
3 **Li** 6.941	4 **Be** 9.012											5 **B** 10.811	6 **C** 12.011	7 **N** 14.007	8 **O** 16.00	9 **F** 19.00	10 **Ne** 20.179
11 **Na** 22.99	12 **Mg** 24.30											13 **Al** 26.98	14 **Si** 28.09	15 **P** 30.974	16 **S** 32.06	17 **Cl** 35.453	18 **Ar** 39.948
19 **K** 39.10	20 **Ca** 40.08	21 **Sc** 44.96	22 **Ti** 47.90	23 **V** 50.94	24 **Cr** 51.00	25 **Mn** 54.93	26 **Fe** 55.85	27 **Co** 58.93	28 **Ni** 58.69	29 **Cu** 63.55	30 **Zn** 65.39	31 **Ga** 69.72	32 **Ge** 72.59	33 **As** 74.92	34 **Se** 78.96	35 **Br** 79.90	36 **Kr** 83.80
37 **Rb** 85.47	38 **Sr** 87.62	39 **Y** 88.91	40 **Zr** 91.22	41 **Nb** 92.91	42 **Mo** 95.94	43 **Tc** (98)	44 **Ru** 101.1	45 **Rh** 102.91	46 **Pd** 105.42	47 **Ag** 107.87	48 **Cd** 112.41	49 **In** 114.82	50 **Sn** 118.71	51 **Sb** 121.75	52 **Te** 127.60	53 **I** 126.91	54 **Xe** 131.29
55 **Cs** 132.91	56 **Ba** 137.33	57 *****La** 138.91	72 **Hf** 178.49	73 **Ta** 180.95	74 **W** 183.85	75 **Re** 186.21	76 **Os** 190.2	77 **Ir** 192.22	78 **Pt** 195.08	79 **Au** 196.97	80 **Hg** 200.59	81 **Ti** 204.38	82 **Pb** 207.2	83 **Bi** 208.98	84 **Po** (209)	85 **At** (210)	86 **Rn** (222)
87 **Fr** (223)	88 **Ra** 226.02	89 †**Ac** 227.03	104 **Rf** (261)	105 **Db** (262)	106 **Sg** (263)	107 **Bh** (262)	108 **Hs** (265)	109 **Mt** (266)	110 **§** (269)	111 **§** (272)	112 **§** (277)						

§ Not yet named

***** Lanthanide Series

58 **Ce** 140.12	59 **Pr** 140.91	60 **Nd** 144.24	61 **Pm** (145)	62 **Sm** 150.4	63 **Eu** 151.97	64 **Gd** 157.25	65 **Tb** 158.93	66 **Dy** 162.50	67 **Ho** 164.93	68 **Er** 167.26	69 **Tm** 168.93	70 **Yb** 173.04	71 **Lu** 174.97

† Actinide Series

90 **Th** 232.04	91 **Pa** 231.04	92 **U** 238.03	93 **Np** 237.05	94 **Pu** (244)	95 **Am** (243)	96 **Cm** (247)	97 **Bk** (247)	98 **Cf** (251)	99 **Es** (252)	100 **Fm** (257)	101 **Md** (258)	102 **No** (259)	103 **Lr** (260)

Practice Exam 2

Section I: Multiple-Choice Questions

Time: 90 minutes

75 questions

45% of total grade

No calculators allowed

This section consists of 75 multiple-choice questions. Mark your answers carefully on the answer sheet.

General Instructions

Do not open this booklet until you are told to do so by the proctor.

Be sure to write your answers for Section I on the separate answer sheet. Use the test booklet for your scratch work or notes, but remember that no credit will be given for work, notes, or answers written only in the test booklet. After you have selected an answer, blacken thoroughly the corresponding circle on the answer sheet. To change an answer, erase your previous mark completely, and then record your new answer. Mark only one answer for each question.

Example   Sample Answer

The Pacific is   Ⓐ Ⓑ ● Ⓓ Ⓔ

    A.   a river

    B.   a lake

    C.   an ocean

    D.   a sea

    E.   a gulf

To discourage haphazard guessing on this section of the exam, a quarter of a point is subtracted for every wrong answer, but no points are subtracted if you leave the answer blank. Even so, if you can eliminate one or more of the choices for a question, it may be to your advantage to guess.

Because it is not expected that all test takers will complete this section, do not spend too much time on difficult questions. Answer first the questions you can answer readily, and then, if you have time, return to the difficult questions later. Don't get stuck on one question. Work quickly but accurately. Use your time effectively. The preceding table is provided for your use in answering questions in Section I.

GO ON TO THE NEXT PAGE

Directions: Each group of lettered answer choices below refers to the numbered statements or questions that immediately follow. For each question or statement, select the one lettered choice that is the best answer and fill in the corresponding circle on the answer sheet. An answer choice may be used once, more than once, or not at all in each set of questions.

Questions 1–5

    A. SO_2
    B. SiH_4
    C. CO_2
    D. CaO
    E. NO

1. In which of the choices is there polar double bonding in a nonpolar molecule?

2. Which of the molecule is a major contributor to acid rain?

3. Which of the molecules has been linked with depletion of the ozone layer?

4. Which of the molecules has four sp^3 hybrid bonds?

5. Which compound is a basic anhydride?

6. Which of the following solutions would show the greatest conductivity at 30°C?

    A. 0.20 M $Ca(NO_3)_2$
    B. 0.25 M HCl
    C. 0.30 M NaOH
    D. 0.10 M NaCl
    E. 0.40 M CH_3OH

7. Unknown element X combines with oxygen to form the compound XO_2. If 44.0 grams of element X combines with 8.00 grams of oxygen, what is the atomic mass of element X?

    A. 16 amu
    B. 44 amu
    C. 88 amu
    D. 176 amu
    E. 352 amu

8. Which of the following does NOT show hydrogen bonding?

    A. ammonia, NH_3
    B. hydrazine, N_2H_4
    C. hydrogen peroxide, H_2O_2
    D. dimethyl ether, CH_3OCH_3
    E. methyl alcohol, CH_3OH

9. Sulfur trioxide gas dissociates into sulfur dioxide gas and oxygen gas at 1250°C. In an experiment, 3.60 moles of sulfur trioxide were placed into an evacuated 3.0-liter flask. The concentration of sulfur dioxide gas measured at equilibrium was found to be 0.20 M. What is the equilibrium constant, K_c, for the reaction?

    A. 1.6×10^{-4}
    B. 1.0×10^{-3}
    C. 2.0×10^{-3}
    D. 4.0×10^{-3}
    E. 8.0×10^{-3}

Questions 10–14

    A. amide
    B. amine
    C. ketone
    D. thiol
    E. salt

10.

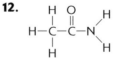

11.

12.

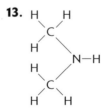

13.

14.

$$H-\underset{\underset{H}{|}}{\overset{\overset{H}{|}}{C}}-\underset{\underset{H}{|}}{\overset{\overset{H}{|}}{C}}-S-H$$

15. Which of the following is not capable of reacting with molecular oxygen?

- A. SO_2
- B. SO_3
- C. NO
- D. N_2O
- E. P_4O_6

16. Given a molecule with the general formula AB_2, which one of the following would be the most useful in determining whether the molecule was bent or linear?

- A. ionization energies
- B. electron affinities
- C. dipole moments
- D. electronegativities
- E. bond energies

17. For the reaction

$$2NO_{(g)} + O_{2(g)} \rightarrow 2NO_{2(g)}$$

which two of the following possible intermediate mechanisms would support this reaction?

- (1) $2NO_{(g)} \rightarrow N_2O_{2(g)}$
- (2) $NO_{(g)} + O_{2(g)} \rightarrow NO_{3(g)}$
- (3) $2NO_{2(g)} \rightarrow N_2O_{2(g)} + O_{2(g)}$
- (4) $NO_{3(g)} + NO_{(g)} \rightarrow 2NO_{2(g)}$
- (5) $NO_{3(g)} \rightarrow NO_{(g)} + O_{2(g)}$

- A. 1 and 2
- B. 2 and 3
- C. 3 and 4
- D. 2 and 4
- E. 1 and 4

18. An unknown ionic compound AB_2 is dissolved in water at a certain temperature and is determined to have a solubility of 2.0×10^{-2} M. What is the K_{sp} of AB_2?

- A. 6.0×10^{-6}
- B. 3.2×10^{-5}
- C. 6.0×10^{-2}
- D. 6.0×10^{-2}
- E. 3.2×10^{2}

19. Given the information from Question #18, what is the equilibrium concentration of A^{2+} when $AB_{2(s)}$ is added to 2.0 M XB, a soluble ionic compound?

- A. 3.2×10^{-8} M
- B. 1.0×10^{-6} M
- C. 2.0×10^{-6} M
- D. 4.0×10^{-6} M
- E. 8.0×10^{-6} M

20. Which of the following choices represents $^{239}_{94}Pu$ producing a positron?

- A. $^{239}_{94}Pu \rightarrow ^{235}_{94}Pu + ^{4}_{2}He$
- B. $^{239}_{94}Pu \rightarrow ^{0}_{-1}e \rightarrow + ^{239}_{93}Np$
- C. $^{239}_{94}Pu + ^{0}_{-1}e \rightarrow ^{239}_{93}Np$
- D. $^{239}_{94}Pu \rightarrow ^{239}_{93}Np + ^{0}_{1}e$
- E. $^{239}_{94}Pu + ^{4}_{2}He \rightarrow ^{235}_{92}U$

21. The valence electron configuration of element A is $3s^2 3p^1$ and that of B is $3s^2 3p^4$. What is the probable empirical formula for a compound of the two elements?

- A. A_2B
- B. AB_2
- C. A_3B_2
- D. A_2B_3
- E. AB

22. The K_{sp} of lead(II) chloride is 2.4×10^{-4}. What conclusion can be made about the concentration of $[Cl^-]$ in a solution of lead chloride if $[Pb^{2+}] = 1.0$ M?

- A. $[Cl^-]$ can have any value.
- B. $[Cl^-]$ cannot be greater than $K_{sp}^{1/2}$.
- C. $[Cl^-]$ cannot be less that $K_{sp}^{1/2}$.
- D. $[Cl^-]$ cannot be equal to $K_{sp}^{1/2}$.
- E. $[Cl^-]$ must also be equal to 1.0 M.

GO ON TO THE NEXT PAGE

23. For the following reaction

$$Zn_{(s)} + 2Ag^+_{(aq)} \rightarrow Zn^{2+}_{(aq)} + 2Ag_{(s)}$$

The standard voltage $E°_{cell}$ has been calculated to be 1.56 volts. To decrease the voltage of the cell to 1.00 volt, one could

A. increase the size of the zinc electrode
B. reduce the coefficients of the reactions so that it reads

$$\tfrac{1}{2} Zn_{(s)} + Ag^+_{(aq)} \rightarrow \tfrac{1}{2} Zn^{2+}_{(aq)} + Ag_{(s)}$$

C. decrease the concentration of the silver ion in solution
D. increase the concentration of the silver ion in solution
E. decrease the concentration of the zinc ion in solution

24. The silver ion in the complex $[Ag(CN)_2]^-$ has a coordination number of

A. 2
B. 3
C. 4
D. 5
E. 6

25. Which of the following would NOT act as a Brønsted base?

A. HSO_4^-
B. SO_4^{2-}
C. NH_4^+
D. NH_3
E. H_2O

26. Balance the following equation using the lowest possible whole-number coefficients.

$$NH_3 + CuO \rightarrow Cu + N_2 + H_2O$$

The sum of the coefficients is

A. 9
B. 10
C. 11
D. 12
E. 13

27. A freshman chemist analyzed a sample of copper(II) sulfate pentahydrate for water of hydration by weighing the hydrate, heating it to convert it to anhydrous copper(II) sulfate, and then weighing the anhydrate. The % H_2O was determined to be 30.%. The theoretical value is 33%. Which of the following choices is definitely NOT the cause of the error?

A. After the student weighed the hydrate, a piece of rust fell from the tongs into the crucible.
B. Moisture driven from the hydrate condensed on the inside of the crucible cover before the student weighed the anhydride.
C. All the weighings were made on a balance that was high by 10%.
D. The original sample contained some anhydrous copper(II) sulfate.
E. The original sample was wet.

28. Given the following information:

Reaction 1: $H_{2(g)} + \tfrac{1}{2} O_{2(g)} \rightarrow H_2O_{(l)}$
$\triangle H° = -286$ kJ

Reaction 2: $CO_{2(g)} \rightarrow C_{(s)} + O_{2(g)}$
$\triangle H° = 394$ kJ

Reaction 3: $2CO_{2(g)} + H_2O_{(l)} \rightarrow C_2H_{2(g)} + \tfrac{5}{2} O_{2(g)}$
$\triangle H° = 1300$ kJ

Find $\triangle H°$ for the reaction $C_2H_{2(g)} \rightarrow 2C_{(s)} + H_{2(g)}$

A. -226 kJ
B. -113 kJ
C. 113 kJ
D. 226 kJ
E. 452 kJ

29. Which of the following would be the most soluble in water?

A. carbon tetrachloride
B. methane
C. octane
D. methyl ethyl ketone
E. ethyl alcohol

30. According to the Law of Dulong and Petit, the best prediction for the specific heat of technetium (Tc), atomic mass = 100., is

A. 0.10 J/g · °C
B. 0.25 J/g · °C
C. 0.50 J/g · °C
D. 0.75 J/g · °C
E. 1.0 J/g · °C

31. Which of the following would express the approximate density of carbon dioxide gas at 0°C and 2.00 atm pressure (in grams per liter)?

A. 2 g/L
B. 4 g/L
C. 6 g/L
D. 8 g/L
E. none of the above

32. For a substance that remains a gas under the conditions listed, deviation from the ideal gas law would be most pronounced at

A. −100°C and 5 atm
B. −100°C and 1.0 atm
C. 0°C and 1.0 atm
D. 100°C and 1.0 atm
E. 100°C and 5.0 atm

33. Which of the following series of elements is listed in order of increasing atomic radius?

A. Na, Mg, Al, Si
B. C, N, O, F
C. O, S, Se, Te
D. I, Br, Cl, F
E. K, Kr, O, Au

34. When subjected to the flame test, a solution that contains K^+ ions produces the color

A. yellow
B. violet
C. crimson
D. green
E. orange

35. Carbon monoxide gas is combusted in the presence of oxygen gas into carbon dioxide. $\triangle H$ for this reaction is −283 kJ. Which of the following would NOT increase the rate of reaction?

(1) raising the temperature
(2) lowering the temperature
(3) increasing the pressure
(4) decreasing the pressure
(5) adding a catalyst

A. 1 and 3
B. 2 and 4
C. 2 and 3
D. 1 and 4
E. 5

36. Which one of the following is a nonpolar molecule with one or more polar bonds?

A. H–Br
B. Cl–Be–Cl
C. H–H
D. H–O–H
E. K–Cl

37. The bond energy of Br-Br is 192 kJ/mole, and that of Cl–Cl is 243 kJ/mole. What is the approximate Cl–Br bond energy?

A. 54.5 kJ/mole
B. 109 kJ/mole
C. 218 kJ/mole
D. 435 kJ/mole
E. 870 kJ/mole

Practice Exam 2

GO ON TO THE NEXT PAGE

38. Which of the following is the correct Lewis structure for the ionic compound $Ca(ClO_2)_2$?

A.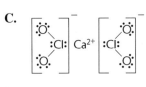

B.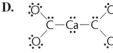

C.

D.

E.

39. Which of the following liquids has the highest vapor pressure at 25°C?

  A. carbon tetrachloride, CCl_4
  B. hydrogen peroxide, H_2O_2
  C. water, H_2O
  D. dichloromethane, CH_2Cl_2
  E. trichloromethane, $CHCl_3$

40. An imaginary metal crystallizes in a cubic lattice. The unit cell edge length is 100. picometers (1 picometer = 1×10^{-12} meters). The density of this metal is 200. g/cm^3. The atomic mass of the metal is 60.2 g/mol. How many of these metal atoms are there within a unit cell?

  A. 1
  B. 2
  C. 4
  D. 6
  E. 12

41. When 5.92 grams of a nonvolatile, nonionizing compound is dissolved in 186 grams of water, the freezing point (at normal pressure) of the resulting solution is –0.592°C. What is the molecular weight of the compound?

  A. 10.0 g/mol
  B. 100. g/mol
  C. 110. g/mol
  D. 200. g/mol
  E. 210. g/mol

For Questions 42–46, consider the following system at equilibrium:

$$2N_2O_{(g)} \longleftrightarrow 2N_{2\,(g)} + O_{2\,(g)} \qquad \Delta H = +163 \text{ kJ}$$

and select from the following choices:

  A. to the right
  B. to the left
  C. neither
  D. in both directions
  E. cannot be determined from information provided

42. In which direction will the system move in order to reestablish equilibrium if N_2O is added?

43. In which direction will the system move in order to reestablish equilibrium if O_2 is removed?

44. In which direction will the system move in order to reestablish equilibrium if the volume is decreased?

45. In which direction will the system move in order to reestablish equilibrium if the temperature is raised?

46. In which direction will the system move in order to reestablish equilibrium if a catalyst is added?

47. Acetaldehyde, CH_3CHO, decomposes into methane gas and carbon monoxide gas. This is a second-order reaction (rate is proportional to the concentration of the reactant). The rate of decomposition at 140°C is 0.10 mole · liter^{-1} · sec^{-1} when the concentration of acetaldehyde is 0.010 mole · liter^{-1}. What is the rate of the reaction when the concentration of acetaldehyde is 0.050 mole/liter?

  A. 0.50 mole · liter^{-1} · sec^{-1}
  B. 1.0 mole · liter^{-1} · sec^{-1}
  C. 1.5 mole · liter^{-1} · sec^{-1}
  D. 2.0 mole · liter^{-1} · sec^{-1}
  E. 2.5 mole · liter^{-1} · sec^{-1}

For Questions 48 and 49, refer to the following diagram:

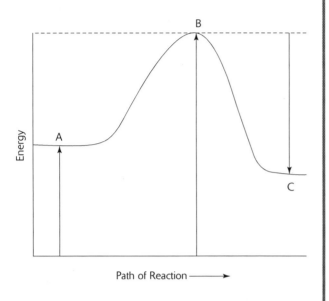

48. The activation energy is represented by

  A. A
  B. B
  C. C
  D. B – A
  E. B – C

49. The enthalpy of the reaction is represented by

  A. B – (C – A)
  B. B
  C. C – A
  D. B – C
  E. A – (B – C)

50. Solid carbon reacts with carbon dioxide gas to produce carbon monoxide gas. At 1,500°C, the reaction is found to be at equilibrium with a K_p value of 0.50 and a total pressure of 3.5 atm. What is the proper expression for the partial pressure (in atmospheres) of the carbon dioxide gas?

  A. $\dfrac{-0.50 + \sqrt{\left[(0.50)^2 - 4(1)(-3.5)\right]}}{2(1)}$

  B. $\dfrac{-0.50 + \sqrt{\left[(0.50)^2 - 4(1)(-1.75)\right]}}{2(1)}$

  C. $\dfrac{-0.50 + \sqrt{\left[(0.50) - 4(1)(-1.75)\right]}}{2(1)}$

  D. $\dfrac{-0.50 + \sqrt{\left[(0.50)^2 - 2(1)(3.5)\right]}}{2(1)}$

  E. $\dfrac{-0.50 + \sqrt{\left[(0.50)^2 + 4(1)(1.75)\right]}}{2(-1)}$

51. Will a precipitate form when one mixes 75.0 mL of 0.050 M K_2CrO_4 solution with 75.0 mL of 0.10 M $Sr(NO_3)_2$? K_{sp} for $SrCrO_4 = 3.6 \times 10^{-5}$

  A. Yes, a precipitate will form, $Q > K_{sp}$.
  B. Yes, a precipitate will form, $Q < K_{sp}$.
  C. Yes, a precipitate will form, $Q = K_{sp}$.
  D. No, a precipitate will not form, $Q > K_{sp}$.
  E. No, a precipitate will not form, $Q < K_{sp}$.

52. All of the following choices are strong bases EXCEPT

  A. CsOH
  B. RbOH
  C. $Ca(OH)_2$
  D. $Ba(OH)_2$
  E. $Mg(OH)_2$

GO ON TO THE NEXT PAGE

53. Given the following standard molar entropies measured at 25°C and 1 atm pressure, calculate $\triangle S°$ in $(J \cdot mol^{-1} \cdot K^{-1})$ for the reaction

$$2Al_{(s)} + 3MgO_{(s)} \rightarrow 3Mg_{(s)} + Al_2O_{3(s)}$$

Substance	S°
$Al_{(s)}$	28.0 J · mol⁻¹· K⁻¹
$MgO_{(s)}$	27.0 J · mol⁻¹· K⁻¹
$Mg_{(s)}$	33.0 J · mol⁻¹ · K⁻¹
$Al_2O_{3(s)}$	51.0 J · mol⁻¹ · K⁻¹

    A. $-29.0\ J \cdot mol^{-1} \cdot K^{-1}$
    B. $-13.0\ J \cdot mol^{-1} \cdot K^{-1}$
    C. $13.0\ J \cdot mol^{-1} \cdot K^{-1}$
    D. $69.0\ J \cdot mol^{-1} \cdot K^{-1}$
    E. $139\ J \cdot mol^{-1} \cdot K^{-1}$

54. Given for the reaction $Hg_{(l)} \rightarrow Hg_{(g)}$ that $\triangle H° = 63.0\ kJ \cdot mole^{-1}$ and $\triangle S° = 100.\ J \cdot K^{-1} \cdot mole^{-1}$, calculate the normal boiling point of Hg.

    A.   6.30 K
    B.   63.0 K
    C. 6.30×10^2 K
    D. 6.30×10^3 K
    E.   cannot be determined from the information provided

55. When $NH_{3(aq)}$ is added to a solution containing $Zn^{2+}_{(aq)}$, a white precipitate appears. Upon addition of more $NH_{3(aq)}$, the precipitate dissolves. The precipitate is most likely

    A. $Zn(OH)_2$
    B. $Zn(NH_3)_4^{2+}$
    C.   Zn
    D. $Zn(NH_3)_2$
    E. $Zn(NH_4)_2$

56. What mass of copper would be produced by the reduction of the $Cu^{2+}_{(aq)}$ ion by passing 96.487 amperes of current through a solution of copper(II) chloride for 100.00 minutes? (1 Faraday = 96,487 coulombs)

    A.   95.325 g
    B.   190.65 g
    C.   285.98 g
    D.   381.30 g
    E.   cannot be determined from the information provided

57. A cell has been set up as shown in the following diagram, and $E°$ has been measured as 1.00 V at 25°C. Calculate $\triangle G°$ for the reaction.

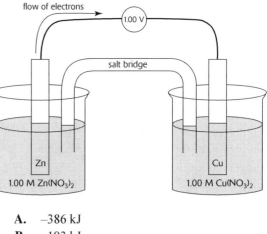

    A. -386 kJ
    B. -193 kJ
    C.   1.00 kJ
    D.   193 kJ
    E.   386 kJ

Questions 58–62

    A.   alcohol
    B.   aldehyde
    C.   carboxylic acid
    D.   ester
    E.   ether

58.

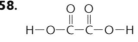

59.

60.

61.

62.

Questions 63–65

A. $_0^0\gamma$

B. $_1^1H$

C. $_0^1n$

D. $_2^4He$

E. $2\,_0^1n$

63. $_{26}^{54}Fe + ? \rightarrow _{26}^{56}Fe + 2\,_1^1H$

64. $_{29}^{65}Cu + _0^1n \rightarrow _{29}^{64}Cu + ?$

65. $_7^{14}N + _1^1H \rightarrow _8^{15}O + ?$

66. The half-life of C is 5770 years. What percent of the original radioactivity would be present after 28,850 years?

A. 1.56%

B. 3.12%

C. 6.26%

D. 12.5%

E. 25.0%

For Questions 67 and 68, consider the following molecules:

$$C_2Cl_2 \quad C_2HCl \quad C_2H_2Cl_2 \quad C_2HCl_5$$

67. How many of the molecules contain two pi bonds between the carbon atoms?

A. 0

B. 1

C. 2

D. 3

E. 4

68. How many of the molecules contain at least one sigma bond?

A. 0

B. 1

C. 2

D. 3

E. 4

69. A certain gas had a volume of 3.0 liters and a pressure of 3.0 atmospheres. The pressure on the gas was reduced to 1.0 atmosphere, and the gas was allowed to expand. How much work was involved in this process?

A. $-9.0 \, L \cdot atm$

B. $-6.0 \, L \cdot atm$

C. $-3.0 \, L \cdot atm$

D. $3.0 \, L \cdot atm$

E. $6.0 \, L \cdot atm$

70. Which of the following is NOT a typical property of a particle?

A. mass

B. kinetic energy

C. momentum

D. amplitude

E. All are typical particle properties.

71. In which of the following reactions does $\triangle H°_f = \triangle H°_{rxn}$?

A. $O_{(g)} + O_{2(g)} \rightarrow O_{3(g)}$

B. $H_{2(g)} + S_{(rhombic)} \rightarrow H_2S_{(g)}$

C. $H_{2(g)} + FeO_{(s)} \rightarrow H_2O_{(l)} + Fe_{(s)}$

D. $C_{(diamond)} + O_{2(g)} \rightarrow CO_{2(g)}$

E. none of the reactions

GO ON TO THE NEXT PAGE

72. On a particular day at 9:00 AM a student filled three balloons (all of equal size) with three different gases- one with hydrogen, another with air, and another with sulfur hexafluoride. Five hours later she came back and observed the balloons.

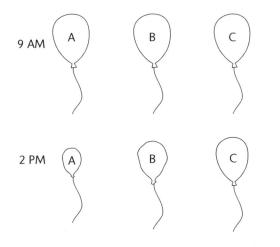

With all other factors being held constant, which of the following could be true given the following reasons?

A. Balloon A could be filled with hydrogen gas since hydrogen would effuse out the balloon membrane holes more quickly than air molecules could effuse in.

B. Balloon B could be filled with hydrogen since air would effuse through the balloon membrane holes at the same rate that hydrogen would effuse out as long as the two gases were at the same temperature.

C. Balloon A could be filled with sulfur hexafluoride because it is heavier than air and would cause the gas to escape through membrane holes through the process of osmosis.

D. Balloon C could be filled with air because it is always warmer at 2:00 PM than at 9:00 AM.

E. It is impossible to tell which balloon contains what gas with the given information.

73. Which of the following would NOT be a correct resonance structure for the isocyanate ion, CNO^-?

A. $[:C≡N-\ddot{\ddot{O}}:]^-$

B. $[\ddot{C}=N=\ddot{O}]^-$

C. $[:\ddot{C}-N≡O:]^-$

D. $[:C≡N=\ddot{O}]^-$

E. All choices are correct resonance structures.

74. Which of the following salts forms a basic solution when dissolved in water?

A. KCl

B. NH_4NO_3

C. Li_2SO_4

D. Na_2CO_3

E. AlI_3

75. Which of the following might be expected to have geometric isomers?

A. $Au(NH_3)^{2+}$

B. $Zn(H_2O)_2(OH)_2$

C. $Zn(NH_3)_4^{2+}$

D. $Co(NH_3)_4Cl_2$

E. $Pt(NH_3)_4^{2+}$

IF YOU FINISH BEFORE TIME IS CALLED, CHECK YOUR WORK ON THIS SECTION ONLY. DO NOT WORK ON ANY OTHER SECTION IN THE TEST.

PERIODIC TABLE OF THE ELEMENTS

1 **H** 1.0079																	2 **He** 4.0026
3 **Li** 6.941	4 **Be** 9.012											5 **B** 10.811	6 **C** 12.011	7 **N** 14.007	8 **O** 16.00	9 **F** 19.00	10 **Ne** 20.179
11 **Na** 22.99	12 **Mg** 24.30											13 **Al** 26.98	14 **Si** 28.09	15 **P** 30.974	16 **S** 32.06	17 **Cl** 35.453	18 **Ar** 39.948
19 **K** 39.10	20 **Ca** 40.08	21 **Sc** 44.96	22 **Ti** 47.90	23 **V** 50.94	24 **Cr** 51.00	25 **Mn** 54.93	26 **Fe** 55.85	27 **Co** 58.93	28 **Ni** 58.69	29 **Cu** 63.55	30 **Zn** 65.39	31 **Ga** 69.72	32 **Ge** 72.59	33 **As** 74.92	34 **Se** 78.96	35 **Br** 79.90	36 **Kr** 83.80
37 **Rb** 85.47	38 **Sr** 87.62	39 **Y** 88.91	40 **Zr** 91.22	41 **Nb** 92.91	42 **Mo** 95.94	43 **Tc** (98)	44 **Ru** 101.1	45 **Rh** 102.91	46 **Pd** 105.42	47 **Ag** 107.87	48 **Cd** 112.41	49 **In** 114.82	50 **Sn** 118.71	51 **Sb** 121.75	52 **Te** 127.60	53 **I** 126.91	54 **Xe** 131.29
55 **Cs** 132.91	56 **Ba** 137.33	57 *****La** 138.91	72 **Hf** 178.49	73 **Ta** 180.95	74 **W** 183.85	75 **Re** 186.21	76 **Os** 190.2	77 **Ir** 192.22	78 **Pt** 195.08	79 **Au** 196.97	80 **Hg** 200.59	81 **Ti** 204.38	82 **Pb** 207.2	83 **Bi** 208.98	84 **Po** (209)	85 **At** (210)	86 **Rn** (222)
87 **Fr** (223)	88 **Ra** 226.02	89 †**Ac** 227.03	104 **Rf** (261)	105 **Db** (262)	106 **Sg** (263)	107 **Bh** (262)	108 **Hs** (265)	109 **Mt** (266)	110 **§** (269)	111 **§** (272)	112 **§** (277)						

§ Not yet named

* Lanthanide Series

58 **Ce** 140.12	59 **Pr** 140.91	60 **Nd** 144.24	61 **Pm** (145)	62 **Sm** 150.4	63 **Eu** 151.97	64 **Gd** 157.25	65 **Tb** 158.93	66 **Dy** 162.50	67 **Ho** 164.93	68 **Er** 167.26	69 **Tm** 168.93	70 **Yb** 173.04	71 **Lu** 174.97

† Actinide Series

90 **Th** 232.04	91 **Pa** 231.04	92 **U** 238.03	93 **Np** 237.05	94 **Pu** (244)	95 **Am** (243)	96 **Cm** (247)	97 **Bk** (247)	98 **Cf** (251)	99 **Es** (252)	100 **Fm** (257)	101 **Md** (258)	102 **No** (259)	103 **Lr** (260)

GO ON TO THE NEXT PAGE

STANDARD REDUCTION POTENTIALS IN AQUEOUS SOLUTION AT 25°C

Half-reaction			$E°(V)$
$F_{2\,(g)} + 2\,e^-$	$\rightarrow$	$2\,F^-$	2.87
$Co^{3+} + e^-$	$\rightarrow$	Co^{2+}	1.82
$Au^{3+} + 3\,e^-$	$\rightarrow$	$Au_{(s)}$	1.50
$Cl_{2\,(g)} + 2\,e^-$	$\rightarrow$	$2\,Cl^-$	1.36
$O_{2\,(g)} + 4\,H^+ + 4\,e^-$	$\rightarrow$	$2\,H_2O_{(l)}$	1.23
$Br_{2\,(l)} + 2\,e^-$	$\rightarrow$	$2\,Br^-$	1.07
$2\,Hg^{2+} + 2\,e^-$	$\rightarrow$	Hg_2^{2+}	0.92
$Hg^{2+} + 2\,e^-$	$\rightarrow$	$Hg_{(l)}$	0.85
$Ag^+ + e^-$	$\rightarrow$	$Ag_{(s)}$	0.80
$Hg_2^{2+} + 2\,e^-$	$\rightarrow$	$2\,Hg_{(l)}$	0.79
$Fe^{3+} + e^-$	$\rightarrow$	Fe^{2+}	0.77
$I_{2\,(s)} + 2\,e^-$	$\rightarrow$	$2\,I^-$	0.53
$Cu^+ + e^-$	$\rightarrow$	$Cu_{(s)}$	0.52
$Cu^{2+} + 2\,e^-$	$\rightarrow$	$Cu_{(s)}$	0.34
$Cu^{2+} + e^-$	$\rightarrow$	Cu^+	0.15
$Sn^{4+} + 2\,e^-$	$\rightarrow$	Sn^{2+}	0.15
$S_{(s)} + 2\,H^+ + 2\,e^-$	$\rightarrow$	$H_2S_{(g)}$	0.14
$2\,H^+ + 2\,e^-$	$\rightarrow$	$H_{2(g)}$	0.00
$Pb^{2+} + 2\,e^-$	$\rightarrow$	$Pb_{(s)}$	−0.13
$Sn^{2+} + 2\,e^-$	$\rightarrow$	$Sn_{(s)}$	−0.14
$Ni^{2+} + 2\,e^-$	$\rightarrow$	$Ni_{(s)}$	−0.25
$Co^{2+} + 2\,e^-$	$\rightarrow$	$Co_{(s)}$	−0.28
$Cd^{2+} + 2\,e^-$	$\rightarrow$	$Cd_{(s)}$	−0.40
$Cr^{3+} + e^-$	$\rightarrow$	Cr^{2+}	−0.41
$Fe^{2+} + 2\,e^-$	$\rightarrow$	$Fe_{(s)}$	−0.44
$Cr^{3+} + 3\,e^-$	$\rightarrow$	$Cr_{(s)}$	−0.74
$Zn^{2+} + 2\,e^-$	$\rightarrow$	$Zn_{(s)}$	−0.76
$2\,H_2O_{(l)} + 2\,e^-$	$\rightarrow$	$H_{2(g)} + 2\,OH^-$	−0.83
$Mn^{2+} + 2\,e^-$	$\rightarrow$	$Mn_{(s)}$	−1.18
$Al^{3+} + 3\,e^-$	$\rightarrow$	$Al_{(s)}$	−1.66
$Be^{2+} + 2\,e^-$	$\rightarrow$	$Be_{(s)}$	−1.70
$Mg^{2+} + 2\,e^-$	$\rightarrow$	$Mg_{(s)}$	−2.37
$Na^+ + e^-$	$\rightarrow$	$Na_{(s)}$	−2.71
$Ca^{2+} + 2\,e^-$	$\rightarrow$	$Ca_{(s)}$	−2.87
$Sr^{2+} + 2\,e^-$	$\rightarrow$	$Sr_{(s)}$	−2.89
$Ba^{2+} + 2\,e^-$	$\rightarrow$	$Ba_{(s)}$	−2.90
$Rb^+ + e^-$	$\rightarrow$	$Rb_{(s)}$	−2.92
$K^+ + e^-$	$\rightarrow$	$K_{(s)}$	−2.92
$Cs^+ + e^-$	$\rightarrow$	$Cs_{(s)}$	−2.92
$Li^+ + e^-$	$\rightarrow$	$Li_{(s)}$	−3.05

Note: Unless otherwise stated, assume that for all questions involving solutions and/or chemical equations, the system is in water at room temperature.

ADVANCED PLACEMENT CHEMISTRY EQUATIONS AND CONSTANTS

ATOMIC STRUCTURE

$$E = hv \qquad c = \lambda v$$

$$\lambda = \frac{h}{mv} \qquad p = mv$$

$$E_n = \frac{-2.178 \times 10^{-18}}{n^2} \text{ joule}$$

EQUILIBRIUM

$$K_a = \frac{[H^+][A^-]}{[HA]}$$

$$K_b = \frac{[OH^-][HB^+]}{[B]}$$

$$K_w = [OH^-][H^+] = 1.0 \times 10^{-14} \text{ @ } 25°C$$
$$= K_a \times K_b$$

$$pH = -\log[H^+], \quad pOH = -\log[OH^-]$$

$$14 = pH + pOH$$

$$pH = pK_a + \log\frac{[A^-]}{[HA]}$$

$$pOH = pK_b + \log\frac{[HB^+]}{[B]}$$

$$pK_a = -\log K_a, \quad pK_b = -\log K_b$$

$$K_p = K_c (RT)^{\Delta n}$$

where Δn = moles product gas − moles reactant gas

THERMOCHEMISTRY/KINETICS

$$\Delta S° = \Sigma S° \text{ products} - \Sigma S° \text{ reactants}$$

$$\Delta H° = \Sigma \Delta H_f° \text{ products} - \Sigma \Delta H_f° \text{ reactants}$$

$$\Delta G° = \Sigma \Delta G_f° \text{ products} - \Sigma \Delta G_f° \text{ reactants}$$

$$\Delta G° = \Delta H° - T\Delta S°$$
$$= -RT \ln K = -2.303 \, RT \log K$$
$$= -n \, \mathcal{F} \, E°$$

$$\Delta G = \Delta G° + RT \ln Q = \Delta G° + 2.303 \, RT \log Q$$
$$q = mc\Delta T$$

$$C_p = \frac{\Delta H}{\Delta T}$$

$$\ln[A]_t - \ln[A]_0 = -kt$$

$$\frac{1}{[A]_t} - \frac{1}{[A]_0} = kt$$

$$\ln k = \frac{-E_a}{R}\left(\frac{1}{T}\right) + \ln A$$

E = energy v = velocity
v = frequency n = principal quantum number
λ = wavelength
p = momentum m = mass

Speed of light, $c = 3.0 \times 10^8 \text{ m} \cdot \text{s}^{-1}$

Planck's constant, $h = 6.63 \times 10^{-34} \text{ J} \cdot \text{s}$

Boltzmann's constant, $k = 1.38 \times 10^{-23} \text{ J} \cdot \text{K}^{-1}$

Avogadro's number $= 6.022 \times 10^{23} \text{ mol}^{-1}$

Electron charge, $e = -1.602 \times 10^{-19} \text{ coulomb}$

1 electron volt per atom $= 96.5 \text{ kJ} \cdot \text{mol}^{-1}$

Equilibrium Constants
K_a (weak acid)
K_b (weak base)
K_w (water)
K_p (gas pressure)
K_c (molar concentrations)

$S°$ = standard entropy
$H°$ = standard enthalpy
$G°$ = standard free energy
$E°$ = standard reduction potential
T = temperature
n = moles
m = mass
q = heat
c = specific heat capacity
C_p = molar heat capacity at constant pressure
E_a = activation energy
k = rate constant
A = frequency factor

Faraday's constant, $\mathcal{F} = 96,500$ coulombs per mole of electrons

Gas constant, $R = 8.31 \text{ J} \cdot \text{mol}^{-1} \cdot \text{K}^{-1}$
$= 0.0821 \text{ L} \cdot \text{atm} \cdot \text{mol}^{-1} \cdot \text{K}^{-1}$
$= 8.31 \text{ volt} \cdot \text{coulomb} \cdot \text{mol}^{-1} \cdot \text{K}^{-1}$

GO ON TO THE NEXT PAGE

Practice Exam 2

GASES, LIQUIDS, AND SOLUTIONS

$$PV = nRT$$

$$\left(P + \frac{n^2a}{V^2}\right)(V - nb) = nRT$$

$$P_A = P_{total} \times X_A, \text{ where } X_A = \frac{\text{moles A}}{\text{total moles}}$$

$$P_{total} = P_A + P_B + P_C + \ldots$$

$$n = \frac{m}{M}$$

$$K = {}^{\circ}C + 273$$

$$\frac{P_1V_1}{T_1} = \frac{P_2V_2}{T_2}$$

$$D = \frac{m}{V}$$

$$u_{rms} = \sqrt{\frac{3kT}{m}} = \sqrt{\frac{3RT}{m}}$$

$$KE \text{ per molecule} = \tfrac{1}{2}mv^2$$

$$KE \text{ per mole} = \tfrac{3}{2}RT$$

$$\frac{r_1}{r_2} = \sqrt{\frac{M_2}{M_1}}$$

molarity, M = moles solute per liter solution

molality, m = moles solute per kilogram solvent

$$\Delta T_f = i \cdot K_f \times \text{molality}$$

$$\Delta T_b = i \cdot K_b \times \text{molality}$$

$$\pi = i \cdot M \cdot R \cdot T$$

$$A = a \cdot b \cdot c$$

P = pressure
V = volume
T = temperature
n = number of moles
D = density
m = mass
v = velocity

u_{rms} = root-mean-square speed
KE = kinetic energy
r = rate of effusion
M = molar mass
π = osmotic pressure
i = van't Hoff factor
K_f = molal freezing-point depression constant
K_b = molal boiling-point elevation constant
A = absorbance
a = molar absorptivity
b = path length
c = concentration
Q = reaction quotient
I = current (amperes)
q = charge (coulombs)
t = time (seconds)
E° = standard reduction potential
K = equilibrium constant

OXIDATION-REDUCTION; ELECTROCHEMISTRY

$$Q = \frac{[C]^c[D]^d}{[A]^a[B]^b}, \text{ where } a\,A + b\,B \rightarrow c\,C + d\,D$$

$$I = \frac{q}{t}$$

$$E_{cell} = E^{\circ}_{cell} - \frac{RT}{n\mathscr{F}}\ln Q = E^{\circ}_{cell} - \frac{0.0592}{n}\log Q @ 25{}^{\circ}C$$

$$\log K = \frac{n \cdot E^{\circ}}{0.0592}$$

Gas constant, $R = 8.31 \text{ J} \cdot \text{mol}^{-1} \cdot \text{K}^{-1}$
$\qquad = 0.0821 \text{ L} \cdot \text{atm} \cdot \text{mol}^{-1} \cdot \text{K}^{-1}$
$\qquad = 8.31 \text{ volt} \cdot \text{coulomb} \cdot \text{mol}^{-1} \cdot \text{K}^{-1}$
Boltzmann's constant, $k = 1.38 \times 10^{-23} \text{ J} \cdot \text{K}^{-1}$
K_f for $H_2O = 1.86 \text{ K} \cdot \text{kg} \cdot \text{mol}^{-1}$
K_b for $H_2O = 0.512 \text{ K} \cdot \text{kg} \cdot \text{mol}^{-1}$
$1 \text{ atm} = 760 \text{ mm Hg}$
$\qquad = 760 \text{ torr}$
STP $= 0.000{}^{\circ}$ C and 1.000 atm
Faraday's constant, $\mathscr{F} = 96,500$ coulombs per
mole of electrons

Section II: Free-Response Questions

CHEMISTRY

Section II

Total time—90 minutes

Part A

Time—40 minutes

YOU MAY USE YOUR CALCULATOR FOR PART A

CLEARLY SHOW THE METHOD USED AND STEPS INVOLVED IN ARRIVING AT YOUR ANSWERS. It is to your advantage to do this because you may obtain partial credit if you do and you will receive little or no credit if you do not. Attention should be paid to significant figures.

Answer Question 1 below. The Section II score weighting for this question is 20%.

1. Ethylamine reacts with water as follows:

$$C_2H_5NH_{2(aq)} + H_2O_{(l)} \rightarrow C_2H_5NH^+_{(aq)} + OH^-_{(aq)}$$

The base-dissociation constant, K_b, for the ethylamine ion is 5.6×10^{-4}.

(a) A student carefully measures out 65.987 mL of a 0.250 M solution of ethylamine. Calculate the OH^- ion concentration.

(b) Calculate the pOH of the solution.

(c) Calculate the % ionization of the ethylamine in the solution in part (a).

(d) What would be the pH of a solution made by adding 15.000 grams of ethylammonium bromide ($C_2H_5NH_3Br$) to 250.00 mL of a 0.100-molar solution of ethylamine. (The addition of the solid does not change the solution volume.)

(e) If a student adds 0.125 grams of solid silver nitrate to the solution in part (a), will silver hydroxide form as a precipitate? The value of K_{sp} for silver hydroxide is 1.52×10^{-8}.

Answer EITHER Question 2 or 3 below. Only one of these two questions will be graded. If you start both questions, be sure to cross out the question you do not want graded. The Section II score weighting for the question you choose is 20%.

2. $$2Cu_{(s)} + \tfrac{1}{2} O_{2(g)} \rightarrow Cu_2O_{(s)} \qquad \triangle H°_f = -168.6 \text{ kJ} \cdot \text{mol}^{-1}$$

Copper reacts with oxygen to produce copper(I) oxide, as represented by the equation above. A 100.0 g sample of $Cu_{(s)}$ is mixed with 12.0 L of $O_{2(g)}$ at 2.50 atm and 298K.

(a) Calculate the number of moles of each of the following before the reaction begins.

  (i) $Cu_{(s)}$

  (ii) $O_{2(g)}$

GO ON TO THE NEXT PAGE

(b) Identify the limiting reactant when the mixture is heated to produce $Cu_2O_{(s)}$. Support your answer with calculations.

(c) Calculate the number of moles of $Cu_2O_{(s)}$ produced when the reaction proceeds to completion.

(d) The standard free energy of formation, $\triangle G°_f$, of $Cu_2O_{(s)}$ is -146 kJ $\cdot$ mol^{-1} at 298K.

    (i) Calculate the standard entropy of formation, $\triangle S°_f$, of $Cu_2O_{(s)}$ at 298K. Include units with your answer.

    (ii) Given the standard enthalpy of formation, $\triangle H°_f$ and the standard entropy of formation, $\triangle S°_f$, which one is considered to be more responsible for the spontaneity of forming Cu_2O?

3. Radon-222 can be produced from the α-decay of radium-226.

    (a) Write the nuclear reaction.

    (b) Calculate $°E$ (in kJ) when 7.00 g of $^{226}_{88}Ra$ decays.

        $^{4}_{2}He = 4.0015$ g/mole

        $^{222}_{86}Rn = 221.9703$ g/mole

        $^{226}_{88}Ra = 225.9771$ g/mole

    (c) Calculate the mass defect of $^{226}_{88}Ra$.

        1 mole protons = 1.00728 g

        1 mole neutrons = 1.00867 g

        atomic mass $^{226}_{88}Ra = 225.9771$ g/mole

    (d) Calculate the binding energy (in kJ/mole) of $^{226}_{88}Ra$.

    (e) $^{226}_{88}Ra$ has a half-life of 1.62×10^3 yr. Calculate the first-order rate constant.

    (f) Calculate the fraction of $^{226}_{88}Ra$ that will remain after 100.0 yr.

CHEMISTRY

Part B

Time—50 minutes

NO CALCULATORS MAY BE USED FOR PART B

Answer Question 4 below. The Section II score weight for this question is 15%.

4. Write the formulas to show the reactants and the products for any FIVE of the laboratory situations described below. Answers to more than five choices will not be graded. In all cases, a reaction occurs. Assume that solutions are aqueous unless otherwise indicated. Represent substances in solution as ions if the substances are extensively ionized. Omit formulas for any ions or molecules that are unchanged by the reaction. You need not balance the equations.

Example: A strip of magnesium is added to a solution of silver nitrate.

Ex.	$Mg + Ag^+ \rightarrow Mg^2 + Ag$

(a) Methanol is mixed with acetic acid and then gently warmed.

(b) A 9M nitric acid solution is added to a solution of potassium carbonate.

(c) Calcium oxide is heated in an environment of sulfur trioxide gas.

(d) Iron(III) nitrate is added to a strong sodium hydroxide solution.

(e) Solid copper(II) oxide is dropped into sulfuric acid.

(f) Carbon dioxide gas is heated in the presence of solid magnesium oxide.

(g) Hydrochloric acid is added to a sodium carbonate solution.

(h) Small pieces of aluminum are added to a solution of copper(II) sulfate.

GO ON TO THE NEXT PAGE

Answer BOTH Question 5 AND Question 6 below. Both of these questions will be graded. The Section II score weighting for these questions is 30% (15% each).

5.

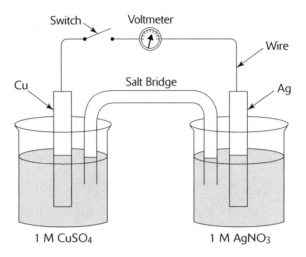

1 M CuSO₄   **1 M AgNO₃**

A student places a copper electrode in a 1 M solution of $CuSO_4$ and in another beaker places a silver electrode in a 1 M solution of $AgNO_3$. $E°_{red}$ for silver is +0.7991 volts while the $E°_{red}$ of copper is +0.337 volts. A salt bridge composed of Na_2SO_4 connects the two beakers. The voltage measured across the electrodes is found to be +0.42 volts.

(a) In the diagram above, label the electrode that is the anode. Justify your answer.

(b) In the diagram above, draw an arrow indicating the direction of the electron flow in the external circuit when the switch is closed. Justify your answer.

(c) Describe what is happening at the cathode. Include any equations that may be important.

(d) Write the balanced overall cell equation and determine $E°_{cell}$.

(e) Write the standard cell notation.

(f) The student adds 4 M ammonia to the copper sulfate solution, producing the complex ion $Cu(NH_3)_4^{2+}{}_{(aq)}$. The student remeasures the cell potential and discovers the voltage to be 0.88 volts at 25°C. Show how a student would determine the $Cu^{2+}{}_{(aq)}$ concentration after the ammonia had been added. Do not do any calculations.

6. Common oxides of nitrogen are NO, NO_2, N_2O, and N_2O_4. Using principles of chemical bonding and molecular geometry, answer each of the following. Lewis electron-dot diagrams and sketches of molecules may be helpful as part of your explanations.

(a) Draw the Lewis structures for any two of these oxides of nitrogen. In each case, the oxygen(s) are terminal atoms.

(b) Which of the oxides 'violates' the octet rule? Explain your answer.

(c) Draw the resonance structures for N_2O.

(d) Which bonds in N_2O_4 are polar and which are nonpolar? In the case of the polar bonds, which atom acts as the positive pole?

(e) Compare the structure of NO with that of NO_2.

(f) The bond energy for N—O is 222 kJ/mol; for N—N it is 159 kJ/mol; for N–O it is 222 kJ/mol; and for N=O it is 607 kJ/mol. Estimate the $\triangle H$ for the dimerization of $NO_{2(g)}$.

Answer EITHER Question 7 or 8 below. Only one of these two questions will be graded. If you start both questions, be sure to cross out the question you do not want graded. The Section II score weighting for the question you choose is 15%.

7. Solids can be classified into four categories: ionic, metallic, covalent network, and molecular. Choose one of the four categories listed and for that category identify the basic structural unit; describe the nature of the force both within the unit and between units; cite the basic properties of melting point, conduction of electricity, solubility, hardness, and conduction of heat for that type of solid; give an example of the type of solid; and describe a laboratory means of identifying the solid.

8. Answer the following questions about ammonia, $NH_{3(g)}$ and methane gas, $CH_{4(g)}$. Assume that both gases exhibit ideal behavior.

   (a) Draw the complete Lewis structure (electron-dot diagram) for the ammonia and methane molecules.

   (b) Identify the shape of each molecule.

   (c) One of the gases dissolves readily in water to form a solution with a pH above 7. Identify the gas and account for this observation by writing a chemical equation.

   (d) A 1.5 mole sample of methane gas is placed in a piston at a constant temperature. Sketch the expected plot of volume vs. pressure, holding temperature constant.

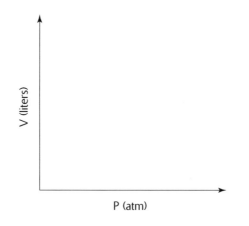

   (e) Samples of ammonia and methane gas are placed in 2 liter containers at the conditions indicated in the diagram below.

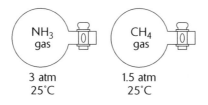

       (i) Indicate whether the average kinetic energy of the ammonia molecules is greater than, equal to, or less than the average kinetic energy of the methane molecules. Justify your answer.

       (ii) Indicate whether the root-mean square speed of the methane molecules is greater than, equal to, or less than the root-mean-square speed of the ammonia molecules. Justify your answer.

       (iii) Indicate whether the number of ammonia molecules is greater than, equal to, or less than the number of methane molecules. Justify your answer.

Answer Key for Practice Exam 2

Section I: Multiple-Choice Questions

1. C	**26.** D	**51.** A
2. A	**27.** E	**52.** E
3. E	**28.** A	**53.** C
4. B	**29.** E	**54.** C
5. D	**30.** B	**55.** A
6. A	**31.** B	**56.** B
7. D	**32.** A	**57.** B
8. D	**33.** C	**58.** C
9. D	**34.** B	**59.** A
10. E	**35.** B	**60.** E
11. C	**36.** B	**61.** B
12. A	**37.** C	**62.** D
13. B	**38.** C	**63.** D
14. D	**39.** D	**64.** E
15. B	**40.** B	**65.** A
16. C	**41.** B	**66.** B
17. D	**42.** A	**67.** C
18. B	**43.** A	**68.** E
19. E	**44.** B	**69.** B
20. D	**45.** A	**70.** D
21. D	**46.** C	**71.** B
22. B	**47.** E	**72.** A
23. C	**48.** D	**73.** D
24. A	**49.** C	**74.** D
25. C	**50.** B	**75.** D

Predicting Your AP Score

The table below shows historical relationships between students' results on the multiple-choice portion (Section I) of the AP Chemistry exam and their overall AP score. The AP score ranges from 1 to 5, with 3, 4, or 5 generally considered to be passing. Over the years, around 60% of the students who take the AP Chemistry Exam receive a 3, 4, or 5.

After you've taken the multiple-choice practice exam under timed conditions, count the number of questions you got correct. From this number, subtract the number of wrong answers times $\frac{1}{4}$. Do NOT count items left blank as wrong. Then refer to this table to find your "probable" overall AP score. For example, if you get 39 questions correct, based on historical statistics, you have a 25% chance of receiving an overall score of 3, a 63% chance of receiving an overall score of 4, and a 12% chance of receiving an overall score of 5. Note that your actual results may be different from the score this table predicts. Also, remember that the free-response section represents 55% of your AP score.

No attempt is made here to combine your specific results on the practice AP Chemistry free-response questions (Section II) with your multiple-choice results (which is beyond the scope of this book and for which no data is available). However, you should have your AP chemistry instructor review your essays before you take the AP Chemistry Exam so that he or she can give you additional pointers.

Number of Multiple-Choice Questions Correct*	Overall AP Score				
	1	2	3	4	5
47 to 75	0%	0%	1%	21%	78%
37 to 46	0%	0%	25%	63%	12%
24 to 36	0%	19%	69%	12%	0%
13 to 23	15%	70%	15%	0%	0%
0 to 12	86%	14%	0%	0%	0%
% of Test Takers Receiving Score	21%	22%	25%	15%	17%

*Corrected for wrong answers

Answers and Explanations for Practice Exam 2

1. **(C)** Oxygen is more electronegative than carbon, resulting in polar bonding. Because there are no unshared pairs of electrons for carbon, a linear molecule results. Linear molecules are nonpolar when both peripheral atoms are the same.

$$\ddot{\underset{..}{O}}=C=\ddot{\underset{..}{O}}$$

2. **(A)** 70% of acid rain comes from sulphur dioxide (SO_2), which dissolves into the water to form sulphuric acid. The rest comes from various oxides of nitrogen (mainly NO_2 and NO_3, collectively called NO_x).

$$:\ddot{\underset{..}{O}}-\ddot{S}=\ddot{\underset{..}{O}}: \longleftrightarrow :\ddot{\underset{..}{O}}=\ddot{S}-\ddot{\underset{..}{O}}:$$

3. **(E)** Produced in internal combustion engines and electrical generating stations, NO (nitric oxide or nitrogen monoxide) has been implicated in the depletion of the ozone layer, formation of photochemical smog, and acid rain (SO_2 is linked with acid rain but not depletion of the ozone layer). Nitric oxide reacts with and depletes ozone: $NO + O_3 \longleftrightarrow NO_2 + O_2$. More recently, however, NO has been shown to be involved in a seemingly limitless range of biological functions such as controlling blood circulation, regulating the activity of the brain and other organs and as part of the body's immune system.

4. **(B)**

$$\begin{array}{c} H \\ | \\ H-\underset{|}{\overset{Si}{\diagdown}}H \\ | \\ H \end{array}$$

Silicon, in order to bond four hydrogen atoms to itself, must exhibit sp^3 hybridization.

5. **(D)** Adding water to calcium oxide produces calcium hydroxide ($CaO + H_2O \rightarrow Ca(OH)_2$).

6. **(A)** $Ca(NO_3)_2$ ionizes into three moles of ions per mole of compound

$$Ca(NO_3)_{2(aq)} \rightarrow Ca^{2+}{}_{(aq)} + 2NO_3{}^-{}_{(aq)}$$

For a 0.20 M solution of $Ca(NO_3)_2$ there would be 0.60 moles of ions per liter which would allow the greatest electrical conductivity. CH_3OH is an organic molecule and does not ionize.

7. **(D)** 8.00 g of oxygen atoms represent 0.500 moles.

$$\frac{8.00 \text{ g O}}{0.500 \text{ mole O}} \times \frac{2 \text{ moles O}}{1 \text{ mole } X} \times \frac{44.0 \text{ g } X}{8.00 \text{ g O}} = 176 \text{ g } X \text{ / mole } X$$

8. **(D)** Hydrogen bonding is a very strong intermolecular force that occurs between molecules containing an H atom that is bonded to a fluorine, oxygen, or nitrogen atom. In Choice (D), the hydrogens are bonded to carbon, not to F, O, or N.

9. **(D)** **Step 1:** Write the balanced equation in equilibrium:

$$2SO_{3\,(g)} \longleftrightarrow 2SO_{2\,(g)} + O_{2\,(g)}$$

Step 2: Write the equilibrium expression:

$$K_c = \frac{[SO_2]^2 [O_2]}{[SO_3]^2}$$

Step 3: Create a chart showing initial and final concentrations.

Species	Initial Concentration	Final Concentration
SO_3	$\dfrac{3.60 \text{ moles}}{3 \text{ liters}} = 1.20 \text{ M}$	1.20M – 0.20 M = 1.00 M
SO_2	0 M	0.20 M
O_2	0 M	0.10 M

Step 4: Substitute the final equilibrium concentrations into the equilibrium expression.

$$K_c = \frac{\left[SO_2\right]^2\left[O_2\right]}{\left[SO_3\right]^2} = \frac{(0.20)^2(0.10)}{(1.00)^2} = 4.0 \times 10^{-3}$$

10. (E) Salts are composed of positive and negative ions.

M = Metal

The name of this compound is potassium propionate.

11. (C) The functional group of a ketone is

$$\begin{array}{c} O \\ \| \\ -C- \end{array}$$

The name of this ketone is methyl ethyl ketone.

12. (A) The functional group of an amide is

$$\begin{array}{c} O \\ \| \\ -C-N< \end{array}$$

The name of this amide is acetamide.

13. (B) The functional group of an amine is

$$\begin{array}{c} | \\ -N- \end{array}$$

The name of this amine is dimethylamine.

14. (D) The functional group of a thiol is

$$-S-H$$

The name of this thiol is ethanethiol.

15. (B) In SO_3, the sulfur has a +6 oxidation number; the sulfur cannot be oxidized further. The other elements bound to oxygen in the other choices have oxidation numbers less than their maximum value and can undergo further oxidation.

16. (C) When presented with a generic formula, such as AB_2, the best way to answer the question is to use familiar examples that satisfy the conditions of the question. In CO_2, a linear molecule, the two dipoles cancel each other, resulting in a nonpolar molecule. However, in H_2O, the two dipoles do not cancel each other out and results in a net dipole moment and a bent molecule. For both CO_2 and H_2O, we have data on ionization energy, electron affinity, electronegativity, and bond energy, but these are of no use by themselves in determining the geometry of the species.

17. (D) All intermediate mechanisms must add up to yield the original, overall balanced equation.

$$\frac{\begin{array}{l} NO_{(g)} + O_{2(g)} \rightarrow \cancel{NO_{3(g)}} \\ \cancel{NO_{3(g)}} + NO_{(g)} \rightarrow 2NO_{2(g)} \end{array}}{2NO_{(g)} + O_{2(g)} \rightarrow 2NO_{2(g)}}$$

18. (B) $AB_{2(s)} \longleftrightarrow A^{2+}_{(aq)} + 2B^-_{(aq)}$

$[A^{2+}] = s$, $[B^-] = 2[A^{2+}] = 2s$

$K_{sp} = [A^{2+}][B^-]^2 = (s)(2s)^2 = 4s^3$

$\phantom{K_{sp}} = 4(2.0 \times 10^{-2})^3 = 4(8.0 \times 10^{-6}) = 32 \times 10^{-6} = 3.2 \times 10^{-5}$

The reason the [B⁻] = 2.0 M is because 1 mole of AB₂ dissociates to give one mole of A⁺ and two moles of B⁻.

19. (E)

$$\left[A^{2+}\right] = \frac{K_{sp}}{\left[B^-\right]^2} = \frac{32 \times 10^{-6}}{(2.0)^2} = 8.0 \times 10^{-6}\,M$$

20. (D) The positron is a particle with the same mass as the electron but the opposite charge. The net effect of positron emission is to change a proton to a neutron. Begin by writing the nuclear equation

$^{239}_{94}Pu \rightarrow\, ^0_1e +\, ^A_Z X$

Remember that the total of the A and Z values must be the same on both sides of the equation.

Solve for the Z value of X: $Z + 1 = 94$, so $Z = 93$

Solve for the A value of X: $A + 0 = 239$, so $A = 239$

Therefore, you have $^{239}_{93}X$, or $^{239}_{93}Np$

21. (D) Element A keys out to be Al, which, being a metal in Group IIIA, would have a +3 charge. Element B would key out as sulfur, a nonmetal with a charge of –2, giving the formula Al_2S_3, or A_2B_3.

22. (B) Begin by writing the equilibrium equation.

$$PbCl_{2\,(aq)} \longleftrightarrow Pb^{2+}_{(aq)} + 2Cl^-_{(aq)}$$

Next, write the equilibrium expression.

$K_{sp} = [Pb^{2+}][Cl^-]^2$

In reference to the chloride ion concentration, rewrite the expression for $[Cl^-]$:

$$\left[Cl^-\right] = \left(\frac{K_{sp}}{\left[Pb^{2+}\right]}\right)^{1/2}$$

If we substitute 1.0 M for $[Pb^{2+}]$, then $[Cl^-] = K_{sp}^{1/2}$

At any value greater than this expression, $PbCl_{2(s)}$ will precipitate, removing $Cl^-_{(aq)}$ from solution.

23. (C) The question concerns the effect of changing standard conditions of a cell to nonstandard conditions. To calculate the voltage of a cell under nonstandard conditions, use the Nernst equation

$$E = E° - \frac{0.0591}{n} \log Q = E° - \frac{0.0591}{2} \log \frac{\left[Zn^{2+}\right]}{\left[Ag^+\right]^2}$$

where $E°$ represents the cell voltage under standard conditions, E represents the cell voltage under nonstandard conditions, n represents the number of moles of electrons passing through the cell, and Q represents the reaction quotient.

Decreasing the $[Ag^+]$ increases Q. Increasing Q increases $\log Q$. Increasing $\log Q$ decreases $-\log Q$, which decreases E.

24. (A) The central metal ion forms only two bonds to ligands, so the coordination number is 2.

25. (C) A Brønsted base is a species that can accept a proton in an acid-base reaction. The ammonium ion donates a proton

$$NH_4^+{}_{(aq)} + OH^-{}_{(aq)} \longleftrightarrow NH_{3\,(aq)} + H_2O_{(l)}$$

26. (D) $2NH_3 + 3CuO \rightarrow 3Cu + N_2 + 3H_2O$

$2 + 3 + 3 + 1 + 3 = 12$

27. (E) The wetness of the original sample increases the initial weight of the hydrate. It does not decrease the final weight of the anhydrate (even though the net effect is the same). Using some fictitious numbers to answer this question (let 100 g = mass of the hydrate and 67 g = mass of the anhydrate): (100 g – 67 g)/100 g = 33 g/100g = 33% water. If the original sample was wet, then we could show the initial mass of the hydrate as, say, 167 g. The final mass of 67 g won't change because the impurity was water, which evaporates in the experiment. So we have: (167 g – 67 g)/167 g = 100 g/167g. This fraction is greater than 50% and therefore greater than the theoretical value of 33%.

28. (A) When doubling the coefficients of reaction 2 in order to cancel the CO_2 and O_2, be sure to double $\triangle H°$ to +788 kJ.

$\cancel{H_2O_{(l)}} \rightarrow H_{2(g)} + \cancel{\tfrac{1}{2}O_{2(g)}}$	$\Delta H° = -286$ kJ
$\cancel{2CO_{2(g)}} \rightarrow 2C_{(s)} + \cancel{2O_{2(g)}}$	$\Delta H° = +788$ kJ
$C_2H_{2(g)} + \cancel{\tfrac{5}{2}O_{2(g)}} \rightarrow \cancel{2CO_{2(g)}} + \cancel{H_2O_{(l)}}$	$\Delta H° = -1300$ kJ
$C_2H_{2(g)} \rightarrow H_{2(g)} + 2C_{(s)}$	$\Delta H° = -226$ kJ

29. (E) Ethyl alcohol (C_2H_5OH) is the only one that contains hydrogen bonding.

30. (B) The Law of Dulong and Petit states that

molar mass x specific heat ≈ 25 J/mole · °C

You know that technetium has an atomic mass of 100.

$(100.) (x) \approx 25$ J/mole · °C

$x \approx 0.25$ J/g · °C

31. (B) First calculate the volume the CO_2 gas would occupy at 2.00 atm using the relationship

$$\frac{P_1V_1}{T_1} = \frac{P_2V_2}{T_2}$$

Because the temperature is remaining constant and assuming that we are using 1 mole of gas, we can use $P_1V_1 = P_2V_2$, where initial conditions are at STP and final conditions are at 0°C and 2.00 atm.

$(1.00 \text{ atm}) (22.4 \text{ liters}) = (2.00 \text{ atm}) (V_2)$

$V_2 = 11.2$ liters

Because the amount of gas has not changed from the initial STP conditions (1 mole or 44.01 grams), the density of the gas at 2.00 atm and 0°C would be

$$\frac{44.01 \text{ grams}}{11.2 \text{ liters}} \approx 4 \text{ g} / \text{L}$$

Another approach to this problem (that would require a calculator) would be to use the ideal gas law, $PV = nRT$.

$$\text{density} = \frac{g}{V} = \frac{P \cdot MM}{RT}$$

$$= \frac{200 \text{ atm} \cdot 44.01 \text{ g} \cdot \text{mole}^{-1}}{0.0821 \text{ L} \cdot \text{atm} \cdot \text{mole}^{-1} \cdot \text{K}^{-1} \cdot 273 \text{ K}} \approx 4 \text{ g} / \text{L}$$

32. (A) The van der Waals constant *a* corrects for the attractive forces between gas molecules. The constant *b* corrects for particle volume. The attractive forces between gas molecules become pronounced when the molecules are closer together. Conditions which favor this are low temperatures (–100°C) and high pressures (5.0 atm).

33. (C) Atomic radius increases as one moves down a column (or group).

34. (B) Refer to the Flame Color chart found in *CliffsAP Chemistry,* 3rd Edition.

35. (B) Begin by writing the equation:

$$CO_{(g)} + \tfrac{1}{2} O_{2(g)} \rightarrow CO_{2(g)} + 283 \text{ kJ heat}$$

Decreasing the temperature would decrease the number of effective collisions between $CO_{(g)}$ and $O_{2(g)}$. Decreasing the pressure (accomplished by either increasing the volume or decreasing the number of molecules) would also favor decreased effective collisions. Note that this problem was NOT at equilibrium.

36. (B) The Cl atom is more electronegative than the Be atom, resulting in a polar bond. However, because the molecule is linear and the two ends are identical, the overall molecule is nonpolar.

37. (C) If the polarity of the bond A–B is about the same as those of the nonpolar bonds A–A and B–B, then the bond energy of A–B can be taken as the average of the bond energies of A–A and B–B; (192 + 243) / 2 ≈ 218 kJ/mole.

38. (C) To draw Lewis diagrams:

1. Find total # of valence e^-.

2. Arrange atoms—singular atom is usually in the middle.

3. Form bonds between atoms ($2e^-$).

4. Distribute remaining e^- to give each atom an octet (there are exceptions).

5. If there aren't enough e^- to go around, form double or triple bonds.

To find total # of valence e^- for polyatomic ions:

1. Add $1e^-$ for each negative charge.

2. Subtract $1e^-$ for each positive charge.

3. Place brackets around the ion and label the charge.

39. (D) You can rule out Choice B, hydrogen peroxide, and Choice C, water, because the very strong hydrogen bonds between their molecules lowers the vapor pressure (the ease at which the liquid evaporates). Although Answer A, carbon tetrachloride, the only nonpolar molecule in the list, has only dispersion forces present between molecules, Choice D, dichloromethane, has the lowest molecular weight and consequently the lowest amount of dispersion forces.

40. (B) First, calculate the mass of one cell, 100. pm on an edge:

$$\frac{200.\text{ g}}{1\text{ cm}^3} \times \left(\frac{100\text{ cm}}{1\text{ m}}\right)^3 \times \left(\frac{1\text{ m}}{10^{12}\text{ pm}}\right)^3 \times \left(\frac{100\text{ pm}}{1}\right)^3$$

$$= 2.00 \times 10^{-22}\text{ g / cell}$$

Next, calculate the mass of one metal atom:

$$\frac{60.2\text{ g}}{1\text{ mole}} \times \frac{1\text{ mole}}{6.02 \times 10^{23}\text{ atoms}} = 10.0 \times 10^{-23}\text{ g / atom}$$

$$= 1.00 \times 10^{-22}\text{ g / atom}$$

Finally, calculate the number of metal atoms in one cell:

$$\frac{2.00 \times 10^{-22}\text{ g} \cdot \text{cell}^{-1}}{1.00 \times 10^{-22}\text{ g} \cdot \text{atom}^{-1}} = 2\text{ atoms / cell}$$

41. (B) This problem can be solved using the factor-label method. The freezing point depression constant (k_f) for water is $1.86°\text{C} \cdot m^{-1}$.

$$\frac{0.592°\text{C}}{1} \times \frac{1\text{ mole solute}}{1.86°\text{C} \cdot \text{kg H}_2\text{O}} \times \frac{186\text{ g H}_2\text{O}}{5.92\text{ g solute}} \times \frac{1\text{ kg H}_2\text{O}}{1000\text{ g H}_2\text{O}}$$

$$= 0.0100\text{ mol / g} = 100.\text{ g / mol}$$

42. (A) If a system at equilibrium is disturbed by adding a gaseous species (reactant or product), the reaction will proceed in such a direction as to consume part of the added species.

43. (A) If a system at equilibrium is disturbed by removing a gaseous species (reactant or product), the reaction will proceed in such a direction as to restore part of the removed species.

44. (B) When the volume of an equilibrium system is decreased, reaction takes place in the direction that decreases the total number of moles of gas.

45. (A) Because $\triangle H$ is a positive value, the forward reaction is endothermic. An increase in temperature causes the endothermic reaction to occur.

46. (C) A catalyst has no effect on equilibrium. By adding a catalyst, the activation energy of both the forward and reverse rates will be lowered, but there will be no effect on equilibrium.

47. (E) Begin this problem by writing a balanced equation.

$$CH_3CHO_{(g)} \rightarrow CH_{4(g)} + CO_{(g)}$$

Next, write a rate expression.

rate = $k(\text{conc. CH}_3\text{CHO})^2$

Because you know the rate and the concentration of CH_3CHO, solve for k, the rate-specific constant.

$$k = \frac{\text{rate}}{\left(\text{conc. CH}_3\text{CHO}\right)^2} \rightarrow \frac{0.10\text{ mole} \cdot \text{liter}^{-1} \cdot \text{sec}^{-1}}{\left(0.01\text{ mole / liter}\right)^2}$$

$$= 1.0 \times 10^3\text{ liters} \cdot \text{mole}^{-1} \cdot \text{sec}^{-1}$$

Finally, substitute the rate-specific constant and the new concentration into the rate expression.

$$\text{rate} = \frac{1.0 \times 10^{-3}\text{ liter}}{1\text{ mole} \cdot \text{sec}} \times \left(\frac{0.050\text{ mole}}{1\text{ liter}}\right)^2 = 2.5\text{ moles} \cdot \text{liter}^{-1} \cdot \text{sec}^{-1}$$

48. (D) The activation energy is the amount of energy that the reactants must absorb from the system in order to react. In the reaction diagram, the reactants begin at A. The reactants must absorb the energy from A to B in order to form the activated complex. The energy necessary to achieve this activated complex is the distance from A to B in the diagram and is mathematically the difference (B − A).

49. (C) The enthalpy of the reaction, $\triangle H$, is the difference between the enthalpies of the products and the enthalpies of the reactants.

$$\triangle H = \Sigma H_{products} - \Sigma H_{reactants}$$

The products are represented at point C and the reactants are represented at point A, so the change in enthalpy is $C - A$.

50. (B) Step 1: Write the balanced equation.

$$C_{(s)} + CO_{2\,(g)} \longleftrightarrow 2CO_{(g)}$$

Step 2: Write the equilibrium expression.

$$K_p = \frac{(P_{CO})^2}{P_{CO_2}} = 0.50$$

Step 3: Express the two unknowns, pressure of CO and pressure of CO_2, in terms of a single unknown, pressure of CO.

$$P_{total} = P_{CO} + P_{CO_2} = 3.5 \text{ atm}$$
$$P_{CO_2} = 3.5 \text{ atm} - P_{CO}$$

Step 4: Rewrite the equilibrium expression in terms of the single unknown.

$$K_p = 0.50 = \frac{(P_{CO})^2}{3.5 - P_{CO}}$$

Step 5: Rewrite this relationship in terms of the quadratic equation so that you can solve for the unknown x, the pressure of the CO.

$$0.50 = x^2/(3.5 - x) \qquad x^2 = 0.50(3.5 - x)$$

$$x^2 = 1.75 - 0.50x$$

Putting this equation into the standard form, $ax^2 + bx + c = 0$, you get

$$x^2 + 0.50x - 1.75 = 0$$

Step 6: Use the quadratic equation to solve for x.

$$x = \frac{-0.50 \pm \sqrt{(0.50)^2 - 4(1)(-1.75)}}{2(1)}$$

51. (A) Recognize that this problem is one involving the ion product, Q. We calculate Q in the same manner as K_{sp}, except that we use initial concentrations of the species instead of equilibrium concentrations. We then compare the value of Q to that of K_{sp}.

If $Q < K_{sp}$—no precipitate

If $Q = K_{sp}$—no precipitate

If $Q > K_{sp}$—a precipitate forms

At this point you can rule out Choices B, C, and D because they do not make sense. If you have forgotten how to do the problem mathematically, you should guess now since you have a 50% chance of getting the answer right.

Step 1: Realize that this problem involves a possible double displacement, the possible precipitate being either KNO_3 or $SrCrO_4$. Rule out the KNO_3 because all nitrates are soluble and because you were provided with the K_{sp} for $SrCrO_4$. To answer these questions, you must know your solubility rules!

Step 2: Write the net ionic equation.

$$Sr^{2+}_{(aq)} + CrO_4^{2-}_{(aq)} \rightarrow SrCrO_{4(s)}$$

Step 3: Write the equilibrium expression.

$K_{sp} = [Sr^{2+}][CrO_4^{2-}]$

Step 4: Determine the initial concentrations of the ions that may form the precipitate in the mixed solution. Because the initial reactant solution volumes each double, their initial concentrations are each cut in half.

The total liters of solution = 0.075 + 0.075 = 0.15 liter. Therefore,

$$[Sr^{2+}] = \frac{7.5 \times 10^{-3} \text{ mole}}{0.15 \text{ liter}} = 0.050 \text{ M}$$

$$[CrO_4^{2-}] = \frac{3.8 \times 10^{-3} \text{ mole}}{0.15 \text{ liter}} = 0.025 \text{ M}$$

Step 5: Determine Q, the ion product.

$Q = [Sr^{2+}][CrO_4^{2-}] = (0.050)(0.025) = 1.3 \times 10^{-3}$

Therefore, because Q (1.3×10^{-3}) > K_{sp} (3.6×10^{-5}), a precipitate will form.

52. (E) All hydroxides of the Group I metals are strong bases. The hydroxides of the heavier group II metals (Ca, Sr, and Ba) are also strong bases. $Mg(OH)_2$ is not very soluble in water, yielding relatively little $OH^-_{(aq)}$.

53. (C)

$\triangle S° = \Sigma S°_{products} - \Sigma S°_{reactants}$

$\triangle S° = [3(33.0) + 51.0] - [2(28.0) + 3(27.0)] = 13.0 \text{ J} \cdot \text{mol}^{-1} \cdot \text{K}^{-1}$

54. (C) At equilibrium $Hg_{(l)} \longleftrightarrow Hg_{(g)}$, which represents the condition of boiling, and at equilibrium $\triangle G° = 0$. The word *normal* in the question refers to conditions at 1 atm of pressure, which is reflected in the notation for standard conditions for $\triangle S°$ and $\triangle H°$. Therefore, using the Gibbs-Helmholtz equation, $\triangle G° = \triangle H° - T\triangle S°$, we can substitute 0 for $\triangle G°$ and solve for T.

$$T = \frac{\triangle H°}{\triangle S°} = \frac{63,000 \cdot \text{mole}^{-1}}{100 \text{ J} \cdot \text{K}^{-1} \cdot \text{mole}^{-1}} = 6.30 \times 10^2 \text{ K}$$

55. (A) In water solutions, NH_3 forms OH^- ions. Insoluble hydroxides such as $Zn(OH)_2$ can be precipitated by adding NH_3:

$$Zn^{2+}_{(aq)} + 2NH_{3(aq)} + 2H_2O_{(l)} \rightarrow Zn(OH)_{2(s)} + 2NH_4^+_{(aq)}$$

56. (B) Step 1: Write the reaction that would occur at the cathode.

$$Cu^{2+}_{(aq)} + 2e^- \rightarrow Cu_{(s)}$$

Step 2: This problem can be solved by using the factor-label method:

(Note all of the conversions factors that you should be comfortable with.)

$$\frac{96.487 \text{ amperes}}{1} \times \frac{100.0 \text{ minutes}}{1} \times \frac{60 \text{ seconds}}{1 \text{ minute}} \times \frac{1 \text{ coulomb}}{1 \text{ ampere} \cdot \text{second}} \times \frac{1 \text{ Faraday}}{96,487 \text{ coulombs}} \times \frac{1 \text{ mole } e^-}{1 \text{ Faraday}}$$

$$\times \frac{1 \text{ mole Cu}}{2 \text{ moles } e^-} \times \frac{63.55 \text{ g Cu}}{1 \text{ mole Cu}} = 190.65 \text{ g Cu}$$

57. (B) The formula you need for this problem is $\triangle G° = -n\mathscr{F}E°$. The Faraday constant, $\mathscr{F}$, is equal to 9.65×10^4 joules $\cdot$ volt^{-1} $\cdot$ mole^{-1}. n is the number of electrons transferred between oxidizing and reducing agents in a balanced redox equation.

Step 1: Write the balanced redox equation.

$$Zn_{(s)} + Cu^{2+}_{(aq)} \rightarrow Zn^{2+}_{(aq)} + Cu_{(s)}$$

Step 2: Identify the variables needed for the equation.

$\triangle G° = ?$ $\qquad \mathscr{F} = 9.65 \times 10^4$ joules $\cdot$ volt^{-1} $\cdot$ mole^{-1}

$\qquad n = 2 \qquad E° = 1.00$ volt

Step 3: Substitute into the equation and solve.

$$\Delta G° = \frac{-\left(2 \; \text{moles} \, e^-\right)}{1} \times \frac{9.65 \times 10^4 \; \text{joules}}{\text{volt} \cdot \text{mole} \, e^-} \times \frac{1.00 \; \text{volt}}{1}$$
$$= -1.93 \times 10^5 \; \text{joules} = -193 \; \text{kJ}$$

58. (C) The functional group of a carboxylic acid is

$$\overset{\displaystyle O}{\underset{\displaystyle }{\overset{\displaystyle \|}{—C—OH}}}$$

The name of this compound is oxalic acid, which is an aliphatic dicarboxylic acid.

59. (A) The functional group of an alcohol is

$$—O—H$$

The name of this alcohol is ethyl alcohol.

60. (E) The functional group of an ether is

$$—O—$$

The name of this ether is diethyl ether.

61. (B) The functional group of an aldehyde is

$$\overset{\displaystyle O}{\overset{\displaystyle \|}{—C—H}}$$

The name of this aldehyde is acetaldehyde.

62. (D) The functional group of an ester is

$$\overset{\displaystyle O}{\overset{\displaystyle \|}{—C—O—}}$$

The name of this ester is *n*-octyl acetate, which is the odor of oranges. Esters are formed from the reaction of a carboxylic acid with an alcohol.

63. (D) Think of the yield sign (arrow) as an equal sign. The superscript represents the mass number. The sum of the mass numbers on both sides of the arrow must be equal. The subscript represents the atomic number, and as with mass numbers, the sum of the numbers on both sides of the arrow must be equal.

mass number: $54 + \underline{4} = 56 + 2(1)$

atomic number: $26 + \underline{2} = 26 + 2(1)$

$$^{54}_{26}\text{Fe} + ^{4}_{2}\textbf{He} \rightarrow ^{56}_{26}\text{Fe} + 2\,^{1}_{1}\text{H}$$

64. **(E)**

mass number: $65 + 1 = 64 + 2(1)$

atomic number: $29 + 0 = 29 + 2(0)$

$_{29}^{65}\text{Cu} + _{0}^{1}\text{n} \rightarrow _{29}^{64}\text{Cu} + \mathbf{2}\,_{0}^{1}\mathbf{n}$

65. **(A)**

mass number: $14 + 1 = 15 + \underline{0}$

atomic number: $7 + 1 = 8 + \underline{0}$

$_{7}^{14}\text{N} + _{1}^{1}\text{H} \rightarrow _{8}^{15}\text{O} + _{0}^{0}\boldsymbol{\gamma}$

66. **(B)** This problem can be solved using the factor-label method:

$$\frac{28{,}850\ \cancel{\text{years}}}{1} \times \frac{1\ \text{half}-\text{life}}{5770\ \cancel{\text{years}}} = 5.00\ \text{half}-\text{lives}$$

In 5 half-lives, the radioactivity is reduced by

$(\frac{1}{2})^{5} = \frac{1}{32} \approx \frac{3}{100} \approx 3\%$

67. **(C)** A triple bond contains one sigma and two pi bonds. Two of the compounds (C_2Cl_2 and C_2HCl) contain a triple bond.

$$\text{Cl}-\text{C} \equiv \text{C}-\text{Cl} \qquad \text{H}-\text{C} \equiv \text{C}-\text{Cl}$$

68. **(E)** A single bond is a sigma bond. All compounds contain at least one sigma bond.

69. **(B)** Begin by recognizing that you will need the following relationship: work $= -P\triangle V$

Next, identify initial and final conditions.

$P_f = 1.0$ atm (final pressure is always used to solve for w)

$V_i = 3.0$ liters

V_f is determined by using the relationship $P_1V_1 = P_2V_2$

$(3.0$ atm$)$ $(3.0$ liters$) = (1.0$ atm$)$ (V_f)

$V_f = 9.0$ liters

$\triangle V = V_f - V_i = 9.0$ liters $- 3.0$ liters $= 6.0$ liters

$w = -P\triangle V$

$= -(1.0$ atm$)$ $(6.0$ liters$) = -6.0$ L $\cdot$ atm

70. **(D)** In the macroscopic world, wave and particle properties are mutually exclusive. At the atomic level, objects exhibit characteristic properties of both waves and particles. The amplitude of a wave is the measure of the magnitude of the maximum disturbance in the medium during one wave cycle, and is measured in units depending on the type of wave.

71. **(B)** The formation of hydrogen sulfide from hydrogen gas and sulfur conforms to the definition of both standard enthalpy of reaction and standard enthalpy of formation since the heat change that is measured is for the formation of one mole of compound from the elements in their standard state. In Choice (D), diamond is not the stable allotrope of carbon—it is graphite.

72. **(A)** The MM of hydrogen gas is ≈ 2 g · mol^{-1}, that of sulfur hexafluoride ≈ 146 g · mol^{-1} and that of air is ≈ 29 g · mol^{-1}

Gas	Atomic Mass		Number of Atoms		Molecular Mass		Percent		Weight of Dry Air
Oxygen	16	x	2	=	32	x	21%	=	7
Nitrogen	14	x	2	=	28	x	78%	=	+22
Total									**29**

At a constant temperature, lighter gas molecules diffuse faster than heavier molecules. The reverse is true which might make one conclude that Balloon C is filled with sulfur hexafluoride.

73. **(D)** Because nitrogen is a second row element, it cannot exceed an octet. Since Choice (D) shows nitrogen with 10 valence electrons, it cannot be correct.

74. **(D)** Refer to the following chart.

	Anions (–)	Cations (+)
Acidic	HSO_4^-, $H_2PO_4^-$	NH_4^+, Mg^{2+}, Al^{3+} transition metal ions
Basic	$C_2H_3O_2^-$, CN^-, CO_3^{2-}, F^-, HCO_3^-, HPO_4^{2-}, HS^-, NO_2^-, PO_4^{3-}, S^{2-}	none
Neutral	Cl^-, Br^-, I^-, ClO_4^-, NO_3^-, SO_4^{2-}	Li^+, Na^+, K^+, Ca^{2+}, Ba^{2+}

75. **(D)** Geometric isomers are chemical compounds having the same molecular formula but with different geometric configurations, as when atoms or groups of atoms are attached in different spatial arrangements on either side of a double bond. Linear and tetrahedral complexes cannot form geometric isomers. The gold complex would be linear. Zinc complexes are tetrahedral because Zn^{2+} has 10 electrons in its $3d$ sublevel with no d orbitals available for forming dsp^2 hybrids. The platinum complex is square planar but all ligands are identical. Cobalt complexes are octahedral. Examples of some geometric isomers for $Co(NH_3)_4Cl_2$ include

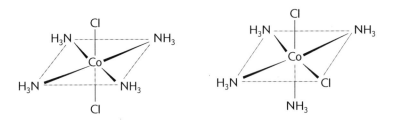

Section II: Free-Response Questions

Scoring Guidelines

One point deduction for mathematical error (maximum once per question)

One point deduction for error in significant figures (maximum once per question and the number of significant figures must be correct within +/– one digit)

Part A:

Question 1

1. Ethylamine reacts with water as follows:

$$C_2H_5NH_{2(aq)} + H_2O_{(l)} \rightarrow C_2H_5NH_3^+{}_{(aq)} + OH^-{}_{(aq)}$$

The base-dissociation constant, K_b, for the ethylamine ion is 5.6×10^{-4}.

(a) A student carefully measures out 65.987 mL of a 0.250 M solution of ethylamine. Calculate the OH^- ion concentration.

Step 1: Rewrite the balanced equation for the ionization of ethylamine. $C_2H_5NH_2 + H_2O \longleftrightarrow C_2H_5NH_3^+ + OH^-$	1 point for correctly balanced equation.
Step 2: Write the expression for the base-dissociation constant. $K_b = \dfrac{\left[C_2H_5NH_3^+\right]\left[OH^-\right]}{\left[C_2H_5NH_2\right]} = 5.6 \times 10^{-4}$	1 point for correct K_b expression.
Step 3: Create a chart showing initial and final concentrations (at equilibrium) of the involved species. Let x be the amount of $C_2H_5NH_3^+$ that forms from $C_2H_5NH_2$. Because $C_2H_5NH_3^+$ is in a 1:1 molar ratio with OH^-, $[OH^-]$ also equals x. <table><tr><th>Species</th><th>Initial Concentration</th><th>Final Concentration at Equilibrium</th></tr><tr><td>$C_2H_5NH_2$</td><td>0.250 M</td><td>0.250 − x</td></tr><tr><td>$C_2H_5NH_3^+$</td><td>0 M</td><td>x</td></tr><tr><td>OH^-</td><td>0 M</td><td>x</td></tr></table>	
Step 4: Substitute the equilibrium concentrations from the chart into the equilibrium expression and solve for x. $K_b = \dfrac{\left[C_2H_5NH_3^+\right]\left[OH^-\right]}{\left[C_2H_5NH_2\right]}$ $5.6 \times 10^{-4} = \dfrac{(x)(x)}{0.250 - x}$ $x^2 = (5.6 \times 10^{-4})(0.250 - x)$	1 point for correct equilibrium expression.

(continued)

Assume that $[C_2H_5NH_2]$ remains constant at 0.250 M; $x = [OH^-] = 0.012$ M *The 65.987 mL is not needed because concentration is* *independent of the amount of solution measured.*	1 point for correct $[OH]^-$.

(b) Calculate the pOH of the solution.

pOH = −log $[OH^-]$ pOH = −log (0.012) = 1.92	1 point for correct pOH.

(c) Calculate the % ionization of the ethylamine in the solution in part (a).

$\% = \dfrac{\text{part}}{\text{whole}} \times 100\% = \dfrac{0.012}{0.250} \times 100\% = 4.8\%$	1 point for correct % ionization.

(d) What would be the pH of a solution made by adding 15.000 grams of ethylammonium bromide ($C_2H_5NH_3Br$) to 250.00 mL of a 0.100-molar solution of ethylamine. (The addition of the solid does not change the solution volume.)

Step 1: Note that when $C_2H_5NH_3Br$ dissolves in water, it dissociates into $C_2H_5NH_3^+$ and Br^-. Furthermore, $C_2H_5NH_3^+$ is a weak acid. **Step 2:** Rewrite the balanced equation at equilibrium for the reaction. $C_2H_5NH_3^+ \longleftrightarrow C_2H_5NH_2 + H^+$	1 point for correctly balanced equation.
Step 3: Write the equilibrium expression: $K_a = \dfrac{K_w}{K_b} = \dfrac{10^{-14}}{5.6 \times 10^{-4}} = 1.8 \times 10^{-11}$	1 point for correct equilibrium expression.
Step 4: Calculate the initial concentrations of the species of interest. $[C_2H_5NH_2] = 0.100$ M $[C_2H_5NH_3^+] = \dfrac{15.000 \text{ g } C_2H_5NH_3Br}{1} \times \dfrac{1 \text{ mole } C_2H_5NH_3^+}{126.05 \text{ g } C_2H_5NH_3Br}$ $\times \dfrac{1}{0.250 \text{ liter}} = 0.476$ M	1 point for correct calculation of $[C_2H_5NH_3^+]$.
$[H^+] = 0$	

Step 5:

Species	Initial Concentration	Final Concentration at Equilibrium
$C_2H_5NH_2$	0.100 M	$0.100 + x$
$C_2H_5NH_3^+$	0.476 M	$0.476 - x$
H^+	0 M	x

$$\frac{\left[C_2H_5NH_2\right]\left[H^+\right]}{\left[C_2H_5NH_3^+\right]} = K_a$$

$$\frac{(0.100+x)(x)}{(0.476-x)} = 1.8 \times 10^{-11}$$

The "+x" and "−x" drop out of the equation since x is much, much smaller than the initial concentrations of both the weak acid and its conjugate base.

$$\frac{(0.100)(x)}{(0.476)} = 1.8 \times 10^{-11}$$

$x = (H^+) = 8.57 \times 10^{-11}$

pH = −log (8.57×10^{-11}) = 10.07	1 point for correct pH.

(e) If a student adds 0.125 grams of solid silver nitrate to the solution in part (a), will silver hydroxide form as a precipitate? The value of K_{sp} for silver hydroxide is 1.52×10^{-8}.

Step 1: Write the equation in equilibrium for the dissociation of AgOH. $AgOH_{(aq)} \longleftrightarrow Ag^+_{(aq)} + OH^-_{(aq)}$	1 point for correct equation.
Step 2: Calculate the concentration of the ions present. $\left[Ag^+\right] = \dfrac{0.125 \text{ g AgBr}}{0.065987 \text{L}} \times \dfrac{1 \text{ mole AgBr}}{187.772 \text{ g AgBr}} \times \dfrac{1 \text{ mole Ag}^+}{1 \text{ mole AgBr}} = 0.0101 M$	1 point for correct calculation of [Ag$^+$].
[OH$^-$] = 0.012 M	
Step 3: Solve for the ion product, Q. $Q = [Ag^+][OH^-] = (0.0101)(0.012) = 1.21 \times 10^{-4}$	1 point for correct calculation of Q.
K_{sp} AgOH = 1.52×10^{-8} Because $Q > K_{sp}$, AgOH will precipitate.	1 point for correct interpretation of Q and K_{sp}.

Question 2

$$2Cu_{(s)} + \frac{1}{2} O_{2(g)} \rightarrow Cu_2O_{(s)} \qquad \triangle H°_f = -168.6 \text{ kJ} \cdot \text{mol}^{-1}$$

2. Copper reacts with oxygen to produce copper(I) oxide, as represented by the equation above. A 100.0 g sample of $Cu_{(s)}$ is mixed with 12.0 L of $O_{2(g)}$ at 2.50 atm and 298K.

   (a) Calculate the number of moles of each of the following before the reaction begins.

   (i) $Cu_{(s)}$

n Cu = 100.0 g̶ ̶C̶u̶ $\times \dfrac{1 \text{ mol Cu}}{64.546 \text{ g̶ ̶C̶u̶}}$ = 1.549 mol Cu	1 point for correct number of moles of Cu.

   (ii) $O_{2(g)}$

$PV = nRT$ $n \text{ O}_2 = \dfrac{PV}{RT} = \dfrac{2.50 \text{ a̶t̶m̶} \times 12.0 \text{ L̶} \cdot \text{mol} \cdot \text{K̶}}{0.0821 \text{ L̶} \cdot \text{a̶t̶m̶} \cdot 298 \text{ K̶}} = 1.23 \text{ mol O2}$	1 point for correct number of moles of O2(g).

   (b) Identify the limiting reactant when the mixture is heated to produce $Cu_2O_{(s)}$. Support your answer with calculations.

$n \text{ O}_2 \text{ reacting} = 1.549 \text{ m̶o̶l̶ ̶C̶u̶} \times \dfrac{0.5 \text{ mol O}_2}{2 \text{ m̶o̶l̶e̶ ̶C̶u̶}} = 0.3873 \text{ mol O}_2$	1 point for identifying the limiting reactant.
Initially there were 1.23 mol of O_2; however, only 0.3873 mol of O_2 reacted. Therefore, there is an excess of oxygen gas; thereby, copper is the limiting reactant.	1 point for supporting the conclusion with proper calculations and reasoning.

   (c) Calculate the number of moles of $Cu_2O_{(s)}$ produced when the reaction proceeds to completion.

$n \text{ Cu}_2\text{O} = 1.549 \text{ m̶o̶l̶ ̶C̶u̶} \times \dfrac{1 \text{ mol Cu}_2\text{O}}{2 \text{ m̶o̶l̶ ̶C̶u̶}}$ = 0.7745 mol Cu$_2$O	1 point for correct number of moles of Cu$_2$O.

   (d) The standard free energy of formation, $\triangle G°_f$, of $Cu_2O_{(s)}$ is -146 kJ $\cdot$ mol^{-1} at 298K.

   (i) Calculate the standard entropy of formation, $\triangle S°_f$, of $Cu_2O_{(s)}$ at 298K. Include units with your answer.

$\triangle G°_f = \triangle H°_f - T\triangle S°_f$ $-146 \text{ kJ} \cdot \text{mol}^{-1} = -168.6 \text{ kJ} \cdot \text{mol}^{-1} - (298 \text{ K})\triangle S°f$ $23 \text{ kJ} \cdot \text{mol}^{-1} = -(298 \text{ K})\triangle S°_f$ $\triangle S°_f = \dfrac{23 \text{ kJ} \cdot \text{mol}^{-1}}{-298 \text{ K}} = -0.077 \text{ kJ} \cdot \text{mol}^{-1} \cdot \text{K}^{-1}$	1 point for correct setup for determining $\triangle S°_f$. 1 point for correct $\triangle S°_f$ including units.

(ii) Given the standard enthalpy of formation, $\triangle H^\circ_f$ and the standard entropy of formation, $\triangle S^\circ_f$, which one is considered to be more responsible for the spontaneity of forming Cu_2O?

Generally, $\triangle H^\circ_f$ is more important when deciding on spontaneity. The reaction is exothermic ($\triangle H^\circ_f = -168.6$ kJ · mol^{-1}) which favors spontaneity. Because $\triangle S^\circ_f$ is negative (-0.077 kJ · mol^{-1} · K^{-1}), the system becomes more ordered as the reaction proceeds which will not increase the spontaneity of the reaction.	1 point for correctly identifying $\triangle H^\circ_f$ and correct interpretation that addresses the signs.

Question 3

3. Radon-222 can be produced from the α-decay of radium-226.

    (a) Write the nuclear reaction.

$^{226}_{88}Ra \rightarrow \, ^{222}_{86}Rn + \, ^{4}_{2}He$	1 point for correct nuclear reaction.

    (b) Calculate $\triangle E$ (in kJ) when 7.00 g of $^{226}_{88}Ra$ decays.

$\triangle E = \triangle mc^2 = 9.00 \times 10^{10}\, kJ \cdot g^{-1} \times \triangle m$	1 point for correct formula for determining $\triangle E$.
$\triangle m$ = mass products – mass reactants = (4.0015 g + 221.9703 g) – 225.9771 g = –0.0053 g	1 point for correct $\triangle m$.
$\triangle E = \dfrac{7.00 \text{ g } ^{226}_{88}Ra}{1} \times \dfrac{1 \text{ mole } ^{226}_{88}Ra}{225.9771 \text{ g } ^{226}_{88}Ra}$ $\times \dfrac{-0.0053 \text{ g}}{1 \text{ mole } ^{226}_{88}Ra} \times \dfrac{9.00 \times 10^{10}\, kJ}{g}$ $= -1.5 \times 10^7\, kJ$	1 point for correct calculation of $\triangle E$.

    (c) Calculate the mass defect of $^{226}_{88}Ra$.

88 moles protons = 88 × 1.00728 g = 88.6406 g 226 – 88 = 138 neutrons 138 moles neutrons = 138 × 1.00867 g = 139.196 g total = 88.6406 g + 139.196 g = 227.837 g	1 point for correct setup for determining mass defect.
mass defect = 227.837 g – 225.9771 g = 1.860 g	1 point for correct answer.

    (d) Calculate the binding energy (kJ/mole) of $^{226}_{88}Ra$.

$\triangle E = \dfrac{9.00 \times 10^{10}\, kJ}{g} \times \dfrac{1.860 \text{ g}}{1 \text{ mole}} = 1.67 \times 10^{11}\, kJ\,/\,mole$	1 point for correct setup. 1 point for correct $\triangle E$.

    (e) $^{226}_{88}Ra$ has a half-life of 1.62×10^3 yr. Calculate the first-order constant.

$k = \dfrac{0.693}{1.62 \times 10^3\, yr} = 4.28 \times 10^{-4}\, yr$	1 point for correct calculation of k.

    (f) Calculate the fraction of $^{226}_{88}Ra$ that will remain after 100.0 yr.

$\ln \dfrac{x_o}{x} = kt = 4.28 \times 10^{-4}\, yr^{-1} \times 100.0\, yr = 4.28 \times 10^{-2}\, yr$ $e^{0.0428} = 1.04 = \dfrac{x_o}{x}$	1 point for correct setup.
fraction remaining: $\dfrac{x}{x_o} = \dfrac{1}{1.04} = 0.962 = 96.2\%$	1 point for correct answer.

Part B:

Question 4

(For a complete list of reaction types you will encounter, refer to *CliffsAP Chemistry*, 3rd Edition.)

4. Students choose five of the eight reactions. Only the answers in the boxes are graded (unless clearly marked otherwise). Each correct answer earns 3 points, 1 point for reactants and 2 points for products. All products must be correct to earn both product points. Equations do not need to be balanced and phases need not be indicated. Any spectator ions on the reactant side nullify the 1 possible reactant point, but if they appear again on the product side, there is no product-point penalty. A fully molecular equation (when it should be ionic) earns a maximum of 1 point. Ion charges must be correct.

(a) Methanol is mixed with acetic acid and then gently warmed.

| $CH_3OH + CH_3COOH \rightarrow CH_3COOCH_3 + H_2O$ | 1 point for reactant(s), 2 points for product(s). |
| | Acid added to an alcohol produces an ester (condensation reaction). |

(b) A 9M nitric acid solution is added to a solution of potassium carbonate.

| $H^+ + CO_3^{2-} \rightarrow H_2CO_3$ | 1 point for reactant(s), 2 points for product(s). |
| | Strong acid + salt of a weak acid yields the salt of the strong acid plus a weak acid. The salt of the strong acid in this case is potassium nitrate. Because both potassium ion and nitrate ion are spectator ions, they don't appear in the net ionic equation. |

(c) Calcium oxide is heated in an environment of sulfur trioxide gas.

| $CaO + SO_3 \rightarrow CaSO_4$ | 1 point for reactant(s), 2 points for product(s). |
| | Metallic oxide + nonmetallic oxide $\rightarrow$ salt |

(d) Iron(III) nitrate is added to a strong sodium hydroxide solution.

| $Fe^{3+} + OH^- \rightarrow Fe(OH)_3$ | 1 point for reactant(s), 2 points for product(s). |
| | Reaction refers to solubility rules. Iron(III) hydroxide is not soluble. |

(e) Solid copper (II) oxide is dropped into sulfuric acid.

$CuO + H^+ \rightarrow Cu^{2+} + H_2O$	1 point for reactant(s), 2 points for product(s).
	A basic anhydride + acid $\rightarrow$ salt + water.
	The negative ion (sulfate ion) of the salt produced in this reaction is a spectator ion and does not appear.

(f) Carbon dioxide gas is heated in the presence of solid magnesium oxide.

| $CO_2 + MgO \rightarrow MgCO_3$ | 1 point for reactant(s), 2 points for product(s). |
| | Acidic anhydride + basic anhydride Æ salt |

(g) Hydrochloric acid is added to a sodium carbonate solution.

$H^+ + CO_3^{2-} \rightarrow CO_2 + H_2O$	1 point for reactant(s), 2 points for product(s).
	An acid + a carbonate $\rightarrow$ salt + CO_2 + water
	Both the positive and negative ions (sodium and chloride ions) of the salt produced in this reaction are spectator ions and do not appear.

(h) Small pieces of aluminum are added to a solution of copper(II) sulfate.

$Cu^{2+} + Al \rightarrow Cu + Al^{3+}$	1 point for reactant(s), 2 points for product(s).
	Oxidation-reduction

Question 5

5. A student places a copper electrode in a 1 M solution of $CuSO_4$ and in another beaker places a silver electrode in a 1 M solution of $AgNO_3$. $E°_{red}$ for silver is +0.7991 volts while the $E°_{red}$ of copper is +0.337 volts. A salt bridge composed of Na_2SO_4 connects the two beakers. The voltage measured across the electrodes is found to be +0.42 volts.

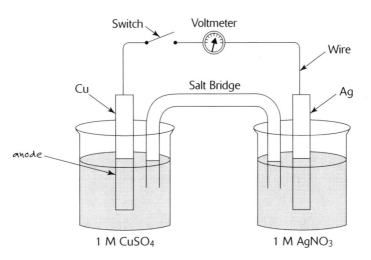

(a) In the diagram above, label the electrode that is the anode. Justify your answer.

Oxidation occurs at the anode. Silver is lower in the activity series than copper. Alternatively, you can say that because $E°_{ox}$ Cu > $E°_{ox}$ Ag, copper is the site of oxidation and thus is the anode. Therefore, the oxidation half-reaction is ox: $Cu_{(s)} \rightarrow Cu^{2+}_{(aq)} + 2e^-$	1 point for correct labeling of electrode. 1 point for correct explanation.

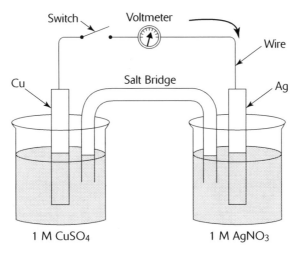

(b) In the diagram above, draw an arrow indicating the direction of the electron flow in the external circuit when the switch is closed. Justify your answer.

In a spontaneous (voltaic) cell, electrons flow from the anode toward the cathode.	1 point for arrow drawn correctly. 1 point for correct explanation.

(c) Describe what is happening at the cathode. Include any equations that may be important.

Reduction always occurs at the cathode. Note that $E°_{red}$ for silver is +0.7991 volts while that of copper +0.337 volts. This means that copper metal is higher in the activity series than the silver metal, so copper metal will reduce the silver ion. The equation that describes reduction (or the cathode reaction)	1 point for correct explanation.
is therefore red: $Ag^+_{(aq)} + e^- \rightarrow Ag_{(s)}$	1 point for correct reduction equation.

(d) Write the balanced overall cell equation and determine $E°_{cell}$.

ox: $Cu_{(s)} \rightarrow Cu^{2+}_{(aq)} + 2e^-$ $\quad E°_{ox} = -0.337$ red: $2Ag^+_{(aq)} + 2e^- \rightarrow 2Ag_{(s)}$ $\quad E°_{red} = +0.7991$ $\overline{Cu_{(s)} + 2Ag^+_{(aq)} \rightarrow Cu^{2+}_{(aq)} + 2Ag_{(s)}} \quad E°_{cell} = 0.462$	1 point for correct cell equation. 1 point for $E°_{cell}$.

(e) Write the standard cell notation.

$Cu_{(s)} | Cu^{2+}_{(aq)} \| Ag^+_{(aq)} | Ag_{(s)}$	1 point for correct notation.

(f) The student adds 4 M ammonia to the copper sulfate solution, producing the complex ion $Cu(NH_3)_4^{2+}_{(aq)}$. The student remeasures the cell potential and discovers the voltage to be 0.88 volts at 25°C. Show how a student would determine the $Cu^{2+}_{(aq)}$ concentration after the ammonia had been added. Do not do any calculations.

Because the cell is not operating under standard conditions, the Nernst equation would need to be used. The formula for the Nernst equation is $E_{cell} = E°_{cell} - \dfrac{0.0592}{n} \log Q$ at 25°C where $Q = \dfrac{[Cu^{2+}_{(aq)}]}{[Ag^+_{(aq)}]^2} = \dfrac{x}{1^2} = x$ Substituting what we know at this point gives $0.88 = 0.46 - \dfrac{0.0592}{2} \log x$	1 point for correctly identifying the need to use the Nernst equation and setting it up.

Question 6

6. Common oxides of nitrogen are NO, N_2O, NO_2 and N_2O_4. Using principles of chemical bonding and molecular geometry, answer each of the following. Lewis electron-dot diagrams and sketches of molecules may be helpful as part of your explanations.

(a) Draw the Lewis structures for any two of these oxides of nitrogen. In each case, the oxygen(s) are terminal atoms.

$:N\equiv N-\ddot{O}:$ $\cdot\ddot{N}\equiv\ddot{O}:$ (NO₂ structure) (N₂O₄ structure)	1 point for any two Lewis structures drawn correctly.

(b) Which of the oxides 'violates' the octet rule. Explain your answer.

NO and NO_2 Molecules containing an odd number of electrons do not follow the octet rule. In the case of NO_2 there are 17 valence electrons, while NO has 11 valence electrons. 'Free radicals' are paramagnetic and show a weak attraction toward a magnetic field.	1 point for correctly identifying NO and NO_2 and for a correct explanation (must identify both).

(c) Draw the resonance structures for N_2O.

$:N\equiv N-\ddot{O}:$ ⟷ $:\ddot{N}=N=\ddot{O}:$ ⟷ $:\ddot{N}-N\equiv O:$	1 point for each resonance structure drawn correctly.

(d) Which bonds in N_2O_4 are polar and which are nonpolar? In the case of the polar bonds, which atom acts as the positive pole?

(N₂O₄ structure) The N-N bond is nonpolar. The N-O and the N=O bonds are polar. Because oxygen is more electronegative than nitrogen, the nitrogen is acting as the positive pole.	1 point for identifying correctly which bond are polar and which are nonpolar. 1 point for correctly identifying N as the positive pole.

(e) Compare the structure of NO with that of NO_2.

The Lewis structure of NO is $\ddot{N}=\ddot{O} \longleftrightarrow \ddot{N}=\dot{O}$ NO has a bond order of 2.5 and would be linear. The nitrogen to oxygen bond distance in NO would be shorter than the nitrogen to oxygen bond distance in NO_2.	
Both of the N–O bonds in NO_2 would have a bond order of 1.5. In NO_2, resonance structure would exist where both N–O bonds are the same length—intermediate in length between a single and double bond. The large bond angle in NO_2 is due to a lone electron (single electron—not a lone pair) in the ideal trigonal planar geometry.	1 point for correct explanation.

(f) The bond energy for N–O is 222 kJ/mol; for N–N it is 159 kJ/mol; N–O = 222 kJ/mol; and for N=O it is 607 kJ/mol. Estimate the $\triangle H$ for the dimerization of $NO_{2(g)}$.

The reaction for the dimerization of $NO_{2(g)}$ is $2NO_{2(g)} \rightarrow N_2O_{4(g)}$ No bonds need to be broken in the NO_2 molecule. The only bond that needs to be formed is the N-N bond in the N_2O_4 molecule; therefore, $\triangle H = -159$ kJ.	1 point for correct calculation.

Question 7

7. Solids can be classified into four categories: ionic, metallic, covalent network, and molecular. Choose one of the four categories listed and for that category identify the basic structural unit; describe the nature of the force both within the unit and between units; cite the basic properties of melting point, conduction of electricity, solubility, hardness, and conduction of heat for that type of solid; give an example of the type of solid; and describe a laboratory means of identifying the solid.

Note: Although the directions only required one category, all four will be presented. Count each correct box in the column as 1 point for the category that you chose.

Characteristic	Ionic	Metallic	Covalent Network	Molecular
Structural unit	Ions	Cations surrounded by mobile "sea" of electrons	Atoms	Polar or nonplar molecules
Force within units	Covalent bond within polyatomic ion	Atomic forces between subatomic particles	Atomic forces between subatomic particles	Covalent bond
Force between units	Ionic bond, electrostatic attraction	Metallic bond	Covalent bond	Dipole-dipole dispersion (London); H bonds; dipole-induced; dipole
Melting point	High	Variable	Very high	Nonpolar-low; polar-high
Conduction of electricity	In water solution or molten state	Always conducts	Does not conduct	Does not conduct
Solubility	Solubility in water varies	Not soluble	Not soluble	Nonpolar-insoluble in water; polar–some degree of solubility in water; solubility in organic solvents varies
Hardness	Hard, brittle	Variable, malleable, ductile	Very hard	Soft
Conduction of heat	Poor	Good	Poor, except diamond	Poor
Examples	NaCl, $CaCl_2$	Cu, Fe, Au	SiO_2, $C_{(diamond)}$	H_2O-polar; CO_2-nonpolar
Lab tests	Conducts in pure state when molten or in H_2O of ionizing solvents	Always conducts	Extremely hard; nonconductor	Low M.P.; nonconductor

Question 8

8. Answer the following questions about ammonia, $NH_{3(g)}$ and methane gas, $CH_{4(g)}$. Assume that both gases exhibit ideal behavior.

(a) Draw the complete Lewis structure (electron-dot diagram) for the ammonia and methane molecules.

$H - \ddot{N}$ structure with H's; $H - C - H$ structure with H's	1 point for each correct, complete Lewis structure.

(b) Identify the shape of each molecule.

Ammonia, (NH_3) has a pyramidal shape. Methane, (CH_4) has a tetrahedral shape.	1 point for each correct shape.

(c) One of the gases dissolves readily in water to form a solution with a pH above 7. Identify the gas and account for this observation by writing a chemical equation.

The gas that produces a pH greater than 7 when added to water is ammonia, NH_3. The reaction that accounts for this is $NH_{3\,(g)} + H_2O_{(l)} \longleftrightarrow NH_{4\ (aq)}^+ + OH^-_{\,(aq)}$	1 point for correctly identifying NH_3 and a correct explanation.

(d) A 1.5 mole sample of methane gas is placed in a piston at a constant temperature. Sketch the expected plot of volume vs. pressure holding temperature constant.

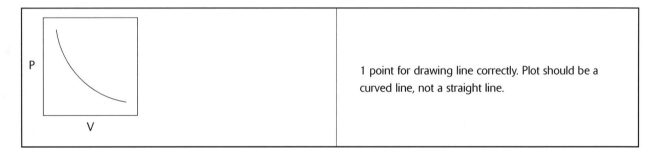

	1 point for drawing line correctly. Plot should be a curved line, not a straight line.

(e) Samples of ammonia and methane gas are placed in 2 L containers at the conditions indicated in the diagram below.

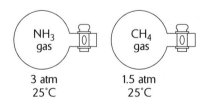

(i) Indicate whether the average kinetic energy of the ammonia molecules in greater than, equal to, or less than the average kinetic energy of the methane molecules. Justify your answer.

According to kinetic-molecular theory, if two different gases are at the same temperature, their molecules have the same average kinetic energy. Average kinetic energy is proportional to temperature.	1 point for correct answer and explanation.

(ii) Indicate whether the root-mean-square speed of the methane molecules is greater than, equal to, or less than the root-mean-square speed of the ammonia molecules. Justify your answer.

The average kinetic energy, ε, is related to the *root-mean-square* (rms) speed u through the equation: $\varepsilon = \frac{1}{2}\,mu^2$ Because the MM of CH_4 (16) is slightly less than that of NH_3 (17), the root-mean-square speed of CH_4 is slightly higher than that of NH_3. Root-mean-square speed is inversely proportional to the square root of the molar mass of the gas.	1 point for correct answer and explanation.

(iii) Indicate whether the number of ammonia molecules is greater than, equal to, or less than the number of methane molecules. Justify your answer.

According to the diagram in (e), ammonia with a pressure of 3 atm would have twice the number of molecules as methane would with a pressure of 1.5 atm—all other factors being held constant.	1 point for correct answer and explanation.

Multiple-Choice Answer Sheet for Practice Exam 3

Remove this sheet and use it to mark your answers.
Answer sheets for "Section II: Free-Response Questions" can be found at the end of this book.

Section I
Multiple-Choice Questions

1 Ⓐ Ⓑ Ⓒ Ⓓ Ⓔ
2 Ⓐ Ⓑ Ⓒ Ⓓ Ⓔ
3 Ⓐ Ⓑ Ⓒ Ⓓ Ⓔ
4 Ⓐ Ⓑ Ⓒ Ⓓ Ⓔ
5 Ⓐ Ⓑ Ⓒ Ⓓ Ⓔ
6 Ⓐ Ⓑ Ⓒ Ⓓ Ⓔ
7 Ⓐ Ⓑ Ⓒ Ⓓ Ⓔ
8 Ⓐ Ⓑ Ⓒ Ⓓ Ⓔ
9 Ⓐ Ⓑ Ⓒ Ⓓ Ⓔ
10 Ⓐ Ⓑ Ⓒ Ⓓ Ⓔ
11 Ⓐ Ⓑ Ⓒ Ⓓ Ⓔ
12 Ⓐ Ⓑ Ⓒ Ⓓ Ⓔ
13 Ⓐ Ⓑ Ⓒ Ⓓ Ⓔ
14 Ⓐ Ⓑ Ⓒ Ⓓ Ⓔ
15 Ⓐ Ⓑ Ⓒ Ⓓ Ⓔ
16 Ⓐ Ⓑ Ⓒ Ⓓ Ⓔ
17 Ⓐ Ⓑ Ⓒ Ⓓ Ⓔ
18 Ⓐ Ⓑ Ⓒ Ⓓ Ⓔ
19 Ⓐ Ⓑ Ⓒ Ⓓ Ⓔ
20 Ⓐ Ⓑ Ⓒ Ⓓ Ⓔ
21 Ⓐ Ⓑ Ⓒ Ⓓ Ⓔ
22 Ⓐ Ⓑ Ⓒ Ⓓ Ⓔ
23 Ⓐ Ⓑ Ⓒ Ⓓ Ⓔ
24 Ⓐ Ⓑ Ⓒ Ⓓ Ⓔ
25 Ⓐ Ⓑ Ⓒ Ⓓ Ⓔ

26 Ⓐ Ⓑ Ⓒ Ⓓ Ⓔ
27 Ⓐ Ⓑ Ⓒ Ⓓ Ⓔ
28 Ⓐ Ⓑ Ⓒ Ⓓ Ⓔ
29 Ⓐ Ⓑ Ⓒ Ⓓ Ⓔ
30 Ⓐ Ⓑ Ⓒ Ⓓ Ⓔ
31 Ⓐ Ⓑ Ⓒ Ⓓ Ⓔ
32 Ⓐ Ⓑ Ⓒ Ⓓ Ⓔ
33 Ⓐ Ⓑ Ⓒ Ⓓ Ⓔ
34 Ⓐ Ⓑ Ⓒ Ⓓ Ⓔ
35 Ⓐ Ⓑ Ⓒ Ⓓ Ⓔ
36 Ⓐ Ⓑ Ⓒ Ⓓ Ⓔ
37 Ⓐ Ⓑ Ⓒ Ⓓ Ⓔ
38 Ⓐ Ⓑ Ⓒ Ⓓ Ⓔ
39 Ⓐ Ⓑ Ⓒ Ⓓ Ⓔ
40 Ⓐ Ⓑ Ⓒ Ⓓ Ⓔ
41 Ⓐ Ⓑ Ⓒ Ⓓ Ⓔ
42 Ⓐ Ⓑ Ⓒ Ⓓ Ⓔ
43 Ⓐ Ⓑ Ⓒ Ⓓ Ⓔ
44 Ⓐ Ⓑ Ⓒ Ⓓ Ⓔ
45 Ⓐ Ⓑ Ⓒ Ⓓ Ⓔ
46 Ⓐ Ⓑ Ⓒ Ⓓ Ⓔ
47 Ⓐ Ⓑ Ⓒ Ⓓ Ⓔ
48 Ⓐ Ⓑ Ⓒ Ⓓ Ⓔ
49 Ⓐ Ⓑ Ⓒ Ⓓ Ⓔ
50 Ⓐ Ⓑ Ⓒ Ⓓ Ⓔ

51 Ⓐ Ⓑ Ⓒ Ⓓ Ⓔ
52 Ⓐ Ⓑ Ⓒ Ⓓ Ⓔ
53 Ⓐ Ⓑ Ⓒ Ⓓ Ⓔ
54 Ⓐ Ⓑ Ⓒ Ⓓ Ⓔ
55 Ⓐ Ⓑ Ⓒ Ⓓ Ⓔ
56 Ⓐ Ⓑ Ⓒ Ⓓ Ⓔ
57 Ⓐ Ⓑ Ⓒ Ⓓ Ⓔ
58 Ⓐ Ⓑ Ⓒ Ⓓ Ⓔ
59 Ⓐ Ⓑ Ⓒ Ⓓ Ⓔ
60 Ⓐ Ⓑ Ⓒ Ⓓ Ⓔ
61 Ⓐ Ⓑ Ⓒ Ⓓ Ⓔ
62 Ⓐ Ⓑ Ⓒ Ⓓ Ⓔ
63 Ⓐ Ⓑ Ⓒ Ⓓ Ⓔ
64 Ⓐ Ⓑ Ⓒ Ⓓ Ⓔ
65 Ⓐ Ⓑ Ⓒ Ⓓ Ⓔ
66 Ⓐ Ⓑ Ⓒ Ⓓ Ⓔ
67 Ⓐ Ⓑ Ⓒ Ⓓ Ⓔ
68 Ⓐ Ⓑ Ⓒ Ⓓ Ⓔ
69 Ⓐ Ⓑ Ⓒ Ⓓ Ⓔ
70 Ⓐ Ⓑ Ⓒ Ⓓ Ⓔ
71 Ⓐ Ⓑ Ⓒ Ⓓ Ⓔ
72 Ⓐ Ⓑ Ⓒ Ⓓ Ⓔ
73 Ⓐ Ⓑ Ⓒ Ⓓ Ⓔ
74 Ⓐ Ⓑ Ⓒ Ⓓ Ⓔ
75 Ⓐ Ⓑ Ⓒ Ⓓ Ⓔ

PERIODIC TABLE OF THE ELEMENTS

1	2	3	4	5	6	7	8	9	10	11	12	13	14	15	16	17	18
1 **H** 1.0079																	2 **He** 4.0026
3 **Li** 6.941	4 **Be** 9.012											5 **B** 10.811	6 **C** 12.011	7 **N** 14.007	8 **O** 16.00	9 **F** 19.00	10 **Ne** 20.179
11 **Na** 22.99	12 **Mg** 24.30											13 **Al** 26.98	14 **Si** 28.09	15 **P** 30.974	16 **S** 32.06	17 **Cl** 35.453	18 **Ar** 39.948
19 **K** 39.10	20 **Ca** 40.08	21 **Sc** 44.96	22 **Ti** 47.90	23 **V** 50.94	24 **Cr** 51.00	25 **Mn** 54.93	26 **Fe** 55.85	27 **Co** 58.93	28 **Ni** 58.69	29 **Cu** 63.55	30 **Zn** 65.39	31 **Ga** 69.72	32 **Ge** 72.59	33 **As** 74.92	34 **Se** 78.96	35 **Br** 79.90	36 **Kr** 83.80
37 **Rb** 85.47	38 **Sr** 87.62	39 **Y** 88.91	40 **Zr** 91.22	41 **Nb** 92.91	42 **Mo** 95.94	43 **Tc** (98)	44 **Ru** 101.1	45 **Rh** 102.91	46 **Pd** 105.42	47 **Ag** 107.87	48 **Cd** 112.41	49 **In** 114.82	50 **Sn** 118.71	51 **Sb** 121.75	52 **Te** 127.60	53 **I** 126.91	54 **Xe** 131.29
55 **Cs** 132.91	56 **Ba** 137.33	57 **＊La** 138.91	72 **Hf** 178.49	73 **Ta** 180.95	74 **W** 183.85	75 **Re** 186.21	76 **Os** 190.2	77 **Ir** 192.22	78 **Pt** 195.08	79 **Au** 196.97	80 **Hg** 200.59	81 **Ti** 204.38	82 **Pb** 207.2	83 **Bi** 208.98	84 **Po** (209)	85 **At** (210)	86 **Rn** (222)
87 **Fr** (223)	88 **Ra** 226.02	89 **†Ac** 227.03	104 **Rf** (261)	105 **Db** (262)	106 **Sg** (263)	107 **Bh** (262)	108 **Hs** (265)	109 **Mt** (266)	110 **§** (269)	111 **§** (272)	112 **§** (277)						

＊ Lanthanide Series

58 **Ce** 140.12	59 **Pr** 140.91	60 **Nd** 144.24	61 **Pm** (145)	62 **Sm** 150.4	63 **Eu** 151.97	64 **Gd** 157.25	65 **Tb** 158.93	66 **Dy** 162.50	67 **Ho** 164.93	68 **Er** 167.26	69 **Tm** 168.93	70 **Yb** 173.04	71 **Lu** 174.97

† Actinide Series

90 **Th** 232.04	91 **Pa** 231.04	92 **U** 238.03	93 **Np** 237.05	94 **Pu** (244)	95 **Am** (243)	96 **Cm** (247)	97 **Bk** (247)	98 **Cf** (251)	99 **Es** (252)	100 **Fm** (257)	101 **Md** (258)	102 **No** (259)	103 **Lr** (260)

§ Not yet named

Practice Exam 3

Section I: Multiple-Choice Questions

Time: 90 minutes

75 questions

45% of total grade

No calculators allowed

This section consists of 75 multiple-choice questions. Mark your answers carefully on the answer sheet.

General Instructions

Do not open this booklet until you are told to do so by the proctor.

Be sure to write your answers for Section I on the separate answer sheet. Use the test booklet for your scratch work or notes, but remember that no credit will be given for work, notes, or answers written only in the test booklet. After you have selected an answer, blacken thoroughly the corresponding circle on the answer sheet. To change an answer, erase your previous mark completely, and then record your new answer. Mark only one answer for each question.

Example   Sample Answer

The Pacific is   Ⓐ Ⓑ ● Ⓓ Ⓔ

    A. a river
    B. a lake
    C. an ocean
    D. a sea
    E. a gulf

To discourage haphazard guessing on this section of the exam, a quarter of a point is subtracted for every wrong answer, but no points are subtracted if you leave the answer blank. Even so, if you can eliminate one or more of the choices for a question, it may be to your advantage to guess.

Because it is not expected that all test takers will complete this section, do not spend too much time on difficult questions. Answer first the questions you can answer readily, and then, if you have time, return to the difficult questions later. Don't get stuck on one question. Work quickly but accurately. Use your time effectively. The preceding table is provided for your use in answering questions in Section I.

GO ON TO THE NEXT PAGE

Directions: Each group of lettered answer choices below refers to the numbered statements or questions that immediately follow. For each question or statement, select the one lettered choice that is the best answer and fill in the corresponding circle on the answer sheet. An answer choice may be used once, more than once, or not at all in each set of questions.

Questions 1–3

    A. F
    B. Co
    C. Sr
    D. Be
    E. O

1. Which has the lowest ionization energy?

2. Of those elements with negative oxidation states, which has the fewest such states?

3. Which has the smallest ionic radius?

4. What is the net number of Na^+ and Cl^- ions in the NaCl unit cell?

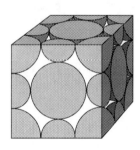

    A. 4
    B. 8
    C. 12
    D. 16
    E. 18

5. Which of the following statements is NOT correct?

    A. At constant temperature, the pressure of a certain amount of gas increases with increasing volume.
    B. At constant volume, the pressure of a certain amount of gas increases with increasing temperature.
    C. At constant pressure, the volume of a certain amount of gas increases with increasing temperature.
    D. In dealing with gas laws, the most convenient scale of temperature to use is the Kelvin temperature scale.
    E. Equal numbers of molecules of all gases exert about the same pressure at a certain temperature and volume.

6. Which of the following reactions results in the formation of a coordinate covalent bond?

    A. $NH_4^+ + H^+ \rightarrow NH_5^{2+}$
    B. $CH_3OH + H^+ \rightarrow CH_3-OH_2^+$
    C. $Cl + Br \rightarrow ClBr$
    D. $H^+ + OH^- \rightarrow H_2O$
    E. $CH_3^+ + Br^- \rightarrow CH_3Br$

Questions 7–10

$$A_{(g)} + 2B_{(g)} + 3C_{(g)} \rightarrow 4D_{(g)} + 5E_{(g)}$$

$$\text{rate of formation of } E = \frac{d[E]}{dt} k[A]^2[B]$$

7. If one were to double the concentration of B, the rate of the reaction shown above would increase by a factor of

    A. ½
    B. 1
    C. 2
    D. 4
    E. 8

8. $\dfrac{-d[B]}{dt}$ is equal to

    A. $\dfrac{-d[A]}{dt}$

    B. $\dfrac{-d[C]}{dt}$

    C. $\dfrac{-d\,½[D]}{dt}$

    D. $\dfrac{d\,⅕[E]}{dt}$

    E. none of these

9. To decrease the rate constant k, one could

    A. increase [E]
    B. decrease [B]
    C. decrease the temperature
    D. increase the volume
    E. increase the pressure

10. If one were to reduce the volume of a container to $\frac{1}{3}$ of its original volume, the rate of the reaction would increase by a factor of

A. 3
B. 9
C. 16
D. 27
E. Reducing the volume of the container has no effect on the rate.

11. Which one of the following is NOT an assumption of the kinetic theory of gases?

A. Gas particles are negligibly small.
B. Gas particles undergo a decrease in kinetic energy when passed from a region of high pressure to a region of low pressure.
C. Gas particles are in constant motion.
D. Gas particles don't attract each other.
E. Gas particles undergo elastic collisions.

12. Given the following reaction

$$N_2O_{4\,(g)} \longleftrightarrow 2NO_{2\,(g)} \qquad \Delta H° = 58.0 \text{ kJ}$$

Which of the following changes would cause the equilibrium to shift to the left?

A. add N_2O_4
B. remove NO_2
C. add N_2 to the system, thereby increasing the pressure
D. increase the volume
E. decrease the temperature

13. If a 10. cm^3 sample of unknown contains 1 cm^3 of 0.1 M $AlCl_3$, then the concentration of Al^{3+} in the unknown is about

A. 0.001 M
B. 0.01 M
C. 0.1 M
D. 1 M
E. 10 M

Questions 14–17 refer to the following isomers:

A. *trans*-2-butene

B. 1-butene

C. 2-methylpropene

D. *cis*-2-butene

E. isomethyl butane

14.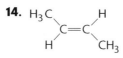

15.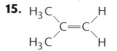

16. H_3C ... CH_3
$C=C$
H ... H

17. CH_3CH_2 ... H
$C=C$
H ... H

18. For the reaction

$$Ni_{(s)} \left| Ni^{+2}_{(aq)} \right\| Ag^{+}_{(aq)} \left| Ag_{(s)} \right.$$

and given that

$$Ni^{2+}_{(aq)} + 2e^- \rightarrow Ni_{(s)} \quad E°_{red} = -0.25 \text{ volt}$$
$$Ag^{+}_{(aq)} + e^- \rightarrow Ag_{(s)} \quad E°_{red} = 0.80 \text{ volt}$$

which of the following statements is true?

A. The reaction is spontaneous, $E° = 1.05$ volts.
B. The reaction is nonspontaneous, $E° = -1.05$ volts.
C. The reaction is spontaneous, $E° = -1.05$ volts.
D. The reaction is spontaneous, $E° = 0.55$ volt.
E. The reaction is nonspontaneous, $E° = -0.55$ volt.

GO ON TO THE NEXT PAGE

19. What would be the proper setup to determine the vapor pressure of a solution at 25°C that has 45 grams of $C_6H_{12}O_6$, glucose (MM = 180 g · mol^{-1}), dissolved in 72 grams of H_2O? The vapor pressure of pure water at 25°C is 23.8 torr.

  A. 23.8 − (72/18) + (45/180)

  B. 23.8 − (0.0588)(23.8)

  C. (0.0588 + 23.8) / (72/18)

  D. ((72/18) + (45/180))/23.8

  E. none of the setups are correct

20. Which formula correctly represents the diamminediaquadibromochromium(III) ion?

  A. $[Cr(H_2O)_2(NH_3)_2Br_2]^+$

  B. $[(NH_3)_2(H_2O)Br_2Cr]^{3+}$

  C. $[Cr(H_2O)_2(NH_3)_2Br_2]^{3+}$

  D. $[(NH_3)_2(H_2O)_2Br^{2+}Cr]^+$

  E. $[Cr(H_2O)_2(NH_3)Br_2]^{2+}$

21. The hybridization of the central atom in NH_2^- would be

  A. sp

  B. sp^2

  C. sp^3

  D. sp^3d

  E. sp^3d^2

22. A radioactive isotope has a half-life of 6.93 years and decays by beta emission. Determine the approximate fraction of the sample that is left undecayed at the end of 11.5 years.

  A. 1%

  B. 5%

  C. 30%

  D. 75%

  E. 99%

23. When the following equation is balanced, using smallest whole-number coefficients,

$$Cr_2O_7^{2-}{}_{(aq)} + Cl^-{}_{(aq)} \rightarrow Cr^{3+}{}_{(aq)} + Cl_{2(g)}$$

(acidic solution)

the sum of all coefficients is

  A. 4

  B. 8

  C. 16

  D. 33

  E. 37

24. An atom whose atomic radius is 0.43 nm crystallizes with a body-centered cubic unit cell. What is the approximate length of a side of the cell? ($\sqrt{3}$ = 1.73).

  A. 0.1 nm

  B. 0.5 nm

  C. 0.9 nm

  D. 1.8 nm

  E. 4.0 nm

25. The following is the spectrochemical series of common ligands arranged in order of increasing $\triangle$ (energy gap). Which of the following complexes of Ti^{3+} would exhibit the shortest wavelength absorption in the visible spectrum?

$$Cl^- < F^- < H_2O < NH_3 < en < NO_2^- \text{ (N-bonded)} < CN^-$$

  A. $[Ti(H_2O)_6]^{3+}$

  B. $[Ti(en)_3]^{3+}$

  C. $[TiCl_6]^{3-}$

  D. $[TiF_6]^{3-}$

  E. $[Ti(NH_3)_6]^{3-}$

26. What is the formula of a compound formed by combining 50. grams of element X (atomic weight = 100.) and 32 grams of oxygen gas?

  A. XO_2

  B. XO_4

  C. X_4O

  D. X_2O

  E. XO

Questions 27–30

A student performed an experiment to determine the molar mass (MM) of a volatile liquid by determining its vapor density. She placed a small amount of a volatile liquid into a flask of known volume then covered the flask with aluminum foil that had been punctured with a small pin. She then placed the apparatus into a boiling water bath and allowed the liquid to vaporize (see figure below).

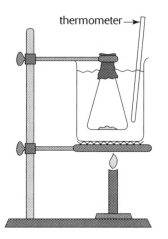

Choose from the following choices to answer questions 27–30:

   A.   The mass of the condensate would be larger than expected because it would include the mass of the vapor and the mass of the liquid. MM would be higher than expected.

   B.   The mass of the condensate would be larger than expected because it would include the mass of the vapor and the mass of the drops of water. MM would be higher than expected.

   C.   The calculated mass of vapor would be smaller than expected because some of the vapor would have escaped from the flask prior to the flask being weighed. MM would be too small.

   D.   Because the temperature of the water bath did not equal the temperature of the vapor, the temperature value used would be too large since the sample was collected at a lower temperature than the boiling water. MM would be too large.

   E.   There would be no effect on the MM.

In each of the following questions the student made an error in her procedure. Determine how each error would have affected the MM.

  27. She removed the flask prematurely from the hot water bath leaving some of the unknown in the liquid phase.

  28. Upon complete vaporization of the liquid sample, she removed the flask from the boiling water bath before allowing it a chance to reach the temperature of the hot water.

  29. She was not careful to keep the aluminum foil on the flask while it was cooling.

  30. She did not dry off the flask properly and left a few drops of water on the outside of the flask.

  31. A piece of metal weighing 418.6 grams was put into a boiling water bath. After 10 minutes, the metal was immediately placed in 250.0 grams of water at 40.0°C. The maximum temperature that the system reached was 50.0°C. What is the specific heat of the metal? (The specific heat of water is 4.186 J/g · °C.)

   A.   0.500 J/g · °C
   B.   1.00 J/g · °C
   C.   2.00 J/g · °C
   D.   4.00 J/g · °C
   E.   8.00 J/g · °C

  32. The critical temperature is

   A.   the temperature below which a gas undergoes cooling when expanded into a vacuum.

   B.   the temperature at which a gas liquefies at one atmosphere pressure.

   C.   the temperature at which the average kinetic energy of the molecules is a maximum.

   D.   the temperature above which it is impossible to liquefy a gas.

   E.   the temperature at which a liquid turns into a solid.

GO ON TO THE NEXT PAGE

33. In expanding from 5.00 to 6.00 liters at a constant pressure of 2.00 atmospheres, a gas absorbs 505.64 joules of energy (101.32 joules = 1 liter · atm). The change in energy, $\triangle E$, for the gas is

   A. 50.66 J
   B. 101.32 J
   C. 303.00 J
   D. 505.64 J
   E. 606.00 J

34. What would be the O–C–O bond angle in oxalic acid?

$$\text{H}-\text{O}-\overset{\displaystyle \text{O}}{\overset{\|}{\text{C}}}-\overset{\displaystyle \text{O}}{\overset{\|}{\text{C}}}-\text{O}-\text{H}$$

   A. 60°
   B. 90°
   C. 109°
   D. 120°
   E. 180°

35. What is the partial pressure of helium when 8.0 grams of helium and 16 grams of oxygen are in a container with a total pressure of 5.00 atm?

   A. 0.25 atm
   B. 1.00 atm
   C. 1.50 atm
   D. 2.00 atm
   E. 4.00 atm

Questions 36–38

A student had 5 test tubes each filled with a different reagent as shown.

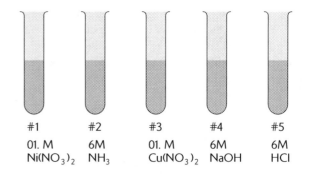

#1	#2	#3	#4	#5
01. M	6M	01. M	6M	6M
$Ni(NO_3)_2$	NH_3	$Cu(NO_3)_2$	NaOH	HCl

36. The student mixed small samples from two of the tubes and formed a dark blue solution. Which two tubes were mixed together?

   A. 1 and 2
   B. 2 and 3
   C. 3 and 4
   D. 4 and 5
   E. 1 and 3

37. The student mixed small samples from two of the tubes and formed a green precipitate. Which two tubes were mixed together?

   A. 1 and 2
   B. 2 and 3
   C. 3 and 4
   D. 4 and 5
   E. 1 and 4

38. The student mixed small samples from two of the tubes and a considerable amount of heat was produced. Which two tubes were mixed together?

   A. 1 and 2
   B. 2 and 3
   C. 3 and 4
   D. 4 and 5
   E. 1 and 4

39. Which of the following configurations represents a neutral transition element?

A. $1s^2 2s^2 2p^2$
B. $1s^2 2s^2 2p^6 3s^2 3p^4$
C. $1s^2 2s^2 3s^2$
D. $1s^2 2s^2 2p^6 3s^2 3p^6 3d^8 4s^2$
E. $1s^2 2s^2 2p^6 3s^2 3p^6 3d^{10} 4s^2 4p^6$

40. Arrange the following ionic compounds in order of decreasing lattice energy: KBr, LiF, MgO

A. $KBr > LiF > MgO$
B. $MgO > LiF > KBr$
C. $KBr > MgO > LiF$
D. $MgO > KBr > LiF$
E. $LiF > KBr > MgO$

41. The electronegativity of carbon is 2.5, whereas that of oxygen is 3.5. What type of bond would you expect to find in carbon monoxide?

A. nonpolar covalent
B. polar covalent
C. covalent network
D. ionic
E. delta

42. If $\triangle H$ is positive and $\triangle S$ is negative, then $\triangle G$ is always

A. positive
B. negative
C. negative at low temperatures; positive at high temperatures
D. positive at low temperatures; negative at high temperatures
E. cannot be determined from the information provided

43. Arrange the following ions in order of increasing ionic radius: Mg^{2+}, F^-, and O^{2-}.

A. O^{2-}, F^-, Mg^{2+}
B. Mg^{2+}, O^{2-}, F^-
C. Mg^{2+}, F^-, O^{2-}
D. O^{2-}, Mg^{2+}, F^-
E. F^-, O^{2-}, Mg^{2+}

44. Calculate $\triangle H$ for the synthesis of ethyne (C_2H_2) gas given the following reactions and enthalpy changes

$$H_{2(g)} + \tfrac{1}{2} O_{2(g)} \rightarrow H_2O_{(l)} \quad \triangle H = -286 \text{ kJ}$$
$$C_2H_{2(g)} + \tfrac{5}{2} O_{2(g)} \rightarrow 2CO_{2(g)} + H_2O_{(l)} \quad \triangle H = -1300 \text{ kJ}$$
$$C_{(s)} + O_{2(g)} \rightarrow CO_{2(g)} \quad \triangle H = -395 \text{ kJ}$$

A. -1981 kJ
B. -681 kJ
C. -619 kJ
D. 224 kJ
E. 619 kJ

45. Which one of the following is correct?

A. $KClO_3$, potassium perchlorate
B. CuO, copper oxide
C. $Al_3(SO_3)_2$, aluminum sulfate
D. $MgPO_4$, magnesium phosphate
E. $Na_2Cr_2O_7$, sodium dichromate

Questions 46 and 47 refer to 2, 3-pentadiol which has four possible structures:

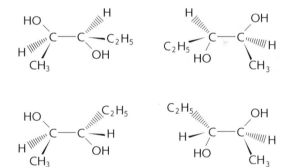

46. Which of the structures are enantiomers?

A. 1 and 2
B. 2 and 3
C. 1 and 4
D. 1 and 3; 2 and 4
E. 1 and 2; 3 and 4

47. Which of the structures are diastereomers?

A. 1, 2 and 3
B. 1 and 4; 2 and 3
C. 1 and 2; 3 and 4
D. 1 and 3; 2 and 4; 1 and 4; 2 and 3
E. all structures are diastereomers of each other

48. A certain metal crystallizes in a face-centered cube measuring 4.00×10^2 picometers on each edge. What is the radius of the atom? (1 picometer (pm) = 1×10^{-12} meter)

   A. 141 pm
   B. 173 pm
   C. 200. pm
   D. 282 pm
   E. 565 pm

49. The geometry of XeF_4 would most likely be

   A. tetrahedral
   B. pyramidal
   C. square planar
   D. T-shaped
   E. trigonal bipyramidal

50. A student was given 31.5 mg of $Ba(OH)_2 \cdot 8H_2O$ (M.W. = 315 g · mol^{-1}). She wanted to make a solution that was 0.10 M in OH$^-$. How much water should she add to make the solution?

   A. 1.0 mL
   B. 2.0 mL
   C. 4.0 mL
   D. 8.0 mL
   E. 99 mL

51. Which of the following compounds would be most soluble in an acidic solution?

   A. SiC
   B. PbI_2
   C. AgCl
   D. $BaSO_4$
   E. $CaCO_3$

52. At 37°C and 1.00 atm of pressure, nitrogen dissolves in the blood at a solubility of 6.0×10^{-4} M. If a diver breathes compressed air where nitrogen gas constitutes 80. mole % of the gas mixture and the total pressure at this depth is 3.0 atm, what is the concentration of nitrogen in her blood?

   A. 1.4×10^{-4} M
   B. 6.0×10^{-4} M
   C. 1.0×10^{-3} M
   D. 1.4×10^{-3} M
   E. 6.0×10^{-3} M

53. The condensation of a gas to a liquid would most likely have

   A. positive $\triangle H$ and positive $\triangle S$
   B. negative $\triangle H$ and positive $\triangle S$
   C. positive $\triangle H$ and negative $\triangle S$
   D. negative $\triangle H$ and negative $\triangle S$
   E. cannot be determined because temperature and pressures are not given

54. The rate-determining step of a several-step reaction mechanism has been determined to be

$$3X_{(g)} + 2Y_{(g)} \rightarrow 4Z_{(g)}$$

When 3.0 moles of gas X and 2.0 moles of gas Y are placed in a 5.0-liter vessel, the initial rate of the reaction is found to be 0.45 mole/liter · min. What is the rate constant for the reaction?

   A. $\dfrac{0.45}{\left(\dfrac{3.0}{5.0}\right)^3 \left(\dfrac{2.0}{5.0}\right)^2}$

   B. $\dfrac{0.45}{(3.0)(2.0)}$

   C. $\dfrac{0.45}{\left(\dfrac{3.0}{5.0}\right)^2 \left(\dfrac{2.0}{5.0}\right)^3}$

   D. $\dfrac{0.45}{\left(\dfrac{3.0}{5.0}\right)\left(\dfrac{2.0}{5.0}\right)}$

   E. $\dfrac{(3.0)^3 (2.0)^3}{0.45}$

55. Given the following aqueous solutions

0.15 m $CaCl_2$ 0.050 m NaCl   0.10 m H_2SO_4
0.30 m $C_6H_{12}O_6$

arrange them in order of increasing freezing point (lowest f.p. to highest f.p.).

   A. 0.15 m $CaCl_2$ > 0.050 m NaCl > 0.10 m H_2SO_4 > 0.30 m $C_6H_{12}O_6$
   B. 0.30 m $C_6H_{12}O_6$ > 0.10 m H_2SO_4 > 0.050 m NaCl > 0.15 m $CaCl_2$
   C. 0.10 m H_2SO_4 > 0.30 m $C_6H_{12}O_6$ > 0.15 m $CaCl_2$ = 0.050 m NaCl
   D. 0.15 m $CaCl_2$ = 0.10 m H_2SO_4 = 0.30 m $C_6H_{12}O_6$ = 0.050 m NaCl
   E. 0.15 m $CaCl_2$ > 0.10 m H_2SO_4 = 0.30 m $C_6H_{12}O_6$ > 0.050 m NaCl

For Questions 56 and 57, use the following information:

A student prepared a 1.00 M acetic acid solution ($HC_2H_3O_2$). The student found the pH of the solution to be 2.00.

56. What is the K_a value for the solution?

A. 3.00×10^{-7}
B. 2.00×10^{-6}
C. 2.00×10^{-5}
D. 1.00×10^{-4}
E. 1.00×10^{-3}

57. What is the approximate % dissociation of the acetic acid? (Use the 5% rule.)

A.   0.050%
B.   1.0%
C.   1.5%
D.   2.0%
E.   2.5%

58. Carbon-14 decays through

A.   electron capture
B.   beta emission
C.   positron emission
D.   alpha emission
E.   It does not decay, it is very stable.

59. Copper(II) iodate has a solubility of 3.3×10^{-3} M at 25°C. Calculate its K_{sp} value.

A. 1.4×10^{-7}
B. 1.1×10^{-5}
C. 3.3×10^{-3}
D. 5.1×10^{-1}
E. 3.3×10^{3}

60. Which of the following reactions would most likely produce the titration curve represented below?

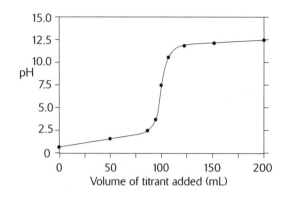

A. $H_2SO_4 + NH_3$
B. $KOH + HC_2H_3O_2$
C. $HC_7H_5O_2 + CH_3NH_2$
D. $HNO_3 + NaOH$
E. $HNO_2 + NaOH$

61. Arrange the following oxyacids in order of decreasing acid strength.

$$HClO, HIO, HBrO, HClO_3, HClO_2$$

A. $HClO > HIO > HBrO > HClO_3 > HClO_2$
B. $HClO > HClO_2 > HClO_3 > HBrO > HIO$
C. $HBrO > HClO > HClO_2 > HClO_3$
D. $HBrO > HClO > HClO_3 > HClO_2 > HIO$
E. $HClO_3 > HClO_2 > HClO > HBrO > HIO$

Questions 62–66

A.   Max Planck
B.   Niels Bohr
C.   Werner Heisenberg
D.   Louis de Broglie
E.   Wolfgang Pauli

62. No two electrons in an atom can have the same set of four quantum numbers.

63. The theory that electrons travel in discrete orbits around the atom's nucleus, with the chemical properties of the element being largely determined by the number of electrons in the outer orbits. The idea that an electron could drop from a higher-energy orbit to a lower one, emitting a photon.

GO ON TO THE NEXT PAGE

64. Wave-particle duality of nature.

65. Energy can only be absorbed or released in whole-number multiples of $h\nu$.

66. The simultaneous determination of both the position and momentum of a particle each has an inherent uncertainty, the product of these being not less than a known constant.

67. A student wants to make up 250 mL of an HNO_3 solution that has a pH of 2.00. How many milliliters of the 2.00 M HNO_3 should the student use? (The remainder of the solution is pure water.)

  A. 0.50 mL
  B. 0.75 mL
  C. 1.0 mL
  D. 1.3 mL
  E. This can't be done. The 2.00 M acid is weaker than the solution required.

68. Metallic crystals are formed by elements which have

  A. high ionization energies
  B. low ionization energies
  C. high electron affinities
  D. bond-dissociation energy
  E. high electronegativities

69. Calculate the approximate standard free energy change for the ionization of hydrofluoric acid, HF ($K_a = 1 \times 10^{-3}$), at 25°C.

  A. −9 kJ
  B. −4 kJ
  C. 0.05 kJ
  D. 4 kJ
  E. 20 kJ

70.

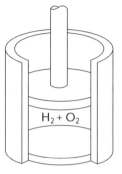

A mixture of hydrogen and oxygen gases in a cylinder were ignited. As the reaction occurred, the piston rose and the system lost 700 J of heat to its surroundings. It was determined that the expanding gas did 300 J of work on the surroundings as the piston pushed against the atmosphere. What is the change in the internal energy of the system?

  A. −1000 J
  B. −400 J
  C. 0 J
  D. 400 J
  E. 1000 J

71. Find $E°$ for a cell composed of silver and gold electrodes in 1 molar solutions of their respective ions: $E°_{red}$ Ag = +0.80 volts; $E°_{red}$ Au = +1.68 volts.

  A. −0.44 volt
  B. 0 volt
  C. 0.44 volt
  D. 0.88 volt
  E. 2.48 volt

72. Given the following information, which of the statements is true?

$$Cu^{2+}_{(aq)} + e^- \rightarrow Cu^+_{(aq)} \qquad E°_{red} = 0.34 \text{ V}$$
$$2H^+_{(aq)} + 2e^- \rightarrow H_{2(g)} \qquad E°_{red} = 0.00 \text{ V}$$
$$Fe^{2+}_{(aq)} + 2e^- \rightarrow Fe_{(s)} \qquad E°_{red} = -0.44 \text{ V}$$
$$Ni_{(s)} \rightarrow Ni^{2+}_{(aq)} + 2e^- \qquad E°_{ox} = 0.25 \text{ V}$$

  A. $Cu^{2+}_{(aq)}$ is the strongest oxidizing agent
  B. $Cu^{2+}_{(aq)}$ is the weakest oxidizing agent
  C. $Ni_{(s)}$ is the strongest oxidizing agent
  D. $Fe_{(s)}$ is the weakest reducing agent
  E. $H^+_{(aq)}$ is the strongest oxidizing agent

73. An electric current is applied to an aqueous solution of $FeCl_2$ and $ZnCl_2$. Which of the following reactions occurs at the cathode?

A. $Fe^{2+}_{(aq)} + 2e^- \rightarrow Fe_{(s)}$ $E°_{red} = -0.44$ V

B. $Fe_{(s)} \rightarrow Fe^{2+}_{(aq)} + 2e^-$ $E°_{ox} = 0.44$ V

C. $Zn^{2+}_{(aq)} + 2e^- \rightarrow Zn_{(s)}$ $E°_{red} = -0.76$ V

D. $Zn_{(s)} \rightarrow Zn^{2+}_{(aq)} + 2e^-$ $E°_{ox} = 0.76$ V

E. $2H_2O_{(l)} \rightarrow O_{2(g)} + 4H^+_{(aq)} + 4e^-$ $E°_{ox} = -1.23$ V

74. Data was obtained for the decomposition of NO_2 according to the following reaction

$$2NO_{2(g)} \rightarrow 2NO_{(g)} + O_{2(g)}$$

and a plot of $1/[NO_2]$ vs. time produced the following slope

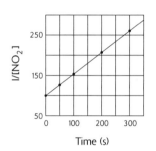

The reaction is

A. 0 order

B. 1st order

C. 2nd order

D. 3rd order

E. cannot be determined with information provided

75. How much 2.0 M H_2SO_4 would be required to make 500 mL of 0.50 M H_2SO_4?

A. 100 mL

B. 125 mL

C. 250 mL

D. 500 mL

E. 1000 mL

IF YOU FINISH BEFORE TIME IS CALLED, CHECK YOUR WORK ON THIS SECTION ONLY. DO NOT WORK ON ANY OTHER SECTION IN THE TEST.

PERIODIC TABLE OF THE ELEMENTS

1 H 1.0079																	2 He 4.0026
3 Li 6.941	4 Be 9.012											5 B 10.811	6 C 12.011	7 N 14.007	8 O 16.00	9 F 19.00	10 Ne 20.179
11 Na 22.99	12 Mg 24.30											13 Al 26.98	14 Si 28.09	15 P 30.974	16 S 32.06	17 Cl 35.453	18 Ar 39.948
19 K 39.10	20 Ca 40.08	21 Sc 44.96	22 Ti 47.90	23 V 50.94	24 Cr 51.00	25 Mn 54.93	26 Fe 55.85	27 Co 58.93	28 Ni 58.69	29 Cu 63.55	30 Zn 65.39	31 Ga 69.72	32 Ge 72.59	33 As 74.92	34 Se 78.96	35 Br 79.90	36 Kr 83.80
37 Rb 85.47	38 Sr 87.62	39 Y 88.91	40 Zr 91.22	41 Nb 92.91	42 Mo 95.94	43 Tc (98)	44 Ru 101.1	45 Rh 102.91	46 Pd 105.42	47 Ag 107.87	48 Cd 112.41	49 In 114.82	50 Sn 118.71	51 Sb 121.75	52 Te 127.60	53 I 126.91	54 Xe 131.29
55 Cs 132.91	56 Ba 137.33	57 *La 138.91	72 Hf 178.49	73 Ta 180.95	74 W 183.85	75 Re 186.21	76 Os 190.2	77 Ir 192.22	78 Pt 195.08	79 Au 196.97	80 Hg 200.59	81 Ti 204.38	82 Pb 207.2	83 Bi 208.98	84 Po (209)	85 At (210)	86 Rn (222)
87 Fr (223)	88 Ra 226.02	89 †Ac 227.03	104 Rf (261)	105 Db (262)	106 Sg (263)	107 Bh (262)	108 Hs (265)	109 Mt (266)	110 § (269)	111 § (272)	112 § (277)						

§ Not yet named

* Lanthanide Series

58 Ce 140.12	59 Pr 140.91	60 Nd 144.24	61 Pm (145)	62 Sm 150.4	63 Eu 151.97	64 Gd 157.25	65 Tb 158.93	66 Dy 162.50	67 Ho 164.93	68 Er 167.26	69 Tm 168.93	70 Yb 173.04	71 Lu 174.97

† Actinide Series

90 Th 232.04	91 Pa 231.04	92 U 238.03	93 Np 237.05	94 Pu (244)	95 Am (243)	96 Cm (247)	97 Bk (247)	98 Cf (251)	99 Es (252)	100 Fm (257)	101 Md (258)	102 No (259)	103 Lr (260)

STANDARD REDUCTION POTENTIALS IN AQUEOUS SOLUTION AT 25°C

Half-reaction			$E°$(V)
$F_2{}_{(g)} + 2\,e^-$	→	$2\,F^-$	2.87
$Co^{3+} + e^-$	→	Co^{2+}	1.82
$Au^{3+} + 3\,e^-$	→	$Au_{(s)}$	1.50
$Cl_2{}_{(g)} + 2\,e^-$	→	$2\,Cl^-$	1.36
$O_2{}_{(g)} + 4\,H^+ + 4\,e^-$	→	$2\,H_2O_{(l)}$	1.23
$Br_2{}_{(l)} + 2\,e^-$	→	$2\,Br^-$	1.07
$2\,Hg^{2+} + 2\,e^-$	→	$Hg_2{}^{2+}$	0.92
$Hg^{2+} + 2\,e^-$	→	$Hg_{(l)}$	0.85
$Ag^+ + e^-$	→	$Ag_{(s)}$	0.80
$Hg_2{}^{2+} + 2\,e^-$	→	$2\,Hg_{(l)}$	0.79
$Fe^{3+} + e^-$	→	Fe^{2+}	0.77
$I_2{}_{(s)} + 2\,e^-$	→	$2\,I^-$	0.53
$Cu^+ + e^-$	→	$Cu_{(s)}$	0.52
$Cu^{2+} + 2\,e^-$	→	$Cu_{(s)}$	0.34
$Cu^{2+} + e^-$	→	Cu^+	0.15
$Sn^{4+} + 2\,e^-$	→	Sn^{2+}	0.15
$S_{(s)} + 2\,H^+ + 2\,e^-$	→	$H_2S_{(g)}$	0.14
$2\,H^+ + 2\,e^-$	→	$H_2{}_{(g)}$	0.00
$Pb^{2+} + 2\,e^-$	→	$Pb_{(s)}$	−0.13
$Sn^{2+} + 2\,e^-$	→	$Sn_{(s)}$	−0.14
$Ni^{2+} + 2\,e^-$	→	$Ni_{(s)}$	−0.25
$Co^{2+} + 2\,e^-$	→	$Co_{(s)}$	−0.28
$Cd^{2+} + 2\,e^-$	→	$Cd_{(s)}$	−0.40
$Cr^{3+} + e^-$	→	Cr^{2+}	−0.41
$Fe^{2+} + 2\,e^-$	→	$Fe_{(s)}$	−0.44
$Cr^{3+} + 3\,e^-$	→	$Cr_{(s)}$	−0.74
$Zn^{2+} + 2\,e^-$	→	$Zn_{(s)}$	−0.76
$2\,H_2O_{(l)} + 2\,e^-$	→	$H_2{}_{(g)} + 2\,OH^-$	−0.83
$Mn^{2+} + 2\,e^-$	→	$Mn_{(s)}$	−1.18
$Al^{3+} + 3\,e^-$	→	$Al_{(s)}$	−1.66
$Be^{2+} + 2\,e^-$	→	$Be_{(s)}$	−1.70
$Mg^{2+} + 2\,e^-$	→	$Mg_{(s)}$	−2.37
$Na^+ + e^-$	→	$Na_{(s)}$	−2.71
$Ca^{2+} + 2\,e^-$	→	$Ca_{(s)}$	−2.87
$Sr^{2+} + 2\,e^-$	→	$Sr_{(s)}$	−2.89
$Ba^{2+} + 2\,e^-$	→	$Ba_{(s)}$	−2.90
$Rb^+ + e^-$	→	$Rb_{(s)}$	−2.92
$K^+ + e^-$	→	$K_{(s)}$	−2.92
$Cs^+ + e^-$	→	$Cs_{(s)}$	−2.92
$Li^+ + e^-$	→	$Li_{(s)}$	−3.05

Note: Unless otherwise stated, assume that for all questions involving solutions and/or chemical equations, the system is in water at room temperature.

GO ON TO THE NEXT PAGE

ADVANCED PLACEMENT CHEMISTRY EQUATIONS AND CONSTANTS

ATOMIC STRUCTURE

$$E = hv \qquad c = \lambda v$$

$$\lambda = \frac{h}{mv} \qquad p = mv$$

$$E_n = \frac{-2.178 \times 10^{-18}}{n^2} \text{ joule}$$

EQUILIBRIUM

$$K_a = \frac{[H^+][A^-]}{[HA]}$$

$$K_b = \frac{[OH^-][HB^+]}{[B]}$$

$$K_w = [OH^-][H^+] = 1.0 \times 10^{-14} \text{ @ } 25°C$$

$$= K_a \times K_b$$

$$pH = -\log[H^+], \; pOH = -\log[OH^-]$$

$$14 = pH + pOH$$

$$pH = pK_a + \log\frac{[A^-]}{[HA]}$$

$$pOH = pK_b + \log\frac{[HB^+]}{[B]}$$

$$pK_a = -\log K_a, \; pK_b = -\log K_b$$

$$K_p = K_c(RT)^{\Delta n}$$

where Δn = moles product gas – moles reactant gas

THERMOCHEMISTRY/KINETICS

$$\Delta S° = \Sigma S° \text{ products} - \Sigma S° \text{ reactants}$$

$$\Delta H° = \Sigma \Delta H_f° \text{ products} - \Sigma \Delta H_f° \text{ reactants}$$

$$\Delta G° = \Sigma \Delta G_f° \text{ products} - \Sigma \Delta G_f° \text{ reactants}$$

$$\Delta G° = \Delta H° - T\Delta S°$$

$$= -RT \ln K = -2.303 \, RT \log K$$

$$= -n \, \mathscr{F} \, E°$$

$$\Delta G = \Delta G° + RT \ln Q = \Delta G° + 2.303 \, RT \log Q$$

$$q = mc\Delta T$$

$$C_p = \frac{\Delta H}{\Delta T}$$

$$\ln[A]_t - \ln[A]_0 = -kt$$

$$\frac{1}{[A]_t} - \frac{1}{[A]_0} = kt$$

$$\ln k = \frac{-E_a}{R}\left(\frac{1}{T}\right) + \ln A$$

E = energy $\qquad v$ = velocity
v = frequency $\qquad n$ = principal quantum
λ = wavelength $\qquad\qquad$ number
p = momentum $\qquad m$ = mass

Speed of light, $c = 3.0 \times 10^8 \text{ m} \cdot \text{s}^{-1}$

Planck's constant, $h = 6.63 \times 10^{-34} \text{ J} \cdot \text{s}$

Boltzmann's constant, $k = 1.38 \times 10^{-23} \text{ J} \cdot \text{K}^{-1}$

Avogadro's number $= 6.022 \times 10^{23} \text{ mol}^{-1}$

Electron charge, $e = -1.602 \times 10^{-19}$ coulomb

1 electron volt per atom $= 96.5 \text{ kJ} \cdot \text{mol}^{-1}$

Equilibrium Constants

K_a (weak acid)
K_b (weak base)
K_w (water)
K_p (gas pressure)
K_c (molar concentrations)

$S°$ = standard entropy
$H°$ = standard enthalpy
$G°$ = standard free energy
$E°$ = standard reduction potential
T = temperature
n = moles
m = mass
q = heat
c = specific heat capacity
C_p = molar heat capacity at constant pressure
E_a = activation energy
k = rate constant
A = frequency factor

Faraday's constant, $\mathscr{F} = 96{,}500$ coulombs per mole of electrons

Gas constant, $R = 8.31 \text{ J} \cdot \text{mol}^{-1} \cdot \text{K}^{-1}$

$$= 0.0821 \text{ L} \cdot \text{atm} \cdot \text{mol}^{-1} \cdot \text{K}^{-1}$$

$$= 8.31 \text{ volt} \cdot \text{coulomb} \cdot \text{mol}^{-1} \cdot \text{K}^{-1}$$

GASES, LIQUIDS, AND SOLUTIONS

$$PV = nRT$$

$$\left(P + \frac{n^2a}{V^2}\right)(V - nb) = nRT$$

$$P_A = P_{total} \times X_A, \text{ where } X_A = \frac{\text{moles A}}{\text{total moles}}$$

$$P_{total} = P_A + P_B + P_C + \ldots$$

$$n = \frac{m}{M}$$

$$K = {}^\circ C + 273$$

$$\frac{P_1V_1}{T_1} = \frac{P_2V_2}{T_2}$$

$$D = \frac{m}{V}$$

$$u_{rms} = \sqrt{\frac{3kT}{m}} = \sqrt{\frac{3RT}{m}}$$

$$KE \text{ per molecule} = \tfrac{1}{2}mv^2$$

$$KE \text{ per mole} = \tfrac{3}{2}RT$$

$$\frac{r_1}{r_2} = \sqrt{\frac{M_2}{M_1}}$$

molarity, M = moles solute per liter solution
molality, m = moles solute per kilogram solvent

$$\Delta T_f = i \cdot K_f \times \text{molality}$$

$$\Delta T_b = i \cdot K_b \times \text{molality}$$

$$\pi = i \cdot M \cdot R \cdot T$$

$$A = a \cdot b \cdot c$$

P = pressure
V = volume
T = temperature
n = number of moles
D = density
m = mass
v = velocity

u_{rms} = root-mean-square speed
KE = kinetic energy
r = rate of effusion
M = molar mass
π = osmotic pressure
i = van't Hoff factor
K_f = molal freezing-point depression constant
K_b = molal boiling-point elevation constant
A = absorbance
a = molar absorptivity
b = path length
c = concentration
Q = reaction quotient
I = current (amperes)
q = charge (coulombs)
t = time (seconds)
E° = standard reduction potential
K = equilibrium constant

OXIDATION-REDUCTION; ELECTROCHEMISTRY

$$Q = \frac{[C]^c [D]^d}{[A]^a [B]^b}, \text{ where } a\,A + b\,B \rightarrow c\,C + d\,D$$

$$I = \frac{q}{t}$$

$$E_{cell} = E^\circ{}_{cell} - \frac{RT}{n\mathscr{F}}\ln Q = E^\circ{}_{cell} - \frac{0.0592}{n}\log Q \text{ @ } 25^\circ C$$

$$\log K = \frac{n \cdot E^\circ}{0.0592}$$

Gas constant, $R = 8.31 \text{ J} \cdot \text{mol}^{-1} \cdot \text{K}^{-1}$
$= 0.0821 \text{ L} \cdot \text{atm} \cdot \text{mol}^{-1} \cdot \text{K}^{-1}$
$= 8.31 \text{ volt} \cdot \text{coulomb} \cdot \text{mol}^{-1} \cdot \text{K}^{-1}$
Boltzmann's constant, $k = 1.38 \times 10^{-23} \text{ J} \cdot \text{K}^{-1}$
K_f for $H_2O = 1.86 \text{ K} \cdot \text{kg} \cdot \text{mol}^{-1}$
K_b for $H_2O = 0.512 \text{ K} \cdot \text{kg} \cdot \text{mol}^{-1}$
1 atm = 760 mm Hg
= 760 torr
STP = 0.000° C and 1.000 atm
Faraday's constant, $\mathscr{F} = 96{,}500$ coulombs per mole of electrons

GO ON TO THE NEXT PAGE

Section II: Free-Response Questions

CHEMISTRY

Section II

Total time—90 minutes

Part A

Time—40 minutes

YOU MAY USE YOUR CALCULATOR FOR PART A

CLEARLY SHOW THE METHOD USED AND STEPS INVOLVED IN ARRIVING AT YOUR ANSWERS. It is to your advantage to do this, because you may obtain partial credit if you do and you will receive little or no credit if you do not. Attention should be paid to significant figures.

Answer Question 1 below. The Section II score weighting for this question is 20%.

1. 250.0 grams of solid copper(II) nitrate is placed in an empty 4.0-liter flask. Upon heating the flask to 250°C, some of the solid decomposes into solid copper(II) oxide, gaseous nitrogen(IV) oxide, and oxygen gas. At equilibrium, the pressure is measured and found to be 5.50 atmospheres.

   (a) Write the balanced equation for the reaction.

   (b) Calculate the number of moles of oxygen gas present in the flask at equilibrium.

   (c) Calculate the number of grams of solid copper(II) nitrate that remained in the flask at equilibrium.

   (d) Write the equilibrium expression for K_p and calculate the value of the equilibrium constant.

   (e) If 420.0 grams of the copper(II) nitrate had been placed into the empty flask at 250°C, what would the total pressure have been at equilibrium?

Answer EITHER Question 2 or 3 below. Only one of these two questions will be graded. If you start both questions, be sure to cross out the question you do not want graded. The Section II score weighting for the question you choose is 20%.

2. The reaction $2NO_{2(g)} + Cl_{2(g)} \rightarrow 2NO_2Cl_{(g)}$ was studied at 20°C and the following data were obtained:

Experiment	Initial $[NO_2]$ (mole · liter^{-1})	Initial $[Cl_2]$ (mole · liter^{-1})	Initial Rate of Increase of $[NO_2Cl]$ (mole · liter^{-1} · sec^{-1})
1	0.100	0.005	1.35×10^{-7}
2	0.100	0.010	2.70×10^{-7}
3	0.200	0.010	5.40×10^{-7}

   (a) Write the rate law for the reaction.

   (b) What is the overall order for the reaction? Explain.

   (c) Calculate the rate-specific constant, including the correct units.

   (d) In Experiment 3, what is the initial rate of decrease of $[Cl_2]$?

   (e) Propose a mechanism for the reaction that is consistent with the rate law expression you found in part (a).

3. A student wanted to determine the molecular weight of a monoprotic, solid acid, symbolized as HA. The student carefully measured out 25.000 grams of HA and dissolved it in distilled H_2O to bring the volume of the solution to exactly 500.00 mL. The student next measured out several fifty-mL aliquots of the acid solution and then titrated them against standardized 0.100 M NaOH solution. The results of the three titrations are given in the following table:

Trial	mL of HA Solution	mL of NaOH Solution
1	49.12	87.45
2	49.00	84.68
3	48.84	91.23

(a) Calculate the average number of moles of HA in the fifty-mL aliquots.

(b) Calculate the molecular weight of the acid, HA.

(c) Calculate the pH of the fifty-mL aliquot solution (assume complete ionization).

(d) Calculate the pOH of the fifty-mL aliquot solution (assume complete ionization).

(e) Discuss how each of the following errors would affect the determination of the molecular weight of the acid, HA.

    (i) The balance that the student used in measuring out the 25.000 grams of HA was reading 0.010 grams too low.

    (ii) There was an impurity in the acid, HA.

    (iii) The NaOH solution used in titration was actually 0.150 M instead of 0.100 M.

CHEMISTRY

Part B

Time—50 minutes

NO CALCULATORS MAY BE USED FOR PART B

Answer Question 4 below. The Section II score weight for this question is 15%.

4. Write the formulas to show the reactants and the products for any FIVE of the laboratory situations described below. Answers to more than five choices will not be graded. In all cases, a reaction occurs. Assume that solutions are aqueous unless otherwise indicated. Represent substances in solution as ions if the substances are extensively ionized. Omit formulas for any ions or molecules that are unchanged by the reaction. You need not balance the equations.

Example: A strip of magnesium is added to a solution of silver nitrate.

Ex.	$Mg + Ag^+ \longrightarrow Mg^2 + Ag$

(a) A solution of aluminum nitrate is added to a solution of sodium phosphate.

(b) Hot steam is mixed with propene gas.

(c) Manganese dioxide (acting as a catalyst) is added to a solid sample of potassium chlorate and the mixture is then heated.

(d) Hydroiodic acid is mixed with solid calcium carbonate.

(e) A piece of aluminum is dropped into a solution of lead chloride.

(f) Solid calcium oxide is added to silicon dioxide and the mixture is heated strongly.

(g) A concentrated potassium hydroxide solution is added to solid aluminum hydroxide.

(h) Chloromethane is bubbled through a solution of warm ammonia.

Answer BOTH Question 5 AND Question 6 below. Both of these questions will be graded. The Section II score weighting for these questions is 30% (15% each).

5. A student was given three flasks that were labeled X, Y, and Z. Each flask contained one of the following solutions: 1.0 M $AgNO_3$, 1.0 M $Pb(NO_3)_2$ or 1.0 M $Al_2(SO_4)_3$.

The student was also given three flasks that were labeled A, B and C. One of these flasks contained 1.0 M NaOH, another contained 1.0 M K_2CrO_4, and another contained 1.0 M NaI. This information is summarized in the diagram below.

Each flask contains one of the following solutions:
1.0M $AgNO_3$
1.0M $Pb(NO_3)_2$
1.0M $Al_2(SO_4)_3$

X Y Z

Each flask contains one of the following solutions:
1.0M NaOH
1.0M K_2CrO_4
1.0M NaI

A B C

(a) The student combined samples from flask X and flask A and noticed a brick-red precipitate.

   (i) Identify the solutions in flask X and flask A.

   (ii) Write the balanced chemical reaction that occurred when solutions X and A were mixed. Omit formulas for any ions or molecules that were unchanged by the reaction.

(b) When samples from flask X and B were mixed, a brown precipitate was formed.

   (i) Identify the solution in flask B.

   (ii) Write the chemical reaction that occurred when solutions from flasks X and B were mixed.

(c) How would you be able to determine for sure which flask contained $PbNO_3$?

(d) Write the net ionic equation for the reaction that would produce PbI_2.

(e) What test could you do to confirm that the flask that did not produce PbI_2 (either Y or Z) contained $Al_2(SO_4)_3$?

6. Explain each of the following in terms of (1) inter- and intra-atomic or molecular forces and (2) structure.

(a) ICl has a boiling point of 97°C, whereas NaCl has a boiling point of 1400°C.

(b) $KI_{(s)}$ is very soluble in water, whereas $I_{2(s)}$ has a solubility of only 0.03 grams per 100 grams of water.

(c) Solid Ag conducts an electric current, whereas solid $AgNO_3$ does not.

(d) PCl_3 has a measurable dipole moment, whereas PCl_5 does not.

(e) The carbon-to-carbon bond energy in C_2H_5Cl is less than it is in C_2H_3Cl.

Answer EITHER Question 7 or 8 below. Only one of these two questions will be graded. If you start both questions, be sure to cross out the question you do not want graded. The Section II score weighting for the question you choose is 15%.

7. Butadiene, C_4H_6, is a planar molecule that has the following carbon-carbon bond lengths in Å (10^{-10}m):

$$H_2C=CH—CH=CH_2$$
$$1.34 \quad 1.48 \quad 1.34$$

(a) Predict the approximate bond angles around each of the carbon atoms.

(b) Predict the hybridization of the carbon atoms. Explain your reasoning.

(c) Sketch the 3-dimensional structure of the molecule.

(d) How many total sigma and pi bonds are in this molecule?

(e) Compare the bond lengths shown above with established average bond lengths for C—C at 1.54 Å and C=C at 1.34 Å. Explain any differences.

(f) Are there any *cis-* or *trans-* isomers for this compound? Explain your reason(s).

(g) Replace the CH_2 (one only) group in the above structure with CHCl. Draw and label all geometric isomers that the new compound may have.

GO ON TO THE NEXT PAGE

8. The first three ionization energies (I_1, I_2, and I_3) for beryllium and neon are given in the following table:

(kJ/mole)	I_1	I_2	I_3
Be	900	1,757	14,840
Ne	2,080	3,963	6,276

(a) Write the complete electron configuration for beryllium and for neon.

(b) Draw the Lewis diagrams for Be and Ne.

(c) Explain any trends or significant discrepancies found in the ionization energies for beryllium and neon.

(d) If chlorine gas is passed into separate containers of heated beryllium and heated neon, explain what compounds (if any) might be formed, and explain your answer in terms of the electron configurations of these two elements.

(e) An unknown element, X, has the following three ionization energies:

(kJ/mole)	I_1	I_2	I_3
X	419	3,069	4,600

(f) On the basis of the ionization energies given, what is most likely to be the compound produced when chlorine reacts with element X and explain your reasoning.

Answer Key for Practice Exam 3

Section I: Multiple-Choice Questions

1. C		**26.** B		**51.** E	
2. A		**27.** A		**52.** D	
3. D		**28.** D		**53.** D	
4. B		**29.** C		**54.** A	
5. A		**30.** B		**55.** E	
6. B		**31.** A		**56.** D	
7. C		**32.** D		**57.** B	
8. C		**33.** C		**58.** B	
9. C		**34.** D		**59.** A	
10. D		**35.** E		**60.** D	
11. B		**36.** B		**61.** E	
12. E		**37.** E		**62.** E	
13. B		**38.** D		**63.** B	
14. A		**39.** D		**64.** D	
15. C		**40.** B		**65.** A	
16. D		**41.** B		**66.** C	
17. B		**42.** A		**67.** D	
18. A		**43.** C		**68.** B	
19. B		**44.** D		**69.** E	
20. A		**45.** E		**70.** A	
21. C		**46.** E		**71.** D	
22. C		**47.** D		**72.** A	
23. D		**48.** A		**73.** A	
24. C		**49.** C		**74.** C	
25. B		**50.** B		**75.** B	

Predicting Your AP Score

The table below shows historical relationships between students' results on the multiple-choice portion (Section I) of the AP Chemistry exam and their overall AP score. The AP score ranges from 1 to 5, with 3, 4, or 5 generally considered to be passing. Over the years, around 60% of the students who take the AP Chemistry Exam receive a 3, 4, or 5.

After you've taken the multiple-choice practice exam under timed conditions, count the number of questions you got correct. From this number, subtract the number of wrong answers times $\frac{1}{4}$. Do NOT count items left blank as wrong. Then refer to this table to find your "probable" overall AP score. For example, if you get 39 questions correct, based on historical statistics, you have a 25% chance of receiving an overall score of 3, a 63% chance of receiving an overall score of 4, and a 12% chance of receiving an overall score of 5. Note that your actual results may be different from the score this table predicts. Also, remember that the free-response section represents 55% of your AP score.

No attempt is made here to combine your specific results on the practice AP Chemistry free-response questions (Section II) with your multiple-choice results (which is beyond the scope of this book and for which no data is available). However, you should have your AP chemistry instructor review your essays before you take the AP Chemistry Exam so that he or she can give you additional pointers.

Number of Multiple-Choice Questions Correct*	Overall AP Score				
	1	2	3	4	5
47 to 75	0%	0%	1%	21%	78%
37 to 46	0%	0%	25%	63%	12%
24 to 36	0%	19%	69%	12%	0%
13 to 23	15%	70%	15%	0%	0%
0 to 12	86%	14%	0%	0%	0%
% of Test Takers Receiving Score	21%	22%	25%	15%	17%

*Corrected for wrong answers

Answers and Explanations for Practice Exam 3

1. **(C)** Shielding and large ionic radius minimize electrostatic attraction.

2. **(A)** F has only one negative oxidation state (-1).

3. **(D)** Be^{2+} has electrons in the first energy level only.

4. **(B)** NaCl crystallizes face-centered-cubic.

$$\left(\frac{1}{4} \, Na^+ \text{ per edge} \right) \times \left(12 \text{ edges} \right) = 3 \, Na^+$$

$$\left(1 \, Na^+ \text{ per center} \right) \times \left(1 \text{ center} \right) = 1 \, Na^+$$

$$\left(\frac{1}{8} \, Cl^- \text{ per corner} \right) \left(8 \text{ corners} \right) = 1 \, Cl^-$$

$$\left(\frac{1}{2} \, Cl^- \text{ per face} \right) \left(6 \text{ faces} \right) = 3 \, Cl^-$$

$$\overline{\qquad 8 \text{ total ions} \qquad}$$

5. **(A)** Remember Boyle's Law: As the volume decreases (at constant temperature), the pressure increases.

6. **(B)** In this case, a lone electron pair on oxygen forms a bond to H^+. A coordinate covalent bond (also known as a dative covalent bond) is a special type of covalent bond in which the shared electrons come from one of the atoms only. After the bond has been formed, its strength is no different from that of a covalent bond. Coordinate covalent bonds are formed when a Lewis base (an electron donor) donates a pair of electrons to a Lewis acid (an electron acceptor); the resultant compound is then called an adduct (a compound formed by the addition reaction between two molecules). The process of forming a dative bond is called coordination.

7. **(C)** In examining the rate expression, note that B is first-order, so the rate is directly proportional to the concentration of the reactant. Holding [A] constant and doubling [B] would double the rate.

8. **(C)** The term $-d[B]/dt$ represents the rate of decrease in the concentration of B as time elapses. For every mole of B that is lost on the reactant side, $\frac{1}{2} \times 4$, or 2 moles of D are gained on the product side over the same amount of time (dt).

9. **(C)** The rate constant is independent of the concentration of the reactants. However, k depends on two factors:

   - The nature of the reaction. "Fast" reactions typically have large rate constants.
   - The temperature. Usually k increases with an increase in temperature; k and temperature are directly proportional.

10. **(D)** The overall order of the reaction is the sum of the orders of the individual reactants. Only gas concentrations are affected by changes in container volume. Here, $[A]^2[B]^1 = 2 + 1 = 3$. For reactions with an overall order of 3, the rate is proportional to the cube of the concentration of the reactants: $3^3 = 27$.

11. **(B)** The postulates of the kinetic theory are:

    - Gases are composed of tiny, invisible molecules that are widely separated from one another in empty space.
    - The molecules are in constant, continuous, random, and straight-line motion.
    - The molecules collide with one another, but the collisions are perfectly elastic (no net loss of energy).
    - The pressure of a gas is the result of collisions between the gas molecules and the walls of the container.
    - The average kinetic energy of all the molecules collectively is directly proportional to the absolute temperature of the gas. Equal numbers of molecules of any gas have the same average kinetic energy at the same temperature.

12. **(E)** The sign of $\triangle H°$ is positive, therefore the reaction is endothermic (heat is a reactant). Lowering the temperature will shift the equilibrium in the direction that produces heat (to the left). Adding N_2 will not shift equilibrium because N_2 is neither a product nor reactant. All other choices will cause the equilibrium to shift to the right.

13. (B) The Al^{3+} has been diluted tenfold:

$$\frac{0.1 \text{ M} \times 1 \text{ cm}^3}{10. \text{ cm}^3} = 0.01 \text{ M}$$

14. (A) Geometrical isomers are compounds that have the same molecular formula and the same groups bonded to one another but differ in the spatial arrangement of the groups. In the *trans* form of this compound, the two methyl groups are on opposite sides.

15. (C) The location of the double bond along an alkene chain is indicated by a prefix number that designates the number of the carbon atom that is part of the double bond and is nearest an end of the chain. The chain is always numbered from the end that gives the smallest number prefix.

16. (D) In the *cis* isomer, the two methyl groups are on the same side of the double bond.

17. (B) All four carbons lie on a continuous chain with the double bond coming after the #1 carbon on the chain.

18. (A)

$$Ni_{(s)} \big| Ni^{2+}_{(aq)} \big\| Ag^{+}_{(aq)} \big| Ag_{(s)}$$

$$\text{anode (oxidation)} \big\| \text{cathode (reduction)}$$

$$Ni_{(s)} \rightarrow Ni^{2+}_{(aq)} + 2e^- \big\| 2Ag^{+}_{(aq)} + 2e^- \rightarrow 2Ag_{(s)}$$

By convention, in the representation of the cell, the anode is represented on the left and the cathode on the right. The anode is the electrode at which oxidation occurs (AN OX), and the cathode is the electrode at which reduction takes place (RED CAT). The single vertical line ($|$) indicates contact between the electrode and solution. The double vertical lines ($\|$) represent the porous partition, or salt bridge, between the two solutions in the two half-cells. The ion concentration or pressures of a gas are enclosed in parentheses.

Take the two equations that decoded the standard cell notation and include the $E^{\circ}_{reduction}$ and the $E^{\circ}_{oxidation}$ voltages:

(Be sure to change the sign of the cell potential for the nickel reaction because you're representing it as an oxidation reaction.)

ox: $Ni_{(s)} \rightarrow Ni^{2+}_{(aq)} + 2e^-$	$E^{\circ}_{ox} = 0.25$ volt
red: $2Ag^{+}_{(aq)} + 2e^- \rightarrow 2Ag_{(s)}$	$E^{\circ}_{red} = +0.80$ volt
$Ni_{(s)} + 2Ag^{+}_{(aq)} \rightarrow Ni^{2+}_{(aq)} + 2Ag_{(s)}$	$E^{\circ}_{cell} = +1.05$ volts

19. (B) According to Raoult's Law, the vapor pressure above a solution that contains a nonvolatile solute is equal to the mole fraction of the solvent times the vapor pressure of the pure solvent:

$$P_1 = i \cdot X_1 \cdot P_1^{\circ}$$

where P_1 = vapor pressure of the solvent with added solute, X_1 = mole fraction of solvent, P_1° = vapor pressure of the pure solvent, and i = # moles after the solution / # moles before solution.

Convert 45 grams of glucose into moles by dividing by the molecular weight of glucose (180)

45 grams glucose × 1 mole glucose / 180 grams glucose = 0.25 moles glucose

Convert 72 grams of H_2O to moles H_2O by dividing by the molecular weight of H_2O (18)

72 grams H_2O × 1 mole H_2O / 18 grams H_2O = 4 moles H_2O

Determine the mole fraction of solute glucose

mole fraction of glucose = moles glucose / total moles = 0.25 / 4.25 = 0.0588

Using Raoult's Law, determine the vapor pressure of the solution.

$$P_1^{\circ} - X_2 P_1^{\circ} = P_1 = 23.8 - (0.0588)(23.8) = 23.8 - 1.4 = 22.4 \text{ torr}$$

20. (A) The (III) indicates that the central positive ion should have a +3 charge. In adding up the charges for the ligand you get:

$$2H_2O = 0$$
$$2NH_3 = 0$$
$$2(Br^-) = -2$$
$$1(Cr^{+?}) = ?$$

$$\overline{\qquad\qquad + 1 \text{ (overall charge of compound)}}$$

Therefore, the Cr ion must have a charge of +3.

Choice (D) also yields a +3 charge for Cr, and yet does not conform to standard methods of writing complex ion formulas.

21. (C) Begin by drawing the Lewis structure

$$\left[\text{H} :\ddot{\text{N}}: \text{H}\right]^-$$

Next, determine the electron-pair geometry around N using VSEPR rules. Because there are four electrons pairs around N, the electron-pair geometry is tetrahedral (or sp^3 hybridization).

22. (C) To solve this problem, use the equation

$$\log\frac{X_o}{X} = \frac{k \cdot t}{2.30} \quad \text{or} \quad \ln\frac{X_o}{X} = k \cdot t$$

with the corresponding half-life $t_{1/2} = 0.693/k$, where X_o is the number of original radioactive nuclei and X represents the number of radioactive nuclei at time t. k represents the first-order rate constant. Substituting into the equation yields

$$\log\frac{X_o}{X} = \frac{(0.693/6.93 \text{ years})(11.5 \text{ years})}{2.30} = 0.5$$

$$\frac{X_o}{X} \approx 3$$

$$\frac{X}{X_o} \approx \frac{1}{3} \times 100\% \approx 33\% \text{ that remained unreacted}$$

An alternative method would be to consider that two half lives of wait-time would leave 25% of the original isotope. 2×6.93 is ≈ 14. 11.5 years is a bit less than 14, so a bit more than 25% of the isotope remains . . . $\approx 30\%$.

23. (D)

$$6e^- + 14H^+_{(aq)} + Cr_2O_7^{2-}{}_{(aq)} \rightarrow 2Cr^{3+}{}_{(aq)} + 7H_2O_{(l)}$$
$$6Cl^-_{(aq)} \rightarrow 3Cl_{2(g)} + 6e^-$$

$$\overline{14H^+_{(aq)} + Cr_2O_7^{2-}{}_{(aq)} + 6Cl^-_{(aq)} \rightarrow 2Cr^{3+}{}_{(aq)} + 7H_2O_{(l)} + 3Cl_{2(g)}}$$

24. (C) The body-centered cubic cell looks like this:

Body-centered cubic

The formula that relates the atomic radius (r) to the length of one edge (s) of the cube for a body-centered cubic cell is $4r = s\sqrt{3}$.

$$4\,(0.43) = s \cdot (1.73)$$
$$1.72 = s\,(1.73)$$
$$s \approx 0.9$$

25. (B) The wavelength of the absorption is determined by the magnitude of the splitting between the *d*-orbital energies in the field of the surrounding ligands. The larger the splitting, the shorter the wavelength of the absorption corresponding to the transition of the electron from the lower- to the higher-energy orbital. The splitting will be the largest for ethylenediamine (en), the ligand that is highest in the spectrochemical series.

26. (B) According to the information given, you have 0.50 mole of element X (50. g/100. g · mole^{-1} = 0.50 mole). For the oxygen, remember that you will use 16g/mole for the atomic weight, giving you 2.0 moles of oxygen atoms. A 0.50:2.0 molar ratio is the same as a 1:4 molar ratio, so the answer is XO_4.

27. (A)

28. (D)

29. (C)

30. (B)

31. (A)

q of system $= -\,q$ of surroundings

heat lost by metal = heat gained by water

$q = (\text{mass})\,(\triangle T)\,(C_p)$

$-(x\ \text{J/g} \cdot {}^\circ\text{C}) \times (418.6.\ \text{g metal})\,(50.0^\circ\text{C} - 100.0^\circ\text{C}) = (4.186\ \text{J/g} \cdot {}^\circ\text{C}) \times (250.0\ \text{g H}_2\text{O}) \times (50.0^\circ\text{C} - 40.0^\circ\text{C})$

$x = 0.500\ \text{J/g} \cdot {}^\circ\text{C}$

32. (D) The critical temperature, T_c, of a material is the temperature above which distinct liquid and gas phases do not exist. As the critical temperature is approached, the properties of the gas and liquid phases become the same. Above the critical temperature, there is only one phase.

33. (C) The first law of thermodynamics states that $\triangle E = q + w$. Because $w = -P_{ext} \cdot \triangle V$, the equation can be stated as

$\triangle E = \triangle H - P_{ext} \cdot \triangle V$

$\triangle V = 6 \text{ L} - 5 \text{ L} = 1 \text{ L of expansion}$

$\triangle E = 505.64 \text{ joules} - (2.00 \text{ atm} \cdot 1 \text{ liters} \cdot 101.32 \text{ J/L} \cdot \text{atm})$

$= 303.00 \text{ J}$

34. (D) Count the double bond around the central carbons atom as a single electron pair when determining geometry or bond angle. There are a total of 3 electron pairs around each C atom—counting the double bond as just one electron pair. The result is trigonal planar geometry with a bond angle of 120°.

35. (E) Use the formula

$$P_1 = \frac{n_1}{n_{total}} P_{total}$$

derived from Dalton's Law of Partial Pressures. Find the number of moles of the two gases first.

$$\frac{8.0 \text{ g He}}{1} \times \frac{1 \text{ mole He}}{4.0 \text{ g He}} = 2.0 \text{ moles He}$$

$$\frac{16.0 \text{ g O}_2}{1} \times \frac{1 \text{ mole O}_2}{32 \text{ g O}_2} = 0.50 \text{ mole O}_2$$

$n_{total} = 2.0 \text{ moles} + 0.50 \text{ moles} = 2.5 \text{ moles}$

$$P_{He} = \frac{2.0 \text{ moles}}{2.5 \text{ moles}} \times 5.00 \text{ atm} = 4.00 \text{ atm}$$

36. (B) The Cu^{2+} ion is blue. $Cu(NH_3)_4^{2+}$ would be formed by adding $Cu(NO_3)_2$ with NH_3. The Cu-NH_3 complex ion is dark blue.

37. (E) The Ni^{2+} ion is green. The precipitate formed was $Ni(OH)_2$.

38. (D) A neutralization reaction between a strong acid and a strong base produces heat.

39. (D) The transition elements are filling the d orbitals. When completely filled, the d orbitals hold a maximum of 10 electrons.

40. (B) Lattice energy is defined as the energy required to separate completely the ions in an ionic solid. Because electrostatic attraction between oppositely charged ions increases with the charge on the ions, Mg^{2+} and O^{2-} would have the greatest electrostatic attraction and the largest lattice energy. Because the radius of a Li^+ ion is smaller than the radius of a K^+ ion and an F^- has a smaller ionic radius than Br^-, the distance between the ions would be less in LiF than in KBr. Electrostatic attraction increases as internuclear distance between ions decreases...meaning that smaller ions such as Li^+ and F^- form stronger bonds.

41. (B) Electronegativity differences less that 1.7 are classified as covalent. Unequal differences in sharing electrons are known as polar covalent.

42. (A) The question involves the equation for free energy:

$\triangle G = \triangle H - T\triangle S$. Under the conditions stated in the question, the reaction is nonspontaneous at all temperatures and the reverse reaction is spontaneous. An example of this would be the synthesis of ozone from oxygen: $3O_{2(g)} \rightarrow 2O_{3(g)}$

43. (C) Note that all the ions have 10 electrons; that is, they are all isoelectronic with neon. Because they all have the same number of electrons, the only factor that will determine their size will be the nuclear charge—the greater the nuclear charge, the smaller the radius. Therefore, magnesium, with a nuclear charge of +2, has the smallest radius among these ions.

44. (D) Begin by writing the balanced reaction:

$$2C_{(s)} + H_{2(g)} \rightarrow C_2H_{2(g)}$$

Next, rearrange the given reactions remembering to change sign when reversing direction according to Hess's Law. Also remember to double $\triangle H$ when doubling the coefficients in order to cancel terms.

$$\begin{array}{ll} H_{2(g)} + \cancel{\tfrac{1}{2}O_{2(g)}} \rightarrow \cancel{H_2O_{(l)}} & \triangle H = -286 \text{ kJ} \\ \cancel{2CO_{2(g)}} + \cancel{H_2O_{(l)}} \rightarrow C_2H_{2(g)} + \cancel{\tfrac{5}{2}O_{2(g)}} & \triangle H = 1300 \text{ kJ} \\ 2C_{(s)} + \cancel{2O_{2(g)}} \rightarrow \cancel{2CO_{2(g)}} & \triangle H = -790 \text{ kJ} \\ \hline 2C_{(s)} + H_{2(g)} \rightarrow C_2H_{2(g)} & \triangle H = 224 \text{ kJ} \end{array}$$

45. (E) In Choice A, $KClO_3$ is potassium chlorate, not perchlorate. In Choice B, CuO is copper(II) oxide, to distinguish it from copper(I) oxide (Cu_2O). In Choice C, the formula for aluminum sulfate is $Al_2(SO_4)_3$. In Choice D, the formula for magnesium phosphate is $Mg_3(PO_4)_2$. If you missed these, review inorganic nomenclature in your textbook or *CliffsAP Chemistry,* 3rd Edition.

46. (E) Enantiomers are mirror images that are NOT superimposable.

47. (D) Diastereomers are stereoisomers that are not mirror images of each other.

48. (A)

Face-centered cubic

The formula which relates the radius of an atom "r" to the length of the side "s" of the unit cell for a face-centered cubic cell is

$4r = s\sqrt{2}$.

$$r = \frac{400. \text{ pm } \sqrt{2}}{4} = 100. (1.414) = 141 \text{ pm}$$

49. (C) The Lewis structure of XeF_4 is

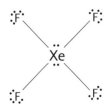

Because Xe has 12 electrons in its valence shell we would expect an octahedral disposition of the six electron pairs, two of which are nonbonded pairs. Because nonbonded pairs have a larger volume requirement than bonded pairs, we would expect the nonbonded pair to be opposite one another, leading to a square planar arrangement of the molecule.

50. (B)

$$\frac{31.5 \ \text{mg} \ Ba(OH)_2 \cdot 8H_2O}{1} \times \frac{1 \ g}{10^3 \ \text{mg}} = 3.15 \times 10^{-2} \ g \ Ba(OH)_2 \cdot 8H_2O$$

$$\frac{3.15 \times 10^{-2} \ g \ Ba(OH)_2 \cdot 8H_2O}{315 \ g \ Ba(OH)_2 \cdot 8H_2O \ / \ mol} = 1.00 \times 10^{-4} \ mol \ Ba(OH)_2 \cdot 8H_2O$$

$Ba(OH)_2 \cdot 8H_2O$ contains 2 moles of OH^-

$$\frac{1.00 \times 10^{-4} \ mol \ Ba(OH)_2 \cdot 8H_2O}{1} \times \frac{2 \ mol \ OH^-}{1 \ mol \ Ba(OH)_2 \cdot 8H_2O}$$

$$= 2.00 \times 10^{-4} \ mol \ OH^-$$

Therefore, $\dfrac{2.00 \times 10^{-4} \ mol \ OH^-}{0.10 \ M \ OH^-} = 2.0 \times 10^{-3}$ liters $= 2.0$ mL

51. (E) $CaCO_3$ dissolves in acid solutions because CO_3^{2-} is a basic anion:

$$CaCO_{3(s)} \longleftrightarrow Ca^{2+}_{(aq)} + CO_{3}^{2-}{}_{(aq)}$$
$$CO_{3}^{2-}{}_{(aq)} + 2H^+_{(aq)} \longleftrightarrow H_2CO_{3(aq)}$$
$$H_2CO_{3(aq)} \rightarrow CO_{2(g)} + H_2O_{(l)}$$
$$\overline{CaCO_{3(s)} + 2H^+_{(aq)} \rightarrow Ca^{2+}_{(aq)} + CO_{2(g)} + H_2O_{(l)}}$$

The solubility of $AgCl$ is unaffected by changes in pH since Cl^- is the anion of a strong acid and therefore has negligible basicity. HSO_4^- is an acidic anion. Cl^- and SO_4^{2-} are neutral anions.

52. (D) Determine k by using Henry's Law, $C = kP$

$$k = \frac{\text{concentration} \ N_2}{\text{pressure} \ N_2} = \frac{6.0 \times 10^{-4} \ M}{1.00 \ atm} = 6.0 \times 10^{-4} \ M \cdot atm^{-1}$$

To solve the problem

$$P = 0.80 \times 3.0 \ atm = 2.4 \ atm$$

$$C = kP = \frac{6.0 \times 10^{-4} \ moles}{liter \cdot atm} \times \frac{2.4 \ atm}{1} = 1.4 \times 10^{-3} \ M$$

53. (D) The condensation of a gas releases energy which would result in a negative $\triangle H$. During the process of condensation, the system goes from a state of high disorder (gas) to a state of higher order (liquid) causing a decrease in entropy resulting in a negative $\triangle S$.

54. (A) Given a reaction mechanism, the order with respect to each reactant is its coefficient in the chemical equation for that step. The slowest step is the rate-determining step, so

$$\text{rate} = k[X]^3[Y]^2$$

$$k = \frac{\text{rate}}{[X]^3[Y]^2} = \frac{0.45 \ \ \text{mole} \ / \ \text{liter} \cdot \text{min}}{\left(\dfrac{3.0 \ \text{moles}}{5.0 \ \text{liters}}\right)^3 \left(\dfrac{2.0 \ \text{moles}}{5.0 \ \text{liters}}\right)^2}$$

55. (E) $0.15 \ m \ CaCl_2 = 0.45 \ m$ in particles; $0.050 \ m \ NaCl = 0.10 \ m$ in particles; $0.10 \ m \ H_2SO_4 = 0.30 \ m$ in particles; and $0.30 \ m \ C_6H_{12}O_6 = 0.30 \ m$ in particles. The higher the molality in total particles, the lower the freezing point. Freezing point depression is determined by the equation: $\triangle T = k_f \times m \times i$; where k_f is the molal freezing-point depression constant, m is the concentration of the solute in molality units, and i is the van't Hoff factor (actual number of particles in solution after dissociation/number of formula units initially dissolved in solution).

56. (D) Step 1: Write the balanced equation in a state of equilibrium.

$$HC_2H_3O_{2(aq)} \longleftrightarrow H^+_{(aq)} + C_2H_3O_2^-_{(aq)}$$

Step 2: Write the equilibrium expression.

$$K_a = \frac{[H^+][C_2H_3O_2^-]}{[HC_2H_3O_2]}$$

Step 3: Use the pH of the solution to determine $[H^+]$.

$pH = -\log[H^+] = 2.00$

$H^+ = 10^{-2.00} = 0.0100$ M

Step 4: Determine $[C_2H_3O_2^-]$

The molar ratio of $[H^+]$ to $[C_2H_3O_2^-]$ is 1:1, $[C_2H_3O_2^-] = 0.0100$ M also.

Step 5: Substitute the concentrations into the equilibrium expression.

$[HC_2H_3O_2] = 1.00 - 0.01 = 0.99$ M. The final acetic acid concentration is approximately equal to its initial concentration because acetic acid is a weak acid.

$$K_a = \frac{[H^+][C_2H_3O_2^-]}{[HC_2H_3O_2]} = \frac{(0.0100)^2}{0.99} \approx 1.00 \times 10^{-4}$$

57. (B) Step 1: Write the generic formula for % dissociation.

$$\% \text{ dissociation} = \frac{part}{whole} \times 100\% = \frac{M\ HC_2H_3O_2 \text{ dissociated}}{M\ HC_2H_3O_2 \text{ available}} \times 100\%$$

Step 2: Substitute the known information into the generic equation and solve.

$$\% \text{ dissociation} = \frac{0.0100\ M}{0.99\ M} \times 100\% \approx 1.00\%$$

Note: The 5% rule states that the approximation $a - x \approx a$ is valid if $x < 0.05a$.

58. (B) Carbon-14 has 6 protons and 8 neutrons giving a neutron-to-proton ratio of 1.3:1. Elements with low atomic numbers normally have stable nuclei with approximately equal numbers of neutrons and protons. Thus, C-14 with a high neutron-to-proton ratio results in the emission of a beta particle (high speed electron):

$$^{14}_6C \rightarrow {}^0_{-1}e + {}^{14}_7N$$

Beta particle emission results in the lowering of the neutron-to-proton ratio.

59. (A) Step 1: Write the equation for the dissociation of copper(II) iodate.

$$Cu(IO_3)_{2(s)} \rightarrow Cu^{2+}_{(aq)} + 2\ IO_3^-_{(aq)}$$

Step 2: Write down the concentrations during the process of dissociation.

3.3×10^{-3} M $Cu(IO_3)_{2(aq)} \rightarrow 3.3 \times 10^{-3}$ M $Cu^{2+}_{(aq)} + 2(3.3 \times 10^{-3}$M $IO_3^-_{(aq)})$

$[Cu^{2+}] = 3.3 \times 10^{-3}$ M

$[IO_3^-] = 6.6 \times 10^{-3}$ M

Step 3: Write the equilibrium expression.

$K_{sp} = [Cu^{2+}][IO_3^-]^2$

Step 4: Substitute the equilibrium concentration into the K_{sp} expressions.

$K_{sp} = (3.3 \times 10^{-3})(6.6 \times 10^{-3})^2 = 1.4 \times 10^{-7}$

60. (D) Nitric acid (HNO₃) is a strong acid and sodium hydroxide (NaOH) is a strong base. The curve is steep as it reaches the end point. Choice (A) is a strong acid + a weak base. Choice (B) and (E) are strong bases + weak acids. Choice (C) is a weak acid + a weak base.

61. (E) For a series of oxyacids of the same structure that differ only in the halogen, the acid strength increases with the electronegativity of the halogen. Because the electronegativity of the halogens increases as we move up the column, the order at this point would be HClO > HBrO > HIO. For a series of oxyacids containing the same halogen, the H–O bond polarity, and hence the acid strength, increases with the oxidation states of the chlorine; i.e., +1, +3, and +5, respectively. And thus, the correct order for decreasing acid strength is HClO₃ > HClO₂ > HClO > HBrO > HIO.

62. (E)

63. (B)

64. (D)

65. (A)

66. (C)

67. (D) Step 1: Calculate the number of moles of H⁺ in 250 mL of a HNO₃ solution which has a pH of 2.00. HNO₃ is a monoprotic acid, pH = –log[H⁺], so 2.00 = –log[H⁺] and [H⁺] = 1.00 × 10⁻² M.

$$\text{mole } H^+ = \frac{1.00 \times 10^{-2} \text{ mole } H^+}{1 \text{ liter}} \times \frac{0.25 \text{ liter}}{1}$$

$$= 2.5 \times 10^{-3} \text{ mole } H^+$$

Step 2: Determine the number of milliliters of concentrated HNO₃ solution that is needed.

$$\frac{2.5 \times 10^{-3} \text{ mole } H^+}{1} \times \frac{1000 \text{ mL sol'n}}{2.00 \text{ mole } H^+} = 1.3 \text{ mL sol'n}$$

68. (B) Metals have ionization energies (or ionization potentials) that are much lower than those of the nonmetals since a smaller amount of energy is required to remove an electron from a metal than from a nonmetal. Removal of an electron(s) is called oxidation. Nonmetals, on the other hand, have high electron affinities compared to metals and tend to gain electrons. Gain of electrons is called reduction.

69. (E) At equilibrium, $\triangle G = 0 = \triangle G° + 2.303 \, RT \log K$

(at equilibrium $Q = K$)

$\triangle G° = -2.303 \, (8.314 \, J \cdot K^{-1}) \, (298K) \, (\log 1 \times 10^{-3})$

Rounding,

$\sim -2.3 \, (8.3) \, (300) \, (-3.0) \approx 20 \text{ kJ}$

70. (A) The formula that is used to determine change in internal energy is $\triangle E = q + w$, where $\triangle E$ is the change in internal energy, q is the heat added to or released from the system, and w is the work on or by the system. Both the heat lost by the system and the work done by the system on its surroundings are negative in sign. Therefore, $\triangle E = q + w = (700J) + (-300J) = -1000$ J. Thus, 1000 J of energy has been transferred from the system to the surroundings.

71. (D) Notice that $E°_{red}$ for silver is lower than $E°_{red}$ for gold. This means that because silver is higher in the activity series, silver metal will reduce the gold ion.

Step 1: Write the net cell reaction:

$Ag_{(s)} + Au^+_{(aq)} \rightarrow Ag^+_{(aq)} + Au_{(s)}$

Step 2: Write the two half-reactions and include the E°_{red} and E°_{ox} values.

ox: $Ag_{(s)} \longleftrightarrow Ag^+_{(aq)} + e^-$ $E^\circ_{ox} = -0.80$ volt

red: $Au^+_{(aq)} + e^- \longleftrightarrow Au_{(s)}$ $E^\circ_{red} = 1.68$ volts

_____

$Ag_{(s)} + Au^+_{(aq)} \longleftrightarrow Ag^+_{(aq)} + Au_{(s)}$ $E^\circ = +0.88$ volt

Because the sign of E° is positive, the reaction will proceed spontaneously.

72. (A) The more positive the E°_{red} value, the greater the tendency for the substance to be reduced, and conversely, the less likely it is to be oxidized. It would help in this example to reverse the last equation so it can be easily compared to the other E°_{red} values. The last equation becomes $Ni^{2+}_{(aq)} + 2e^- \rightarrow Ni_{(s)}$; $E^\circ_{red} = -0.25$ V.

The equation with the largest E°_{red} is $Cu^{2+}_{(aq)} + e^- \rightarrow Cu^+_{(aq)}$; $E^\circ_{red} = 0.34$ V. Thus, $Cu^{2+}_{(aq)}$ is the strongest oxidizing agent of those listed because it has the greatest tendency to be reduced. Conversely, $Cu^+_{(aq)}$ would be the weakest reducing agent. $Fe^{2+}_{(aq)}$ would be the weakest oxidizing agent because it would be the most difficult species to reduce. Conversely, $Fe_{(s)}$ would be the strongest reducing agent.

73. (A) Reduction occurs at the cathode. You can eliminate choices (B), (D), and (E) because these reactions are oxidations. E°_{red} for $Fe^{2+}_{(aq)}$ is -0.44 V, and E°_{red} for $Zn^{2+}_{(aq)}$ is -0.76 V. Because $Fe^{2+}_{(aq)}$ has the more positive E°_{red} of the two choices, $Fe^{2+}_{(aq)}$ is the more easily reduced and therefore plates out on the cathode.

74. (C) A second-order reaction depends on the reactant concentration raised to the second power or on the concentrations of two different reactants, each raised to the first power. The rate law is given by rate $= k[A]^2$ which can be derived into the equation

$$\frac{1}{[A]_t} = k \cdot t + \frac{1}{[A]_o}$$

and has the form of a straight line ($y = mx + b$). The plot of $1/[A]_t$ vs. t will yield a straight line with a slope equal to k and a y-intercept equal to $1/[A]_o$.

75. (B) Use the equation $M_1V_1 = M_2V_2$, where the 1 represents initial conditions (before dilution) and the 2 represents final conditions (after dilution). In this case

$$V_1 = \frac{M_2 V_2}{M_1} = \frac{(0.50 \text{ M})(500 \text{ mL})}{(2.0 \text{ M})} = 125 \text{ mL}$$

Section II: Free-Response Questions

Scoring Guidelines

One point deduction for mathematical error (maximum once per question)

One point deduction for error in significant figures (maximum once per question and the number of significant figures must be correct within +/− one digit)

Part A:

Question 1

1. 250.0 grams of solid copper(II) nitrate is placed in an empty 4.0-liter flask. Upon heating the flask to 250°C, some of the solid decomposes into solid copper(II) oxide, gaseous nitrogen(IV) oxide, and oxygen gas. At equilibrium, the pressure is measured and found to be 5.50 atmospheres.

   (a) Write the balanced equation for the reaction.

$2Cu(NO_3)_{2(s)} \longrightarrow 2CuO_{(s)} + 4NO_{2(g)} + O_{2(g)}$	1 point for correct balanced equation.

   (b) Calculate the number of moles of oxygen gas present in the flask at equilibrium.

$PV = nRT$ $T = 250°C + 273 = 523K$	1 point for correct equation and correct temperature.
$n = \dfrac{PV}{RT} = \dfrac{(5.50 \text{ atm})(4.0 \text{ liters})}{(0.0821 \text{ liter} \cdot \text{atm} / \text{mol} \cdot \text{K})(523\text{K})}$ $= 0.51$ moles gas	1 point for correct number of total moles of gas.
4 mol NO_2 + 1 mol O_2 = 5 mol total gas $\dfrac{0.51 \text{ mole gas}}{1} \times \dfrac{1 \text{ mole } O_2}{5 \text{ moles gas}} = 0.10 \text{ mole } O_2$	1 point for correct number of moles of O_2.

   (c) Calculate the number of grams of solid copper(II) nitrate that remained in the flask at equilibrium.

moles of $Cu(NO_3)_2$ that decomposed: $\dfrac{0.10 \text{ mole } O_2}{1} \times \dfrac{2 \text{ moles } Cu(NO_3)_2}{1 \text{ mole } O_2}$ $= 0.20 \text{ mole } Cu(NO_3)_2$ mass of $Cu(NO_3)_2$ that decomposed: $\dfrac{0.20 \text{ mole } Cu(NO_3)_2}{1} \times \dfrac{187.57 \text{ g } Cu(NO_3)_2}{1 \text{ mole } Cu(NO_3)_2}$ $= 38 \text{ g } Cu(NO_3)_2$	1 point for correct number of grams of $Cu(NO_3)_2$.
mass of $Cu(NO_3)_2$ that remains in flask: 250.0 $Cu(NO_3)_2$ originally − 38 g $Cu(NO_3)_2$ that decomposed = 212 g $Cu(NO_3)_2$ that remains	1 point for correct number of grams of $Cu(NO_3)_2$ that remained.

(d) Write the equilibrium expression for K_p and calculate the value of the equilibrium constant.

$K_p = (\text{pressure } NO_2)^4 \times (\text{pressure } O_2)$	1 point for correct equilibrium expression.
$\dfrac{4 \text{ moles } NO_{2(g)}}{5 \text{ total moles gas}} \times \dfrac{5.50 \text{ atm}}{1} = 4.40 \text{ atm } NO_2$	1 point for correct number of atm of NO_2.
$5.50 \text{ atm}_{tot} - 4.40 \text{ atm}_{NO_2} = 1.10 \text{ atm } O_2$ $K_p = (4.40)^4 (1.10) = 412.$	1 point for correct value of K_p.

(e) If 420.0 grams of the copper(II) nitrate had been placed into the empty flask at 250°C, what would the total pressure have been at equilibrium?

Because the temperature was kept constant, as was the size of the flask, and because some of the original 250.0 grams of $Cu(NO_3)_2$ was left as solid in the flask at equilibrium, any extra $Cu(NO_3)_2$ introduced into the flask would remain as solid—there would be no substantial change in the pressure. The amount of pure solid does not affect equilibrium (as long as *some* solid remains at equilibrium).	1 point for correct conclusion.

Question 2

2. The reaction $2NO_{2(g)} + Cl_{2(g)} \rightarrow 2NO_2Cl_{(g)}$ was studied at 20°C and the following data were obtained

Experiment	Initial [NO$_2$] (mole · liter^{-1})	Initial [Cl$_2$] (mole · liter^{-1})	Initial Rate of Increase of [NO$_2$Cl] (mole · liter^{-1} · sec^{-1})
1	0.100	0.005	1.35×10^{-7}
2	0.100	0.010	2.70×10^{-7}
3	0.200	0.010	5.40×10^{-7}

(a) Write the rate law for the reaction.

rate = $k[NO_2]^n[Cl_2]^m$ Expt. 1: rate = 1.35×10^{-7} mole/(liter · sec) = $k(0.100 \text{ M})^n(0.0050 \text{ M})^m$ Expt. 2: rate = 2.70×10^{-7} mole/(liter · sec) = $k(0.100\text{M})^n(0.010 \text{ M})^m$ Expt. 3: rate = 5.4×10^{-7} mole/(liter · sec) = $k(0.200 \text{ M})^n(0.010 \text{ M})^m$ $\dfrac{\text{rate 2}}{\text{rate 1}} = \dfrac{2.70 \times 10^{-7} \text{ mole}/(\text{liter} \cdot \text{sec})}{1.35 \times 10^{-7} \text{ mole}/(\text{liter} \cdot \text{sec})}$ $= \dfrac{k(0.100 \text{ M})^n (0.010 \text{ M})^m}{k(0.0100 \text{ M})^n (0.0050 \text{ M})^m}$ $2.00 = (2.0)^m \qquad m = 1$ $\dfrac{\text{rate 3}}{\text{rate 2}} = \dfrac{5.40 \times 10^{-7} \text{ mole}/(\text{liter} \cdot \text{sec})}{2.70 \times 10^{-7} \text{ mole}/(\text{liter} \cdot \text{sec})}$ $= \dfrac{k(0.200 \text{ M})^n (0.010 \text{ M})^m}{k(0.100 \text{ M})^n (0.010 \text{ M})^m}$ $2.00 = (2.00)^n$ $n = 1$	1 point for correct setup for determining rate law.
rate = $k[NO_2]^1[Cl_2]^1$	1 point for correct rate law.

(b) What is the overall order for the reaction? Explain.

overall order = $m + n = 1 + 1 = 2$	1 point for correct determination of the overall order.
The rate is proportional to the product of the concentrations of the two reactants: $2NO_{2(g)} + Cl_{2(g)} \rightarrow 2NO_2Cl_{(g)}$ $\text{rate} = \dfrac{-\Delta[NO_2]}{\Delta t} = k[NO_2][Cl_2]$ or $\text{rate} = \dfrac{-2\Delta[Cl_2]}{\Delta t} = k[NO_2][Cl_2]$	1 point for correct explanation.

(c) Calculate the rate-specific constant, including the correct units.

rate = $k[NO_2][Cl_2]$	1 point for correct setup.
$k = \dfrac{\text{rate}}{[NO_2][Cl_2]}$ $= \dfrac{1.35 \times 10^{-7} \text{ mole} \cdot \text{liter}^{-1} \cdot \text{sec}^{-1}}{(0.100 \text{ mole} \cdot \text{liter}^{-1})(0.005 \text{ mole} \cdot \text{liter}^{-1})}$ $= 2.7 \times 10^{-4} \text{ liter}/(\text{mole} \cdot \text{sec})$	1 point for correct answer with proper units.

(d) In Experiment 3, what is the initial rate of decrease of $[Cl_2]$?

$2 NO_{2(g)} + Cl_{2(g)} \rightarrow 2NO_2Cl_{(g)}$	1 point for correct setup to determine initial rate of decrease.
$\dfrac{-d[Cl_2]}{dt} = \dfrac{1}{2}\left(\dfrac{d[NO_2Cl]}{dt}\right)$ $= \dfrac{-(5.40 \times 10^{-7})}{2}$ $= -2.70 \times 10^{-7} \text{ mole} \cdot \text{liter} \cdot \text{sec}^{-1}$	1 point for correct answer.

(e) Propose a mechanism for the reaction that is consistent with the rate law expression you found in part (a) and showing how you derived it.

The proposed mechanism must satisfy two requirements: (1) The sum of the steps must give a balanced equation. (2) The mechanism must agree with the experimentally determined rate law. $NO_{2(g)} + Cl_{2(g)} \xrightarrow{k_1} NO_2Cl_{(g)} + Cl_{(g)}$ slow $Cl_{(g)} + NO_{2(g)} \xrightarrow{k_2} NO_2Cl_{(g)}$ fast	1 point for correct explanation of how the mechanism was determined.
Requirement 1: $NO_{2(g)} + Cl_{2(g)} \rightarrow NO_2Cl_{(g)} + \cancel{Cl_{(g)}}$ $\cancel{Cl_{(g)}} + NO_{2(g)} \rightarrow NO_2Cl_{(g)}$ $\overline{2NO_{2(g)} + Cl_{2(g)} \rightarrow 2NO_2Cl_{(g)}}$ Requirement 2: $NO_{2(g)} + Cl_{2(g)} \rightarrow NO_2Cl_{(g)} + Cl_{(g)}$ is the rate-determining step. This step is bimolecular. rate $= k_1[NO_2][Cl_2]$ as found in part (a). **Note:** Meeting these two requirements does not prove that this *is* the mechanism for the reaction— only that it *could* be.	1 point for a correct mechanism.

Question 3

3. A student wanted to determine the molecular weight of a monoprotic, solid acid, symbolized as HA. The student carefully measured out 25.000 grams of HA and dissolved it in distilled H_2O to bring the volume of the solution to exactly 500.00 mL. The student next measured out several fifty-mL aliquots of the acid solution and then titrated it against standardized 0.100 M NaOH solution. The results of the three titrations are given in the following table:

Trial	mL of HA Solution	mL of NaOH Solution
1	49.12	87.45
2	49.00	84.68
3	48.84	91.23

(a) Calculate the number of moles of HA in the fifty-mL aliquots.

At the end of titration, moles of HA = moles of NaOH average volume of NaOH $= \dfrac{87.45 + 84.68 + 91.23}{3}$ $= 87.79$ mL	1 point for proper setup.
moles HA = moles NaOH = $V_{NaOH} \times M_{NaOH}$ $= \dfrac{0.08779 \text{ liter}}{1} \times \dfrac{0.100 \text{ mole}}{1 \text{ liter}} = 8.78 \times 10^{-3}$ mole	1 point for correct number of moles of HA.

(b) Calculate the molecular weight of the acid, HA.

average mL of HA solution = $\dfrac{49.12 + 49.00 + 48.84}{3} = 48.99$ mL	1 point for proper setup.
$MW = \dfrac{48.99 \text{ mL HA sol'n}}{8.78 \times 10^{-3} \text{ mole HA}} \times \dfrac{25.00 \text{ g HA}}{500.00 \text{ mL HA sol'n}}$ $= 279$ g / mole	1 point for correct MW.

(c) Calculate the pH of the fifty-mL aliquot solution (assume complete ionization).

moles H^+ = moles HA due to complete ionization of the acid $[H^+] = \dfrac{\text{moles } H^+}{\text{liters solution}} = \dfrac{8.78 \times 10^{-3} \text{ mole } H^+}{0.04899 \text{ liter HA sol'n}}$ $= 0.179$ M	1 point for proper setup.
pH = $-\log$ [0.179] = 0.747	1 point for correct pH.

(d) Calculate the pOH of the fifty-mL aliquot solution (assume complete ionization).

pOH = 14.000 − pH = 14.000 − 0.747 = 13.253	1 point for correct pOH.

(e) Discuss how each of the following errors would affect the determination of the molecular weight of the acid, HA.

(i) The balance that the student used in measuring out the 25.000 grams of HA was reading 0.010 grams too low.

Student would think they had 25.000 grams when there were actually 25.010 grams. In the calculation of molecular weight (grams/mole), the grams would be too low, so the effect would be a lower MW than expected.	1 point for correct explanation.

(ii) There was an impurity in the acid, HA.

Student would have less HA than expected. In the calculation of molecular weight (g/mole), there would be less HA available than expected. Therefore, in the titration against NaOH, it would take less NaOH than expected to reach the equivalence point. This error would cause a larger MW than expected because the denominator moles) would be smaller. The results assume that the impurity does not have more H⁺/mass of impurity than the HA.	1 point for correct explanation.

(iii) The NaOH solution used in titration was actually 0.150 M instead of 0.100 M.

It would take less NaOH to reach the equivalence point because the NaOH is stronger. Because it would take less NaOH, the number of moles of NaOH would be less than expected, causing the denominator (moles) to be smaller than expected, making the calculated MW larger than expected. **Note:** Using volume averages in the design of this particular experiment can lead to inaccuracy. A better design would be to calculate three values for molecular weight from three separate runs and average the results.	1 point for correct explanation.

Part B:

Question 4

(For a complete list of reactive types that you will encounter, refer to *CliffsAP Chemistry,* 3rd Edition)

(a) A solution of aluminum nitrate is added to a solution of sodium phosphate.

$Al^{3+} + PO_4^{3-} \rightarrow AlPO_4$	1 point for reactant(s), 2 points for product(s).
	Precipitation reaction due to phosphate ion's general insolubility.

(b) Hot steam is mixed with propene gas.

$C_3H_6 + H_2O \rightarrow C_3H_7OH$	1 point for reactant(s), 2 points for product(s).
	$$\begin{array}{ccc} H & H & H \\ | & | & | \\ H-C-C-C-H \\ | & | & | \\ H & OH & H \end{array}$$
	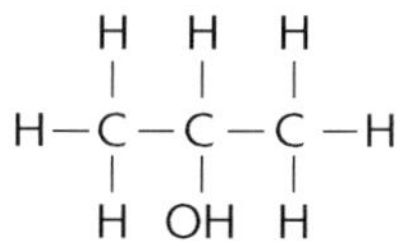 Organic addition.

(c) Manganese dioxide (acting as a catalyst) is added to a solid sample of potassium chlorate and the mixture is then heated.

$KClO_3 \xrightarrow{MnO_2} KCl + O_2$	1 point for reactant(s), 2 points for product(s).
	Decomposition ($AB \rightarrow A + B$).

(d) Hydroiodic acid is mixed with solid calcium carbonate.

$H^+ + CO_3^{2-} \rightarrow HCO_3^-$ or $H^+ + CO_3^{2-} \rightarrow H_2CO_3$ or $H^+ + CO_3^{2-} \rightarrow CO_2 + H_2O$	1 point for reactant(s), 2 points for product(s).
	Acid + carbonate $\rightarrow$ salt + CO_2 + water. Iodide and calcium ions are spectator ions.

(e) A piece of aluminum is dropped into a solution of lead chloride.

$Al + Pb^{2+} \rightarrow Al^{3+} + Pb$	1 point for reactant(s), 2 points for product(s).
	Redox.

(f) Solid calcium oxide is added to silicon dioxide and the mixture is heated strongly.

$CaO + SiO_2 \rightarrow CaSiO_3$	1 point for reactant(s), 2 points for product(s).
	Synthesis ($A + B \rightarrow AB$).

(g) A concentrated potassium hydroxide solution is added to solid aluminum hydroxide.

	1 point for reactant(s), 2 points for product(s).
$OH^- + Al(OH)_3 \rightarrow Al(OH)_4^-$	Complex ions. Ligands are generally electron pair donors (Lewis bases). Important ligands are NH_3, CN^-, and OH^-. Ligands bond to a central atom that is usually the positive ion of a transition metal, forming complex ions and coordination compounds.

(h) Chloromethane is bubbled through a solution of warm ammonia.

	1 point for reactant(s), 2 points for product(s).
$CH_3Cl + NH_3 \rightarrow CH_3NH_3 + Cl^-$	Organic substitution.

Question 5

5. A student was given three flasks that were labeled X, Y, and Z. Each flask contains one of the following solutions: 1.0 M $AgNO_3$, 1.0 M $Pb(NO_3)_2$, or 1.0 M $Al_2(SO_4)_3$.

The student was also given three flasks that were labeled A, B and C. One of these flasks contained 1.0 M NaOH, another contained 1.0 M K_2CrO_4 and another contained 1.0 M NaI. This information is summarized in the diagram below.

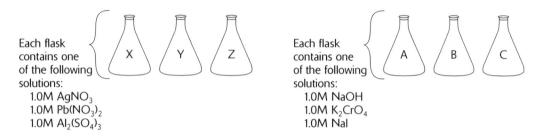

Each flask contains one of the following solutions:
1.0M $AgNO_3$
1.0M $Pb(NO_3)_2$
1.0M $Al_2(SO_4)_3$

Each flask contains one of the following solutions:
1.0M NaOH
1.0M K_2CrO_4
1.0M NaI

(a) The student combined samples from flask X and flask A and noticed a brick-red precipitate.

    (i) Identify the solutions in flasks X and A.

The brick-red precipitate was identified as silver chromate; thus, flask X must be $AgNO_3$ and flask A must be K_2CrO_4.	1 point for correct identification of X and 1 point for correct identification of A.

    (ii) Write the balanced chemical reaction that occurred when solutions X and A were mixed. Omit formulas for any ions or molecules that were unchanged by the reaction.

$2Ag^+_{(aq)} + CrO_4^{2-}_{(aq)} \rightarrow Ag_2CrO_{4(s)}$	1 point for correct formula and 1 point if balanced properly.

(b) When samples from flask X and B were mixed a brown precipitate was formed.

    (i) Identify the solution in flask B.

The brown precipitate was identified as silver hydroxide. Therefore B must be NaOH.	1 point for correctly identifying flask B as containing NaOH.

    (ii) Write the chemical reaction that occurred when solutions from flasks X and B were mixed.

$Ag^+_{(aq)} + OH^-_{(aq)} \rightarrow AgOH_{(s)}$	1 point for correct formulas and 1 point if balanced properly.

(c) How would you be able to determine for sure which flask contained $Pb(NO_3)_2$?

Because I was able to determine that A contained K_2CrO_4 and B contained NaOH, by default flask C must contain NaI. I would mix samples from flask C with samples from flasks Y and Z. Since lead iodide (PbI_2) is a yellow precipitate, the flask when mixed with sample from flask C that produced a yellow precipitate would contain $Pb(NO_3)_2$.	1 point for correct logic.

(d) Write the net ionic equation for the reaction that would produce PbI_2.

$Pb^{2+}_{(aq)} + 2I^-_{(aq)} \rightarrow PbI_{2(s)}$	1 point for correctly balanced equation.

(e) What test could you do to confirm that the flask that did not produce PbI_2 (either Y or Z) contained $Al_2(SO_4)_3$?

Aluminum hydroxide is a white precipitate. If I take samples from the flask that did not produce PbI_2, and mix it with a sample from flask B which I know contains NaOH, I should produce the white aluminum hydroxide precipitate.	1 point for correct explanation and logic.

Question 6

6. Explain each of the following in terms of (1) inter- and intra- atomic or molecular forces and (2) structure.

(a) ICl has a boiling point of 97°C, whereas NaCl has a boiling point of 1400°C.

ICl is a covalently bonded, molecular solid; NaCl is an ionic solid.	
There are dipole forces between ICl molecules but electrostatic forces between Na^+ and Cl^- ions.	
Dipole forces in ICl are much weaker that the ionic bonds in NaCl.	1 point each for any two of the reasons listed on the left.
I and Cl are similar in electronegativity—generates only partial δ^+ and δ^- around molecule.	
Na and Cl differ greatly in electronegativity—greater electrostatic force.	
When heated slightly, ICl boils because energy supplied (heat) overcomes weak dipole forces.	

(b) $KI_{(s)}$ is very soluble in water, whereas $I_{2(s)}$ has a solubility of only 0.03 grams per 100 grams of water.

KI is an ionic solid, held together by ionic bonds.	
I_2 is a molecular solid, held together by covalent bonds.	
KI dissociates into K^+ and I^- ions.	1 point each for any two of the reasons listed on the left.
I_2 slightly dissolves in water, maintaining its covalent bond.	
Solubility rule: Like dissolves like. H_2O is polar; KI is polar; I_2 is not polar.	

(c) Solid Ag conducts an electric current, whereas solid $AgNO_3$ does not.

Ag is a metal.	
$AgNO_3$ is an ionic solid.	
Ag structure consists of Ag^+ cations surrounded by mobile or "free" electrons.	1 point each for any two of the reasons listed on the left.
$AgNO_3$ structure consists of Ag^+ cations electrostatically attracted to NO_3^- polyatomic anions—no free or mobile electrons.	

(d) PCl_3 has a measurable dipole moment, whereas PCl_5 does not.

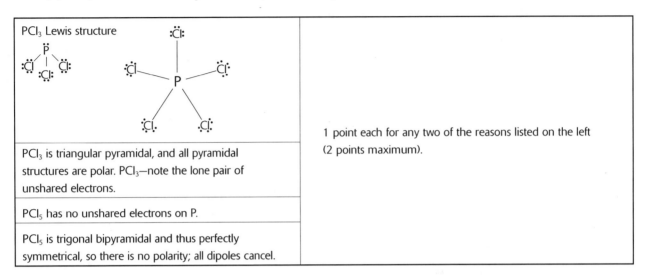

PCl₃ Lewis structure	1 point each for any two of the reasons listed on the left (2 points maximum).
PCl_3 is triangular pyramidal, and all pyramidal structures are polar. PCl_3—note the lone pair of unshared electrons.	
PCl_5 has no unshared electrons on P.	
PCl_5 is trigonal bipyramidal and thus perfectly symmetrical, so there is no polarity; all dipoles cancel.	

(e) The carbon-to-carbon bond energy in C_2H_5Cl is less than it is in C_2H_3Cl.

C_2H_3Cl has a double bond between the carbon atoms (see diagram below) whereas C_2H_5Cl contains a single bond between the carbon atoms (see diagram below). Less energy is required to break a single bond than a double bond.	1 point for indicating that C_2H_5Cl has a single bond between the carbon atoms and that C_2H_3Cl has a double bond between the carbon atoms.
	1 point for indicating that a double bond requires more energy to break than a single bond.

Question 7

7. Butadiene, C_4H_6, is a planar molecule that has the following carbon-carbon bond lengths in Å (10^{-10}m).

$$H_2C\underset{1.34}{=}CH\underset{1.48}{-}CH\underset{1.34}{=}CH_2$$

(a) Predict the approximate bond angles around each of the carbon atoms.

All bond angles around the carbon atoms should be approximately 120°.	1 point for correct bond angle.

(b) Predict the hybridization of the carbon atoms. Explain your reasoning.

All carbon atoms should exhibit sp^2 hybridization. sp^2 hybridization results in three equivalent hybrids directed to the corners of an equilateral triangle, leaving one p orbital perpendicular to the plane of the hybrids.	1 point for correct hybridization.
	1 point for correct interpretation.

(c) Sketch the 3-dimensional structure of the molecule.

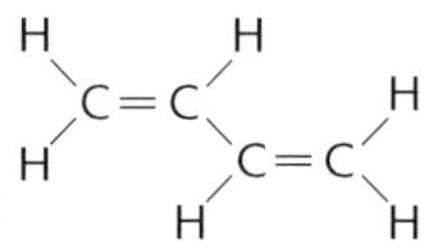	1 point for correct structure.

(d) How many total sigma and pi bonds are in this molecule?

Each double bond consists of one sigma and one pi bond. Each single bond consists of one sigma bond. Therefore because there are two double bonds and seven single bonds, there are nine sigma bonds and two pi bonds.	1 point for correct number of sigma bonds.
	1 point for correct number of pi bonds.

(e) Compare the bond lengths shown above with established average bond lengths for C—C at 1.54 Å and C=C at 1.34 Å. Explain any differences.

The shorter C–C single bond distance in butadiene comes about because the two carbon atoms in the bond are sp^2 hybridized.	1 point for correct explanation.

(f) Are there any *cis-*, *trans-* isomers for this compound? Explain your reason(s).

No. Because the two carbon C=C groups have identical constituents (H atom) on one of the carbon atoms in each double bond.	1 point for correct explanation.

(g) Replace the CH_2 (one only) group in the above structure with CHCl. Draw and label all geometric isomers that the new compound may have.

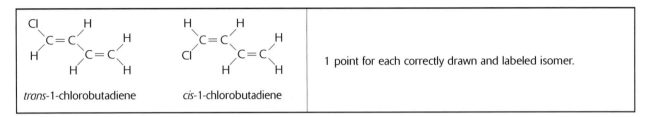

trans-1-chlorobutadiene *cis*-1-chlorobutadiene	1 point for each correctly drawn and labeled isomer.

Question 8

The first three ionization energies (I_1, I_2, and I_3) for beryllium and neon are given in the following table.

(kJ/mole)	I_1	I_2	I_3
Be	900	1,757	14,840
Ne	2,080	3,963	6,276

(a) Write the complete electron configuration for beryllium and for neon.

Be: $1s^2 2s^2$ Ne: $1s^2 2s^2 2p^6$	1 point each for correct electron configuration.

(b) Draw the Lewis diagrams for Be and Ne.

B̈e :N̈e:	1 point each for correct Lewis diagram.

(c) Explain any trends or significant discrepancies found in the ionization energies for beryllium and neon.

■ In the case of both beryllium and neon, ionization energies increase as one moves from I_1 to I_2 to I_3. ■ The general trend is for ionization energy to increase as one moves from left to right across the periodic table and to decrease as one moves down; this is the reverse of the trend one finds in examining the atomic radius. ■ Both beryllium and neon are in the second period. ■ Beryllium: There is generally not enough energy available in chemical reactions to remove inner electrons, as noted by the significantly higher third ionization energy. ■ Beryllium: The Be^{2+} ion is a very stable species with a noble-gas configuration, so removing a third electron from beryllium requires significantly greater energy. ■ Neon: Neon is an inert element with a full complement of 8 electrons in its valence shell. ■ Neon: It is significantly more difficult to remove neon's most loosely held electron (I_1) than that of beryllium's (I_1). This trend is also noted when examining I_2's and I_3's. ■ Neon: Neon also has a greater nuclear charge than beryllium, which if all factors are held constant, would result in a smaller atomic radius.	1 point each for any of the concepts listed to the left.

(d) If chlorine gas is passed into separate containers of heated beryllium and heated neon, explain what compounds (if any) might be formed, and explain your answer in terms of the electron configurations of these two elements.

The only compound formed would be $BeCl_2$. The Be atom readily loses 2 electrons to form the stable Be^{2+} ion. The third ionization energy is too high to form Be^{3+}. The electron affinity of neon is very low because it has a stable octet of electrons in its valence shell and the ionization energies of neon are too high.	1 point for any of the points listed to the left.

(e) An unknown element, X, has the following three ionization energies:

(kJ/mole)	I_1	I_2	I_3
X	419	3,069	4,600

On the basis of the ionization energies given, what is most likely to be the compound produced when chlorine reacts with element X and provide explanation.

The first ionization energy (I_1) of element X is relatively low when compared to I_2 and I_3. This means that X is probably a member of the Group I alkali metals. Thus, the formation of X^{2+} and X^{3+} would be difficult to achieve. Therefore, the formula is most likely to be XCl.	1 point for correct answer of XCl and 1 point for correct explanation.

Multiple-Choice Answer Sheet for Practice Exam 4

Remove this sheet and use it to mark your answers.
Answer sheets for "Section II: Free-Response Questions" can be found at the end of this book.

Section I
Multiple-Choice Questions

CUT HERE

1 Ⓐ Ⓑ Ⓒ Ⓓ Ⓔ	26 Ⓐ Ⓑ Ⓒ Ⓓ Ⓔ	51 Ⓐ Ⓑ Ⓒ Ⓓ Ⓔ
2 Ⓐ Ⓑ Ⓒ Ⓓ Ⓔ	27 Ⓐ Ⓑ Ⓒ Ⓓ Ⓔ	52 Ⓐ Ⓑ Ⓒ Ⓓ Ⓔ
3 Ⓐ Ⓑ Ⓒ Ⓓ Ⓔ	28 Ⓐ Ⓑ Ⓒ Ⓓ Ⓔ	53 Ⓐ Ⓑ Ⓒ Ⓓ Ⓔ
4 Ⓐ Ⓑ Ⓒ Ⓓ Ⓔ	29 Ⓐ Ⓑ Ⓒ Ⓓ Ⓔ	54 Ⓐ Ⓑ Ⓒ Ⓓ Ⓔ
5 Ⓐ Ⓑ Ⓒ Ⓓ Ⓔ	30 Ⓐ Ⓑ Ⓒ Ⓓ Ⓔ	55 Ⓐ Ⓑ Ⓒ Ⓓ Ⓔ
6 Ⓐ Ⓑ Ⓒ Ⓓ Ⓔ	31 Ⓐ Ⓑ Ⓒ Ⓓ Ⓔ	56 Ⓐ Ⓑ Ⓒ Ⓓ Ⓔ
7 Ⓐ Ⓑ Ⓒ Ⓓ Ⓔ	32 Ⓐ Ⓑ Ⓒ Ⓓ Ⓔ	57 Ⓐ Ⓑ Ⓒ Ⓓ Ⓔ
8 Ⓐ Ⓑ Ⓒ Ⓓ Ⓔ	33 Ⓐ Ⓑ Ⓒ Ⓓ Ⓔ	58 Ⓐ Ⓑ Ⓒ Ⓓ Ⓔ
9 Ⓐ Ⓑ Ⓒ Ⓓ Ⓔ	34 Ⓐ Ⓑ Ⓒ Ⓓ Ⓔ	59 Ⓐ Ⓑ Ⓒ Ⓓ Ⓔ
10 Ⓐ Ⓑ Ⓒ Ⓓ Ⓔ	35 Ⓐ Ⓑ Ⓒ Ⓓ Ⓔ	60 Ⓐ Ⓑ Ⓒ Ⓓ Ⓔ
11 Ⓐ Ⓑ Ⓒ Ⓓ Ⓔ	36 Ⓐ Ⓑ Ⓒ Ⓓ Ⓔ	61 Ⓐ Ⓑ Ⓒ Ⓓ Ⓔ
12 Ⓐ Ⓑ Ⓒ Ⓓ Ⓔ	37 Ⓐ Ⓑ Ⓒ Ⓓ Ⓔ	62 Ⓐ Ⓑ Ⓒ Ⓓ Ⓔ
13 Ⓐ Ⓑ Ⓒ Ⓓ Ⓔ	38 Ⓐ Ⓑ Ⓒ Ⓓ Ⓔ	63 Ⓐ Ⓑ Ⓒ Ⓓ Ⓔ
14 Ⓐ Ⓑ Ⓒ Ⓓ Ⓔ	39 Ⓐ Ⓑ Ⓒ Ⓓ Ⓔ	64 Ⓐ Ⓑ Ⓒ Ⓓ Ⓔ
15 Ⓐ Ⓑ Ⓒ Ⓓ Ⓔ	40 Ⓐ Ⓑ Ⓒ Ⓓ Ⓔ	65 Ⓐ Ⓑ Ⓒ Ⓓ Ⓔ
16 Ⓐ Ⓑ Ⓒ Ⓓ Ⓔ	41 Ⓐ Ⓑ Ⓒ Ⓓ Ⓔ	66 Ⓐ Ⓑ Ⓒ Ⓓ Ⓔ
17 Ⓐ Ⓑ Ⓒ Ⓓ Ⓔ	42 Ⓐ Ⓑ Ⓒ Ⓓ Ⓔ	67 Ⓐ Ⓑ Ⓒ Ⓓ Ⓔ
18 Ⓐ Ⓑ Ⓒ Ⓓ Ⓔ	43 Ⓐ Ⓑ Ⓒ Ⓓ Ⓔ	68 Ⓐ Ⓑ Ⓒ Ⓓ Ⓔ
19 Ⓐ Ⓑ Ⓒ Ⓓ Ⓔ	44 Ⓐ Ⓑ Ⓒ Ⓓ Ⓔ	69 Ⓐ Ⓑ Ⓒ Ⓓ Ⓔ
20 Ⓐ Ⓑ Ⓒ Ⓓ Ⓔ	45 Ⓐ Ⓑ Ⓒ Ⓓ Ⓔ	70 Ⓐ Ⓑ Ⓒ Ⓓ Ⓔ
21 Ⓐ Ⓑ Ⓒ Ⓓ Ⓔ	46 Ⓐ Ⓑ Ⓒ Ⓓ Ⓔ	71 Ⓐ Ⓑ Ⓒ Ⓓ Ⓔ
22 Ⓐ Ⓑ Ⓒ Ⓓ Ⓔ	47 Ⓐ Ⓑ Ⓒ Ⓓ Ⓔ	72 Ⓐ Ⓑ Ⓒ Ⓓ Ⓔ
23 Ⓐ Ⓑ Ⓒ Ⓓ Ⓔ	48 Ⓐ Ⓑ Ⓒ Ⓓ Ⓔ	73 Ⓐ Ⓑ Ⓒ Ⓓ Ⓔ
24 Ⓐ Ⓑ Ⓒ Ⓓ Ⓔ	49 Ⓐ Ⓑ Ⓒ Ⓓ Ⓔ	74 Ⓐ Ⓑ Ⓒ Ⓓ Ⓔ
25 Ⓐ Ⓑ Ⓒ Ⓓ Ⓔ	50 Ⓐ Ⓑ Ⓒ Ⓓ Ⓔ	75 Ⓐ Ⓑ Ⓒ Ⓓ Ⓔ

PERIODIC TABLE OF THE ELEMENTS

1																	2
H 1.0079																	**He** 4.0026
3 **Li** 6.941	4 **Be** 9.012											5 **B** 10.811	6 **C** 12.011	7 **N** 14.007	8 **O** 16.00	9 **F** 19.00	10 **Ne** 20.179
11 **Na** 22.99	12 **Mg** 24.30											13 **Al** 26.98	14 **Si** 28.09	15 **P** 30.974	16 **S** 32.06	17 **Cl** 35.453	18 **Ar** 39.948
19 **K** 39.10	20 **Ca** 40.08	21 **Sc** 44.96	22 **Ti** 47.90	23 **V** 50.94	24 **Cr** 51.00	25 **Mn** 54.93	26 **Fe** 55.85	27 **Co** 58.93	28 **Ni** 58.69	29 **Cu** 63.55	30 **Zn** 65.39	31 **Ga** 69.72	32 **Ge** 72.59	33 **As** 74.92	34 **Se** 78.96	35 **Br** 79.90	36 **Kr** 83.80
37 **Rb** 85.47	38 **Sr** 87.62	39 **Y** 88.91	40 **Zr** 91.22	41 **Nb** 92.91	42 **Mo** 95.94	43 **Tc** (98)	44 **Ru** 101.1	45 **Rh** 102.91	46 **Pd** 105.42	47 **Ag** 107.87	48 **Cd** 112.41	49 **In** 114.82	50 **Sn** 118.71	51 **Sb** 121.75	52 **Te** 127.60	53 **I** 126.91	54 **Xe** 131.29
55 **Cs** 132.91	56 **Ba** 137.33	57 *****La** 138.91	72 **Hf** 178.49	73 **Ta** 180.95	74 **W** 183.85	75 **Re** 186.21	76 **Os** 190.2	77 **Ir** 192.22	78 **Pt** 195.08	79 **Au** 196.97	80 **Hg** 200.59	81 **Ti** 204.38	82 **Pb** 207.2	83 **Bi** 208.98	84 **Po** (209)	85 **At** (210)	86 **Rn** (222)
87 **Fr** (223)	88 **Ra** 226.02	89 †**Ac** 227.03	104 **Rf** (261)	105 **Db** (262)	106 **Sg** (263)	107 **Bh** (262)	108 **Hs** (265)	109 **Mt** (266)	110 **§** (269)	111 **§** (272)	112 **§** (277)						

§ Not yet named

* Lanthanide Series

58 **Ce** 140.12	59 **Pr** 140.91	60 **Nd** 144.24	61 **Pm** (145)	62 **Sm** 150.4	63 **Eu** 151.97	64 **Gd** 157.25	65 **Tb** 158.93	66 **Dy** 162.50	67 **Ho** 164.93	68 **Er** 167.26	69 **Tm** 168.93	70 **Yb** 173.04	71 **Lu** 174.97

† Actinide Series

90 **Th** 232.04	91 **Pa** 231.04	92 **U** 238.03	93 **Np** 237.05	94 **Pu** (244)	95 **Am** (243)	96 **Cm** (247)	97 **Bk** (247)	98 **Cf** (251)	99 **Es** (252)	100 **Fm** (257)	101 **Md** (258)	102 **No** (259)	103 **Lr** (260)

Practice Exam 4

Section I: Multiple-Choice Questions

Time: 90 minutes

75 questions

45% of total grade

No calculators allowed

This section consists of 75 multiple-choice questions. Mark your answers carefully on the answer sheet.

General Instructions

Do not open this booklet until you are told to do so by the proctor.

Be sure to write your answers for Section I on the separate answer sheet. Use the test booklet for your scratch work or notes, but remember that no credit will be given for work, notes, or answers written only in the test booklet. After you have selected an answer, blacken thoroughly the corresponding circle on the answer sheet. To change an answer, erase your previous mark completely, and then record your new answer. Mark only one answer for each question.

Example   Sample Answer

The Pacific is   Ⓐ Ⓑ ● Ⓓ Ⓔ

    A.   a river
    B.   a lake
    C.   an ocean
    D.   a sea
    E.   a gulf

To discourage haphazard guessing on this section of the exam, a quarter of a point is subtracted for every wrong answer, but no points are subtracted if you leave the answer blank. Even so, if you can eliminate one or more of the choices for a question, it may be to your advantage to guess.

Because it is not expected that all test takers will complete this section, do not spend too much time on difficult questions. Answer first the questions you can answer readily, and then, if you have time, return to the difficult questions later. Don't get stuck on one question. Work quickly but accurately. Use your time effectively. The preceding table is provided for your use in answering questions in Section I.

GO ON TO THE NEXT PAGE

Directions: Each group of lettered answer choices below refers to the numbered statements or questions that immediately follow. For each question or statement, select the one lettered choice that is the best answer and fill in the corresponding circle on the answer sheet. An answer choice may be used once, more than once, or not at all in each set of questions.

Questions 1–3

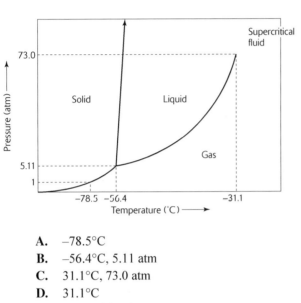

A.   −78.5°C
B.   −56.4°C, 5.11 atm
C.   31.1°C, 73.0 atm
D.   31.1°C
E.   none of the above

1. What does the phase diagram above show to be the normal boiling point of carbon dioxide?

2. Which point represents the critical point?

3. Which point represents the triple point?

4. What is the IUPAC name for the following cycloalkane?

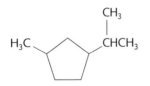

A.   Methyl-propylcyclopentane
B.   1-Methyl-3-isopropylcyclopentane
C.   Methyl-propylcycloalkane
D.   1-Isopropyl-3-methylcyclopentane
E.   1-Propyl-4-methylcyclopentane

5. Within a period, an increase in atomic number is usually accompanied by

A.   a decrease in atomic radius and an increase in electronegativity.
B.   an increase in atomic radius and an increase in electronegativity.
C.   a decrease in atomic radius and a decrease in electronegativity.
D.   an increase in atomic radius and a decrease in electronegativity.
E.   None of these answer choices is correct.

6. How many moles of solid $Ca(NO_3)_2$ should be added to 450 milliliters of 0.35 M $Al(NO_3)_3$ to increase the concentration of the NO_3^- ion to 1.7 M? (*Assume that the volume of the solution remains constant.*)

A.   0.07 mole
B.   0.15 mole
C.   0.29 mole
D.   0.45 mole
E.   0.77 mole

7. Which of the following would be spontaneous?

A.   the decomposition of iron(II) oxide to iron metal and oxygen gas
B.   heat transfer from an ice cube to a room maintained at a temperature of 27°C
C.   expansion of a gas to fill the available volume
D.   the decomposition of sodium chloride
E.   freezing of water at 2°C

8. Calculate the rate constant for the radioactive disintegration of an isotope that has a half-life of 6930 years.

A. 1.00×10^{-5} yr^{-1}
B. 1.00×10^{-4} yr^{-1}
C. 1.00×10^{-3} yr^{-1}
D. 1.00×10^{3} yr^{-1}
E. 1.00×10^{4} yr^{-1}

9. How many electrons can be accommodated in all the atomic orbitals that correspond to the principal quantum number 4?

    A. 2
    B. 8
    C. 18
    D. 32
    E. 40

10. A certain organic compound has a vapor pressure of 132 mm Hg at 54°C. To determine the vapor pressure of 2.00 moles of the compound at 37°C, taking the heat of vaporization for the compound to be 4.33×10^4 J/mole, you would use

    A. the Arrhenius equation
    B. the Clausius-Clapeyron equation
    C. the combined gas laws
    D. the ideal gas law
    E. Raoult's Law

11. Excess silver carbonate is added to 500 mL of water and the mixture stirred. Which of the following will cause the equilibrium to shift in the direction that would favor ionization?

    (1) add some $AgNO_3$
    (2) add some NH_3
    (3) add some Na_2CO_3
    (4) add some HNO_3

    A. 1 and 2
    B. 2 and 3
    C. 3 and 4
    D. 1 and 4
    E. 2 and 4

12. The value of K_a for lactic acid, HLac, is 1.5×10^{-5}. What is the value of K_b for the lactate anion, Lac^-?

    A. 1.0×10^{-14}
    B. 8.5×10^{-10}
    C. 6.7×10^{-10}
    D. 8.5×10^{10}
    E. It cannot be determined from the information provided.

13. Solid calcium carbonate decomposes to produce solid calcium oxide and carbon dioxide gas. The value of $\triangle G°$ for this reaction is 130.24 kJ/mole. Calculate $\triangle G$ at 100°C for this reaction if the pressure of the carbon dioxide gas is 1.00 atm.

    A. −998.56 kJ/mole
    B. −604.2 kJ/mole
    C. 56.31 kJ/mole
    D. 130.24 kJ/mole
    E. 256.24 kJ/mole

14. The density of a gas is directly proportional to its

    A. pressure
    B. volume
    C. kinetic energy
    D. temperature
    E. molecular velocity

15. Dinitrogen pentoxide decomposes according to the following balanced equation:

$$N_2O_{5(g)} \rightarrow 2\ NO_{(g)} + \tfrac{1}{2}\ O_{2(g)}$$

The rate of decomposition was found to be 0.80 moles $\cdot$ liter^{-1} $\cdot$ sec^{-1} at a given concentration and temperature. What would the rate be for the formation of oxygen gas under the same conditions?

    A. 0.20 moles $\cdot$ liter^{-1} $\cdot$ sec^{-1}
    B. 0.40 moles $\cdot$ liter $\cdot$ sec^{-1}
    C. 0.80 moles $\cdot$ liter $\cdot$ sec^{-1}
    D. 1.60 moles $\cdot$ liter^{-1} $\cdot$ sec^{-1}
    E. 3.20 moles $\cdot$ liter^{-1} $\cdot$ sec^{-1}

16. Which of the following solutions would be basic?

    A. NH_4I
    B. NaOCl
    C. $Fe(NO_3)_3$
    D. $Ba(NO_3)_2$
    E. NH_4NO_2

GO ON TO THE NEXT PAGE

17. The solubility product constant at 25°C for AgCl is 1.6×10^{-10} and that for AgI is 8.0×10^{-17}. Determine the equilibrium constant for the reaction of silver chloride with $I^-_{(aq)}$.

    A. 1.3×10^{-26}
    B. 5.0×10^{-7}
    C. 1.0×10^{3}
    D. 2.0×10^{6}
    E. 1.3×10^{16}

18. What happens to the velocities of different molecules as the temperature of the gas increases?

    A. The velocities of all component molecules increase equally.
    B. The velocity range among different molecules at higher temperatures is smaller than that at lower temperatures.
    C. The effect on the velocities of the molecules depends on whether the pressure remains constant.
    D. The velocity range among different molecules at higher temperatures is wider than the range at lower temperatures.
    E. None of these answer choices are correct.

19. When 0.600 mole of $BaCl_{2(aq)}$ is mixed with 0.250 mole of $K_3AsO_{4(aq)}$, what is the maximum number of moles of solid $Ba_3(AsO_4)_2$ that could be formed?

    A. 0.125 mole
    B. 0.200 mole
    C. 0.250 mole
    D. 0.375 mole
    E. 0.500 mole

Questions 20–23

    A. HNO_3
    B. Al_2O_3
    C. NO
    D. BF_3
    E. C_2H_6

20. An example of a strong oxidizing agent.

21. An example of a paramagnetic oxide.

22. An example of an amphoteric oxide.

23. An example of a Lewis acid.

24. Element X is found in two forms: 90.0% is an isotope that has a mass of 20.0, and 10.0% is an isotope that has a mass of 22.0. What is the atomic mass of element X?

    A. 20.0
    B. 20.2
    C. 20.8
    D. 21.2
    E. 21.8

25. Element Q occurs in compounds X, Y, and Z. The mass of element Q in 1 mole of each compound is as follows:

Compound	Grams of Q in Compound
X	38.00
Y	95.00
Z	133.00

Element Q is most likely

    A. N
    B. O
    C. F
    D. Ir
    E. Cs

26. Which of the following would have an answer with three significant figures?

    A. $103.1 + 0.0024 + 0.16$
    B. $(3.0 \times 10^4)\,(5.022 \times 10^{-3})\,/\,(6.112 \times 10^2)$
    C. $(4.3 \times 10^5)\,/\,(4.225 + 56.0003 - 0.8700)$
    D. $(1.43 \times 10^3 + 3.1 \times 10^1)\,/\,(4.11 \times 10^{-6})$
    E. $(1.41 \times 10^2 + 1.012 \times 10^4)\,/\,(3.2 \times 10^{-1})$

27. Arrange the following oxides in order of increasing basic character.

$$Cs_2O \quad Na_2O \quad Al_2O_3 \quad Cl_2O_7$$

    A. $Cl_2O_7 < Al_2O_3 < Na_2O < Cs_2O$
    B. $Cs_2O < Al_2O_3 < Cl_2O_7 < Na_2O$
    C. $Cs_2O < Cl_2O_7 < Na_2O < Al_2O_3$
    D. $Al_2O_3 < Cl_2O_7 < Cs_2O < Na_2O$
    E. $Na_2O < Cl_2O_7 < Al_2O_3 < Cs_2O$

28. For $H_2C=CH_{2(g)} + H_{2(g)} \rightarrow H_3C-CH_{3(g)}$, predict the enthalpy given the following bond dissociation energies:

H–C, 413 kJ/mole   H–H, 436 kJ/mole

C=C, 614 kJ/mole   C–C, 348 kJ/mole

    A. −656 kJ/mole

    B. −343 kJ/mole

    C. −289 kJ/mole

    D. −124 kJ/mole

    E. −102 kJ/mole

29. A gas which initially occupies a volume of 6.00 liters at 4.00 atm is allowed to expand to a volume of 14.00 liters at a pressure of 1.00 atm. Calculate the value of work, w, done by the gas on the surroundings.

    A. −8.00 L · atm

    B. −7.00 L · atm

    C. 6.00 L · atm

    D. 7.00 L · atm

    E. 8.00 L · atm

30. The combustion of carbon monoxide yields carbon dioxide. The volume of oxygen gas needed to produce 22 grams of carbon dioxide at STP is

    A. 4.0 liters

    B. 5.6 liters

    C. 11 liters

    D. 22 liters

    E. 32 liters

31. A mixture of nitrogen, hydrogen and ammonia gases are in a sealed container and are at equilibrium. Which of the following changes will affect the reaction quotient (Q_c) but not affect the equilibrium constant (K_c)?

    (1) addition of argon to the system

    (2) addition of a catalyst

    (3) decrease the size of the sealed container

    (4) add more hydrogen and nitrogen gases

    (5) increase the temperature

    A. 1 and 2

    B. 2 and 3

    C. 1 and 3

    D. 3 and 4

    E. all of them

32. A sample of zinc metal reacts completely with excess hydrochloric acid according to the following equation:

$$Zn_{(s)} + 2HCl_{(aq)} \rightarrow ZnCl_{2(aq)} + H_{2(g)}$$

8.00 liters of hydrogen gas at 720. mm Hg is collected over water at 40.°C (vapor pressure of water at 40.°C = 55 mm Hg). How much zinc was consumed by the reaction?

    A. $\dfrac{(720/760)(8.00)}{(0.0821)(313)}$

    B. $\dfrac{(760/720)(313)}{(0.0821)(2)}$

    C. $\dfrac{(665/760)(8.00)(65.39)}{(0.0821)(313)}$

    D. $\dfrac{(665/760)(8.00)}{(65.39)(0.0821)(313)}$

    E. $\dfrac{(8.00)(313)(65.39)}{(665/760)(0.0821)}$

GO ON TO THE NEXT PAGE

33. Hydrogen gas and iodine gas are introduced into a cylinder with a movable piston as shown in the following diagram:

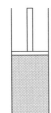

Which of the following would cause a decrease in the reaction rate?

(1) adding neon, holding the volume constant

(2) increase the volume, holding the temperature constant

(3) increase the temperature, holding the volume constant

(4) adding a catalyst

A. 1
B. 2
C. 3
D. 1 and 3
E. 1, 3 and 4

34. Which of the following setups would be used to calculate the wavelength (in meters) of a photon emitted by a hydrogen atom when the electron moves from the $n = 5$ state to the $n = 2$ state? (The Rydberg constant is $R_H = 2.18 \times 10^{-18}$ J. Planck's constant is $h = 6.63 \times 10^{-34}$ J $\cdot$ sec. The speed of light $= 3.00 \times 10^8$ m/sec.)

A. $\left(2.18 \times 10^{-18}\right)\left(\dfrac{1}{5^2} - \dfrac{1}{2^2}\right)\left(6.63 \times 10^{-34}\right)$

B. $\dfrac{\left(6.3 \times 10^{-34}\right)\left(3.00 \times 10^8\right)}{\left(2.18 \times 10^{-18}\right)\left(\dfrac{1}{5^2} - \dfrac{1}{2^2}\right)}$

C. $\dfrac{\left(2.18 \times 10^{-18}\right)\left(3.00 \times 10^8\right)}{\left(6.63 \times 10^{-34}\right)\left(\dfrac{1}{5^2} - \dfrac{1}{2^2}\right)}$

D. $\dfrac{\left(2.18 \times 10^{-18}\right) / \left(3.00 \times 10^8\right)}{\left(6.63 \times 10^{-34}\right)\left(\dfrac{1}{5^2} - \dfrac{1}{2^2}\right)}$

E. $\dfrac{\left(2.18 \times 10^{-18}\right)\left(3.00 \times 10^8\right)}{\left(6.63 \times 10^{-34}\right)\left(\dfrac{1}{5^2} - \dfrac{1}{2^2}\right)}$

35. A characteristic that is unique to the alkali metals is

A. their metallic character.
B. the increase in atomic radius with increasing atomic number.
C. the decrease in ionization energy with increasing atomic number.
D. the noble gas electron configuration of the singly charged positive ion.
E. None of these answer choices are correct.

36. The four quantum numbers (n, l, m_l, and m_s) that describe the valence electron in the cesium atom are

A. 6, 0, −1, +½
B. 6, 1, 1, +½
C. 6, 0, 0, +½
D. 6, 1, 0, +½
E. 6, 0, 1, −½

37. A characteristic of the structure of metallic atoms is that

    A. they tend to share their electrons with other atoms.

    B. their atoms are smaller and more compact than those of nonmetallic elements.

    C. their outermost orbital of electrons is nearly complete, and they attract electrons from other atoms.

    D. the small numbers of electrons in their outermost orbital are weakly held and easily lost.

    E. they have heavier nuclei than nonmetallic atoms.

38. What is the oxidation number of platinum in $[PtCl_6]^{2-}$?

    A. -4
    B. -2
    C. -1
    D. $+4$
    E. $+6$

39. A certain brand of rubbing alcohol is 90 wt. % solution of isopropyl alcohol, C_3H_8O, in water. How many grams of rubbing alcohol contain 9.0 grams of isopropyl alcohol?

    A. 9.0 grams
    B. 10. grams
    C. 11 grams
    D. 90. grams
    E. 1.0×10^2 grams

Questions 40–44

    A. hydrogen bonding
    B. metallic bonding
    C. ionic bonding
    D. dipole forces
    E. van der Waals forces (London dispersion forces)

40. What accounts for the intermolecular forces between CCl_4 molecules?

41. What explains why the boiling point of acetic acid, CH_3COOH, is greater than the boiling point of dimethyl ether, $CH_3—O—CH_3$?

42. What holds solid sodium together?

43. What holds solid ICl together?

44. What holds calcium chloride together?

45. Which of the following choices represents intermolecular forces listed in order from strongest to weakest?

    A. dipole attractions, dispersion forces, hydrogen bonds

    B. hydrogen bonds, dispersion forces, dipole attractions

    C. dipole attractions, hydrogen bonds, dispersion forces

    D. hydrogen bonds, dipole attractions, dispersion forces

    E. dispersion forces, hydrogen bonds, dipole attractions

46. How many milliliters of a 50.0% (by mass) HNO_3 solution, with a density of 2.00 grams per milliliter, are required to make 500. mL of a 2.00 M HNO_3 solution?

    A. 50.0 mL
    B. 63.0 mL
    C. 100. mL
    D. 200. mL
    E. 250. mL

47. What is the percentage (by mass) of NaCl (MM = 58.4) in a 10.0 *m* solution?

    A. $\dfrac{10.0 \times 58.4}{1584}$

    B. $\dfrac{10.0 \times 58.4}{1000.0}$

    C. $\dfrac{2 \times 58.4 \times 10.0}{1000.0}$

    D. $\dfrac{10.0 \times 58.4}{100.00}$

    E. $\dfrac{100 \times 58.4}{1000.00}$

48. A solution of NH_3 dissolved in water is 10.0 *m*. What is the mole fraction of water in the solution?

    A. 1.00/1.18
    B. 1.00/2.18
    C. 0.18/1.00
    D. 0.18/10.0
    E. 1.18

GO ON TO THE NEXT PAGE

49. Which of the following changes will decrease the rate of collisions between gaseous molecules of type A and B in a closed container?

  A.   decrease the volume of the container
  B.   increase the temperature of the system
  C.   add A molecules
  D.   take away B molecules
  E.   add an accelerating catalyst

50. The following data was obtained for the reaction

$$2X + Y \rightarrow 3Z$$

Experiment	X	Y	Rate (mol · liter^{-1} · sec^{-1})
1	3.0	1.5	1.8
2	1.5	3.0	0.45
3	1.5	1.5	0.45

What is the proper rate expression?

  A.   rate = $k[X][Y]$
  B.   rate = $k[Y]^2$
  C.   rate = $k[X]$
  D.   rate = $k[X]^2[Y]$
  E.   rate = $k[X]^2$

51. 6.00 moles of nitrogen gas and 6.00 moles of oxygen gas are placed in a 2.00-liter flask at 500°C and the mixture is allowed to reach equilibrium. What is the concentration, in moles per liter, of nitrogen monoxide at equilibrium if the equilibrium constant is found to be 4.00?

  A.   3.00 M
  B.   6.00 M
  C.   8.00 M
  D.   10.0 M
  E.   12.0 M

52. Lead iodide has a K_{sp} value of 1.08×10^{-7} at 20°C. Calculate its molar solubility at 20°C.

  A. 5.00×10^{-8} M
  B. 3.00×10^{-6} M
  C. 1.00×10^{-4} M
  D. 6.00×10^{-3} M
  E. 3.00×10^{-3} M

53. Given the following reversible equation, determine which species is/are Brønsted acids.

$$CO_3^{2-}{}_{(aq)} + H_2O_{(l)} \longleftrightarrow HCO_3^-{}_{(aq)} + OH^-{}_{(aq)}$$

  A. $CO_3^{2-}{}_{(aq)}$
  B. $H_2O_{(l)}$ and $OH^-{}_{(aq)}$
  C. $H_2O_{(l)}$ and $HCO_3^-{}_{(aq)}$
  D. $CO_3^{2-}{}_{(aq)}$ and $OH^-{}_{(aq)}$
  E. $H_2O_{(l)}$

54. A solution is prepared by adding 0.600 liter of 1.0×10^{-3} M HCl to 0.400 liter of 1.0×10^{-3} M HNO_3. What is the pH of the final solution?

  A.   1.00
  B.   2.00
  C.   3.00
  D.   4.00
  E.   5.00

55. For the given reaction and the following information, calculate $\triangle G°$:

$$2PbO_{(s)} + 2SO_{2(g)} \rightarrow 2PbS_{(s)} + 3O_{2(g)}$$

Species	$\triangle H_f°$ (kJ/mole) at 25°C and 1 atm	S° (J · mole^{-1} · K^{-1}) at 25°C and 1 atm
$PbO_{(s)}$	−218.0	70.0
$SO_{2(g)}$	−297.0	248.0
$PbS_{(s)}$	−100.0	91.0
$O_{2(g)}$	−	205.0

  A.   3.10 kJ
  B.   40.0 kJ
  C.   210.0 kJ
  D.   782.0 kJ
  E.   1830.0 kJ

56. Arrange the following reactions according to increasing $\triangle S°$ values.

  (1) $H_2O_{(g)} \rightarrow H_2O_{(l)}$
  (2) $2HCl_{(g)} \rightarrow H_{2(g)} + Cl_{2(g)}$
  (3) $SiO_{2(s)} \rightarrow Si_{(s)} + O_{2(g)}$

  A.   (1) < (2) < (3)
  B.   (2) < (3) < (1)
  C.   (3) < (1) < (2)
  D.   (1) < (3) < (2)
  E.   (3) < (2) < (1)

57. If $\triangle H°$ and $\triangle S°$ are both negative, then $\triangle G°$ is

   A. always negative.
   B. always positive.
   C. positive at low temperatures and negative at high temperatures.
   D. negative at low temperatures and positive at high temperatures.
   E. zero.

58. When the equation for the following reaction

   $FeCl_2 + KMnO_4 + HCl \rightarrow FeCl_3 + KCl + MnCl_2 + ?H_2O$

   is balanced with the lowest whole-number coefficients, the coefficient for H_2O is

   A. 1
   B. 2
   C. 3
   D. 4
   E. 5

59. Given that

   $$Zn^{2+}_{(aq)} + 2e^- \rightarrow Zn_{(s)} \qquad E°_{red} = -0.76 \text{ V}$$
   $$Cr^{3+}_{(aq)} + 3e^- \rightarrow Cr_{(s)} \qquad E°_{red} = -0.74 \text{ V}$$

   calculate the equilibrium constant K at 25°C for the following balanced reaction:

   $$3Zn_{(s)} + 2Cr^{3+}_{(aq)} \rightarrow 3Zn^{2+}_{(aq)} + 2Cr_{(s)}$$

   A. $K = e^{-0.02}$
   B. $K = e^{0.02}$
   C. $K = e^{4.7}$
   D. $K = e^{8.0}$
   E. cannot be determined from the information provided

For Questions 60–64, choose from the following choices:

   A. $^{201}_{80}Hg + ^{0}_{-1}e \rightarrow ^{201}_{79}Au + ^{0}_{0}\gamma$

   B. $^{11}_{6}C \rightarrow ^{0}_{1}e + ^{11}_{5}B$

   C. $^{237}_{93}Np \rightarrow ^{4}_{2}He + ^{233}_{91}Pa$

   D. $^{235}_{92}U + ^{1}_{0}n \rightarrow ^{141}_{56}Ba + ^{92}_{36}Kr + 3\,^{1}_{0}n$

   E. $^{214}_{83}Bi \rightarrow ^{214}_{84}Po + ^{0}_{-1}e$

60. Alpha (α)-particle production.

61. Beta (β)-particle production.

62. Electron capture.

63. Fission.

64. Positron production.

65. Given the following compounds, arrange them in order of increasing acid strength:

   $$AsH_3 \quad HI \quad NaH \quad H_2O$$

   A. $HI > H_2O > AsH_3 > NaH$
   B. $NaH > AsH_3 > H_2O > HI$
   C. $HI > NaH > AsH_3 > H_2O$
   D. $H_2O > HI > NaH > AsH_3$
   E. $AsH_3 > NaH > HI > H_2O$

66. A crystal of germanium that has been doped with a small amount of aluminum would be classified as a(n)

   A. insulator
   B. alloy
   C. *n*-type semiconductor
   D. *p*-type semiconductor
   E. composite

67. Choose the one FALSE statement.

   A. Nuclei with an even number of protons and an even number of neutrons tend to be stable.
   B. γ-rays are high-energy photons.
   C. Nuclei with too few neutrons per proton tend to undergo positron $\left(^{0}_{1}e\right)$ emission.
   D. Light nuclides are stable when the atomic number (Z) equals the mass number minus the atomic number (A–Z).
   E. Nuclei with too few neutrons per proton tend to undergo β-particle $\left(^{0}_{-1}e\right)$ emission.

GO ON TO THE NEXT PAGE

68. Given the following complexes:

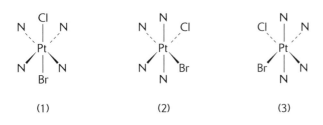

(1)   (2)   (3)

Which of the following is true?

A. #2 and #3 are diasterioisomers; #1 and #2 are enantiomers

B. #2 and #3 are diasterioisomers; #1 and #3 are enantiomers

C. #1 and #2 are diasterioisomers; #2 and #3 are enantiomers

D. #1, #2 and #3 are diasterioisomers; none are enantiomers

E. #1 and #3 are diasterioisomers; #2 and #3 are enantiomers

69. Which of the following would be expected to have a zero dipole moment?

A. NF_3

B. CH_3NH_2

C. H_2O

D. CH_3CH_2Cl

E. PCl_5

70. In which equation would you expect $\triangle E$ and $\triangle H$ to be nearly equal?

A. $2H_{2(g)} + O_{2(g)} \rightarrow 2H_2O_{(l)}$

B. $C_2H_{4(g)} + H_{2(g)} \rightarrow C_2H_{6(g)}$

C. $BrO_3^{-}{}_{(aq)} + 5Br^{-}{}_{(aq)} + 6H^{+}{}_{(aq)} \rightarrow 3Br_{2(aq)} + 3H_2O_{(l)}$

D. $HCOOH_{(aq)} + Br_{2(aq)} \rightarrow 2H^{+}{}_{(aq)} + 2Br^{-}{}_{(aq)} + CO_{2(g)}$

E. $N_2O_{(g)} \rightarrow N_{2(g)} + O_{(g)}$

71. Which of the following molecules would exhibit resonance?

A. $SOCl_2$

B. HNO_3

C. H_2O

D. SO_2Cl_2

E. $COCl_2$

72. Lithium reacts with bromine to form lithium bromide. Which of the following factors would NOT contribute to the overall energy change?

A. first ionization energy for LiBr

B. bond dissociation energy for Br_2

C. electron affinity for Br

D. lattice energy for LiBr

E. all choices contribute to the overall energy change

73. What orbital designation would correspond to the quantum numbers $n = 4$, $l = 2$, and $m_l = 0$?

A. $3d$

B. $4d$

C. $4p$

D. $4f$

E. $5d$

74. Given the following reactions:

$$W + X^+ \rightarrow W^+ + X$$
$$X + Z^+ \rightarrow X^+ + Z$$
$$Y^+ + Z \rightarrow \text{no reaction}$$
$$X + Y^+ \rightarrow X^+ + Y$$

arrange the elements W, X, Y and Z in order of increasing redox activity.

A. $W > X > Y > Z$

B. $X > Y > Z > W$

C. $Y > Z > W > X$

D. $Z > X > W > Y$

E. $Z > Y > X > W$

75. Referring to Question #74, which of the following equations would occur spontaneously?

A. $W^+ + Y \rightarrow W + Y^+$

B. $W^+ + Z \rightarrow W + Z^+$

C. $W + Y^+ \rightarrow W^+ + Y$

D. $Z + Y^+ \rightarrow Z^+ + Y$

E. $W^+ + X^+ \rightarrow W + X$

IF YOU FINISH BEFORE TIME IS CALLED, CHECK YOUR WORK ON THIS SECTION ONLY. DO NOT WORK ON ANY OTHER SECTION IN THE TEST.

PERIODIC TABLE OF THE ELEMENTS

1 **H** 1.0079																	2 **He** 4.0026
3 **Li** 6.941	4 **Be** 9.012											5 **B** 10.811	6 **C** 12.011	7 **N** 14.007	8 **O** 16.00	9 **F** 19.00	10 **Ne** 20.179
11 **Na** 22.99	12 **Mg** 24.30											13 **Al** 26.98	14 **Si** 28.09	15 **P** 30.974	16 **S** 32.06	17 **Cl** 35.453	18 **Ar** 39.948
19 **K** 39.10	20 **Ca** 40.08	21 **Sc** 44.96	22 **Ti** 47.90	23 **V** 50.94	24 **Cr** 51.00	25 **Mn** 54.93	26 **Fe** 55.85	27 **Co** 58.93	28 **Ni** 58.69	29 **Cu** 63.55	30 **Zn** 65.39	31 **Ga** 69.72	32 **Ge** 72.59	33 **As** 74.92	34 **Se** 78.96	35 **Br** 79.90	36 **Kr** 83.80
37 **Rb** 85.47	38 **Sr** 87.62	39 **Y** 88.91	40 **Zr** 91.22	41 **Nb** 92.91	42 **Mo** 95.94	43 **Tc** (98)	44 **Ru** 101.1	45 **Rh** 102.91	46 **Pd** 105.42	47 **Ag** 107.87	48 **Cd** 112.41	49 **In** 114.82	50 **Sn** 118.71	51 **Sb** 121.75	52 **Te** 127.60	53 **I** 126.91	54 **Xe** 131.29
55 **Cs** 132.91	56 **Ba** 137.33	57 ***La** 138.91	72 **Hf** 178.49	73 **Ta** 180.95	74 **W** 183.85	75 **Re** 186.21	76 **Os** 190.2	77 **Ir** 192.22	78 **Pt** 195.08	79 **Au** 196.97	80 **Hg** 200.59	81 **Tl** 204.38	82 **Pb** 207.2	83 **Bi** 208.98	84 **Po** (209)	85 **At** (210)	86 **Rn** (222)
87 **Fr** (223)	88 **Ra** 226.02	89 **†Ac** 227.03	104 **Rf** (261)	105 **Db** (262)	106 **Sg** (263)	107 **Bh** (262)	108 **Hs** (265)	109 **Mt** (266)	110 **§** (269)	111 **§** (272)	112 **§** (277)						

§ Not yet named

58 **Ce** 140.12	59 **Pr** 140.91	60 **Nd** 144.24	61 **Pm** (145)	62 **Sm** 150.4	63 **Eu** 151.97	64 **Gd** 157.25	65 **Tb** 158.93	66 **Dy** 162.50	67 **Ho** 164.93	68 **Er** 167.26	69 **Tm** 168.93	70 **Yb** 173.04	71 **Lu** 174.97
90 **Th** 232.04	91 **Pa** 231.04	92 **U** 238.03	93 **Np** 237.05	94 **Pu** (244)	95 **Am** (243)	96 **Cm** (247)	97 **Bk** (247)	98 **Cf** (251)	99 **Es** (252)	100 **Fm** (257)	101 **Md** (258)	102 **No** (259)	103 **Lr** (260)

* Lanthanide Series

† Actinide Series

GO ON TO THE NEXT PAGE

STANDARD REDUCTION POTENTIALS IN AQUEOUS SOLUTION AT 25°C

Half-reaction			$E°(V)$
$F_{2\,(g)} + 2\,e^-$	$\rightarrow$	$2\,F^-$	2.87
$Co^{3+} + e^-$	$\rightarrow$	Co^{2+}	1.82
$Au^{3+} + 3\,e^-$	$\rightarrow$	$Au_{(s)}$	1.50
$Cl_{2\,(g)} + 2\,e^-$	$\rightarrow$	$2\,Cl^-$	1.36
$O_{2\,(g)} + 4\,H^+ + 4\,e^-$	$\rightarrow$	$2\,H_2O_{(l)}$	1.23
$Br_{2\,(l)} + 2\,e^-$	$\rightarrow$	$2\,Br^-$	1.07
$2\,Hg^{2+} + 2\,e^-$	$\rightarrow$	Hg_2^{2+}	0.92
$Hg^{2+} + 2\,e^-$	$\rightarrow$	$Hg_{(l)}$	0.85
$Ag^+ + e^-$	$\rightarrow$	$Ag_{(s)}$	0.80
$Hg_2^{2+} + 2\,e^-$	$\rightarrow$	$2\,Hg_{(l)}$	0.79
$Fe^{3+} + e^-$	$\rightarrow$	Fe^{2+}	0.77
$I_{2\,(s)} + 2\,e^-$	$\rightarrow$	$2\,I^-$	0.53
$Cu^+ + e^-$	$\rightarrow$	$Cu_{(s)}$	0.52
$Cu^{2+} + 2\,e^-$	$\rightarrow$	$Cu_{(s)}$	0.34
$Cu^{2+} + e^-$	$\rightarrow$	Cu^+	0.15
$Sn^{4+} + 2\,e^-$	$\rightarrow$	Sn^{2+}	0.15
$S_{(s)} + 2\,H^+ + 2\,e^-$	$\rightarrow$	$H_2S_{(g)}$	0.14
$2\,H^+ + 2\,e^-$	$\rightarrow$	$H_{2(g)}$	0.00
$Pb^{2+} + 2\,e^-$	$\rightarrow$	$Pb_{(s)}$	−0.13
$Sn^{2+} + 2\,e^-$	$\rightarrow$	$Sn_{(s)}$	−0.14
$Ni^{2+} + 2\,e^-$	$\rightarrow$	$Ni_{(s)}$	−0.25
$Co^{2+} + 2\,e^-$	$\rightarrow$	$Co_{(s)}$	−0.28
$Cd^{2+} + 2\,e^-$	$\rightarrow$	$Cd_{(s)}$	−0.40
$Cr^{3+} + e^-$	$\rightarrow$	Cr^{2+}	−0.41
$Fe^{2+} + 2\,e^-$	$\rightarrow$	$Fe_{(s)}$	−0.44
$Cr^{3+} + 3\,e^-$	$\rightarrow$	$Cr_{(s)}$	−0.74
$Zn^{2+} + 2\,e^-$	$\rightarrow$	$Zn_{(s)}$	−0.76
$2\,H_2O_{(l)} + 2\,e^-$	$\rightarrow$	$H_{2(g)} + 2\,OH^-$	−0.83
$Mn^{2+} + 2\,e^-$	$\rightarrow$	$Mn_{(s)}$	−1.18
$Al^{3+} + 3\,e^-$	$\rightarrow$	$Al_{(s)}$	−1.66
$Be^{2+} + 2\,e^-$	$\rightarrow$	$Be_{(s)}$	−1.70
$Mg^{2+} + 2\,e^-$	$\rightarrow$	$Mg_{(s)}$	−2.37
$Na^+ + e^-$	$\rightarrow$	$Na_{(s)}$	−2.71
$Ca^{2+} + 2\,e^-$	$\rightarrow$	$Ca_{(s)}$	−2.87
$Sr^{2+} + 2\,e^-$	$\rightarrow$	$Sr_{(s)}$	−2.89
$Ba^{2+} + 2\,e^-$	$\rightarrow$	$Ba_{(s)}$	−2.90
$Rb^+ + e^-$	$\rightarrow$	$Rb_{(s)}$	−2.92
$K^+ + e^-$	$\rightarrow$	$K_{(s)}$	−2.92
$Cs^+ + e^-$	$\rightarrow$	$Cs_{(s)}$	−2.92
$Li^+ + e^-$	$\rightarrow$	$Li_{(s)}$	−3.05

Note: Unless otherwise stated, assume that for all questions involving solutions and/or chemical equations, the system is in water at room temperature.

ADVANCED PLACEMENT CHEMISTRY EQUATIONS AND CONSTANTS

ATOMIC STRUCTURE

$$E = h\nu \qquad c = \lambda\nu$$

$$\lambda = \frac{h}{m\upsilon} \qquad p = m\upsilon$$

$$E_n = \frac{-2.178 \times 10^{-18}}{n^2} \text{ joule}$$

EQUILIBRIUM

$$K_a = \frac{[H^+][A^-]}{[HA]}$$

$$K_b = \frac{[OH^-][HB^+]}{[B]}$$

$$K_w = [OH^-][H^+] = 1.0 \times 10^{-14} \text{ @ 25°C}$$
$$= K_a \times K_b$$

$$pH = -\log[H^+], \quad pOH = -\log[OH^-]$$
$$14 = pH + pOH$$

$$pH = pK_a + \log\frac{[A^-]}{[HA]}$$

$$pOH = pK_b + \log\frac{[HB^+]}{[B]}$$

$$pK_a = -\log K_a, \quad pK_b = -\log K_b$$

$$K_p = K_c(RT)^{\Delta n}$$

where Δn = moles product gas − moles reactant gas

THERMOCHEMISTRY/KINETICS

$$\Delta S° = \Sigma S° \text{ products} - \Sigma S° \text{ reactants}$$

$$\Delta H° = \Sigma \Delta H_f° \text{ products} - \Sigma \Delta H_f° \text{ reactants}$$

$$\Delta G° = \Sigma \Delta G_f° \text{ products} - \Sigma \Delta G_f° \text{ reactants}$$

$$\Delta G° = \Delta H° - T\Delta S°$$
$$= -RT \ln K = -2.303 \, RT \log K$$
$$= -n \, \mathscr{F} \, E°$$

$$\Delta G = \Delta G° + RT \ln Q = \Delta G° + 2.303 \, RT \log Q$$
$$q = mc\Delta T$$

$$C_p = \frac{\Delta H}{\Delta T}$$

$$\ln[A]_t - \ln[A]_0 = -kt$$

$$\frac{1}{[A]_t} - \frac{1}{[A]_0} = kt$$

$$\ln k = \frac{-E_a}{R}\left(\frac{1}{T}\right) + \ln A$$

E = energy $\qquad \upsilon$ = velocity
v = frequency $\qquad n$ = principal quantum
λ = wavelength $\qquad\quad$ number
p = momentum $\qquad m$ = mass

Speed of light, $c = 3.0 \times 10^8 \text{ m} \cdot \text{s}^{-1}$

Planck's constant, $h = 6.63 \times 10^{-34} \text{ J} \cdot \text{s}$

Boltzmann's constant, $k = 1.38 \times 10^{-23} \text{ J} \cdot \text{K}^{-1}$

Avogadro's number $= 6.022 \times 10^{23} \text{ mol}^{-1}$

Electron charge, $e = -1.602 \times 10^{-19} \text{ coulomb}$

1 electron volt per atom $= 96.5 \text{ kJ} \cdot \text{mol}^{-1}$

Equilibrium Constants

K_a (weak acid)
K_b (weak base)
K_w (water)
K_p (gas pressure)
K_c (molar concentrations)

$S°$ = standard entropy
$H°$ = standard enthalpy
$G°$ = standard free energy
$E°$ = standard reduction potential
T = temperature
n = moles
m = mass
q = heat
c = specific heat capacity
C_p = molar heat capacity at constant pressure
E_a = activation energy
k = rate constant
A = frequency factor

Faraday's constant, $\mathscr{F} = 96,500$ coulombs per mole of electrons

Gas constant, $R = 8.31 \text{ J} \cdot \text{mol}^{-1} \cdot \text{K}^{-1}$
$= 0.0821 \text{ L} \cdot \text{atm} \cdot \text{mol}^{-1} \cdot \text{K}^{-1}$
$= 8.31 \text{ volt} \cdot \text{coulomb} \cdot \text{mol}^{-1} \cdot \text{K}^{-1}$

GO ON TO THE NEXT PAGE

GASES, LIQUIDS, AND SOLUTIONS

$$PV = nRT$$

$$\left(P + \frac{n^2a}{V^2}\right)(V - nb) = nRT$$

$$P_A = P_{total} \times X_A, \text{ where } X_A = \frac{\text{moles A}}{\text{total moles}}$$

$$P_{total} = P_A + P_B + P_C + \ldots$$

$$n = \frac{m}{M}$$

$$K = °C + 273$$

$$\frac{P_1V_1}{T_1} = \frac{P_2V_2}{T_2}$$

$$D = \frac{m}{V}$$

$$u_{rms} = \sqrt{\frac{3kT}{m}} = \sqrt{\frac{3RT}{m}}$$

$$KE \text{ per molecule} = \tfrac{1}{2}mv^2$$

$$KE \text{ per mole} = \tfrac{3}{2}RT$$

$$\frac{r_1}{r_2} = \sqrt{\frac{M_2}{M_1}}$$

molarity, M = moles solute per liter solution
molality, m = moles solute per kilogram solvent

$$\Delta T_f = i \cdot K_f \times \text{molality}$$

$$\Delta T_b = i \cdot K_b \times \text{molality}$$

$$\pi = i \cdot M \cdot R \cdot T$$

$$A = a \cdot b \cdot c$$

P = pressure
V = volume
T = temperature
n = number of moles
D = density
m = mass
v = velocity

u_{rms} = root-mean-square speed
KE = kinetic energy
r = rate of effusion
M = molar mass
π = osmotic pressure
i = van't Hoff factor
K_f = molal freezing-point depression constant
K_b = molal boiling-point elevation constant
A = absorbance
a = molar absorptivity
b = path length
c = concentration
Q = reaction quotient
I = current (amperes)
q = charge (coulombs)
t = time (seconds)
$E°$ = standard reduction potential
K = equilibrium constant

OXIDATION-REDUCTION; ELECTROCHEMISTRY

$$Q = \frac{[C]^c[D]^d}{[A]^a[B]^b}, \text{ where } a\,A + b\,B \to c\,C + d\,D$$

$$I = \frac{q}{t}$$

$$E_{cell} = E°_{cell} - \frac{RT}{n\mathscr{F}}\ln Q = E°_{cell} - \frac{0.0592}{n}\log Q @ 25°C$$

$$\log K = \frac{n \cdot E°}{0.0592}$$

Gas constant, $R = 8.31 \text{ J} \cdot \text{mol}^{-1} \cdot \text{K}^{-1}$
$= 0.0821 \text{ L} \cdot \text{atm} \cdot \text{mol}^{-1} \cdot \text{K}^{-1}$
$= 8.31 \text{ volt} \cdot \text{coulomb} \cdot \text{mol}^{-1} \cdot \text{K}^{-1}$
Boltzmann's constant, $k = 1.38 \times 10^{-23} \text{ J} \cdot \text{K}^{-1}$
K_f for $H_2O = 1.86 \text{ K} \cdot \text{kg} \cdot \text{mol}^{-1}$
K_b for $H_2O = 0.512 \text{ K} \cdot \text{kg} \cdot \text{mol}^{-1}$
1 atm = 760 mm Hg
= 760 torr
STP = 0.000° C and 1.000 atm
Faraday's constant, $\mathscr{F} = 96{,}500$ coulombs per mole of electrons

Section II: Free-Response Questions

CHEMISTRY

Section II

Total time—90 minutes

Part A

Time—40 minutes

YOU MAY USE YOUR CALCULATOR FOR PART A

CLEARLY SHOW THE METHOD USED AND STEPS INVOLVED IN ARRIVING AT YOUR ANSWERS. It is to your advantage to do this, since you may obtain partial credit if you do and you will receive little or no credit if you do not. Attention should be paid to significant figures.

Answer Question 1 below. The Section II score weighting for this question is 20%.

1. Magnesium hydroxide has a solubility of 9.24×10^{-4} grams per 100 mL H_2O when measured at 25°C.

   (a) Write a balanced equation representing magnesium hydroxide at equilibrium in a water solution.

   (b) Write an equilibrium expression for magnesium hydroxide in water.

   (c) Calculate the value of K_{sp} at 25°C for magnesium hydroxide.

   (d) Calculate the value of pH and pOH for a saturated solution of magnesium hydroxide at 25°C.

   (e) Show by the use of calculations whether a precipitate would form if one were to add 75.0 mL of a 4.00×10^{-4} M aqueous solution of magnesium chloride to 75.0 mL of a 4.00×10^{-4} M aqueous solution of potassium hydroxide.

Answer EITHER Question 2 or 3 below. Only one of these two questions will be graded. If you start both questions, be sure to cross out the question you do not want graded. The Section II score weighting for the question you choose is 20%.

2. The ferrous ion, $Fe^{2+}_{(aq)}$, reacts with the permanganate ion, $MnO_4^-_{(aq)}$, in an acidic solution to produce the ferric ion, $Fe^{3+}_{(aq)}$. A 6.893 gram sample of ore was mechanically crushed and then treated with concentrated hydrochloric acid, which oxidized all of the iron in the ore to the ferrous ion, $Fe^{2+}_{(aq)}$. Next, the acid solution containing all of the ferrous ions was titrated with 0.100 M $KMnO_4$ solution. The end point was reached when 13.889 mL of the potassium permanganate solution was used.

   (a) Write the oxidation half-reaction.

   (b) Write the reduction half-reaction.

   (c) Write the balanced final redox reaction.

   (d) Identify the oxidizing agent, the reducing agent, the species oxidized, and the species reduced.

   (e) Calculate the number of moles of iron in the sample of ore.

   (f) Calculate the mass percent of iron in the ore.

GO ON TO THE NEXT PAGE

3. A student performed an acid-base titration. The student began Part I of the experiment by determining the exact concentration of a base through the standardization of a basic solution using a primary acidic HCl standard. The student measured out approximately 10 mL of 6.00 M NaOH and diluted it to approximately 600 mL. The student discovered that 48.7 mL of the NaOH solution was needed to neutralize exactly 50.0 mL of a 0.100 M HCl solution.

In Part II of the experiment, the student was given 0.500 grams of an unknown solid acid and titrated it with the known base from Part I. The student added 43.2 mL of the base to the unknown acid but went past the end point and needed to back-titrate with 5.2 mL of the 0.100 M HCl solution to reach the end point. A graph of the titration is presented below.

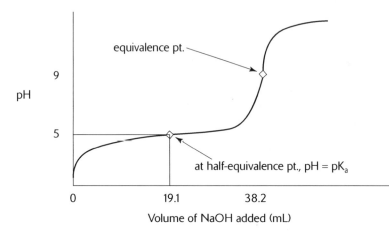

(a) Calculate the molarity of the NaOH solution from Part I.

(b) From the titration curve, determine the K_a or K_a's.

(c) What is the pH of the solution in Part II at the equivalence point?

(d) Calculate K_a of the acid.

(e) Why is the equivalence point not at a pH of 7?

(f) Determine the equivalent mass of the acid.

(g) Given the following list of indicators, which indicator would have been the most appropriate to use for this experiment?

Range	Indicator	Lower Color	Upper Color
0.0–2.5	methyl violet	yellow-green	violet
2.5–4.4	methyl orange	red	yellow
6.0–7.6	bromthymol blue	yellow	blue
8.3–10.0	phenolphthalein	colorless	dark pink

(h) Does the solid acid appear to be monoprotic or diprotic and explain your reasoning using the titration curve.

CHEMISTRY

Part B

Time—50 minutes

NO CALCULATORS MAY BE USED FOR PART B

Answer Question 4 below. The Section II score weight for this question is 15%.

4. Write the formulas to show the reactants and the products for any FIVE of the laboratory situations described below. Answers to more than five choices will not be graded. In all cases, a reaction occurs. Assume that solutions are aqueous unless otherwise indicated. Represent substances in solution as ions if the substances are extensively ionized. Omit formulas for any ions or molecules that are unchanged by the reaction. You need not balance the equations.

Example: A strip of magnesium is added to a solution of silver nitrate.

Ex.	$Mg + Ag^+ \rightarrow Mg^2 + Ag$

(a) Water is added to a flask of solid sodium oxide.

(b) Excess concentrated potassium hydroxide solution is added to a precipitate of zinc hydroxide.

(c) Ethene (ethylene) gas is bubbled through a solution of chlorine.

(d) A chunk of silver was added to a dilute (5 M) nitric acid solution.

(e) A dilute solution of sulfuric acid is added to a solution of barium chloride.

(f) A solution of iron(III) chloride is mixed with a solution of ammonium thiocyanate.

(g) A solution of hydrogen peroxide is warmed.

(h) Finely ground aluminum is added to a solution of copper(II) sulfate.

Answer BOTH Question 5 AND Question 6 below. Both of these questions will be graded. The Section II score weighting for these questions is 30% (15% each).

5. (a) Define the concept of entropy. Be sure to include concepts of state function, units, and magnitude.

(b) From each of the pairs of substances listed, and assuming 1 mole of each substance, choose the one that would be expected to have the lower absolute entropy and explain your reasoning in each case.

(i) $H_2O_{(s)}$ or $SiC_{(s)}$ at the same temperature and pressure.

(ii) $O_{2(g)}$ at 3.0 atm or $O_{2(g)}$ at 1.0 atm, both at the same temperature.

(iii) $NH_{3(l)}$ or $C_6H_{6(l)}$ at the same temperature and pressure.

(iv) $Na_{(s)}$ or $SiO_{2(s)}$.

6. Bromine reacts with a metal (M) as follows:

$$M_{(s)} + Br_{2(g)} \rightarrow MBr_{2(s)}$$

(a) Describe the type of bonding that would occur in $MBr_{2(s)}$.

(b) Define lattice energy. What factors would affect the lattice energy of $MBr_{2(s)}$?

GO ON TO THE NEXT PAGE

(c) If metal M were either magnesium, beryllium, or calcium, arrange the possible compounds in order of increasing lattice energies.

(d) If metal M were either magnesium, sodium, or aluminum (the equations would be different) arrange the resulting compounds in order of increasing lattice energy. Explain your reasoning.

(e) Explain how the heat of the reaction is affected by

    (i) the ionization energy for the metal, M.

    (ii) the size of the ionic radius for the ion, M^{2+}.

Answer EITHER Question 7 or 8 below. Only one of these two questions will be graded. If you start both questions, be sure to cross out the question you do not want graded. The Section II score weighting for the question you choose is 15%.

7. $(P + a)/V^2) (V - b) = R \cdot T$ is the van der Waals equation for one mole of a real gas whereas the ideal gas equation is $PV = nRT$.

(a) Explain the differences between the two equations. What assumptions are made using the ideal gas equation?

(b) Discuss the correctional factor 'a' and the factor(s) that influence its magnitude.

(c) Discuss the correctional factor 'b' and the factor(s) that influence its magnitude.

(d) Given the gases H_2 and HCl, which gas would have a higher value for 'a' and explain your reasoning.

(e) Given the gases H_2 and HCl, which gas would have a higher value for 'b' and explain your reasoning.

(f) Which of the two constants is associated with the boiling point of a substance and explain your reasoning?

8. 3 moles of $PCl_{3(g)}$ and 2 moles of $Cl_{2(g)}$ were introduced into an empty sealed flask and allowed to reach equilibrium with the product, $PCl_{5(g)}$. It was experimentally determined that the overall forward reaction was second order and the reverse reaction was first order in PCl_5.

(a) Write the equilibrium expression for the reaction.

(b) Draw a graph showing how the concentrations of all species change over time until equilibrium is achieved.

(c) Write the rate law for the forward reaction.

(d) List four factors that influence the rate of a reaction and explain each factor using chemical principles.

(e) What is an activated complex?

(f) Explain the concepts behind the Maxwell-Boltzmann distribution and sketch a diagram to explain the concepts.

Answer Key for Practice Exam 4

Section I: Multiple-Choice Questions

1. E	26. D	51. A
2. C	27. A	52. E
3. B	28. D	53. C
4. D	29. A	54. C
5. A	30. B	55. D
6. B	31. D	56. A
7. C	32. C	57. D
8. B	33. B	58. D
9. D	34. B	59. C
10. B	35. D	60. C
11. E	36. C	61. E
12. C	37. D	62. A
13. D	38. D	63. D
14. A	39. B	64. B
15. B	40. E	65. A
16. B	41. A	66. D
17. D	42. B	67. E
18. D	43. D	68. C
19. A	44. C	69. E
20. A	45. D	70. C
21. C	46. B	71. B
22. B	47. A	72. A
23. D	48. A	73. B
24. B	49. D	74. A
25. C	50. E	75. C

Predicting Your AP Score

The table below shows historical relationships between students' results on the multiple-choice portion (Section I) of the AP Chemistry exam and their overall AP score. The AP score ranges from 1 to 5, with 3, 4, or 5 generally considered to be passing. Over the years, around 60% of the students who take the AP Chemistry Exam receive a 3, 4, or 5.

After you've taken the multiple-choice practice exam under timed conditions, count the number of questions you got correct. From this number, subtract the number of wrong answers times ¼. Do NOT count items left blank as wrong. Then refer to this table to find your "probable" overall AP score. For example, if you get a score of 39, based on historical statistics, you have a 25% chance of receiving an overall score of 3, a 63% chance of receiving an overall score of 4, and a 12% chance of receiving an overall score of 5. Note that your actual results may be different from the score this table predicts. Also, remember that the free-response section represents 55% of your AP score.

No attempt is made here to combine your specific results on the practice AP Chemistry free-response questions (Section II) with your multiple-choice results (which is beyond the scope of this book and for which no data is available). However, you should have your AP chemistry instructor review your essays before you take the AP Chemistry Exam so that he or she can give you additional pointers.

Number of Multiple-Choice Questions Correct*	Overall AP Score				
	1	2	3	4	5
47 to 75	0%	0%	1%	21%	78%
37 to 46	0%	0%	25%	63%	12%
24 to 36	0%	19%	69%	12%	0%
13 to 23	15%	70%	15%	0%	0%
0 to 12	86%	14%	0%	0%	0%
% of Test Takers Receiving Score	21%	22%	25%	15%	17%

*Corrected for wrong answers

Answers and Explanations for Practice Exam 4

1. **(E)** "Normal" means 1 atm (760 mm Hg) pressure. Boiling occurs at a temperature at which the substance's vapor pressure becomes equal to the pressure above its surface. On this phase diagram, at 1 atm pressure, there is no intercept on a line separating the liquid phase from the gas phase. In other words, carbon dioxide cannot be liquefied at 1 atm pressure. It is in the liquid form only under very high pressures. At 1.0 atm pressure, solid CO_2 will sublime—that is, go directly to the gas phase.

2. **(C)** The critical point is the point at which the liquid-gas curve ends at a point at which the temperature and pressure have their critical values. Critical temperature is the temperature above which the liquid state of a substance no longer exists. Critical pressure is the pressure at the critical temperature.

3. **(B)** All three phases are in equilibrium at the triple point. The solid CO_2 sublimes if warmed at any pressure below 5.11 atm. Above 5.11 atm, the solid melts if warmed.

4. **(D)** The parent cycloalkane has 5 carbons, thus the ending will be cyclopentane. There are 2 substituents on the cycloalkane- a methyl group and an isopropyl group. Number the cycloalkane with the group having alphabetical priority (isopropyl comes before methyl). Number in the direction that yields the lowest possible number.

5. **(A)** The atomic radius decreases because of increasing effective nuclear charge and electrostatic attraction. There are more protons and electrons; thus, there is an increase in electronegativity. Greater nuclear change creates a greater attraction for electrons, which increases electronegativity.

6. **(B)** The molarity of a solution multiplied by its volume equals the number of moles of solute. In this case, 450 mL of 0.35 M $Al(NO_3)_3$ can be shown as

$$\frac{0.35 \text{ mole Al}(NO_3)_3}{1 \text{ L solution}} \times \frac{0.45 \text{ L solution}}{1}$$
$$= 0.16 \text{ mole Al}(NO_3)_3$$

$Al(NO_3)_3$ is completely soluble, so there would be three times the number of moles of nitrate ions present in the solution because

$$Al(NO_3)_{3(s)} \rightarrow Al^{3+}_{(aq)} + 3NO_3^{-}_{(aq)}$$

Therefore, the number of moles of nitrate ions in the original solution would be $0.16 \times 3 = 0.48$.

The number of moles of nitrate ions needs to be brought up to 0.77 because the volume did not change (it remained at 0.45 liter).

$$\frac{1.7 \text{ moles NO}_3^{-}}{1 \text{ liter solution}} \times \frac{0.45 \text{ liter solution}}{1}$$
$$= 0.77 \text{ mole of NO}_3^{-} \text{ in final solution}$$

The solution begins with 0.48 moles of nitrate ions and must end up with 0.77 moles of nitrate ions; therefore, the solution needs an additional 0.29 mole of nitrate ions:

$(0.77 - 0.48) = 0.29$ mole NO_3^{-} needed

Calcium nitrate, $Ca(NO_3)_2$, produces 2 moles of nitrate ions in solution for each mole of solid calcium nitrate added to the solution. Therefore, because 0.29 mole of NO_3^{-} is needed, you will need $0.29 / 2 \approx 0.15$ mole of solid $Ca(NO_3)_2$.

7. **(C)** All reactions proceed spontaneously in the direction that increases the entropy (disorder) of the system plus surroundings. The entropy of a gas increases when its pressure decreases at constant temperature, while the entropy decreases when pressure increases. The more we expand a gas, the more space the gas molecules will have and so the less ordered they will be.

8. **(B)**

$$k = \frac{\ln 2}{t_{1/2}} = \frac{0.693}{t_{1/2}} = \frac{0.693}{6930 \text{ yr}} = 1.00 \times 10^{-4} \text{ yr}^{-1}$$

9. (D) A principal quantum number of 4 tells you that you are in the fourth energy level. The fourth energy level contains electrons in the *s, p, d,* and *f* orbitals. Counting the maximum numbers of electrons available in each of the four types of sublevels—2 in the *s*, 6 in the *p*, 10 in the *d*, and 14 in the *f*—yields a total of 32. Alternatively, one can use the equation $2n^2$ $(2 \cdot 4^2)$.

10. (B) To do this problem, you would use the Clausius-Clapeyron equation:

$$\log \frac{P_2}{P_1} = \frac{\Delta H_{vap}}{2.303R} \left(\frac{T_2 - T_1}{T_2 T_1} \right)$$

where

$T_1 = 54°C + 273 = 327K$

$T_2 = 37°C + 273 = 310K$

P_1 (132 mm Hg) is the vapor pressure of the liquid at T_1 (327K)

P_2 (x) is the vapor pressure of the liquid at T_2 (310K)

R is a universal gas constant: 8.314 joules/(mole · K)

Although the problem does not require you to solve the equation, it is presented below. Substituting the values of the problem into the equation gives

$$\log \frac{x}{132 \text{ mm Hg}} = \frac{4.33 \times 10^4 \text{ J/mole}}{2.303 \times 8.314 \text{ J/(mole·K)}} \left(\frac{310 \text{ K} - 327 \text{K}}{310 \text{ K} \cdot 327 \text{K}} \right)$$

Simplifying this problem gives you

$$\log \frac{x}{132} = -0.379$$

Solving for *x* yields *x* = 55.2 mm Hg.

Note: The question tells you there are 2.00 moles of the compound. This information is irrelevant to solving the problem because equilibrium vapor pressure is independent of the amount of compound.

11. (E) Begin by writing the equation in equilibrium

$$Ag_2 CO_{3(s)} \longleftrightarrow 2Ag^+_{(aq)} + CO_3^{2-}_{(aq)}$$

HNO_3 is a source of H^+ which would reduce the amount of carbonate ion (the H^+ reacts with the weak base, CO_3^{2-}). NH_3 forms $Ag(NH_3)^{2+}$ removing Ag^+ from solution. Furthermore, according to Le Chatelier's Principle, when the concentration of a species is reduced, the reaction shifts in the direction necessary to reform that species . . . . in this case, toward the right and toward ionization.

12. (C) Remember that for a conjugate acid-base pair, $K_a \times K_b = 10^{-14}$. Therefore,

$$K_b \text{Lac}^- = \frac{10^{-14}}{1.5 \times 10^{-5}} = 6.7 \times 10^{-10}$$

13. (D) $\triangle G°$ represents the free energy at standard conditions: 25°C and 1 atm pressure. $\triangle G$ represents the free energy at nonstandard conditions. In this problem, we have the nonstandard condition of 100°C. In order to solve for the free energy of this reaction, you must use the following equation:

$$\triangle G = \triangle G° + 2.303 \, RT \log Q_p$$

where the constant $R = 8.314$ J · K^{-1}· $mole^{-1}$ and Q_p is called the reaction quotient. The reaction quotient has the same form as the equilibrium constant K_p but uses nonequilibrium pressures.

Step 1: Write a balanced equation:

$$CaCO_{3(s)} \rightarrow CaO_{(s)} + CO_{2(g)}$$

Step 2: Determine the value of Q_p, the reaction quotient:

$$Q_p = P_{CO_{2(g)}} = 1.00$$

Step 3: Substitute into the equation:

$$\triangle G = \triangle G° + 2.303\ RT \log Q_p$$

$$T = 100°C + 273 = 373K$$

$$= 130,240 \text{ J/mole} + 2.303(8.314 \text{ J} \cdot K^{-1} \cdot \text{mole}^{-1})(373K)(\log 1.00)$$

Since log 1.00 = 0, the second term in the equation drops out as zero.

$$= 130,240 \text{ J/mole} = 130.240 \text{ kJ/mole}$$

14. (A)

$$\text{density} = \frac{\text{mass}}{V} = \frac{P \cdot MM}{R \cdot T} = \frac{\text{atm} \cdot \text{g} / \text{mole}}{L \cdot \text{atm} \cdot \text{mole}^{-1} K^{-1} \cdot K}$$

$$= \text{g} / L$$

15. (B) In examining the balanced equation, note that for each mole of N_2O_5 gas that decomposes, ½ mole of O_2 gas is formed. Therefore, the rate of formation of oxygen gas should be half the rate of decomposition of the N_2O_5.

16. (B) Na^+, Ba^{2+}, and I^- are neutral ions. OCl^- and NO_2^- are basic anions. Fe^{3+} and NH_4^+ are acidic cations.

17. (D) Begin by writing the equations which define the equilibrium constants.

$$AgCl_{(s)} \rightarrow Ag^+_{(aq)} + Cl^-_{(aq)} \qquad K_{sp_1} = 1.6 \times 10^{-10} \text{ mol}^2 \cdot L^{-2}$$

$$AgI_{(s)} \rightarrow Ag^+_{(aq)} + I^-_{(aq)} \qquad K_{sp_2} = 8.0 \times 10^{-17} \text{ mol}^2 \cdot L^{-2}$$

Because K_{eq} is needed for the following equation

$AgCl_{(s)} + I^-_{(aq)} \rightarrow AgI_{(s)} + Cl^-_{(aq)}$, and $I^-_{(aq)}$ is found on the reactant side, we need to reverse the equation for the dissociation of $AgI_{(s)}$:

$$Ag^+_{(aq)} + I^-_{(aq)} \rightarrow AgI_{(s)} \qquad K_{sp} = 1/K_{sp_2} = 1.25 \times 10^{16}$$

$$K_{eq} = K_{sp_1} \cdot 1/K_{sp_2} = (1.6 \times 10^{-10})(1.25 \times 10^{16}) = 2.0 \times 10^6$$

18. (D) Whether you can answer this question depends on whether you are acquainted with what is known as the Maxwell-Boltzmann distribution. This distribution describes the way that molecular speeds or energies are shared among the molecules of a gas. If you missed this question, examine the following figure and refer to your textbook for a complete description.

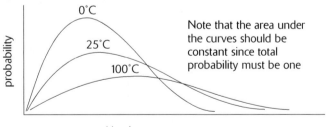

19. (A) Begin by writing a balanced equation:

$$3BaCl_{2(aq)} + 2K_3AsO_{4(aq)} \rightarrow Ba_3(AsO_4)_{2(s)} + 6KCl_{(aq)}$$

Next, realize that this problem is a limiting-reactant problem. That is, one of the two reactants will run out first, and when that happens, the reaction will stop. You need to determine which one of the reactants will run out first. To do this, you need to be able to compare them on a 1:1 basis. But their coefficients are different, so you need to relate both reactants to a common product, say $Ba_3(AsO_4)_2$. Set the problem up like this:

$$\frac{0.600 \text{ mole BaCl}_2}{1} \times \frac{1 \text{ mole Ba}_3(\text{AsO}_4)_2}{3 \text{ moles BaCl}_2} = 0.200 \text{ mole Ba}_3(\text{AsO}_4)_2$$

$$\frac{0.250 \text{ mole K}_3\text{AsO}_4}{1} \times \frac{1 \text{ mole Ba}_3(\text{AsO}_4)_2}{2 \text{ moles K}_3\text{AsO}_4} = 0.125 \text{ mole Ba}_3(\text{AsO}_4)_2$$

Given the two amounts of starting materials, you discover that you can make a maximum of 0.125 moles of $Ba_3(AsO_4)_2$, because at that point you will have exhausted your supply of K_3AsO_4.

20. (A) Oxidation is by definition the loss of electrons by an element; an oxidizing agent is a substance which causes the electrons of the element to be lost during a chemical reaction. An oxidizing agent causes another substance to be oxidized; an oxidizing agent is itself reduced. An example of HNO_3 acting as a strong oxidizing agent is when copper metal (the reducing agent) is dropped into nitric acid. When this occurs, Cu becomes Cu^{2+}, it loses electrons and becomes oxidized.

$$6H^+ + 3Cu^0 + 2HNO_3 \rightarrow 3Cu^{2+} + 2NO + 4H_2O \text{ (in acidic solution)}$$

21. (C) Nitric oxide is the common name for nitrogen monoxide, $NO_{(g)}$. Nitric oxide is a colorless, paramagnetic gas. It has an acrid odor and low solubility in water and is the simplest thermally stable odd-electron molecule known. Because it has a single, unpaired electron, it is paramagnetic. Paramagnetic materials attract and repel like normal magnets when subjected to a magnetic field.

22. (B) Oxides that can act as both acid and base, at different times, are known as amphoteric oxides. Examples of amphoteric oxides include aluminum oxide, zinc oxide, and tin oxide. These amphoteric oxides react as basic oxides with acids and as acidic oxides with bases.

Aluminum oxide reacts with acids: $Al_2O_3 + 6HCl \rightarrow 2AlCl_3 + 3H_2O$

Aluminum oxide reacts with bases: $Al_2O_3 + 2NaOH + H_2O \rightarrow 2NaAl(OH)_4$

Water is also an amphoteric oxide: $H_2O + NH_3 \longleftrightarrow NH_4^+ + OH^-$ and $H_2O + HCl \longleftrightarrow H_3O^+ + Cl^-$

23. (D) BF_3 is a trigonal-planar molecule because electrons can be found in only three places in the valence shell of the boron atom. As a result, the boron atom is sp^2 hybridized, which leaves an empty $2p_z$ orbital on the boron atom. BF_3 can therefore act as an electron-pair acceptor, or Lewis acid. It can use the empty $2p_z$ orbital to pick up a pair of nonbonding electrons from a Lewis base to form a covalent bond. BF_3 therefore reacts with Lewis bases such as NH_3 to form acid-base complexes in which all of the atoms have a filled shell of valence electrons.

24. (B) To solve this problem, multiply the percentage of each isotope by its atomic mass and add those products.

$(0.900 \times 20.0) + (0.100 \times 22.0) = 20.2$ atomic mass of element X

25. (C) All of the numbers are multiples of 19.00 (fluorine). Use the law of multiple proportions.

26. (D)

$$(1.43 \times 10^3 + 3.1 \times 10^1) = 14.3 \times 10^2 + 0.31 \times 10^2 = 14.6 \times 10^2$$

$$= \frac{14.6 \times 10^2}{4.11 \times 10^{-6}} = 3 \text{ s.f. } (3.55 \times 10^8)$$

27. (A) Basic and ionic characteristics of the oxides of the main group elements in their highest oxidation states increases as one moves down a column. Increasing acidic and covalent characteristics increase as one moves to the right.

28. (D)

Begin this problem by drawing a structural diagram:

There are three steps you need to take to do this problem.

Step 1: Decide which bonds need to be broken on the reactant side of the reaction. Add up all the bond energies for the bonds that are broken. Call this subtotal $\triangle H^{\circ}_1$, and assign it a positive value because when energy is absorbed, bonds are broken, an endothermic process. In the example given, a C=C and a H-H bond need to be broken. This becomes 614 kJ/mole + 436 kJ/mole = $\triangle H^{\circ}_1$ = 1050 kJ/mole.

Step 2: Decide which bonds need to be formed on the product side of the reaction, an exothermic process, hence the negative enthalpy value. Add up all of the bond energies for the bonds that are formed. Call this subtotal $\triangle H^{\circ}_2$. Be sure to assign $\triangle H^{\circ}_2$ a negative value because when energy is released, bonds are formed. In the example given, two C–H bonds and a C–C bond need to be formed. This becomes (2 × 413 kJ/mole) + 348 kJ/mole, or 1174 kJ/mole. Remember to assign a negative sign, which makes $\triangle H^{\circ}_2$ = –1174 kJ/mole.

Step 3: Apply Hess's law: $\triangle H^{\circ} = \triangle H^{\circ}_1 + \triangle H^{\circ}_2$

This becomes 1050 kJ/mole + (–1174 kJ/mole) = –124 kJ/mole.

29. (A)

$\triangle V = V_{\text{final}} - V_{\text{initial}} = 14.00 \text{ L} - 6.00 \text{ L} = 8.00 \text{ L}$

$w = -P\triangle V = -(1.00 \text{ atm}) (8.00 \text{ liters}) = -8.00 \text{ L} \cdot \text{atm}$

Because the gas was expanding, w is negative (work was being done by the system). One can have an expansion only if the internal pressure is greater than the external pressure. Thus, there is a limit on how much work a system can do without an external input of energy. If the gas is going to expand to a final volume of 14 liters, then the final internal pressure will be 1.00 atm.

Because $R = 8.31 \text{ J} \cdot \text{mol}^{-1} \cdot \text{K}^{-1} = 0.0821 \text{ L} \cdot \text{atm} \cdot \text{mol}^{-1} \cdot \text{K}^{-1}$, we could convert the units of work to joules if required.

30. (B)

Begin by writing down a balanced equation.

$$2CO_{(g)} + O_{2(g)} \rightarrow 2CO_{2(g)}$$

Next, use the factor-label method to solve the problem.

$$\frac{22 \text{ g CO}_2}{1} \times \frac{1 \text{ mole CO}_2}{44 \text{ g CO}_2} \times \frac{1 \text{ mole O}_2}{2 \text{ moles CO}_2} \times \frac{22.4 \text{ L O}_2}{1 \text{ mole O}_2} = 5.6 \text{ L O}_2$$

31. (D) Choices 3 and 4 will all cause the equilibrium to shift either left or right which causes a change in reactant and product concentrations which changes the value of the reaction quotient. Only a change in the temperature will cause a change in the value of the equilibrium constant. A catalyst or adding an inert gas will not affect either the equilibrium constant or reaction quotient.

32. (C) Begin by listing the information that is known.

$V = 8.00$ liters H_2

$P = 720.$ mm Hg $- 55$ mm Hg $= 665$ mm Hg (corrected for vapor pressure)

$T = 40.°C + 273 = 313K$

Using the ideal gas law, $PV = nRT$, and realizing that one can determine grams from moles, the equation becomes

$$n_{H_2} = \frac{PV}{RT} = \frac{(665 / 760 \text{ atm})(8.00 \text{ L } H_2)}{(0.0821 \text{ L} \cdot \text{atm} / \text{mole} \cdot K)(313K)}$$

Since for every mole of hydrogen produced, one mole of zinc is consumed, the last step would be to convert these moles to grams by multiplying by the molar mass of zinc.

$$\frac{\text{moles } H_2}{1} \cdot \frac{1 \text{ mole Zn}}{1 \text{ mole } H_2} \cdot \frac{65.39 \text{ g Zn}}{1 \text{ mole Zn}} = \frac{(665 / 760)(8.00)(65.39)}{(0.0821)(313)}$$

33. (B) The reaction rate will decrease since reactant concentrations will decrease.

34. (B)

The following relationships are needed to solve this problem:

$$\Delta E = R_H \left(\frac{1}{n_i^2} - \frac{1}{n_f^2} \right) \text{ and } \lambda = \frac{h \cdot c}{\Delta E}$$

Combining these equations to solve for λ gives the equation

$$\lambda = \frac{h \cdot c}{R_H \left(\dfrac{1}{n_i^2} - \dfrac{1}{n_f^2} \right)}$$

$$= \frac{(6.63 \times 10^{-34} \text{ J} \cdot \text{sec})(3.00 \times 10^8 \text{ m} \cdot \text{sec}^{-1})}{(2.18 \times 10^{-18}) \left(\dfrac{1}{5^2} - \dfrac{1}{2^2} \right)}$$

35. (D) The word *unique* in this question means that only the alkali metals possess this particular characteristic. Of the choices listed, D is the only property that is unique to the alkali metals.

36. (C) The valence electron for the cesium atom is in the $6s$ orbital. In assigning quantum numbers, $n =$ principal energy level $= 6$. The quantum number l represents the angular momentum (type of orbital) with s orbitals $= 0$, p orbitals $= 1$, d orbitals $= 2$, and so forth. In this case, $l = 0$. The quantum number m_l is known as the magnetic quantum number and describes the orientation of the orbital in space. For s orbitals (as in this case), m_l always equals 0. For p orbitals, m_l can take on the values of -1, 0, and $+1$. For d orbitals, m_l can take on the values -2, -1, 0, $+1$, and $+2$. The quantum number m_s is known as the electron spin quantum number and can take only two values, $+\frac{1}{2}$ and $-\frac{1}{2}$, depending on the spin of the electron.

37. (D) Metals lose their electrons readily to become positively charged ions with common charges of $+1$, $+2$, or $+3$.

38. (D) Because chlorine is a halogen, it has an oxidation number of -1. And, because there are 6 chlorines, there is a total charge of -6 for the chlorines. The overall charge is -2, so algebraically, $x + (-6) = -2$. Solving this yields $x = +4$. Thus, the charge (or oxidation number) of platinum is $+4$.

39. (B)

$$90. \text{ mass \% alcohol} = \frac{9.0 \text{ g isopropyl alcohol}}{\text{total mass}} \times 100$$

$$\text{total mass} = 10. \text{ g}$$

40. (E) Because CCl_4 is a nonpolar molecule, the only forces present are dispersion forces.

41. (A) Note that for acetic acid there is a hydrogen attached to an oxygen atom (a prerequisite for H bonding) but that for dimethyl ether there is no H atom connected to an F, O, or N atom. Hydrogen bonding is an extremely strong intermolecular force that results in higher boiling points when compared to molecules of similar molar mass without H-bonding.

$$\underset{\text{acetic acid}}{H_3C-\overset{\overset{\displaystyle O}{\|}}{C}-OH} \qquad \underset{\text{dimethyl ether}}{H_3C-O-CH_3}$$

42. (B) Sodium is a metal. Metals are held together in a crystal lattice, which is a network of cations surrounded by a "sea" of mobile electrons.

43. (D) ICl is a polar molecule. Polar molecules have a net dipole—that is, a center of positive charge separated from a center of negative charge. Adjacent polar molecules line up so that the negative end of the dipole on one molecule is as close as possible to the positive end of its neighbor. Under these conditions, there is an electrostatic attraction between adjacent molecules. The key word here is "solid", because if the question just asked for the force holding ICl (the molecule) together, the answer would be covalent bonding.

44. (C) The metallic cations (Ca^{2+}) are electrostatically attracted to the nonmetallic anions (Cl^-).

45. (D) Hydrogen bonds are the strongest of the intermolecular forces listed; dispersion forces are the weakest.

46. (B) This problem can be easily solved using the factor-label method:

$$\frac{500.\ \cancel{mL\ (2.00\ M\ sol'n)}}{1} \times \frac{1\ \cancel{liter(2.00\ M\ sol'n)}}{1000\ \cancel{mL\ (2.00\ M\ sol'n)}}$$

$$\times \frac{2.00\ \cancel{moles\ HNO_3}}{1\ \cancel{liter\ (2.00\ M\ sol'n)}} \times \frac{63.0\ \cancel{g\ HNO_3}}{1\ \cancel{mole\ HNO_3}} \times \frac{100.\ \cancel{g\ 50\%\ sol'n}}{50.0\ \cancel{g\ HNO_3}}$$

$$\times \frac{1\ mL\ 50.0\%\ sol'n}{2.00\ \cancel{g\ 50.0\%\ sol'n}} = 63.0\ mL\ of\ a\ 50.0\%\ sol'n$$

47. (A) This problem can be solved using the factor-label method:

$$\frac{10.0\ \cancel{moles\ NaCl}}{1000.\ g\ H_2O} \times \frac{58.4\ g\ NaCl}{1\ \cancel{mole\ NaCl}} = \frac{584\ g\ NaCl}{1000.\ g\ H_2O}$$

The question is asking for the parts of NaCl per total solution (solute + solvent).

$$\frac{584\ g\ NaCl}{1000.\ g\ H_2O + 584\ g\ NaCl}$$

48. (A) This problem can be solved using the factor-label method:

$$\frac{10.0\ moles\ NH_3}{1\ \cancel{kg\ H_2O}} \times \frac{1\ \cancel{kg\ H_2O}}{1000\ \cancel{g\ H_2O}} \times \frac{18.02\ \cancel{g\ H_2O}}{1\ mole\ H_2O}$$

$$= \frac{0.180\ mole\ NH_3}{1.00\ mole\ H_2O}$$

Total number of moles = 0.180 mole NH_3 + 1.00 mole H_2O

= 1.18 moles sol'n

$$mol\ fraction\ of\ water = \frac{1.00\ mol\ H_2O}{1.18\ mol\ sol'n}$$

49. (D) With all other factors held constant, decreasing the number of molecules decreases the chance of collision. Adding an accelerating catalyst has no effect on the rate of collisions. It lowers the activation energy, thereby increasing the chance for effective molecular collisions. Furthermore, it increases the rate of production.

50. (E) Examine experiments 2 and 3, wherein [X] is held constant. Note that as [Y] doubles (from 1.5 to 3.0), the rate does not change. Hence, the rate is independent of [Y] and the order is 0 for Y.

Now examine experiments 1 and 3, wherein [Y] is held constant. Note that as [X] doubles, the rate is increased by a factor of 4. In this case, the rate is proportional to the square of the concentration of the reactant. This is a second-order reactant.

Combining these reactant orders in a rate equation gives

rate $= k[X]^2[Y]^0 = k[X]^2$

51. (A) **Step 1:** Write the balanced equation at equilibrium.

$$N_{2(g)} + O_{2(g)} \longleftrightarrow 2NO_{(g)}$$

Step 2: Write the equilibrium expression.

$$K_{eq} = \frac{[NO]^2}{[N_2][O_2]} = 4.00$$

Step 3: Create a chart that shows the initial concentrations, the final concentrations, and the changes in concentration. Let x represent the concentration (M) of either N_2 or O_2 (their concentrations are in a 1:1 molar ratio) that is transformed through the reaction into NO.

Species	Initial Concentration (I)	Change in Concentration (C)	Final Concentration (E)
N_2	3.00 M	−x	3.00 − x
O_2	3.00 M	−x	3.00 − x
NO	0 M	+2x	2x

Step 4: Take the concentrations at equilibrium and substitute them into the equilibrium expression.

$$K_{eq} = \frac{[NO]^2}{[N_2][O_2]} = \frac{(2x)^2}{(3.00 - x)^2} = 4.00$$

Step 5: Solve for x by taking the square root of both sides.

$$\frac{2x}{3.00 - x} = 2.00$$

$2x = 6.00 - 2.00x$

$x = 1.50$

Step 6: Plug the value for x into the expression of the equilibrium concentration for NO.

[NO] $= 2x = 2(1.50) = 3.00$ M

Note: You could also solve this problem using equilibrium partial pressures of the gases:

$$K_p = \frac{(P_{NO})^2}{(P_{N_2})(P_{O_2})} = 4.00$$

Use $P = MRT$, where M represents the molar concentration of the gas, n/V.

Try this approach to confirm that [NO] $= 3.00$ M.

52. (E) **Step 1:** Write the equilibrium equation for the dissociation of lead iodide.

$$PbI_{2(s)} \longleftrightarrow Pb^{2+}_{(aq)} + 2I^-_{(aq)}$$

Step 2: Write the equilibrium expression.

$K_{sp} = [Pb^{2+}][I^-]^2 = 1.08 \times 10^{-7}$

Step 3: Set up a chart that expresses initial and final concentrations (at equilibrium) of the $Pb^{2+}_{(aq)}$ and $I^-_{(aq)}$.

Species	Initial Concentration (M)	Final Concentration (M)
Pb^{2+}	0	x
I^-	0	2x

Step 4: Substitute the equilibrium concentrations of the ions into the equilibrium expression.

$K_{sp} = [Pb^{2+}] [I^-]^2 = (x) (2x)^2 = 1.08 \times 10^{-7}$

$4x^3 = 1.08 \times 10^{-7}$

$x^3 = 27.0 \times 10^{-9}$

$x = 3.00 \times 10^{-3}$

53. **(C)** Brønsted acids donate protons (H^+). In the equation, both H_2O and HCO_3^- donate H^+.

54. **(C)** First, determine the volume of the mixture.

0.600 liter + 0.400 liter = 1.000 liter

Next, determine the concentration of each acid.

HCl: $\dfrac{0.600 \text{ liter} \times (1.0 \times 10^{-3} \text{ M})}{1.00 \text{ liter}} = 0.000600 \text{ M}$

HNO_3: $\dfrac{0.400 \text{ liter} \times (1.0 \times 10^{-3} \text{ M})}{1.00 \text{ liter}} = 0.00400 \text{ M}$

Because both acids are strong (and monoprotic), the H^+ concentration is equal to the concentration of the acid. Therefore, $[H^+] = 6.00 \times 10^{-4} \text{ M} + 4.00 \times 10^{-4} \text{ M} = 1.00 \times 10^{-3} \text{ M}$

$pH = -\log[H^+] = -\log(1.00 \times 10^{-3}) = 3.00$

55. **(D)** This problem requires us to use the Gibbs-Helmholtz equation:

$\triangle G^\circ = \triangle H^\circ - T \triangle S^\circ$

Step 1: Using the given information, calculate $\triangle H^\circ$

$\triangle H^\circ = \Sigma \triangle H_f^\circ{}_{products} - \Sigma \triangle H_f^\circ{}_{reactants}$

$= [2(-100.0)] - [2(-218.0) + 2(-297.0)] = 830.0 \text{ kJ/mole}$

Step 2: Calculate $\triangle S^\circ$

$\triangle S^\circ = \Sigma S^\circ{}_{products} - \Sigma S^\circ{}_{reactants}$

$= [2(91.0) + 3(205.0)] - [2(70.0) + 2(248.0)]$

$= 797.0 - 636.0 = 161.0 \text{ J} \cdot \text{mole}^{-1} \cdot \text{K}^{-1} = 0.161 \text{ kJ} \cdot \text{mole}^{-1} \cdot \text{K}^{-1}$

Step 3: Substitute into the Gibbs-Helmholtz equation

$\triangle G^\circ = \triangle H^\circ - T \triangle S^\circ$

$T = 25^\circ\text{C} + 273 = 298\text{K}$

$\dfrac{830.0 \text{ kJ}}{1 \text{ mole}} - \dfrac{298\cancel{K} \cdot (0.161 \text{ kJ})}{\text{mole} \cdot \cancel{K}} = 782.0 \text{ kJ} / \text{mole}$

56. (A) Entropy is a measure of the randomness or disorder of a system. The greater the disorder of a system, the greater its entropy.

In $H_2O_{(g)} \rightarrow H_2O_{(l)}$, the reaction is going from a disordered state (g) to a more ordered state (l); low entropy, $\triangle S < 0$.

In $2HCl_{(g)} \rightarrow H_{2(g)} + Cl_{2(g)}$, the change in entropy will be very small because there are two moles of gas molecules on each side of the equation.

In $SiO_{2(s)} \rightarrow Si_{(s)} + O_{2(g)}$, the system is becoming more disordered, apparent from the presence of gas molecules on the product side; high entropy, $\triangle S > 0$.

57. (D) Examine the Gibbs-Helmholtz equation,

$\triangle G° = \triangle H° - T\triangle S°$, to see the mathematical relationships of negative $\triangle H°$'s and $\triangle S°$'s. At low temperatures the $\triangle H°$ term dominates . . . making $\triangle G°$ negative. At high temperatures, the $-T\triangle S°$ term dominates . . . making $\triangle G°$ positive.

58. (D) Step 1: Decide what elements are undergoing oxidation and what elements are undergoing reduction.

ox: $Fe^{2+} \rightarrow Fe^{3+}$

red: $MnO_4^- \rightarrow Mn^{2+}$

Step 2: Balance each half-reaction with respect to atoms and then charges.

ox: $Fe^{2+} \rightarrow Fe^{3+} + e^-$

Balance the reduction half-reaction using water to balance the O's.

red: $MnO_4^- \rightarrow Mn^{2+} + 4H_2O$

Balance the H atoms with H^+ ions.

red: $MnO_4^- + 8H^+ \rightarrow Mn^{2+} + 4H_2O$

Balance charges with electrons.

red: $MnO_4^- + 8H^+ + 5e^- \rightarrow Mn^{2+} + 4H_2O$

Step 3: Equalize the number of electrons lost and gained. There were $5e^-$ gained in the reduction half-reaction, so there must be $5e^-$ lost in the oxidation half-reaction.

ox: $5Fe^{2+} \rightarrow 5Fe^{3+} + 5e^-$

Step 4: Add the two half-reactions (cancel the electrons).

ox: $5Fe^{2+} \rightarrow 5Fe^{3+} + \cancel{5e^-}$

red: $MnO_4^- + 8H^+ + \cancel{5e^-} \rightarrow Mn^{2+} + 4H_2O$

$\overline{5Fe^{2+} + MnO_4^- + 8H^+ \rightarrow 5Fe^{3+} + Mn^{2+} + 4H_2O}$

59. (C)

Step 1: Determine the oxidation and reduction half-reactions and $E°_{cell}$

ox: $3\left[Zn_{(s)} \rightarrow Zn^{2+}_{(aq)} + 2e^-\right]$ $\qquad E°_{ox} = +0.76\ V$

red: $2\left[Cr^{3+}_{(aq)} + 3e^- \rightarrow Cr_{(s)}\right]$ $\qquad E°_{red} = -0.74\ V$

$\overline{3Zn_{(s)} + 2Cr^{3+}_{(aq)} \rightarrow 3Zn^{2+}_{(aq)} + 2Cr_{(s)} \qquad E°_{cell} = 0.02\ V}$

Step 2: Use the equation (valid only at 25°C):

n is the number of electrons transferred in the half-reaction.

$\ln K = \dfrac{n \cdot E°_{cell}}{0.0257} = \dfrac{(6)\,0.02\ V}{0.0257} = 4.7$

$K = e^{4.7}$

60. **(C)** An alpha particle, $_2^4\text{He}$, is a helium nucleus.

61. **(E)** A β-particle, $_{-1}^0e$, is an electron. An unstable nuclide in β-particle production creates an electron as it releases energy in the decay process. This electron is created from the decay process, rather than being present before the decay occurs.

62. **(A)** Electron capture is a process by which one of the inner-orbital electrons is captured by the nucleus.

63. **(D)** Fission is the process whereby a heavy nucleus splits into two nuclei (not including He nuclei) with smaller mass numbers.

64. **(B)** A positron, $_1^0e$, is a particle with the same mass as an electron but with the opposite charge. The net effect of positron production is to change a proton into a neutron.

65. **(A)** Electronegativity is a measure of the ability of an atom or molecule to attract electrons in the context of a chemical bond. The type of bond formed is largely determined by the difference in electronegativity between the atoms involved. Elements from the left side of the periodic table form the most basic hydrides because the hydrogen in these compounds carries a negative charge. Thus NaH should be the most basic hydride. Na is less electronegative than As, so we expect a stronger base. Because arsenic is a less electronegative element than oxygen, we would expect that AsH_3 would be a weak base toward water. Hydrides of the halogens, as the most electronegative element in each period, would be acidic relative to water.

66. **(D)** A *p*-type semiconductor is obtained by carrying out a process of doping, that is adding a certain type of atoms to the semiconductor in order to increase the number of free (in this case positive) charge carriers. Germanium, like silicon which has a diamond structure, is a Group 4 semiconductor while aluminum is a Group 3 element (as is boron). Each aluminum atom has one less valence electron than needed for bonding to the four neighboring Ge atoms. Therefore, the valence band is partially filled, which accounts for electrical conductivity. Because the doped germanium has more positive holes in the valence band with more vacant orbitals available to which electrons can be excited by an electrical potential, its conductivity will be greater than pure germanium.

67. **(E)** Nuclides with too many neutrons per proton tend to undergo β-particle production. The net effect of β-particle production is to change a neutron to a proton. Positron production occurs for nuclides that are below the zone of stability (those nuclides whose neutron/proton ratios are too small). The net effect of positron emission is to change a proton to a neutron. An example of positron emission would be

$$_{11}^{22}\text{Na} \rightarrow {}_1^0e + {}_{10}^{22}\text{Ne}$$

Examples of β-particle production are

$$_{90}^{234}\text{Th} \rightarrow {}_{91}^{234}\text{Pa} + {}_{-1}^0e \text{ and } {}_{53}^{131}\text{I} \rightarrow {}_{54}^{131}\text{Xe} + {}_{-1}^0e$$

68. **(C)**

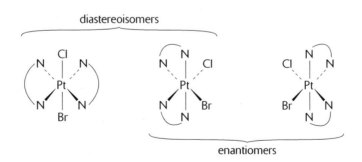

Diasteroisomers, also known as geometric isomers, have different relative orientations of their metal-ligand bonds. Enantiomers are stereoisomers whose molecules are nonsuperposable mirror images of each other. Enantiomers have identical chemical and physical properties except for their ability to rotate the plane of polarized light by equal amounts but in opposite directions. A solution of equal parts of an optically active isomer and its enantiomer is known as a racemic solution and has a net rotation of zero.

69. (E) PCl_5 is trigonal bipyramidal with a zero dipole moment.

70. (C) Refer to the equation $\triangle H = \triangle E + P\triangle V$. The change in enthalpy ($\triangle H$) and the change in total energy ($\triangle E$) of a system are nearly equal when there are no gases involved in a chemical equation. If there are gases in the reaction, then the change in volume ($\triangle V$) is equal to zero; i.e. there are equal numbers of gas molecules on both sides of the equation.

71. (B)

$$:\ddot{O}-N-\ddot{O}-H \longleftrightarrow \ddot{O}=N-\ddot{O}-H$$

72. (A) Ionization energies refer to elements, not compounds.

73. (B) $n = 4$ corresponds to the 4th energy level; $l = 2$ refers to a d orbital, $m_l = 0$ refers to the magnetic quantum number and defines the spatial orientation of the orbital and is not required to answer the question.

74. (A) Any element higher in the activity series will react with the ion of any element lower in the activity series. For example, $Cr + Pb^{2+} \rightarrow Cr^{3+} + Pb$ shows that Cr is more active than lead. $E°_{ox}$ Cr = +0.75 V. $E°_{red}$ Pb^{2+} = −0.13 V. $E°_{tot} = (0.75 - 0.13)$ V = +0.62 V (spontaneous). For the reaction $W + X^+ \rightarrow W^+ + X$, W is higher than X. For the second equation, $X + Z^+ \rightarrow X^+ + Z$, X is higher than Z. For the third reaction, $Y^+ + Z \rightarrow$ no reaction, Y is higher than Z. For the fourth reaction, $X + Y^+ \rightarrow X^+ + Y$, X is higher than Y.

75. (C) W is higher than Y, therefore reaction occurs.

Section II: Free-Response Questions

Scoring Guidelines

One point deduction for mathematical error (maximum once per question)

One point deduction for error in significant figures (maximum once per question and the number of significant figures must be correct within +/– one digit)

Part A:

Question 1

1. Magnesium hydroxide has a solubility of 9.24×10^{-4} grams per 100 mL H_2O when measured at 25°C.

   (a) Write a balanced equation representing magnesium hydroxide in equilibrium in a water solution.

$Mg(OH)_{2(s)} \longleftrightarrow Mg^{2+}_{(aq)} + 2OH^-_{(aq)}$	1 point for correct balanced equation.

   (b) Write an equilibrium expression for magnesium hydroxide in water.

$K_{sp} = [Mg^{2+}][OH^-]^2$	1 point for correct equation.

   (c) Calculate the value of K_{sp} at 25°C for magnesium hydroxide.

MW $Mg(OH)_2$ = 58.32 g/mol $\dfrac{9.24 \times 10^{-4} \text{ g Mg(OH)}_2}{100 \text{ mL H}_2O} \times \dfrac{1 \text{ mole Mg(OH)}_2}{58.32 \text{ g Mg(OH)}_2} \times \dfrac{10^3 \text{ mL H}_2O}{1 \text{ liter H}_2O}$ $= 1.58 \times 10^{-4}$ M $Mg(OH)_2$	1 point for correct M of $Mg(OH)_2$.
$= 1.58 \times 10^{-4}$ M Mg^{2+}	1 point for correct M of Mg^{2+}.
$= 2(1.58 \times 10^{-4}) = 3.16 \times 10^{-4}$ M OH^-	1 point for correct M of OH^-.
$K_{sp} = [Mg^{2+}][OH^-]^2 = (1.58 \times 10^{-4})(3.16 \times 10^{-4})^2$ $= 1.58 \times 10^{-11}$	1 point for correct K_{sp}.

   (d) Calculate the value of pH and pOH for a saturated solution of magnesium hydroxide at 25°C.

pOH = –log $[OH^-]$ $\quad$ = –log (3.16×10^{-4}) = 3.500	1 point for correct pOH.
pH = 14.0 – pOH = 10.5	1 point for correct pH.

(e) Show by the use of calculations whether a precipitate would form if one were to add 75.0 mL of a 4.00×10^{-4} M aqueous solution of magnesium chloride to 75.0 mL of a 4.00×10^{-4} M aqueous solution of potassium hydroxide.

$MgCl_{2(aq)} \rightarrow Mg^{2+}_{(aq)} + 2Cl^{-}_{(aq)}$ $KOH_{(aq)} \rightarrow K^{+}_{(aq)} + OH^{-}_{(aq)}$ Total volume of solution = 75.0 mL + 75.0 mL = 150.0 mL	
$M_1V_1 = M_2V_2$ $(4.00 \times 10^{-4}$ M$)\,(0.0750$ L$) = (x)\,(0.1500$ L$)$ x = $[Mg^{2+}] = 2.00 \times 10^{-4}$ M The same would be true for $[OH^-]$. $Q = [Mg^{2+}]\,[OH^-]^2 = (2.00 \times 10^{-4})(2.00 \times 10^{-4})^2$ = 8.00×10^{-12} $K_{sp} = 1.58 \times 10^{-11}$ A precipitate would NOT form because $Q < K_{sp}$.	1 point for correct determination of Q. 1 point for correct conclusion with supporting evidence on whether a precipitate would form or not.

Question 2

2. The ferrous ion, $Fe^{2+}_{(aq)}$, reacts with the permanganate ion, $MnO_4^-{}_{(aq)}$, in an acidic solution to produce the ferric ion, $Fe^{3+}_{(aq)}$. A 6.893-gram sample of ore was mechanically crushed and then treated with concentrated hydrochloric acid, which oxidized all of the iron in the ore to the ferrous ion, $Fe^{2+}_{(aq)}$. Next, the acid solution containing all of the ferrous ions was titrated with 0.100 M KNO$_4$ solution. The end point was reached when 13.889 mL of the potassium permanganate solution was used.

(a) Write the oxidation half-reaction.

$Fe^{2+}_{(aq)} \rightarrow Fe^{3+}_{(aq)} + e^-$	*OIL (Oxidation is Losing)* 1 point for correct equation.

(b) Write the reduction half-reaction.

$MnO_4^-{}_{(aq)} \rightarrow Mn^{2+}_{(aq)} + 4H_2O_{(l)}$ (balance O's) $MnO_4^-{}_{(aq)} + 8H^+_{(aq)} \rightarrow Mn^{2+}_{(aq)} + 4H_2O_{(l)}$ (balance H's) $MnO_4^-{}_{(aq)} + 8H^+_{(aq)} + 5e^- \rightarrow Mn^{2+}_{(aq)} + 4H_2O_{(l)}$ (balance charge)	1 point for correct balanced equation.

(c) Write the balanced final redox reaction.

ox: $5Fe^{2+} \rightarrow 5Fe^{3+} + 5e^-$ red: $MnO_4^- + 8H^+ + 5e^- \rightarrow Mn^{2+} + 4H_2O$ $\overline{MnO_4^- + 8H^+ + 5Fe^{2+} \rightarrow Mn^{2+} + 4H_2O + 5Fe^{3+}}$	1 point for correct balanced equation.

(d) Identify the oxidizing agent, the reducing agent, the species oxidized, and the species reduced.

oxidizing agent: $MnO_4^-{}_{(aq)}$ a species that accepts electrons from another	1 point for correctly identifying the oxidizing agent.
reducing agent: $Fe^{2+}_{(aq)}$ a species that furnishes electrons to another	1 point for correctly identifying the reducing agent.
species oxidized: $Fe^{2+}_{(aq)}$ **o**xidation is **l**osing (oil)	1 point for correctly identifying the species oxidized.
species reduced: $MnO_4^-{}_{(aq)}$ **r**eduction is **g**aining (rig)	1 point for correctly identifying the species reduced.

(e) Calculate the number of moles of iron in the sample of ore.

$\dfrac{13.889 \text{ mL KMnO}_4}{1} \times \dfrac{1 \text{ liter KMnO}_4 \text{ sol'n}}{1000 \text{ mL KMnO}_4 \text{ sol'n}}$	1 point for correct setup.
$\times \dfrac{0.100 \text{ mole KMnO}_4}{1 \text{ liter KMnO}_4 \text{ sol'n}} \times \dfrac{5 \text{ moles Fe}^{2+}}{1 \text{ mole KMnO}_4}$	
$= 6.94 \times 10^{-3} \text{ mole Fe}^{2+} = 6.94 \times 10^{-3} \text{ mole Fe}$ (because all of the Fe was converted to Fe^{2+})	1 point for correct answer.

(f) Calculate the mass percent of iron in the ore.

$\% = \dfrac{\text{part}}{\text{whole}} \times 100\%$ $= \dfrac{0.00694 \ \cancel{\text{mole Fe}}}{6.893 \ \text{g ore}} \times \dfrac{55.85 \ \text{g Fe}}{1 \ \cancel{\text{mole Fe}}} \times 100\%$ $= 5.62\%$	1 point for correct answer.

Question 3

3. A student performed an acid-base titration. The student began Part I of the experiment by determining the exact concentration of a base through the standardization of a basic solution using a primary acidic HCl standard. The student measured out approximately 10 mL of 6.00 M NaOH and diluted it to approximately 600 mL. The student discovered that 48.7 mL of the NaOH solution was needed to neutralize exactly 50.0 mL of a 0.100 M HCl solution.

In Part II of the experiment, the student was given 0.500 grams of an unknown solid acid and titrated it with the known base from Part I. The student added 43.2 mL of the base to the unknown acid but went past the end point and needed to back-titrate with 5.2 mL of the 0.100 M HCl solution to reach the end point. A graph of the titration is presented below.

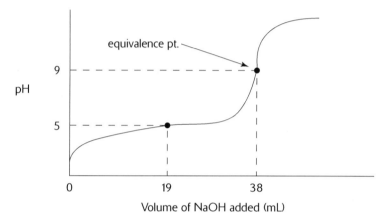

(a) Calculate the molarity of the NaOH solution from Part I.

NaOH + HCl → H₂O + NaCl $50.0 \text{ mL} \times \dfrac{0.100 \text{ mol HCl}}{1000 \text{ mL}} \times \dfrac{1 \text{ mol NaOH}}{1 \text{ mol HCl}} \times \dfrac{1}{0.0487 \text{ L}}$ = 0.103 M NaOH	1 point for correct answer.

(b) From the titration curve, determine the K_a or K_a's.

At the half-equivalence point (19 mL), pH = pK_a. Since the pH at 19 mL was shown to be 5, $K_a = 10^{-pKa} = 1 \times 10^{-5}$	1 point for correct answer.

(c) What is the pH of the solution in Part II at the equivalence point?

According to the titration curve, the pH at the equivalence point appears to be around 9. Therefore, $[OH^-] \approx 10^{-5}$ M.	1 point for correct interpretation of titration curve.

(d) Calculate K_a of the acid.

$[A^-] = \dfrac{(43.2 \text{ mL} \times 0.103 \text{ M}) - (5.2 \text{ mL} \times 0.100 \text{ M})}{43.2 \text{ mL} + 5.2 \text{ mL}}$ $= 0.0812 \text{ M}$	1 point for correct setup for K_a.
$K_a = K_w \cdot \dfrac{[A^-]}{[OH^-]^2} = \dfrac{(1 \times 10^{-14})(0.0812)}{(1 \times 10^{-5})^2}$ $= 8.12 \times 10^{-6}$	1 point for correct calculation and answer for K_a.

(e) Why is the equivalence point not at a pH of 7?

The neutralization reaction is $HA + OH^- \rightarrow A^- + H_2O$, where HA is the weak acid and A^- is its conjugate base. This assumes that HA is a monoprotic acid. Because the principal product of this reaction is the weak base, A^-, the resulting solution will be basic with a pH greater than 7.	1 point for correct explanation.

(f) Determine the equivalent mass of the acid.

$43.2 \text{ mL} \times \dfrac{0.103 \text{ mol OH}^-}{1000 \text{ mL}} = 0.00445 \text{ mol OH}^-$ dispensed from buret $5.2 \text{ mL} \times \dfrac{0.100 \text{ mol H}^+}{1000 \text{ mL}} = 0.00052 \text{ mol H}^+$ used in back titration $(0.00445 - 0.00052)$ mol $= 0.00393$ mol OH^- actually used to neutralize the acid. Since H^+ from the acid reacts in a 1:1 molar ratio with OH^- based on the titration curve, the number of moles of H^+ furnished by the acid must also be 0.00393.	1 point for correct setup.
$\text{equivalent mass} = \dfrac{\text{grams of acid}}{\text{moles of H}^+} = \dfrac{0.500 \text{ g}}{0.00393 \text{ mol}}$ $= 127 \text{ g/mol}$	1 point for correct answer.

(g) Given the following list of indicators, which indicator would have been the most appropriate to use for this experiment?

Range	Indicator	Lower Color	Upper Color
0.0 – 2.5	methyl violet	yellow-green	violet
2.5 – 4.4	methyl orange	red	yellow
6.0 – 7.6	bromthymol blue	yellow	blue
8.3 – 10.0	phenolphthalein	colorless	dark pink

Phenolphthalein would have been a good choice because the pH at the equivalence point falls within the range over which this indicator changes its color.	1 point for correct answer with correct explanation.

(h) Does the solid acid appear to be monoprotic or diprotic and explain your reasoning using the titration curve.

This acid appears to be monoprotic because the titration curve only shows one inflection point as plotted. Another end point (equivalence point) is generally hard to find, using only indicators above pH = 10.5 because the indicator equilibrium reaction $HIn \longleftrightarrow H^+ + In^-$ ($K_{HIn} = 10^{-12}$) interacts and interferes.	1 point for correct answer with correct explanation.

Part B:

Question 4

(For a complete list of reaction types that you will encounter, refer to *CliffsAP Chemistry*, 3rd Edition.)

4. (a) Water is added to a flask of solid sodium oxide.

	1 point for reactant(s), 2 points for product(s).
$Na_2O + H_2O \rightarrow Na^+ + OH^-$	Metallic oxide + H_2O → base (metallic hydroxide)

(b) Excess concentrated potassium hydroxide solution is added to a precipitate of zinc hydroxide.

	1 point for reactant(s), 2 points for product(s).
$OH^- + Zn(OH)_2 \rightarrow Zn(OH)_4^{2-}$ or $Zn(OH)_3^-$ or $ZnO_2^{2-} + H_2O$	Complex ions. *Ligands are generally electron pair donors (Lewis bases) Important ligands to know are NH_3, CN^-, SCN^-, . and OH^- Ligands bond to a central atom that is usually the positive ion of a transition metal, forming complex ions and coordination compounds.*

(c) Ethene (ethylene) gas is bubbled through a solution of chlorine.

	1 point for reactant(s), 2 points for product(s).
$C_2H_4 + Cl_2 \rightarrow C_2H_4Cl_2$	Addition reaction.

(d) A chunk of silver was added to a dilute (5 M) nitric acid solution.

	1 point for reactant(s), 2 points for product(s).
$Ag + H^+ + NO_3^- \rightarrow Ag^+ + NO$ (or NO_2) $+ H_2O$	Redox (remember that strong acids ionize). It is the nitrate ion that often reacts when nitric acid attacks metals, not the hydrogen ion.

(e) A dilute solution of sulfuric acid is added to a solution of barium chloride.

$Ba^{2+} + SO_4^{2-} \rightarrow BaSO_4$ or $HSO_4^- + Ba^{2+} \rightarrow BaSO_4 + H^+$	1 point for reactant(s), 2 points for product(s).
	Precipitation.

(f) A solution of iron (III) chloride is mixed with a solution of ammonium thiocyanate.

	1 point for reactant(s), 2 points for product(s).
$SCN^- + Fe^{3+} \rightarrow Fe(SCN)^{2+}$ or $Fe(SCN)_6{}^{3-}$	Complex ions: *Ligands are generally electron pair donors (Lewis bases). Important ligands to know are NH_3, CN^-, SCN^-, and OH^-. Ligands bond to a central atom that is usually the positive ion of a transition metal, forming complex ions and coordination compounds. On the AP exam, the number of ligands attached to a central metal ion is often twice the oxidation number of the central metal ion.*

(g) A solution of hydrogen peroxide is warmed.

	1 point for reactant(s), 2 points for product(s).
$H_2O_2 \rightarrow H_2O + O_2$	Decomposition.

(h) Finely ground aluminum is added to a solution of copper(II) sulfate.

	1 point for reactant(s), 2 points for product(s).
$Al + Cu^{2+} \rightarrow Al^{3+} + Cu$	Redox.

Question 5

5. (a) Define the concept of entropy. Be sure to include concepts of state function, units, and magnitude.

Entropy, which has the symbol S, is a thermodynamic function that is a measure of the disorder of a system. Entropy, like enthalpy, is a state function. State functions are those quantities whose changed values are determined by their initial and final values. The quantity of entropy of a system depends on the temperature and pressure of the system. The units of entropy are commonly $J \cdot K^{-1} \cdot mole^{-1}$. If S has a $\circ$ (S°), then it is referred to as standard molar entropy and represents the entropy at 298K and 1 atm of pressure; for solutions, it would be at a concentration of 1 molar. The larger the value of the entropy, the greater the disorder of the system.	2 points maximum for definition. Definition must include concept of state function, proper units for entropy, and what comparative large and small values of entropy mean.

(b) From each of the pairs of substances listed, and assuming 1 mole of each substance, choose the one that would be expected to have the lower absolute entropy and explain your reasoning in each case.

(i) $H_2O_{(s)}$ or $SiC_{(s)}$ at the same temperature and pressure.

$SiC_{(s)}$. $H_2O_{(s)}$ is a polar covalent molecule. Between the individual molecules would be hydrogen bonds. $SiC_{(s)}$ exists as a structured and ordered covalent network. Melting point of $SiC_{(s)}$ is much higher than that of $H_2O_{(s)}$, so it would take more energy to vaporize the more ordered $SiC_{(s)}$ than to vaporize $H_2O_{(s)}$.	1 point for correct answer. 1 point for proper explanation.

(ii) $O_{2(g)}$ at 3.0 atm or $O_{2(g)}$ at 1.0 atm, both at the same temperature.

$O_{2(g)}$ at 3.0 atm. At higher pressures, the oxygen molecules have less space to move within and are thus more ordered.	1 point for correct answer. 1 point for proper explanation.

(iii) $NH_{3(l)}$ or $C_6H_{6(l)}$ at the same temperature and pressure.

$NH_{3(l)}$. $NH_{3(l)}$ has hydrogen bonds (favors order). $C_6H_{6(l)}$ has more atoms and so more vibrations—thus greater disorder.	1 point for correct answer. 1 point for proper explanation.

(iv) $Na_{(s)}$ or $SiO_{2(s)}$.

$SiO_{2(s)}$. $Na_{(s)}$ has high entropy. It exhibits metallic bonding, forming soft crystals with high amplitudes of vibration. $SiO_{2(s)}$ forms an ordered, structured covalent network. $SiO_{2(s)}$ has a very high melting point, so more energy is necessary to break the ordered system.	1 point for correct answer. 1 point for proper explanation.

Question 6

6. Bromine reacts with a metal (M) as follows:

$$M_{(s)} + Br_{2(g)} \rightarrow MBr_{2(s)}$$

(a) Describe the type of bonding that would occur in $MBr_{2(s)}$.

An ionic bond can be formed after two or more atoms lose or gain electrons to form an ion. Ionic bonds occur between metals (losing electrons) and nonmetals (gaining electrons). Ions with opposite charges will attract one another creating an ionic bond. Such bonds are stronger than hydrogen bonds, but similar in strength to covalent bonds. Ionic bonding only occurs if the overall energy change for the reaction is favorable (the bonded atoms have a lower energy than the free ones). The larger the energy change the stronger the bond. Pure ionic bonding doesn't actually happen with real atoms. All bonds have a small amount of covalency. The larger the difference in electronegativity, the more ionic the bond.	1 point for description of ionic bonding using at least 2 concepts.

(b) Define lattice energy. What factors would affect the lattice energy of $MBr_{2(s)}$?

The sum of the electrostatic interaction energies between ions in a solid is called the lattice energy of the solid. By convention, the lattice energy refers to the breakup of a crystal into individual ions. It has a positive value because energy is required to separate the electrical charges. The magnitude of a lattice energy is described by Coulomb's Law, L.E. = $Q_1 \cdot Q_2/r$. Lattice energies are largest when the distance between ions is small and when one or both of the charges are large.	1 point for correct definition of lattice energy.
	1 point for at least two factors that affect lattice energy.

(c) If metal M were either magnesium, beryllium, or calcium, arrange the possible compounds in order of increasing lattice energies. Explain your reasoning.

Within a series of compounds that have the same anion but different cations, the order of lattice energies is the same as the order of decreasing cation size. Among the choices possible, the order of increasing lattice energies would be $CaBr_2 < MgBr_2 < BeBr_2$.	1 point for correct order.
	1 point for correct explanation.

(d) If metal M were either magnesium, sodium, or aluminum (the equations would be different) arrange the resulting compounds in order of increasing lattice energy. Explain your reasoning.

Compounds of ions with higher charges have greater lattice energies than compounds of ions with lower charges. In comparing $NaBr$, $MgBr_2$, and $AlBr_3$, the order of charges on the cations is $Al^{3+} > Mg^{2+} > Na^+$, and the order of lattice energies is $NaBr < MgBr_2 < AlBr_3$.	1 point for correct order.
	1 point for correct explanation.

(e) Explain how the heat of the reaction is affected by

(i) the ionization energy for the metal, M.

Ionization energy is the amount of energy that a gaseous atom must absorb so that the outermost electron can be completely separated from the atom. The lower the ionization energy, the more metallic the element. With all factors held constant, energy is required to form the M^{2+} ion (endothermic). With larger ionization energies, the heat of the reaction becomes more positive or more endothermic.	1 point for correct explanation using at least one concept.

(ii) the size of the ionic radius for the ion, M^{2+}.

The ionic radius is estimated from the distance between cations and anions that are adjacent in ion crystals. Positive ions are smaller than the metal atoms from which they are formed. The change that occurs from $M_{(s)} \rightarrow M^{2+}$, which exists as the cation in the ionic solid MBr_2, results in a decrease in the radius. In the calculation of lattice energy, L.E. $= Q_1 \cdot Q_2/r$, the lattice energy is seen to be inversely proportional to the radius, r. Because atomic distances r are decreasing in the reaction, lattice energy is increasing $(-\triangle H)$, which has the effect of making the heat of reaction more negative, or more exothermic. Q_1 and Q_2 being opposite in sign further confirms the fact that bringing cations and anions together is an exothermic process.	2 points for correct answer using concepts of cation charge, cation size, and distance between cations as related by Coulomb's Law.

Question 7

7. $(P + a)/V^2) (V - b) = R \cdot T$ is the van der Waals equation for one mole of a real gas whereas the ideal gas equation is $PV = nRT$.

(a) Explain the differences between the two equations. What assumptions are made using the ideal gas equation?

The behavior of real gases usually agrees with the predictions of the ideal gas equation to within ±5% at normal temperatures and pressures. At low temperatures or high pressures, real gases deviate significantly from ideal gas behavior. The van der Waals equation corrects for these deviations.	1 point for properly explaining the difference between the ideal gas equation and the van der Waals equation.

(b) Discuss the correctional factor "a" and the factor(s) that influence its magnitude.

The ideal gas equation assumes that the force of attraction between gas molecules is zero. The assumption that there is no force of attraction between gas particles is not true. If it was, gases would never condense to form liquids. In reality, there is a small force of attraction between gas molecules that tends to hold the molecules together. This force of attraction has two consequences: (1) gases condense to form liquids at low temperatures, and (2) the pressure of a real gas is sometimes smaller than expected for an ideal gas. The correctional factor "a" corrects for the fact that the pressure of a real gas is smaller than expected from the ideal gas equation.	1 point for explaining "a" correctly and 1 point for supporting evidence.

(c) Discuss the correctional factor "b" and the factor(s) that influence its magnitude.

The kinetic or ideal gas equation assumes that gas particles occupy a negligible fraction of the total volume of the gas and works well at pressures close to 1 atm. However, real gases are not as compressible at high pressures as an ideal gas. The volume of a real gas is therefore larger than expected for the ideal gas equation at high pressures. We correct for the fact that the volume of a real gas is too large at high pressures by subtracting a term from the volume of the real gas before we substitute it into the ideal gas equation.	1 point for explaining "b" correctly and 1 point for supporting evidence.

(d) Given the gases H_2 and HCl, which gas would have a higher value for "a" and explain your reasoning.

HCl would have a higher value for "a" because HCl is a polar molecule and therefore has stronger intermolecular forces than H_2. H_2 is nonpolar with only weak dispersion forces to contend with.	1 point for correct answer and 1 point for supporting the choice with valid reasoning.

(e) Given the gases H_2 and HCl, which gas would have a higher value for "b" and explain your reasoning.

The "b" value corrects for the volume of the molecule. Because HCl is a larger molecule than H_2, HCl would have a slightly larger "b" correctional factor.	1 point for correct answer and 1 point for supporting the choice with valid reasoning.

(f) Which of the two constants is associated with the boiling point of a substance and explain your reasoning?

Compounds for which the force of attraction between particles is strong have large values for "a". When a liquid boils, we would expect that compounds with large values of "a" would have higher boiling points because the force of attraction between gas particles is stronger. We have to go to higher temperatures before we can break the bonds between the molecules in the liquid to form a gas. Gases with very small values of "a," such as H_2 and He, must be cooled to almost absolute zero before they condense to form a liquid.	1 point for correctly identifying the constant "a" with supporting evidence.

Question 8

8. 3 moles of $PCl_{3(g)}$ and 2 moles of $Cl_{2(g)}$ were introduced into an empty sealed flask and allowed to reach equilibrium with the product, $PCl_{5(g)}$. It was experimentally determined that the overall forward reaction was second order and the reverse reaction was first order in PCl_5.

(a) Write the equilibrium expression for the reaction.

$PCl_{3(g)} + Cl_{2(g)} \longleftrightarrow PCl_{5(g)}$	1 point for correct equation.

(b) Draw a graph showing how the concentrations of all species change over time until equilibrium is achieved.

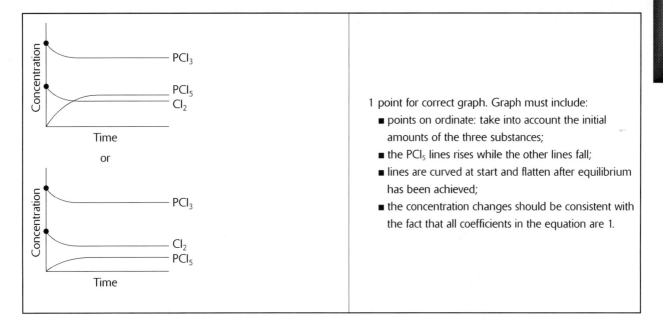

1 point for correct graph. Graph must include:
- points on ordinate: take into account the initial amounts of the three substances;
- the PCl_5 lines rises while the other lines fall;
- lines are curved at start and flatten after equilibrium has been achieved;
- the concentration changes should be consistent with the fact that all coefficients in the equation are 1.

(c) Write the rate law for the forward reaction.

rate = $k[PCl_3] [Cl_2]$	1 point for being first order for each reactant and including k into the equation.

(d) List four factors that influence the rate of a reaction and explain each factor using chemical principles.

■ Nature of the reactants. In the case of solid reactants, if we reduce the physical size of the reactants through grinding, we are in essence increasing the total surface area that collisions can take place. This will have an enhanced effect on rate of product formation. Gaseous reactants have a higher kinetic energy, and therefore the impact energy will be greater resulting in a higher rate of product formation.	
■ A higher concentration of reactants leads to more effective collisions per unit time, which leads to an increasing reaction rate (except for zero order reactions). Similarly, a higher concentration of products tends to be associated with a lower reaction rate.	
■ Medium—The rate of a chemical reaction depends on the medium in which the reaction occurs. It may make a difference whether a medium is aqueous or organic; polar or nonpolar; or liquid, solid, or gaseous.	1 point for each factor (including explanation from points listed).
■ Temperature—Increasing the temperature increases the average kinetic energy of the molecules. This will increase the impact energy enough to overcome the activation energy.	
■ Catalyst—Catalysts lower the activation energy of a chemical reaction and increase the rate of a chemical reaction without being consumed in the process. Catalysts work by increasing the frequency of collisions between reactants, altering the orientation of reactants so that more collisions are effective, reducing intramolecular bonding within reactant molecules, or donating electron density to the reactants. The presence of a catalyst helps a reaction to proceed more quickly to equilibrium. Aside from catalysts, other chemical species can affect a reaction. The quantity of hydrogen ions (the pH of aqueous solutions) can alter a reaction rate. Other chemical species may compete for a reactant or alter orientation, bonding, or electron density, thereby decreasing the rate of a reaction.	

(e) What is an activated complex?

An activated complex is a short-lived, high-energy, unstable intermediate that is formed during a reaction. When chemical substances collide in a reaction, a high-energy, unstable, transitory species known as an activated complex is formed. The activated complex is an unstable arrangement of the atoms which must form either the original reactants or some new products. If the collision is effective it comes apart to form new products and if the collision is ineffective it comes apart to reform the reactants.	1 point for correct explanation using any of the concepts listed.

(f) Explain the concepts behind the Maxwell-Boltzmann distribution and sketch a diagram to explain the concepts.

In order for a molecular collision to be effective it must meet two conditions: (1) the collision must have sufficient enough impact energy to overcome the activation energy. The activation energy is the minimum energy determined by the temperature necessary for the product to form. This impact energy must be sufficient so that (1) bonds can be broken within the reactant molecules and new bonds formed to produce the products and (2) the molecules must also have proper positioning for effective collisions to occur. In any particular mixture of moving molecules, the velocity of the molecules will vary a great deal, from very slow particles (low energy) to very fast particles (high energy). Most of the particles, however, will be moving at a speed very close to the average. The Maxwell-Boltzmann distribution shows how the speeds (and hence the energies) of a mixture of moving particles varies at a particular temperature.	1 point for correct explanation using the concepts listed.
The Maxwell-Boltzmann Distribution 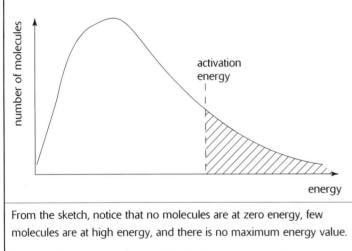	1 point for correct sketch.
From the sketch, notice that no molecules are at zero energy, few molecules are at high energy, and there is no maximum energy value. For a reaction to occur, the particles involved need a minimum amount of energy—the activation energy (E_a). If a particle is not in the shaded area, then it will not have the required energy so it will not be able to participate in the reaction.	

Multiple-Choice Answer Sheet for Practice Exam 5

Remove this sheet and use it to mark your answers.
Answer sheets for "Section II: Free-Response Questions" can be found at the end of this book.

Section I
Multiple-Choice Questions

CUT HERE

1 Ⓐ Ⓑ Ⓒ Ⓓ Ⓔ	26 Ⓐ Ⓑ Ⓒ Ⓓ Ⓔ	51 Ⓐ Ⓑ Ⓒ Ⓓ Ⓔ
2 Ⓐ Ⓑ Ⓒ Ⓓ Ⓔ	27 Ⓐ Ⓑ Ⓒ Ⓓ Ⓔ	52 Ⓐ Ⓑ Ⓒ Ⓓ Ⓔ
3 Ⓐ Ⓑ Ⓒ Ⓓ Ⓔ	28 Ⓐ Ⓑ Ⓒ Ⓓ Ⓔ	53 Ⓐ Ⓑ Ⓒ Ⓓ Ⓔ
4 Ⓐ Ⓑ Ⓒ Ⓓ Ⓔ	29 Ⓐ Ⓑ Ⓒ Ⓓ Ⓔ	54 Ⓐ Ⓑ Ⓒ Ⓓ Ⓔ
5 Ⓐ Ⓑ Ⓒ Ⓓ Ⓔ	30 Ⓐ Ⓑ Ⓒ Ⓓ Ⓔ	55 Ⓐ Ⓑ Ⓒ Ⓓ Ⓔ
6 Ⓐ Ⓑ Ⓒ Ⓓ Ⓔ	31 Ⓐ Ⓑ Ⓒ Ⓓ Ⓔ	56 Ⓐ Ⓑ Ⓒ Ⓓ Ⓔ
7 Ⓐ Ⓑ Ⓒ Ⓓ Ⓔ	32 Ⓐ Ⓑ Ⓒ Ⓓ Ⓔ	57 Ⓐ Ⓑ Ⓒ Ⓓ Ⓔ
8 Ⓐ Ⓑ Ⓒ Ⓓ Ⓔ	33 Ⓐ Ⓑ Ⓒ Ⓓ Ⓔ	58 Ⓐ Ⓑ Ⓒ Ⓓ Ⓔ
9 Ⓐ Ⓑ Ⓒ Ⓓ Ⓔ	34 Ⓐ Ⓑ Ⓒ Ⓓ Ⓔ	59 Ⓐ Ⓑ Ⓒ Ⓓ Ⓔ
10 Ⓐ Ⓑ Ⓒ Ⓓ Ⓔ	35 Ⓐ Ⓑ Ⓒ Ⓓ Ⓔ	60 Ⓐ Ⓑ Ⓒ Ⓓ Ⓔ
11 Ⓐ Ⓑ Ⓒ Ⓓ Ⓔ	36 Ⓐ Ⓑ Ⓒ Ⓓ Ⓔ	61 Ⓐ Ⓑ Ⓒ Ⓓ Ⓔ
12 Ⓐ Ⓑ Ⓒ Ⓓ Ⓔ	37 Ⓐ Ⓑ Ⓒ Ⓓ Ⓔ	62 Ⓐ Ⓑ Ⓒ Ⓓ Ⓔ
13 Ⓐ Ⓑ Ⓒ Ⓓ Ⓔ	38 Ⓐ Ⓑ Ⓒ Ⓓ Ⓔ	63 Ⓐ Ⓑ Ⓒ Ⓓ Ⓔ
14 Ⓐ Ⓑ Ⓒ Ⓓ Ⓔ	39 Ⓐ Ⓑ Ⓒ Ⓓ Ⓔ	64 Ⓐ Ⓑ Ⓒ Ⓓ Ⓔ
15 Ⓐ Ⓑ Ⓒ Ⓓ Ⓔ	40 Ⓐ Ⓑ Ⓒ Ⓓ Ⓔ	65 Ⓐ Ⓑ Ⓒ Ⓓ Ⓔ
16 Ⓐ Ⓑ Ⓒ Ⓓ Ⓔ	41 Ⓐ Ⓑ Ⓒ Ⓓ Ⓔ	66 Ⓐ Ⓑ Ⓒ Ⓓ Ⓔ
17 Ⓐ Ⓑ Ⓒ Ⓓ Ⓔ	42 Ⓐ Ⓑ Ⓒ Ⓓ Ⓔ	67 Ⓐ Ⓑ Ⓒ Ⓓ Ⓔ
18 Ⓐ Ⓑ Ⓒ Ⓓ Ⓔ	43 Ⓐ Ⓑ Ⓒ Ⓓ Ⓔ	68 Ⓐ Ⓑ Ⓒ Ⓓ Ⓔ
19 Ⓐ Ⓑ Ⓒ Ⓓ Ⓔ	44 Ⓐ Ⓑ Ⓒ Ⓓ Ⓔ	69 Ⓐ Ⓑ Ⓒ Ⓓ Ⓔ
20 Ⓐ Ⓑ Ⓒ Ⓓ Ⓔ	45 Ⓐ Ⓑ Ⓒ Ⓓ Ⓔ	70 Ⓐ Ⓑ Ⓒ Ⓓ Ⓔ
21 Ⓐ Ⓑ Ⓒ Ⓓ Ⓔ	46 Ⓐ Ⓑ Ⓒ Ⓓ Ⓔ	71 Ⓐ Ⓑ Ⓒ Ⓓ Ⓔ
22 Ⓐ Ⓑ Ⓒ Ⓓ Ⓔ	47 Ⓐ Ⓑ Ⓒ Ⓓ Ⓔ	72 Ⓐ Ⓑ Ⓒ Ⓓ Ⓔ
23 Ⓐ Ⓑ Ⓒ Ⓓ Ⓔ	48 Ⓐ Ⓑ Ⓒ Ⓓ Ⓔ	73 Ⓐ Ⓑ Ⓒ Ⓓ Ⓔ
24 Ⓐ Ⓑ Ⓒ Ⓓ Ⓔ	49 Ⓐ Ⓑ Ⓒ Ⓓ Ⓔ	74 Ⓐ Ⓑ Ⓒ Ⓓ Ⓔ
25 Ⓐ Ⓑ Ⓒ Ⓓ Ⓔ	50 Ⓐ Ⓑ Ⓒ Ⓓ Ⓔ	75 Ⓐ Ⓑ Ⓒ Ⓓ Ⓔ

CUT HERE

PERIODIC TABLE OF THE ELEMENTS

1																	2
H 1.0079																	**He** 4.0026
3 **Li** 6.941	4 **Be** 9.012											5 **B** 10.811	6 **C** 12.011	7 **N** 14.007	8 **O** 16.00	9 **F** 19.00	10 **Ne** 20.179
11 **Na** 22.99	12 **Mg** 24.30											13 **Al** 26.98	14 **Si** 28.09	15 **P** 30.974	16 **S** 32.06	17 **Cl** 35.453	18 **Ar** 39.948
19 **K** 39.10	20 **Ca** 40.08	21 **Sc** 44.96	22 **Ti** 47.90	23 **V** 50.94	24 **Cr** 51.00	25 **Mn** 54.93	26 **Fe** 55.85	27 **Co** 58.93	28 **Ni** 58.69	29 **Cu** 63.55	30 **Zn** 65.39	31 **Ga** 69.72	32 **Ge** 72.59	33 **As** 74.92	34 **Se** 78.96	35 **Br** 79.90	36 **Kr** 83.80
37 **Rb** 85.47	38 **Sr** 87.62	39 **Y** 88.91	40 **Zr** 91.22	41 **Nb** 92.91	42 **Mo** 95.94	43 **Tc** (98)	44 **Ru** 101.1	45 **Rh** 102.91	46 **Pd** 105.42	47 **Ag** 107.87	48 **Cd** 112.41	49 **In** 114.82	50 **Sn** 118.71	51 **Sb** 121.75	52 **Te** 127.60	53 **I** 126.91	54 **Xe** 131.29
55 **Cs** 132.91	56 **Ba** 137.33	57 ***La** 138.91	72 **Hf** 178.49	73 **Ta** 180.95	74 **W** 183.85	75 **Re** 186.21	76 **Os** 190.2	77 **Ir** 192.22	78 **Pt** 195.08	79 **Au** 196.97	80 **Hg** 200.59	81 **Ti** 204.38	82 **Pb** 207.2	83 **Bi** 208.98	84 **Po** (209)	85 **At** (210)	86 **Rn** (222)
87 **Fr** (223)	88 **Ra** 226.02	89 †**Ac** 227.03	104 **Rf** (261)	105 **Db** (262)	106 **Sg** (263)	107 **Bh** (262)	108 **Hs** (265)	109 **Mt** (266)	110 **§** (269)	111 **§** (272)	112 **§** (277)						

§ Not yet named

* Lanthanide Series

58 **Ce** 140.12	59 **Pr** 140.91	60 **Nd** 144.24	61 **Pm** (145)	62 **Sm** 150.4	63 **Eu** 151.97	64 **Gd** 157.25	65 **Tb** 158.93	66 **Dy** 162.50	67 **Ho** 164.93	68 **Er** 167.26	69 **Tm** 168.93	70 **Yb** 173.04	71 **Lu** 174.97

† Actinide Series

90 **Th** 232.04	91 **Pa** 231.04	92 **U** 238.03	93 **Np** 237.05	94 **Pu** (244)	95 **Am** (243)	96 **Cm** (247)	97 **Bk** (247)	98 **Cf** (251)	99 **Es** (252)	100 **Fm** (257)	101 **Md** (258)	102 **No** (259)	103 **Lr** (260)

Practice Exam 5

Section I: Multiple-Choice Questions

Time: 90 minutes

75 questions

45% of total grade

No calculators allowed

This section consists of 75 multiple-choice questions. Mark your answers carefully on the answer sheet.

General Instructions

Do not open this booklet until you are told to do so by the proctor.

Be sure to write your answers for Section I on the separate answer sheet. Use the test booklet for your scratch work or notes, but remember that no credit will be given for work, notes, or answers written only in the test booklet. After you have selected an answer, blacken thoroughly the corresponding circle on the answer sheet. To change an answer, erase your previous mark completely, and then record your new answer. Mark only one answer for each question.

Example   Sample Answer

The Pacific is   Ⓐ Ⓑ ● Ⓓ Ⓔ

    A. a river
    B. a lake
    C. an ocean
    D. a sea
    E. a gulf

To discourage haphazard guessing on this section of the exam, a quarter of a point is subtracted for every wrong answer, but no points are subtracted if you leave the answer blank. Even so, if you can eliminate one or more of the choices for a question, it may be to your advantage to guess.

Because it is not expected that all test takers will complete this section, do not spend too much time on difficult questions. Answer first the questions you can answer readily, and then, if you have time, return to the difficult questions later. Don't get stuck on one question. Work quickly but accurately. Use your time effectively. The preceding table is provided for your use in answering questions in Section I.

GO ON TO THE NEXT PAGE

Directions: Each group of lettered answer choices below refers to the numbered statements or questions that immediately follow. For each question or statement, select the one lettered choice that is the best answer and fill in the corresponding circle on the answer sheet. An answer choice may be used once, more than once, or not at all in each set of questions.

Questions 1–4

    (A) Mg
    (B) K
    (C) S
    (D) Cl
    (E) Kr

1. Smallest ionic radius.

2. Lowest first ionization energy.

3. The one that would react most actively when placed in water to form a strong base.

4. Greatest electronegativity.

Questions 5–8

    (A) sp
    (B) sp^2
    (C) sp^3
    (D) sp^3d
    (E) sp^3d^2

5. SO_2

6. I_3^-

7. IF_5

8. CH_3OH

For Questions 9–12, use the following graph of ionization energy vs. atomic number:

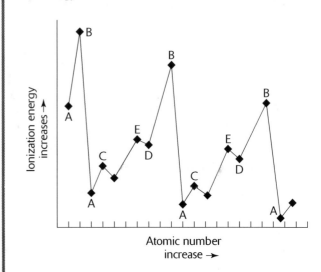

9. Elements with half-filled p orbitals

10. Noble gases

11. Most active metals

12. Beginning of pairing of electrons in the p orbitals

13. The density of a gas is directly proportional to its

    A. temperature
    B. pressure
    C. volume
    D. molecular speed
    E. chemical reactivity

14. Which of the following does NOT represent a possible set of quantum numbers arranged in order n, l, m_l, m_s?

    A. 2, 2, 0, $+\frac{1}{2}$
    B. 2, 1, 0, $-\frac{1}{2}$
    C. 4, 0, 0, $-\frac{1}{2}$
    D. 3, 2, 0, $+\frac{1}{2}$
    E. 4, 3, 1, $+\frac{1}{2}$

15. Which of the following is named incorrectly?

A. Na_2O_2, sodium peroxide
B. Na_2O, sodium oxide
C. NaO_2, sodium superoxide
D. NaO, sodium oxide
E. $NaOH$, sodium hydroxide

16. In the molecule C_2H_2, there are ___ sigma bonds and ___ pi bonds.

A. 1, 4
B. 2, 3
C. 3, 2
D. 4, 1
E. 5, 0

17. Which of the following would NOT easily undergo thermal decomposition?

A. $MgCl_2$
B. $MgCO_3$
C. $Mg(OH)_2$
D. $MgSO_4 \cdot 7H_2O$
E. All choices would easily thermally decompose.

18. A student wished to produce only carbon dioxide and water vapor from the combustion of methane, CH_4. To accomplish this the student should

A. burn CH_4 in limited oxygen.
B. burn CH_4 in a vacuum.
C. burn CH_4 in excess oxygen.
D. burn CH_4 at a very low temperature.
E. burn CH_4 at a very high pressure.

19. Consider the reaction

$$A_{(g)} + B_{(g)} \longleftrightarrow C_{(g)} + D_{(g)}$$

To increase the yield of D, one could

A. decrease the volume of the container.
B. increase the volume of the container.
C. add a catalyst.
D. add a reactant that would absorb C.
E. lower the temperature.

20. The rate constant k for a first order reaction might have which units?

A. $moles \cdot liter^{-1}$
B. $moles \cdot liter$
C. sec^{-1}
D. $moles \cdot liter^{-1} \cdot sec^{-1}$
E. $moles/(liter \cdot sec^2)$

21. Which of the following hydrocarbons would most likely contribute to air pollution?

A. methane
B. ethane
C. propane
D. ethene
E. all would contribute equally

22. A student placed three moles of hydrogen gas and three moles of iodine gas into a 1-liter flask and heated the flask to 300°C. The equilibrium expression would be equal to

A. $K_c = \dfrac{(2x)^2}{(3-x)^2}$

B. $K_c = \dfrac{(2x)^2}{(2-x)^3}$

C. $K_c = \dfrac{x^2}{(2-x)^2}$

D. $K_c = \dfrac{(2x-2)^2}{3-x}$

E. $K_c = \dfrac{(2x)^2}{x-2}$

23. If the equilibrium constant for question #22 was 81, what would be the concentration of the iodine gas at equilibrium?

A. 0.33
B. 2.00
C. 2.45
D. 3.00
E. 9.00

GO ON TO THE NEXT PAGE

Practice Exam 5

24. If the amount of energy required to melt 4.50 grams of ice at 0°C were used to heat 1 gram of water at 5°C, approximately how much steam could be produced? The heat of fusion for H_2O is 335 J/g and the heat of vaporization of water is 2260 J/g.

   A.   0 grams
   B.   0.5 grams
   C.   1.5 grams
   D.   2.5 grams
   E.   5 grams

25. The following graph shows the solubility of ammonium chloride in water. 30 grams of ammonium chloride are added to 1 liter of water. How much more ammonium chloride can be added to the solution until it is saturated at 30°C?

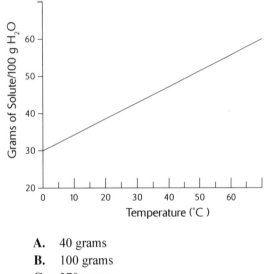

   A.   40 grams
   B.   100 grams
   C.   370 grams
   D.   400 grams
   E.   430 grams

26. Chemical reactions always involve

   A.   release of energy.
   B.   absorption of energy.
   C.   release or absorption of energy.
   D.   release and absorption of energy.
   E.   a change in state.

27. Electromagnetic radiation with a wavelength of 320 nm

   A.   has a higher velocity in a vacuum than does radiation with a wavelength of 400 nm.
   B.   has a higher frequency than radiation with a wavelength 200 nm.
   C.   is in the visible region of the electromagnetic spectrum.
   D.   has a lower energy per photon than does radiation with a wavelength of 100 nm.
   E.   has a slower velocity in a vacuum than does radiation with a wavelength of 400 nm.

28. A student performed a series of experiments and recorded the results.

Experiment	Procedure	Observations
1	A copper wire was placed into a beaker of clear silver nitrate solution.	Two days later she noticed solid silver clinging to the wire. The solution had turned blue.
2	Iron filings were added to the blue solution from Experiment 1.	Two days later she noticed that the iron filings were orange.
3	She dropped a magnesium strip and an iron nail into a 6M solution of HCl.	The magnesium strip produced more hydrogen bubbles than the iron nail.
4	She dropped a small piece of sodium and a small piece of magnesium into warm water. She also added silver, iron, and magnesium metal to samples of warm water.	The sodium reacted more vigorously than did the magnesium. The other metals did not react at all with the warm water.

The order of decreasing strength as a reducing agent based upon the observations is

A. $Ag > Cu > Fe > Mg > Na$
B. $Ag > Na > Cu > Fe > Mg$
C. $Cu > Ag > Fe > Mg > Na$
D. $Na > Cu > Mg > Fe > Ag$
E. $Na > Mg > Fe > Cu > Ag$

29. A student prepares an aqueous solution of NaCl and performs an electrolysis experiment. The products at the cathode would be

A. Na
B. Cl^-
C. Cl_2
D. H_2 and OH^-
E. O_2

30. Substance X is a solid and is mixed with Y which is also a solid. A student wishes to separate the two substances through fractional crystallization. Which property allows the two substances to be separated through this procedure?

A. one substance having a higher vapor pressure than the other
B. one substance having a higher melting point than the other
C. one substance having a higher density than the other
D. one substance having a higher solubility than the other
E. all properties are necessary to separate substances using the technique of fractional crystallization

31. Which of the following statement(s) is true?

I. The mass of the reactants for a particular reaction always equals the mass of the products.
II. The number of moles of product must always equal the number of moles of reactants for any reaction.
III. The volumes of gaseous reactants must always equal the volumes of gaseous products for any reaction.

A. I
B. II
C. III
D. I and II
E. I and III

GO ON TO THE NEXT PAGE

Practice Exam 5

For Questions 32 and 33, refer to the following diagram:

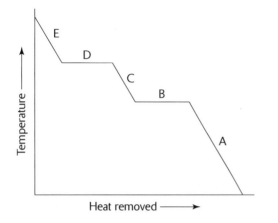

Heat removed ⟶

32. At what point on the graph is melting occurring?

33. At what point on the graph is freezing occurring?

34. Water is often called the 'universal solvent'. The primary reason that water is such a good solvent is due to

    A. its density.
    B. its relatively small size as a molecule.
    C. hydrogen bonding.
    D. a high dielectric constant.
    E. its low molecular weight.

35. A student proceeded to gather the following equipment in order to distill a liquid that was produced by the addition of an acid to a specific solution.

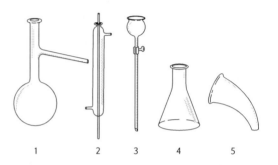

Starting with the piece of equipment which adds acid to the solution and ending with the piece of glassware that contains the distillate, the proper order in connecting the glassware would be

    A. 1-2-3-4-5
    B. 5-4-3-2-1
    C. 3-1-2-5-4
    D. 5-1-4-2-3
    E. 4-2-1-5-3

36. The reaction profile for a two-step reaction is shown below.

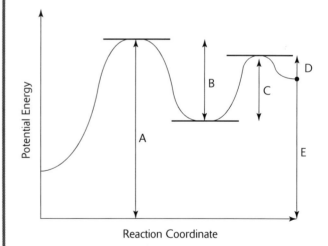

Reaction Coordinate

Which quantity is the most important for determining the rate of the forward reaction?

    A. A
    B. B
    C. C
    D. D
    E. E

37. Which bond is the most stable based on the information below?

Bond	Energy Released in Formation (kJ · mol⁻¹)
H–F	569
H–Cl	432
H–Br	370
H–I	295

    A. H–F
    B. H–Cl
    C. H–Br
    D. H–I
    E. All bonds are equally stable.

38. When water evaporates at constant pressure, the sign of the change in enthalpy

    A. is negative.
    B. is positive.
    C. depends on the temperature.
    D. depends on the volume of the container.
    E. does not exist; that is, the enthalpy change is zero.

39. What is the proper name of $[Co(NH_3)_5Br]Cl_2$?

    A. cobaltpentaamine bromodichloride
    B. pentaaminecobalt(III) bromodichloride
    C. dichlorocobalt(V) bromodichloride
    D. dichloropentaaminecobalt(III) bromide
    E. pentaaminebromocobalt(III) chloride

40. At what temperature does $\triangle G°$ become zero for the following reaction?

$$BaCO_{3(s)} \rightarrow BaO_{(s)} + CO_{2(g)}$$

Species	$\triangle H_f°$ (kJ/mole) at 25°C and 1 atm	S° (J/(mole · K)
$BaCO_{3(s)}$	–1170.	100
$BaO_{(s)}$	–600.	70
$CO_{2(g)}$	–400.	200

    A. 0 K
    B. 1.0×10^1 K
    C. 1.0×10^2 K
    D. 1.0×10^3 K
    E. 1.0×10^4 K

41. A mining company supplies an ore that is 16% chalcocite, Cu_2S, by weight. How many metric tons of ore should be purchased in order to produce 600 metric tons of an alloy containing 13% Cu?

    A. 5.0×10^{-1} metric tons
    B. 1.0×10^1 metric tons
    C. 2.0×10^2 metric tons
    D. 3.0×10^2 metric tons
    E. 6.0×10^2 metric tons

42. What is the charge of Zn in $Zn(H_2O)_3(OH)^+$?

    A. 0
    B. +1
    C. +2
    D. +3
    E. +5

43. If a reactant concentration is doubled, and the reaction rate increases by a factor of 8, the exponent for that reactant in the rate law should be

    A. ¼
    B. ½
    C. 2
    D. 3
    E. 4

Practice Exam 5

GO ON TO THE NEXT PAGE

44. How many grams of NaOH are required to neutralize 700 mL of 3.0 M HCl?

    A. 2.1 grams
    B. 21 grams
    C. 42 grams
    D. 84 grams
    E. 102 grams

45. When 3.00 grams of a certain metal was oxidized, 3.96 grams of its oxide was produced. The specific heat of the metal is 0.250 J/g · °C. What is the approximate atomic weight of this metal?

    A. 35 g/mole
    B. 65 g/mole
    C. 100 g/mole
    D. 170 g/mole
    E. 200 g/mole

46. Calculate the volume of a 36% solution of hydrochloric acid (density = 1.50 g/mL, MM ≈ 36 g/mol) required to prepare 9 liters of a 5 molar solution.

    A. 1 liter
    B. 2 liters
    C. 3 liters
    D. 4 liters
    E. 5 liters

47. Which of the following compounds would be unsaturated?

    A. CH_4
    B. C_2H_2
    C. C_2H_6
    D. C_5H_{12}
    E. C_6H_{14}

48. Which of the following represents an ester?

    A. 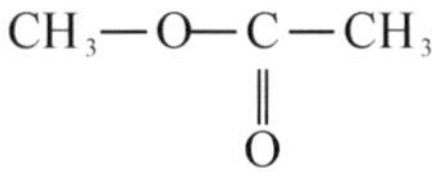
$$CH_3-O-\underset{\underset{O}{\|}}{C}-CH_3$$

    B. CH_3-O-CH_3

    C. 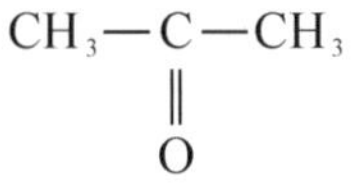
$$CH_3-\underset{\underset{O}{\|}}{C}-CH_3$$

    D. 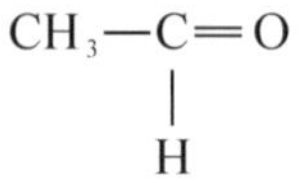
$$CH_3-\underset{\underset{H}{|}}{C}=O$$

    E. 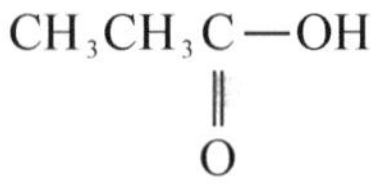
$$CH_3CH_3\underset{\underset{O}{\|}}{C}-OH$$

49. To produce methyl acetate, one would begin with which reactants?

    A. HCOOH and CH_3OH
    B. HCOOH and C_3H_7OH
    C. CH_3CH_2OH and CH_3COOH
    D. C_2H_5OH and HCOOH
    E. CH_3OH and CH_3COOH

50. Calculate the value of $\triangle H$ for the following reaction:

$$H_{2(g)} + F_{2(g)} \rightarrow 2HF_{(g)}$$

Species	Bond Energy (kcal/mole)
F–F	33
H–H	103
H–F	135

    A. −406 kcal/mole
    B. −320 kcal/mole
    C. −271 kcal/mole
    D. −134 kcal/mole
    E. −1.00 kcal/mole

51. How many grams of H_3PO_4 (MM ≈ 100 g/mol) are required to make 100.0 mL of a 0.0333 M H_3PO_4 solution (assume complete or 100% ionization)?

    A. 0.0164 g
    B. 0.164 g
    C. 0.333 g
    D. 0.654 g
    E. 1.31 g

52. An archaeologist discovered some charcoal at an excavation site. He sent the samples to a lab for C-14 dating, knowing that the half-life of C-14 is approximately 5,600 years. The lab reported that the charcoal had 1/8 the amount of C-14 in it that a living sample would have. How many years old was the charcoal?

    A. 700 years
    B. 1,867 years
    C. 8,400 years
    D. 16,800 years
    E. 44,800 years

53. What is the average atomic mass of a hypothetical sample of element X if it is found that 20% of the sample contains an isotope with mass of 100; 50% of the sample contains an isotope of the element with mass of 102; and 30% of the sample contains an isotope of the element with a mass of 105?

    A. 101.0
    B. 101.5
    C. 102.0
    D. 102.5
    E. 103.0

54. A photon was found to have a frequency of 3.00×10^{14} sec^{-1}. Calculate the wavelength of the photon given that the speed of light is 3.00×10^8 m · s^{-1} and 1 meter = 10^9 nanometers.

    A. 1.00×10^{-6} nm
    B. 3.00×10^{-3} nm
    C. 1.00×10^3 nm
    D. 3.00×10^3 nm
    E. 3.00×10^{22} nm

For Questions 55–57: 116.6 grams of magnesium hydroxide is allowed to react with 500 mL of 2M HCl.

55. What is the maximum amount of magnesium chloride that can be produced?

    A. 29.15 g
    B. 58.3 g
    C. 116.6 g
    D. 233.2 g
    E. 466.4 g

56. In reference to problem #55, approximately how much of the excess reagent was left?

    A. 0 grams
    B. 10 grams
    C. 20 grams
    D. 45 grams
    E. 97 grams

57. Suppose only 14.57 grams of magnesium chloride is produced. What would be the % yield?

    A. 10.00%
    B. 15.00%
    C. 25.00%
    D. 50.00%
    E. 95.00%

Use the following information for Questions 58 and 59:

A student prepared a solution of sulfuric acid that contained 980.8 grams of sulfuric acid per liter of solution. At 20°C, the density of the solution was found to be 1.4808 g/mL. The MM of sulfuric acid is 98.08 g/mol.

58. What is the molality of the solution?

    A. 0.15 *m*
    B. 2.50 *m*
    C. 5.00 *m*
    D. 10.00 *m*
    E. 20.00 *m*

GO ON TO THE NEXT PAGE

59. Calculate the mass percent of H_2SO_4 in the solution.

A. 25%
B. 33%
C. 50%
D. 66%
E. 75%

60. It is generally preferable to use absorbance as a measure of absorption rather than % transmittance in most cases because

A. %T cannot be measured as accurately as absorbance.
B. %T is dependant on the power of the incident radiation.
C. absorbance is proportional to the concentration of the solution being analyzed, whereas %T is not.
D. one should actually use % transmittance rather than absorption because some wavelengths are absorbed by the cuvette.
E. it does not matter, both techniques are equally valid.

61. Which of the following is NOT a conjugate acid-base pair?

A. NH_4^+ and NH_3
B. HNO_3 and NO_3^-
C. H_3O^+ and OH^-
D. HCl and Cl^-
E. H_2O and OH^-

62. A gas sample is compressed to half of its original volume and the absolute temperature is increased by 15%. What is the pressure change?

A. 15%
B. 30%
C. 50%
D. 130%
E. 230%

63. The pressure exerted on one mole of an ideal gas at 2.00 atm and 300K is reduced suddenly to 1.00 atm while heat is transferred to maintain the initial temperature of 300K. Calculate the final volume.

A. 6.2 L
B. 12.3 L
C. 24.6 L
D. 48.6 L
E. 92.4 L

64. Using the information from problem #63, which of the following is true?

A. Work is done by the system on the surroundings; heat is absorbed by the system from the surroundings.
B. Work is done by the system on the surroundings; heat is given off by the system to the surroundings.
C. Work is done on the system by the surroundings; heat is absorbed by the system from the surroundings.
D. Work is done on the system by the surroundings; heat is given off by the system to the surroundings.
E. Not enough information is supplied to make a conclusion on the direction of work or heat.

65. What is the name of the branched alkene $CH_3(CH_2)_2C(CH_3)=CHCH_3$?

A. 3-methyl-2-hexene
B. 2-methyl-3-hexene
C. 1-methyl-2,3 diethyl-3-hexene
D. 1-methyl-2,2 diethyl-3-hexene
E. 1,3-dimethyl-3-hexene

66. Phosphoric acid behaves as a triprotic acid, having three ionizable hydrogen atoms. The hydrogen ions are lost sequentially. The chart below provides the ionization constants and their logs.

$H_3PO_{4(aq)}$	$H^+_{(aq)} + H_2PO_4^-{}_{(aq)}$	$K_{a_1} = 7.5 \times 10^{-3}$	$\log K_{a_1} = -2.12$
$H_2PO_4^-{}_{(aq)}$	$H^+_{(aq)} + HPO_4^{2-}{}_{(aq)}$	$K_{a_2} = 6.2 \times 10^{-8}$	$\log K_{a_2} = -7.20$
$HPO_4^{2-}{}_{(aq)}$	$H^+_{(aq)} + PO_4^{3-}{}_{(aq)}$	$K_{a_3} = 1.7 \times 10^{-12}$	$\log K_{a_3} = -11.77$

A 0.300 M solution of K_2HPO_4 is made. The pH of the solution is

A. 2.12
B. 3.60
C. 4.66
D. 7.20
E. 9.49

67. Given the following intermolecular forces—hydrogen bonds, London dispersion forces, ionic interactions and dipole-dipole interactions—if arranged in order from the strongest to the weakest the order would be

A. hydrogen bonds > London dispersion forces > ionic interactions > dipole-dipole interactions
B. London dispersion forces > ionic interactions > dipole-dipole interactions > hydrogen bonds
C. ionic interactions > hydrogen bonds > dipole-dipole interactions > London dispersion forces
D. dipole-dipole interactions > hydrogen bonds > London dispersion forces > ionic interactions
E. dipole-dipole interactions > London dispersion forces > hydrogen bonds > ionic interactions

68. A student wishes to prepare a buffer solution that has a pH of 10.0. The following chart lists five weak bases with their K_b values. Which base would be most appropriate to use in preparing the buffer?

Base	K_b	$-\log(K_b)$
A	2.0×10^{-2}	1.7
B	6.0×10^{-4}	3.2
C	8.0×10^{-8}	7.1
D	1.0×10^{-10}	10
E	2.0×10^{-12}	11.7

A. A
B. B
C. C
D. D
E. E

GO ON TO THE NEXT PAGE

69. A student dissolved 25.00 grams of a protein powder that is used as a dietary supplement in water to make exactly 821 mL of solution. The temperature of the solution was determined to be 27°C. He measured the osmotic pressure exerted by the solution and determined it to be 0.0300 atm. What is the molar mass of the protein?

- **A.** 25,000
- **B.** 50,000
- **C.** 125,000
- **D.** 250,000
- **E.** 500,000

70. Which of the following acids if titrated with an aqueous solution of NaOH will have the highest pH at its end point?

- **A.** H_2SO_4, K_{a_1} – extremely large
- **B.** H_2CrO_4, $K_{a_1} = 5.0$
- **C.** $H_2C_2O_4$, $K_{a_1} = 5.6 \times 10^{-2}$
- **D.** $H_2C_8H_4O_4$, $K_{a_1} = 9.2 \times 10^{-4}$
- **E.** H_2CO_3, $K_{a_1} = 4.5 \times 10^{-7}$

71. A student was performing an experiment in qualitative analysis. Upon addition of HCl to her unknown, she noticed that a white precipitate formed. However, upon heating the solution, the white precipitate dissolved. The precipitate most likely contained

- **A.** Pb^{2+}
- **B.** Hg_2^{2+}
- **C.** Na^+
- **D.** Cr^{3+}
- **E.** SO_4^{2-}

72. A student was investigating five different formulas of a certain class of organic compounds. For each formula the student looked at, he noticed that the % carbon in the compound remained constant. Which class of organic compounds was the student studying?

- **A.** alkanes
- **B.** alkenes
- **C.** alkynes
- **D.** ethers
- **E.** carboxylic acids

73. Which pair of constants listed below is NOT mathematically related?

- **A.** Gibbs free energy—standard cell voltage
- **B.** rate constant—activation energy
- **C.** standard cell voltage—rate constant
- **D.** Gibbs free energy—equilibrium constant
- **E.** standard cell voltage—equilibrium constant

74. A student performed a flame test to determine the identity of a cation. The flame was a bright crimson red. The cation was

- **A.** K^+
- **B.** Na^+
- **C.** Li^+
- **D.** Mg^{2+}
- **E.** H^+

75. A student was testing for the presence of either Fe^{2+} or Fe^{3+}. Which of the following reagents should he use?

- **A.** dimethylglyoxime
- **B.** NaOH
- **C.** $K_3Fe(CN)_6$
- **D.** NH_3
- **E.** Na_2CrO_4

IF YOU FINISH BEFORE TIME IS CALLED, CHECK YOUR WORK ON THIS SECTION ONLY. DO NOT WORK ON ANY OTHER SECTION IN THE TEST.

PERIODIC TABLE OF THE ELEMENTS

1 H 1.0079																		2 He 4.0026
3 Li 6.941	4 Be 9.012											5 B 10.811	6 C 12.011	7 N 14.007	8 O 16.00	9 F 19.00	10 Ne 20.179
11 Na 22.99	12 Mg 24.30											13 Al 26.98	14 Si 28.09	15 P 30.974	16 S 32.06	17 Cl 35.453	18 Ar 39.948
19 K 39.10	20 Ca 40.08	21 Sc 44.96	22 Ti 47.90	23 V 50.94	24 Cr 51.00	25 Mn 54.93	26 Fe 55.85	27 Co 58.93	28 Ni 58.69	29 Cu 63.55	30 Zn 65.39	31 Ga 69.72	32 Ge 72.59	33 As 74.92	34 Se 78.96	35 Br 79.90	36 Kr 83.80
37 Rb 85.47	38 Sr 87.62	39 Y 88.91	40 Zr 91.22	41 Nb 92.91	42 Mo 95.94	43 Tc (98)	44 Ru 101.1	45 Rh 102.91	46 Pd 105.42	47 Ag 107.87	48 Cd 112.41	49 In 114.82	50 Sn 118.71	51 Sb 121.75	52 Te 127.60	53 I 126.91	54 Xe 131.29
55 Cs 132.91	56 Ba 137.33	57 *La 138.91	72 Hf 178.49	73 Ta 180.95	74 W 183.85	75 Re 186.21	76 Os 190.2	77 Ir 192.22	78 Pt 195.08	79 Au 196.97	80 Hg 200.59	81 Ti 204.38	82 Pb 207.2	83 Bi 208.98	84 Po (209)	85 At (210)	86 Rn (222)
87 Fr (223)	88 Ra 226.02	89 †Ac 227.03	104 Rf (261)	105 Db (262)	106 Sg (263)	107 Bh (262)	108 Hs (265)	109 Mt (266)	110 § (269)	111 § (272)	112 § (277)						

§ Not yet named

* Lanthanide Series

58 Ce 140.12	59 Pr 140.91	60 Nd 144.24	61 Pm (145)	62 Sm 150.4	63 Eu 151.97	64 Gd 157.25	65 Tb 158.93	66 Dy 162.50	67 Ho 164.93	68 Er 167.26	69 Tm 168.93	70 Yb 173.04	71 Lu 174.97

† Actinide Series

90 Th 232.04	91 Pa 231.04	92 U 238.03	93 Np 237.05	94 Pu (244)	95 Am (243)	96 Cm (247)	97 Bk (247)	98 Cf (251)	99 Es (252)	100 Fm (257)	101 Md (258)	102 No (259)	103 Lr (260)

Practice Exam 5

GO ON TO THE NEXT PAGE

STANDARD REDUCTION POTENTIALS IN AQUEOUS SOLUTION AT 25°C

Half-reaction		$E°(V)$
$F_2\,_{(g)} + 2\,e^-$	$\rightarrow$ $2\,F^-$	2.87
$Co^{3+} + e^-$	$\rightarrow$ Co^{2+}	1.82
$Au^{3+} + 3\,e^-$	$\rightarrow$ $Au_{(s)}$	1.50
$Cl_2\,_{(g)} + 2\,e^-$	$\rightarrow$ $2\,Cl^-$	1.36
$O_2\,_{(g)} + 4\,H^+ + 4\,e^-$	$\rightarrow$ $2\,H_2O_{(l)}$	1.23
$Br_2\,_{(l)} + 2\,e^-$	$\rightarrow$ $2\,Br^-$	1.07
$2\,Hg^{2+} + 2\,e^-$	$\rightarrow$ Hg_2^{2+}	0.92
$Hg^{2+} + 2\,e^-$	$\rightarrow$ $Hg_{(l)}$	0.85
$Ag^+ + e^-$	$\rightarrow$ $Ag_{(s)}$	0.80
$Hg_2^{2+} + 2\,e^-$	$\rightarrow$ $2\,Hg_{(l)}$	0.79
$Fe^{3+} + e^-$	$\rightarrow$ Fe^{2+}	0.77
$I_2\,_{(s)} + 2\,e^-$	$\rightarrow$ $2\,I^-$	0.53
$Cu^+ + e^-$	$\rightarrow$ $Cu_{(s)}$	0.52
$Cu^{2+} + 2\,e^-$	$\rightarrow$ $Cu_{(s)}$	0.34
$Cu^{2+} + e^-$	$\rightarrow$ Cu^+	0.15
$Sn^{4+} + 2\,e^-$	$\rightarrow$ Sn^{2+}	0.15
$S_{(s)} + 2\,H^+ + 2\,e^-$	$\rightarrow$ $H_2S_{(g)}$	0.14
$2\,H^+ + 2\,e^-$	$\rightarrow$ $H_2\,_{(g)}$	0.00
$Pb^{2+} + 2\,e^-$	$\rightarrow$ $Pb_{(s)}$	−0.13
$Sn^{2+} + 2\,e^-$	$\rightarrow$ $Sn_{(s)}$	−0.14
$Ni^{2+} + 2\,e^-$	$\rightarrow$ $Ni_{(s)}$	−0.25
$Co^{2+} + 2\,e^-$	$\rightarrow$ $Co_{(s)}$	−0.28
$Cd^{2+} + 2\,e^-$	$\rightarrow$ $Cd_{(s)}$	−0.40
$Cr^{3+} + e^-$	$\rightarrow$ Cr^{2+}	−0.41
$Fe^{2+} + 2\,e^-$	$\rightarrow$ $Fe_{(s)}$	−0.44
$Cr^{3+} + 3\,e^-$	$\rightarrow$ $Cr_{(s)}$	−0.74
$Zn^{2+} + 2\,e^-$	$\rightarrow$ $Zn_{(s)}$	−0.76
$2\,H_2O_{(l)} + 2\,e^-$	$\rightarrow$ $H_2\,_{(g)} + 2\,OH^-$	−0.83
$Mn^{2+} + 2\,e^-$	$\rightarrow$ $Mn_{(s)}$	−1.18
$Al^{3+} + 3\,e^-$	$\rightarrow$ $Al_{(s)}$	−1.66
$Be^{2+} + 2\,e^-$	$\rightarrow$ $Be_{(s)}$	−1.70
$Mg^{2+} + 2\,e^-$	$\rightarrow$ $Mg_{(s)}$	−2.37
$Na^+ + e^-$	$\rightarrow$ $Na_{(s)}$	−2.71
$Ca^{2+} + 2\,e^-$	$\rightarrow$ $Ca_{(s)}$	−2.87
$Sr^{2+} + 2\,e^-$	$\rightarrow$ $Sr_{(s)}$	−2.89
$Ba^{2+} + 2\,e^-$	$\rightarrow$ $Ba_{(s)}$	−2.90
$Rb^+ + e^-$	$\rightarrow$ $Rb_{(s)}$	−2.92
$K^+ + e^-$	$\rightarrow$ $K_{(s)}$	−2.92
$Cs^+ + e^-$	$\rightarrow$ $Cs_{(s)}$	−2.92
$Li^+ + e^-$	$\rightarrow$ $Li_{(s)}$	−3.05

Note: Unless otherwise stated, assume that for all questions involving solutions and/or chemical equations, the system is in water at room temperature.

ADVANCED PLACEMENT CHEMISTRY EQUATIONS AND CONSTANTS

ATOMIC STRUCTURE

$$E = hv \qquad c = \lambda v$$

$$\lambda = \frac{h}{mv} \qquad p = mv$$

$$E_n = \frac{-2.178 \times 10^{-18}}{n^2} \text{ joule}$$

EQUILIBRIUM

$$K_a = \frac{[H^+][A^-]}{[HA]}$$

$$K_b = \frac{[OH^-][HB^+]}{[B]}$$

$$K_w = [OH^-][H^+] = 1.0 \times 10^{-14} @ 25°C$$
$$= K_a \times K_b$$

$$pH = -\log[H^+], \ pOH = -\log[OH^-]$$

$$14 = pH + pOH$$

$$pH = pK_a + \log\frac{[A^-]}{[HA]}$$

$$pOH = pK_b + \log\frac{[HB^+]}{[B]}$$

$$pK_a = -\log K_a, \ pK_b = -\log K_b$$

$$K_p = K_c(RT)^{\Delta n}$$

where Δn = moles product gas − moles reactant gas

THERMOCHEMISTRY/KINETICS

$$\Delta S° = \Sigma S° \text{ products} - \Sigma S° \text{ reactants}$$

$$\Delta H° = \Sigma \Delta H_f° \text{ products} - \Sigma \Delta H_f° \text{ reactants}$$

$$\Delta G° = \Sigma \Delta G_f° \text{ products} - \Sigma \Delta G_f° \text{ reactants}$$

$$\Delta G° = \Delta H° - T\Delta S°$$
$$= -RT \ln K = -2.303 \, RT \log K$$
$$= -n \, \mathscr{F} \, E°$$

$$\Delta G = \Delta G° + RT \ln Q = \Delta G° + 2.303 \, RT \log Q$$
$$q = mc\Delta T$$

$$C_p = \frac{\Delta H}{\Delta T}$$

$$\ln[A]_t - \ln[A]_0 = -kt$$

$$\frac{1}{[A]_t} - \frac{1}{[A]_0} = kt$$

$$\ln k = \frac{-E_a}{R}\left(\frac{1}{T}\right) + \ln A$$

E = energy $\qquad v$ = velocity
v = frequency $\qquad n$ = principal quantum
λ = wavelength $\qquad\quad$ number
p = momentum $\quad m$ = mass

Speed of light, $c = 3.0 \times 10^8 \text{ m} \cdot \text{s}^{-1}$

Planck's constant, $h = 6.63 \times 10^{-34} \text{ J} \cdot \text{s}$

Boltzmann's constant, $k = 1.38 \times 10^{-23} \text{ J} \cdot \text{K}^{-1}$

Avogadro's number = $6.022 \times 10^{23} \text{ mol}^{-1}$

Electron charge, $e = -1.602 \times 10^{-19}$ coulomb

1 electron volt per atom = $96.5 \text{ kJ} \cdot \text{mol}^{-1}$

Equilibrium Constants

K_a (weak acid)
K_b (weak base)
K_w (water)
K_p (gas pressure)
K_c (molar concentrations)

$S°$ = standard entropy
$H°$ = standard enthalpy
$G°$ = standard free energy
$E°$ = standard reduction potential
T = temperature
n = moles
m = mass
q = heat
c = specific heat capacity
C_p = molar heat capacity at constant pressure
E_a = activation energy
k = rate constant
A = frequency factor

Faraday's constant, $\mathscr{F} = 96,500$ coulombs per
$\qquad$ mole of electrons

Gas constant, $R = 8.31 \text{ J} \cdot \text{mol}^{-1} \cdot \text{K}^{-1}$
$\qquad\qquad = 0.0821 \text{ L} \cdot \text{atm} \cdot \text{mol}^{-1} \cdot \text{K}^{-1}$
$\qquad\qquad = 8.31 \text{ volt} \cdot \text{coulomb} \cdot \text{mol}^{-1} \cdot \text{K}^{-1}$

GO ON TO THE NEXT PAGE

GASES, LIQUIDS, AND SOLUTIONS

$$PV = nRT$$

$$\left(P + \frac{n^2a}{V^2}\right)(V - nb) = nRT$$

$$P_A = P_{total} \times X_A, \text{ where } X_A = \frac{\text{moles A}}{\text{total moles}}$$

$$P_{total} = P_A + P_B + P_C + \ldots$$

$$n = \frac{m}{M}$$

$$K = {}^\circ C + 273$$

$$\frac{P_1 V_1}{T_1} = \frac{P_2 V_2}{T_2}$$

$$D = \frac{m}{V}$$

$$u_{rms} = \sqrt{\frac{3kT}{m}} = \sqrt{\frac{3RT}{m}}$$

$$KE \text{ per molecule} = \tfrac{1}{2} m v^2$$

$$KE \text{ per mole} = \tfrac{3}{2} RT$$

$$\frac{r_1}{r_2} = \sqrt{\frac{M_2}{M_1}}$$

molarity, M = moles solute per liter solution

molality, m = moles solute per kilogram solvent

$$\Delta T_f = i \cdot K_f \times \text{molality}$$

$$\Delta T_b = i \cdot K_b \times \text{molality}$$

$$\pi = i \cdot M \cdot R \cdot T$$

$$A = a \cdot b \cdot c$$

OXIDATION-REDUCTION; ELECTROCHEMISTRY

$$Q = \frac{[C]^c [D]^d}{[A]^a [B]^b}, \text{ where } a\,A + b\,B \rightarrow c\,C + d\,D$$

$$I = \frac{q}{t}$$

$$E_{cell} = E^\circ_{cell} - \frac{RT}{n\mathscr{F}} \ln Q = E^\circ_{cell} - \frac{0.0592}{n} \log Q \;@\; 25^\circ C$$

$$\log K = \frac{n \cdot E^\circ}{0.0592}$$

P = pressure

V = volume

T = temperature

n = number of moles

D = density

m = mass

v = velocity

u_{rms} = root-mean-square speed

KE = kinetic energy

r = rate of effusion

M = molar mass

π = osmotic pressure

i = van't Hoff factor

K_f = molal freezing-point depression constant

K_b = molal boiling-point elevation constant

A = absorbance

a = molar absorptivity

b = path length

c = concentration

Q = reaction quotient

I = current (amperes)

q = charge (coulombs)

t = time (seconds)

E° = standard reduction potential

K = equilibrium constant

Gas constant, $R = 8.31 \text{ J} \cdot \text{mol}^{-1} \cdot \text{K}^{-1}$

$= 0.0821 \text{ L} \cdot \text{atm} \cdot \text{mol}^{-1} \cdot \text{K}^{-1}$

$= 8.31 \text{ volt} \cdot \text{coulomb} \cdot \text{mol}^{-1} \cdot \text{K}^{-1}$

Boltzmann's constant, $k = 1.38 \times 10^{-23} \text{ J} \cdot \text{K}^{-1}$

K_f for $H_2O = 1.86 \text{ K} \cdot \text{kg} \cdot \text{mol}^{-1}$

K_b for $H_2O = 0.512 \text{ K} \cdot \text{kg} \cdot \text{mol}^{-1}$

1 atm = 760 mm Hg

= 760 torr

STP = 0.000° C and 1.000 atm

Faraday's constant, $\mathscr{F} = 96{,}500$ coulombs per mole of electrons

Section II: Free-Response Questions

CHEMISTRY

Section II

Total time—90 minutes

Part A

Time—40 minutes

YOU MAY USE YOUR CALCULATOR FOR PART A

CLEARLY SHOW THE METHOD USED AND STEPS INVOLVED IN ARRIVING AT YOUR ANSWERS. It is to your advantage to do this, since you may obtain partial credit if you do and you will receive little or no credit if you do not. Attention should be paid to significant figures.

Answer Question 1 below. The Section II score weighting for this question is 20%.

1. Acetic acid, $HC_2H_3O_2$, which is represented as HA, has an acid ionization constant K_a of 1.74×10^{-5}.

   (a) Calculate the hydrogen ion concentration, $[H^+]$, in a 0.50 molar solution of acetic acid.

   (b) Calculate the pH and pOH of the 0.50 molar solution.

   (c) What percent of the acetic acid molecules do not ionize?

   (d) A buffer solution is designed to have a pH of 6.50. What is the $[HA] : [A^-]$ ratio in this system?

   (e) 0.500 liter of a new buffer is made using sodium acetate. The concentration of sodium acetate in this new buffer is 0.35 M. The acetic acid concentration is 0.50 M. Finally, 1.5 grams of LiOH is added to the solution. Calculate the pH of this new buffer.

GO ON TO THE NEXT PAGE

Answer EITHER Question 2 or 3 below. Only one of these two questions will be graded. If you start both questions, be sure to cross out the question you do not want graded. The Section II score weighting for the question you choose is 20%.

2. Methyl alcohol oxidizes to produce methanoic (formic) acid and water according to the following reaction and structural diagram:

$$CH_3OH_{(aq)} + O_{2(g)} \rightarrow HCOOH_{(aq)} + H_2O_{(l)}$$

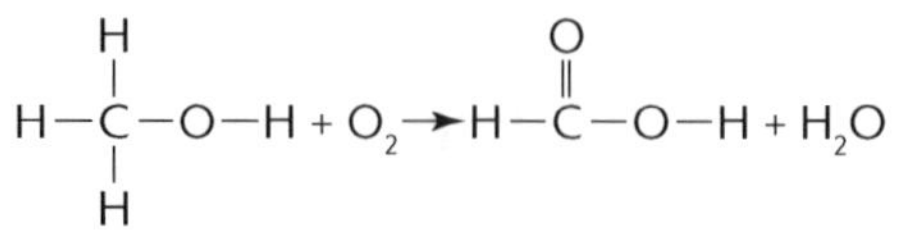

Given the following data:

Substance	$\triangle H_f^\circ$ (kJ/mol)	$S^\circ (J \cdot K^{-1} \cdot mole^{-1})$
$CH_3OH_{(aq)}$	−238.6	129
$O_{2(g)}$	0	205.0
$HCOOH_{(aq)}$	−409	127.0
$H_2O_{(l)}$	−285.84	69.94

(a) Calculate $\triangle H^\circ$ for the oxidation of methyl alcohol.

(b) Calculate $\triangle S^\circ$ for the oxidation of methyl alcohol.

(c) Is the reaction spontaneous at 25°C? Explain your reasoning.

   (i) If the temperature were increased to 100°C, would the reaction be spontaneous?

(d) The heat of fusion of methanoic acid is 12.71 kJ/mole, and its freezing point is 8.3°C. Calculate $\triangle S^\circ$ for the reaction

$$HCOOH_{(l)} \rightarrow HCOOH_{(s)}$$

(e) Calculate the standard molar entropy of $HCOOH_{(s)}$.

   (i) Is the magnitude of S° for $HCOOH_{(s)}$ in agreement with the magnitude of S° for $HCOOH_{(l)}$? (S° for $HCOOH_{(l)} = 109.1 \ J \cdot mole^{-1} \cdot K^{-1}$). Explain your reasoning.

(f) Calculate $\triangle G^\circ$ for the ionization of methanoic acid at 25°C. K_a of methanoic acid = 1.9×10^{-4}.

3. A student constructed a coffee cup calorimeter in the lab as shown in the following diagram:

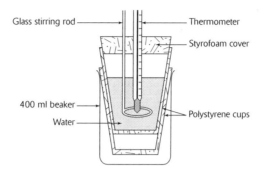

Glass stirring rod — Thermometer
Styrofoam cover
400 ml beaker — Polystyrene cups
Water

The student first determined the heat capacity of the calorimeter by placing 50.0 mL of room temperature distilled water in the calorimeter and determined the temperature of the water to be 23.0°C. He then added 50.0 mL of distilled water measured at 61.0°C to the calorimeter and recorded the temperature of the mixture every 30 seconds. A graph was drawn of the results and is shown below:

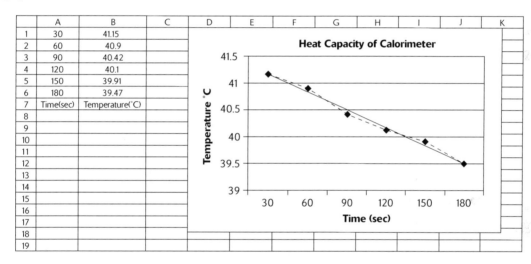

	A	B	C	D	E	F	G	H	I	J	K
1	30	41.15									
2	60	40.9									
3	90	40.42									
4	120	40.1									
5	150	39.91									
6	180	39.47									
7	Time(sec)	Temperature(°C)									
8											
9											
10											
11											
12											
13											
14											
15											
16											
17											
18											
19											

Heat Capacity of Calorimeter

(a) Determine the heat lost by the water (q_{water}). The density of the water was determined to be $1.00 \text{ g} \cdot \text{mL}^{-1}$. The specific heat of water is $4.18 \text{ J/(g} \cdot °\text{C)}$.

(b) Determine the heat gained by the calorimeter ($q_{calorimeter}$).

(c) Determine the calorimeter constant (heat capacity) of the coffee cup calorimeter ($C_{calorimeter}$).

The student then measured temperature changes that occurred when 50.0 mL of 2.00 M HCl at 23.0°C was added to 50.0 mL of 2.00 M NaOH at 23.0°C using the same calorimeter. The highest temperature obtained after mixing the two solutions was 35.6°C. The final density of the solution was $1.00 \text{ g} \cdot \text{mL}^{-1}$.

(d) Write the net ionic equation for the reaction that occurred.

(e) Determine the molar heat of reaction (q_{rxn}).

The student then measured temperature changes that occurred when 50.0 mL of 2.00 M NH₄Cl at 22.9°C was added to 50.0 mL of 2.00 M NaOH at 22.9°C using the same calorimeter. The highest temperature obtained after mixing the two solutions was 24.1°C. The final density of the solution was $1.00 \text{ g} \cdot \text{mL}^{-1}$.

(f) Write the net ionic equation for the reaction that occurred.

(g) Determine the molar heat of reaction (q_{rxn}).

(h) Calculate the enthalpy change per mole for the reaction that would occur using the same calorimeter if one were to mix ammonia with hydrochloric acid.

GO ON TO THE NEXT PAGE

CHEMISTRY

Part B

Time—50 minutes

NO CALCULATORS MAY BE USED FOR PART B

Answer Question 4 below. The Section II score weight for this question is 15%.

4. Write the formulas to show the reactants and the products for any FIVE of the laboratory situations described below. Answers to more than five choices will not be graded. In all cases, a reaction occurs. Assume that solutions are aqueous unless otherwise indicated. Represent substances in solution as ions if the substances are extensively ionized. Omit formulas for any ions or molecules that are unchanged by the reaction. You need not balance the equations.

Example: A strip of magnesium is added to a solution of silver nitrate.

Ex.	$Mg + Ag^+ \longrightarrow Mg^2 + Ag$

(a) A piece of solid magnesium, which is ignited, is added to water.

(b) Methanol is burned completely in air.

(c) Sulfur trioxide gas is bubbled through water.

(d) Iron(III) oxide is added to hydrochloric acid.

(e) Equal volumes of 0.5 M sulfuric acid and 0.5 M sodium hydroxide are mixed.

(f) Acetic acid is added to an aqueous solution of ammonia.

(g) Nitrous acid is added to sodium hydroxide.

(h) Ethanol is heated in the presence of sulfuric acid.

Answer BOTH Question 5 AND Question 6 below. Both of these questions will be graded. The Section II score weighting for these questions is 30% (15% each).

5. As one moves down the halogen column, one notices that the boiling point increases. However, when examining the alkali metal family, one discovers that the melting point decreases as one moves down the column.

(a) Account for the increase in boiling point of the halogens as one moves down the column.

(b) Account for the decrease in melting point of the alkali metals as one moves down the column.

(c) Rank Cs, Li, KCl, I_2, and F_2 in order of decreasing melting point, and explain your reasoning.

6. (a) Write the ground-state electron configuration for the phosphorus atom.

(b) Write the four quantum numbers that describe all the valence electrons in the phosphorus atom.

(c) Explain whether the phosphorus atom, in its ground state, is paramagnetic or diamagnetic.

(d) Phosphorus can be found in such diverse compounds as PCl_3, PCl_5, PCl_4^-, PCl_6^-, and P_4. How can phosphorus, in its ground state, bond in so many different arrangements? Be specific in terms of hybridization, type of bonding, and geometry.

Answer EITHER Question 7 or 8 below. Only one of these two questions will be graded. If you start both questions, be sure to cross out the question you do not want graded. The Section II score weighting for the question you choose is 15%.

7. **(a)** Draw Lewis structures for

   (i) BF_3

   (ii) $TiCl_3$

(b) Determine the molecular geometries including all idealized bond angles for ClNO where the N atom is in the center of the molecule.

(c) Classify XeF_4 as polar or nonpolar and explain why.

(d) Describe the orbital hybridization scheme used by the central atom in its sigma bonding for the following molecules. The central atom is underlined. How many pi bonds are contained in each molecule?

   (i) $\underline{Xe}F_4$

   (ii) $\underline{Xe}F_2$

8. **(a)** Explain the Arrhenius theory of acids and bases.

   (i) Give an example of either an Arrhenius acid or base dissociating in water.

(b) Explain the Brønsted-Lowry theory of acids and bases.

   (i) Give an example of either a Brønsted-Lowry acid or base dissociating in water.

(c) Describe two advantages of the Brønsted-Lowry theory over the Arrhenius theory.

(d) Explain the Lewis theory of acids and bases.

   (i) Give an example of either a Lewis acid or Lewis base.

(e) Discuss how indicators are used in the titration of acids and bases. What factors are used in selecting an appropriate indicator?

Answer Key for Practice Exam 5

Section I: Multiple-Choice Questions

1. A	**26.** C	**51.** C
2. B	**27.** D	**52.** D
3. B	**28.** E	**53.** D
4. D	**29.** D	**54.** C
5. B	**30.** D	**55.** A
6. D	**31.** A	**56.** E
7. E	**32.** B	**57.** D
8. C	**33.** B	**58.** E
9. E	**34.** D	**59.** D
10. B	**35.** C	**60.** C
11. A	**36.** A	**61.** C
12. D	**37.** A	**62.** D
13. B	**38.** B	**63.** C
14. A	**39.** E	**64.** A
15. D	**40.** D	**65.** A
16. C	**41.** E	**66.** E
17. A	**42.** C	**67.** C
18. C	**43.** D	**68.** B
19. D	**44.** D	**69.** A
20. C	**45.** C	**70.** E
21. D	**46.** C	**71.** A
22. A	**47.** B	**72.** B
23. C	**48.** A	**73.** C
24. B	**49.** E	**74.** C
25. C	**50.** D	**75.** C

Predicting Your AP Score

The table below shows historical relationships between students' results on the multiple-choice portion (Section I) of the AP Chemistry exam and their overall AP score. The AP score ranges from 1 to 5, with 3, 4, or 5 generally considered to be passing. Over the years, around 60% of the students who take the AP Chemistry Exam receive a 3, 4, or 5.

After you've taken the multiple-choice practice exam under timed conditions, count the number of questions you got correct. From this number, subtract the number of wrong answers times $\frac{1}{4}$. Do NOT count items left blank as wrong. Then refer to this table to find your "probable" overall AP score. For example, if you get 39 questions correct, based on historical statistics, you have a 25% chance of receiving an overall score of 3, a 63% chance of receiving an overall score of 4, and a 12% chance of receiving an overall score of 5. Note that your actual results may be different from the score this table predicts. Also, remember that the free-response section represents 55% of your AP score.

No attempt is made here to combine your specific results on the practice AP Chemistry free-response questions (Section II) with your multiple-choice results (which is beyond the scope of this book and for which no data is available). However, you should have your AP chemistry instructor review your essays before you take the AP Chemistry Exam so that he or she can give you additional pointers.

Number of Multiple-Choice Questions Correct*	Overall AP Score				
	1	2	3	4	5
47 to 75	0%	0%	1%	21%	78%
37 to 46	0%	0%	25%	63%	12%
24 to 36	0%	19%	69%	12%	0%
13 to 23	15%	70%	15%	0%	0%
0 to 12	86%	14%	0%	0%	0%
% of Test Takers Receiving Score	21%	22%	25%	15%	17%

*Corrected for wrong answers

Answers and Explanations for Practice Exam 5

1. **(A)** Positive ions are smaller than their neutral atoms and negative ions are larger than their neutral atoms. Mg^{2+} is the only ion from the choices with only two principal energy levels of electrons . . . so it is the smallest.

2. **(B)** The ionization potential is the energy that must be supplied to an atom in the gas phase in order to remove an electron. The energy required to remove the first electron is referred to as the first ionization energy for that element. Elements farther to the left and farther down the periodic table generally have lower ionization energies. Of the choices, both K and Kr are farthest down . . . but K is farther to the left.

3. **(B)** $2\ K_{(s)} + 2H_2O_{(l)} \rightarrow 2\ K^+_{(aq)} + 2OH^-_{(aq)} + H_{2(g)}$

   Group 1 metals react *vigorously* with water. The only Group 1 metal of the choices is K.

4. **(D)** Electronegativity is a measure of the tendency of an atom to attract a bonding pair of electrons. Fluorine (the most electronegative element) is assigned a value of 4.0, and values range down to cesium and francium which are the least electronegative at 0.7. Elements in the top right of the periodic table have the highest electronegativity values while elements in the lower left have the smallest electronegatilvity values. Group 18 elements are excluded from the trends due to their stability. Mg, S, and Cl are farthest up, but Cl is farthest to the right.

5. **(B)** One *s* orbital and 2 *p* orbitals are mixed, forming 3 sp^2 hybrid orbitals. This kind of hybridization occurs in molecules with trigonal planar electron geometry (3 electron groups around the central atom) [AX_2E_1, AX_3E_0]. This leaves one *p* orbital to π (pi) bond. The hybrid orbitals overlap in a σ (sigma) bond.

6. **(D)** One *s* orbital, 3 *p* orbitals, and one *d* orbital are mixed, forming 5 sp^3d hybrid orbitals. This kind of hybridization occurs in molecules with trigonal bipyramidal electron geometry (5 electron groups around the central atom) [AX_2E_3, AX_3E_2, AX_4E_1, AX_5E_0]. The hybrid orbitals overlap in a σ (sigma) bond.

7. **(E)** One *s* orbital, 3 *p* orbitals, and 2 *d* orbitals are mixed, forming 6 sp^3d^2 hybrid orbitals. This kind of hybridization occurs in molecules with octahedral electron geometry (6 electron groups around the central atom) [AX_4E_2, AX_5E_1, AX_6E_0]. The hybrid orbitals overlap in a σ (sigma) bond.

8. **(C)** One *s* orbital and 3 *p* orbitals are mixed, forming 4 sp^3 hybrid orbitals. Both the C and O atoms act as "central" atoms. Each is sp^3 hybridized. This kind of hybridization occurs in molecules with tetrahedral electron geometry (4 electron groups around the central atom) [AX_2E_2, AX_3E_1, AX_4E_0]. No *p* orbitals are left to π (pi) bond. The hybrid orbitals still overlap in a σ (sigma) bond.

9. (E) The easiest way to begin this problem is to figure out what points A and points B are (the maximums and minimums). With only one electron in the outer valence shell, the alkali metals lose an electron easily and would result in the lowest ionization energies. Point B, with the highest ionization energies would result from elements with filled valence shells—the noble gases. Because half-filled p orbitals are more stable than a condition when p orbitals are beginning to pair, we would expect to find a slight peak for elements with half-filled p orbitals. We find this condition at points E.

10. (B) The noble gases are relatively nonreactive. This is because they have a complete valence shell. They have little tendency to gain or lose electrons. The noble gases have high ionization energies and negligible electronegativities. The noble gases have low boiling points and are all gases at room temperature.

11. (A) Alkali metals have one electron in their outer shell, which is loosely bound. This gives them the largest atomic radii of the elements in their respective periods. Their low ionization energies result in their metallic properties and high reactivities. An alkali metal can easily lose its valence electron to form the univalent cation. Alkali metals have low electronegativities. They react readily with nonmetals, particularly halogens.

12. (D) The dips at points D in the chart shows the beginning of pairing in the p orbitals and indicates that this first paired electron has a lower ionization potential than atoms which have half-filled p orbitals.

13. (B) Density is defined as mass per volume which is equivalent to

$$\frac{P \times MM}{R \times T}$$

Because "P" is in the numerator, it is directly proportional to density.

14. (A) If $n = 2$, then l must be 0 or 1 (representing either an s or p orbital).

15. (D) Sodium has a +1 oxidation state; oxide has a –2 oxidation state. Na_2O is the formula for sodium oxide.

16. (C) The structural diagram for C_2H_2 is H—C≡C—H. Single bonds are always sigma (total of 2 single bonds). A triple bond consists of 1 sigma and 2 pi bonds.

17. (A) Magnesium chloride is an ionic compound. The amount of heat required to thermally decompose it would be relatively high. The other choices thermally decompose at much lower temperatures. In Choice (B), the carbonate ion breaks down to CO_2. In Choice (C), the hydroxide ion breaks down to H_2O. Finally, the water molecules in Choice (D) evaporate with heat.

18. (C) Hydrocarbon fuels when combusted under actual (nonideal) combustion conditions produce several intermediate products in addition to carbon dioxide and water and include the unburned hydrocarbon, carbon monoxide, oxides of nitrogen, hydroxyl radicals, and the hydrogen ions.

19. (D) This question refers to the Le Chatelier Principle. Because the number of moles of gaseous reactants is equal to the number of moles of gaseous products, changing the volume of the container or changing the pressure will not affect the yield of D. Removing a gaseous product will drive the reaction toward products . . . increasing the yield of D. No information is provided in the question regarding how temperature might affect yield.

20. (C) Rate constants describe the rate of a reaction as a function of starting concentration(s). A first-order rate constant describes a reaction whose rate depends on the concentration of one component only. A first-order rate constant has units of inverse time (usually s^{-1}).

21. (D) Air pollution results from a series of many chemical reactions. Bond strength and bond stability are not the same thing. A triple bond is stronger than a double bond and a double bond is stronger than a single bond. However, the triple bond represents a region of greater inter-atomic electron density than that of a double bond and in turn, the inter-atomic electron density of a double bond is greater than that of a single bond. This means that the electrons binding multiple bonded atoms are more vulnerable to attack by electron-seeking species. Therefore, the reactivity of a double-bonded species (ethene) is greater than found in a single-bonded species. Methane, ethane, and propane contain only single bonds. Attack by an electrophile is different than pulling atoms apart, otherwise known as dissociation.

22. (A) Begin by writing the balanced equation:

$$H_2 + I_2 \longleftrightarrow 2HI$$

Next, write the equilibrium expression

$$K_c = \frac{[HI]^2}{[H_2][I_2]}$$

Let x = moles of H_2 that combine to form HI. x will also represent the moles of I_2 that combine to form HI because H_2 and I_2 are in a 1:1 molar ratio. At equilibrium, $[H_2] = 3 - x$, $[I_2] = 3 - x$, and $[HI] = 2x$.

$$K_c = \frac{(2x)^2}{(3-x)(3-x)} = \frac{(2x)^2}{(3-x)^2}$$

23. (C) Begin by writing the equilibrium expression:

$$81 = \frac{(2x)^2}{(3-x)^2}$$

Next, take the square root of both sides:

$$9 = \frac{2x}{3-x}$$

Cross multiply and solve for x:

$$27 - 9x = 2x \qquad 27 = 11x \qquad x = 2.45$$

24. (B) The word 'approximately' means that we can be fairly safe when rounding numbers as we do the math, considering that the answer choices are fairly far apart. To change 4.50 grams of ice to water would require ~1510 joules ($4.50g \times 335$ J/g). 1 gram of water at 5°C can rise to 100°C as water, absorbing ~4 joules for every 1°C ($95 \times 4 = 380$ J). Therefore, 1510 joules – 380 joules = ~1130 J. 1130 J / 2260 J/g = 0.5 g of water would be converted to steam.

25. (C) The solubility chart shows that at 30°C, that approximately 40 grams of ammonium chloride dissolved in 100 grams of water, or 400 grams would dissolve in 1,000 grams of water. Because 30 grams have already been added, the solution could hold 370 more grams of NH_4Cl until it becomes saturated.

26. (C) Chemical reactions are either endothermic or exothermic (they can't be both).

27. (D) The higher the frequency, the shorter the wavelength. Because all light waves move through a vacuum at the same speed, the number of wave crests passing by a given point in one second depends on the wavelength. That number, also known as the frequency, will be larger for a short-wavelength wave than for a long-wavelength wave. The equation that relates wavelength and frequency is: $\lambda v = v$ where λ is the wavelength, v is the frequency and v is the velocity of the wave. For electromagnetic radiation, the speed is equal to the speed of light, c: and the equation becomes: $\lambda v = c$. The greater the energy, the larger the frequency and the shorter (smaller) the wavelength. It follows therefore that short wavelengths are more energetic than long wavelengths.

28. (E) The stronger reducing and oxidizing agents are the reactants. The weaker reducing and oxidizing agents are the products.

Example: Experiment 1: $Cu_{(s)} + 2Ag^+_{(aq)} \rightarrow Cu^{2+}_{(aq)} + 2Ag_{(s)}$

reducing agent strength: Cu > Ag

oxidizing agent strength: $Ag^+ > Cu^{2+}$

Reaction vs. no reaction can be predicted from relative strength.

Example: Given the reducing agent strength: Fe > Cu > Ag you can predict that Fe will react with metals ions of both Cu and Ag; Cu will only react with the metal ions of Ag; Ag will not react with the metals ions of either Fe or Cu.

29. (D) The equation for the electrolysis of an aqueous solution of NaCl is $2Cl^-_{(aq)} + 2H_2O_{(l)} \rightarrow Cl_{2(g)} + H_{2(g)} + 2OH^-_{(aq)}$. Reduction occurs at the cathode. Reduction involves gaining electrons.

30. (D) Fractional crystallization is a method of refining substances based on differences in solubility. If two or more substances are dissolved in a solvent, they will crystallize out of solution (precipitate) at different rates. Crystallization can be induced by changes in concentration, temperature or other means. Fractional crystallization can be used for purification or analysis.

31. (A) The answer reflects the Law of Conservation of Mass. In order to see why the other two choices are not correct, study the following reaction $2H_{2(g)} + O_{2(g)} \rightarrow 2H_2O_{(g)}$ and notice that the left side of the equation shows 3 moles of reactants while the right side shows 2 moles of products.

32. (B) While a liquid is changing into a crystalline solid at the freezing point, its temperature will not change even though heat is being removed from the sample. This is due to a release of energy by the exothermic change from a liquid to a crystal. Any heat removed to cool the sample is replaced by the heat of fusion given off as the crystal forms. When the liquid reaches the freezing point temperature, some of the liquid begins to form a solid. As more heat is removed, more liquid converts to solid. However, because this releases heat energy, the temperature stays the same. That is, the heat lost by "cooling" is replaced by conversion of liquid to solid. As long as both liquid and solid phase are in equilibrium with each other, the temperature remains at the freezing point. As soon as all of the liquid has been converted to solid, the temperature will start to drop again as the solid cools. It should be noted that the system will follow exactly the same process in reverse if the solid is warmed until it melts.

33. (B) See discussion for Question #32.

34. (D) The primary reason that makes water a good solvent is that it has a high dielectric constant resulting from its nature as a polar molecule. When mixed with ionic compounds, there are favorable ion-dipole interactions in which water is oriented around ions. The electrostatic interactions between ions are weakened because water's dipoles oppose the electric field between ions.

35. (C)

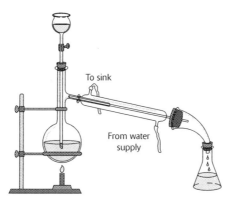

36. (A) The free energy of activation for Step 1 (a) is larger than the activation energy for Step 2 (b) leading to a smaller rate constant. The overall rate of $A \rightarrow C$ is controlled by Step 1 which is the rate-determining step.

37. (A) A chemical bond is more stable when more energy is released at the time the bond forms. Since the most energy is released when HF is formed, the H-F bond will be the most stable.

38. (B) Remember that in an endothermic process, energy is being absorbed. All endothermic changes are defined with a + sign. Going from the liquid to the gaseous phase requires energy and thus is endothermic.

39. (E) NH_3 is a neutral ligand; the bromide and the chloride ion both have a –1 charge. Cobalt would have to have a +3 charge in this compound for the complex compound to be electrically neutral.

40. (D) Using the Gibbs-Helmholz equation, when $\triangle G° = 0$,

$$T = \frac{\Delta H°}{\Delta S°} = \frac{\left[-600. + (-400.) - (-1170.)\right]}{\left[(.07000 + 0.20000) - .10000\right]} = \frac{170}{0.17}$$

$$= 1.00 \times 10^3 \, \text{K}$$

41. (E) Do this problem by using the factor-label method (m.t. stands for metric tons, 1 m.t. = 10^3 kg).

$$\frac{600 \, \text{m.t. alloy}}{1} \times \frac{13 \, \text{m.t. Cu}}{100. \, \text{m.t. alloy}} \times \frac{160 \, \text{m.t. Cu}_2\text{S}}{130 \, \text{m.t. Cu}} \times \frac{100 \, \text{m.t. ore}}{16 \, \text{m.t. Cu}_2\text{S}} = 6.0 \times 10^2 \, \text{m.t. ore}$$

42. (C) Water molecules are neutral. Hydroxide ions (OH^-) have a –1 charge. The overall charge of the complex is +1. Zinc would have to have a +2 charge in order for the complex to end up with a +1 charge. If you let x = charge of the zinc ion, then $+1 = x + 3(0) + 1(-1)$ $x = +2$.

43. (D)

$$\frac{\text{rate}_2}{\text{rate}_1} = \frac{(\text{new conc.})^x}{(\text{old conc.})^x} = \frac{8}{1} = \left(\frac{2 \cdot \text{old conc.}}{\text{old conc.}}\right) = 2^x$$

$$8 = 2^x$$

$$x = 3$$

44. (D) Use the relationship, moles of acid = moles of base. Solve for the moles of acid.

$$\frac{0.700 \, \text{liter acid}}{1} \times \frac{3.0 \, \text{moles acid}}{1 \, \text{liter}} = 2.1 \, \text{moles acid}$$

At neutralization, the moles of acid = moles of base. Therefore,

$$\frac{2.1 \, \text{moles. NaOH}}{1} \times \frac{40.00 \, \text{g NaOH}}{1 \, \text{mole NaOH}} = 84 \, \text{g NaOH}$$

45. (C) The Law of Dulong and Petit states that molar mass × specific heat ≈ 25 J/(mole · °C)

$$\frac{25 \cdot \text{J}}{\text{mole} \cdot °\text{C}} \times \frac{\text{g} \cdot °\text{C}}{0.250 \, \text{J}} \approx 100 \, \text{g} / \text{mol}$$

46. (C) For dilution problems, use the formula $M_1 V_1 = M_2 V_2$; therefore, it is necessary to determine the molarity of the initial solution first.

$$\frac{1.50 \, \text{g sol'n}}{1 \, \text{mL sol'n}} \times \frac{1000 \, \text{mL sol'n}}{1 \, \text{liter sol'n}} \times \frac{36 \, \text{g HCl}}{100 \, \text{g sol'n}} \times \frac{1 \, \text{mole HCl}}{36 \, \text{g HCl}}$$

$$= 15 \, \text{M}$$

Next, use the relationship $M_1 V_1 = M_2 V_2$

(15 M) (x liters) = (5 M) (9 liters) x = 3 liters

47. (B) Hydrocarbons that have double or triple bonds between carbon atoms are called unsaturated hydrocarbons; they are unsaturated in the sense that more hydrogen atoms can be added when H_2 reacts across the double or triple bonds. The only compound in the list with a double or triple bond is C_2H_2, $HC \equiv CH$.

48. (A) Esters have the functional group $\overset{\displaystyle O}{\underset{\displaystyle —C—O—}{\|}}$. The name of this ester is methyl acetate.

49. (E) Methyl acetate is synthesized from acetic acid CH_3COOH and methanol CH_3OH.

50. (D)

bond breaking ($\triangle H_1$)

$$\text{H—H} + \text{F—F} = 103 \, \text{kcal} \cdot \text{mole}^{-1} + 33 \, \text{kcal} \cdot \text{mole}^{-1}$$

$$= 136 \, \text{kcal} \cdot \text{mole}^{-1}$$

bond forming $(\triangle H_2) = 2$ H—F $= 2(-135$ kcal $\cdot$ mole$^{-1})$

$= -270$ kcal $\cdot$ mole^{-1}

$\triangle H° = \triangle H_1 + \triangle H_2 = 136$ kcal $\cdot$ mole$^{-1} + (-270$ kcal $\cdot$ mole$^{-1})$

$= -134$ kcal/mole

51. (C) 100 mL $\times$ (1 L/1000 mL) $\times$ (0.0333 mol/L) $\times$ (100 g/mol) = 0.333 g

52. (D) 1/8 of the original amount of C-14 means that three half-lives have elapsed (½, ¼, ⅛). If each half-life is 5600 years, then $5600 \times 3 = 16{,}800$ years.

53. (D) Multiply the fraction of each isotope by its atomic mass and add the products: $(0.20 \times 100) + (0.50 \times 102) + (0.30 \times 105) = 20 + 51 + 31.5 = 102.5$

54. (C)

$$\text{wavelength}\,(\lambda) = \frac{\text{speed of light}\,(c)}{\text{frequency}\,(v)} = \frac{3.00 \times 10^8\,\text{m} \cdot \text{s}^{-1}}{3.00 \times 10^{14}\,\text{s}^{-1}} \times \frac{10^9\,\text{nanometers}}{1\,\text{meter}} = 1.00 \times 10^3\,\text{nm}$$

55. (A) First, write the balanced equation:

$$Mg(OH)_2 + 2HCl \rightarrow MgCl_2 + 2H_2O$$

Begin by realizing that this is a limiting-reactant problem (you may run out of either $Mg(OH)_2$ or HCl). Both reactants must be considered in how much $MgCl_2$ they can produce. This problem can be done through the factor-label method.

$$\frac{116.6\,\text{g Mg(OH)}_2}{1} \times \frac{1\,\text{mol Mg(OH)}_2}{58.3\,\text{g Mg(OH)}_2} \times \frac{1\,\text{mol MgCl}_2}{1\,\text{mol Mg(OH)}_2} = 2\,\text{mol MgCl}_2$$

$$\frac{500\,\text{mL HCl}}{1} \times \frac{1\,\text{L HCl}}{1000\,\text{mL HCl}} \times \frac{2\,\text{mol HCl}}{1\,\text{L HCl}} \times \frac{1\,\text{mol MgCl}_2}{2\,\text{mol HCl}} = 0.500\,\text{mol MgCl}_2$$

The HCl is the limiting reactant because one can only make 0.500 moles of $MgCl_2$ with it leaving excess $Mg(OH)_2$.

$$\frac{0.500\,\text{mol MgCl}_2}{1} \times \frac{58.3\,\text{g MgCl}_2}{1\,\text{mol MgCl}_2} = 29.15\,\text{g MgCl}_2$$

56. (E) We know that we can only make 29.15 g $MgCl_2$ from the reactants provided. This problem can be solved using the factor-label method.

$$\frac{29.15\,\text{g MgCl}_2}{1} \times \frac{1\,\text{mol MgCl}_2}{95.3\,\text{g MgCl}_2} \times \frac{1\,\text{mol Mg(OH)}_2}{1\,\text{mol MgCl}_2} \times \frac{58.3\,\text{g Mg(OH)}_2}{1\,\text{mol Mg(OH)}_2}$$

$\approx$ 20 grams of $Mg(OH)_2$ consumed. If we started with ~117 g of $Mg(OH)_2$ and we used ~20 grams in the reaction, then ~97 grams would be left over.

Hint: **When the question says "approximately," and the answer choices are fairly far apart as in this example, it is fairly safe to round because you may not use a calculator for this section.**

The problem when rounded looks like

$$\frac{30\,\text{g MgCl}_2}{1} \times \frac{1\,\text{mol MgCl}_2}{90\,\text{g MgCl}_2} \times \frac{1\,\text{mol Mg(OH)}_2}{1\,\text{mol MgCl}_2} \times \frac{60\,\text{g Mg(OH)}_2}{1\,\text{mol Mg(OH)}_2}$$

57. (D)

$$\%\,\text{yield} = \frac{\text{actual yield}}{\text{theoretical yield}} \times 100\%$$

$$= \frac{14.57\,\text{g MgCl}_2}{29.15\,\text{g MgCl}_2} \times 100\% = 50.00\%$$

58. (E)

$$\frac{980.8 \text{ g } H_2SO_4}{1 \text{ L sol'n}} \times \frac{1 \text{ mole } H_2SO_4}{98.08 \text{ g } H_2SO_4} = 10.00 \text{ M}$$

$$\text{density} = \frac{\text{mass}}{\text{volume}} = \frac{1.4808 \text{ g sol'n}}{1 \text{ mL sol'n}} \times \frac{1000 \text{ mL sol'n}}{1 \text{ L sol'n}} = 1480.80 \text{ g / L}$$

Thus, 1 liter of solution weighs 1480.8 g and contains 980.8 grams of sulfuric acid. The mass of water is therefore, 1480.8 – 980.8 = 500.0 g (or 0.5000 kg)

$$\frac{10.00 \text{ moles } H_2SO_4}{0.5000 \text{ kg } H_2O} = 20.00 \text{ m}$$

59. (D) The solution contains 980.8 grams of H_2SO_4 in 1480.8 grams of solution.

$$\frac{980.8 \text{ g } H_2SO_4}{1480.8 \text{ g solution}} \times 100\% \approx 66\%$$

60. (C) This question relates to the Beer Lambert Law, $A = \varepsilon bc$ where A is absorbance, ε is molar absorbtivity, b is the path length, and c is concentration of the sample. This relationship is linear.

61. (C) A Brønsted-Lowry acid will donate one hydrogen ion, and its conjugate base will accept that one hydrogen ion. The difference between the Brønsted-Lowry acid and its conjugate base is only one hydrogen ion, H^+. H_3O^+ and OH^- cannot be a conjugate acid-base pair because H_3O^+ has two more hydrogen ions than OH^-.

62. (D) Let '1' represent the initial state and '2' represent the final state. The number of moles of gas remains constant in this problem. Use the combined form of the ideal gas law to solve for the pressure change.

50% decrease in the volume: $V_2 = V_1 - 0.50V_1 = 0.50V_1$

15% increase in the temperature: $T_2 = T_1 + 0.15T_1 = 1.15T_1$

$$P_2 = P_1 \times \frac{V_1}{V_2} \times \frac{n_2}{n_1} \times \frac{T_2}{T_1} = P_1 \times \frac{V_1}{0.50V_1} \times \frac{n_1}{n_1} \times \frac{1.15 \, T_1}{T_1}$$
$$P_2 = P_1 \times (2) \times (1) \times (1.15) = 2.30 \, P_1$$

Because $P_2 = P_1 + 1.30P_1$, the pressure has increased 130%.

63. (C)

$$V_{final} = (nRT) / P_{final}$$
$$= \frac{(1 \text{ mol})(0.0821 \text{ L} \cdot \text{atm} \cdot K^{-1} \cdot \text{mol}^{-1})(300K)}{(1.00 \text{ atm})} = 24.6 \text{ L}$$

64. (A) When considering a certain volume of gas, that gas can either do work on its environment by expanding (pushing outward, work is positive) or have work done on it by the environment by being compressed (pushed inward, work is negative).

$$V_{initial} = (nRT)/P_{initial}$$
$$= (1 \text{ mol})(0.0821 \text{ L} \cdot \text{atm} \cdot K^{-1} \cdot \text{mol}^{-1})(300K)/(2.00 \text{ atm}) = 12.3 \text{ L}$$

According to the First Law of Thermodynamics, $\triangle q = \triangle E + w$ where q is heat, E is the internal energy of the system, and w is work done by the system. If no heat is added to the system (heat was transferred to maintain the initial temperature of 300K), then

$$\triangle E = q + w = \triangle KE = 0$$

$$w = -P_{ex} \triangle V = -(1.00 \text{ atm})(12.3 \text{ L}) = -12.3 \text{ L} \cdot \text{atm}$$

Work was done by the system on the surroundings because the gas was compressed, therefore

$$q = \triangle E - w = 0 - (-12.3 \text{ L} \cdot \text{atm})$$

$$q = +12.3 \text{ L} \cdot \text{atm}$$

65. (A) The first step is to number the carbons of the longest carbon chain so that the double bond appears on the lowest numbered carbons.

$$CH_3-CH_2-CH_2-\underset{3}{\overset{\overset{\displaystyle CH_3}{\displaystyle |}}{C}}=\underset{2}{CH}-\underset{1}{CH_3}$$

$$\underset{6}{}\ \underset{5}{}\ \underset{4}{}$$

The longest carbon chain contains six carbons, so the compound is a hexene. There is one methyl group on carbon number 3. Combining all the information gives the name 3-methyl-2-hexene.

66. (E) Salts of phosphoric acid can be formed by replacing one, two, or three of the hydrogen ions. For example, KH_2PO_4, sodium dihydrogen phosphate, can be formed by reacting one mole of phosphoric acid with one mole of potassium hydroxide.

$$H_3PO_{4\,(aq)} + OH^-_{(aq)} \longleftrightarrow H_2PO_4^-{}_{(aq)} + H_2O_{(l)}$$

Salts containing the anion HPO_4^{2-} are weakly basic. The tendency of this ion to hydrolyze is greater than its tendency to dissociate.

$$HPO_4^{2-}{}_{(aq)} + H_2O_{(l)} \longleftrightarrow H_2PO_4^-{}_{(aq)} + OH^-_{(aq)}$$

$$K_b = K_w / K_a = 1.00 \times 10^{-14} / 6.2 \times 10^{-8} = 1.6 \times 10^{-7}$$

An amphiprotic salt has a pH that is the average of its pK_2 and pK_3.

Therefore, $pH = \dfrac{(-\log K_2) + (-\log K_3)}{2} = \dfrac{7.20 + 11.77}{2} = 9.49$

67. (C) These are fundamentally electrostatic interactions (ionic interactions, hydrogen bond, dipole-dipole interactions) or electrodynamic interactions (van der Waals/London forces). Electrostatic interactions are classically described by Coulomb's Law, the basic difference between them are the strength of their charge. Ionic interactions are the strongest with integer level charges. Hydrogen bonds have partial charges that are about an order of magnitude weaker. Dipole-dipole interactions also come from partial charges another order of magnitude weaker.

Bond Type	*Relative Strength*
Ionic bonds	1000
Hydrogen bonds	100
Dipole-dipole	10
London forces	1

68. (B) Because the pH of the buffer is 10.0, the pOH would be $14.0 - 10.0 = 4.0$. The pK_b must be within + or – 1 of the pOH of the buffer that must be made.

69. (A) Osmotic pressure of a solution is the force that has to be exerted to halt osmosis. Begin with the formula $\pi V = nRT$, where π represents the pressure measured in atmospheres. $T = 273 + 27°C = 300K$.

Rearranging the formula gives

$$MM = \frac{g \cdot R \cdot T}{\pi \cdot V} = \frac{(25.00\text{ g})(0.0821\text{ L} \cdot \text{atm} \cdot \text{mol}^{-1} \cdot \text{K}^{-1})(300\text{K})}{(0.0300\text{ atm})(0.821\text{ L})}$$

$$= 25{,}000\text{ g} \cdot \text{mol}^{-1}$$

70. (E) The weakest acid will have the lowest K_{a_1} and the strongest conjugate base.

71. (A) The reaction that produced the precipitate is $Pb^{2+}{}_{(aq)} + 2Cl^-_{(aq)} \rightarrow PbCl_{2(s)}$. Lead chloride is a slightly soluble salt, with a solubility of 10 g/L at 20°C. The solubility of $PbCl_2$ increases very rapidly as the temperature rises. At 100°C it has a solubility of 33.5 g/L. However, $PbCl_2$ precipitates very slowly, particularly when other ions that form insoluble chlorides are not present. $PbCl_2$ dissolves in excess chloride ion as a result of the formation of a complex ion, tetrachloroplumbate(II) ion:

$$PbCl_{2\,(s)} + 2Cl^-_{(aq)} \longleftrightarrow \left[PbCl_4\right]^{2-}{}_{(aq)}$$

72. (B) The generic formula for an alkene is C_xH_{2x}. The % carbon in C_2H_4 and $C_{30}H_{60}$ is 85.6%.

73. (C) For Choice A, $\triangle G° = -n\mathscr{F}E°$. For Choice B,

$\ln k = \dfrac{-E_a}{R}\left(\dfrac{1}{T}\right) + \ln A$. For Choice (D), $\Delta G° = -R \cdot T \cdot \ln K$.

For Choice E, $\log K = \dfrac{nE°}{0.0592}$

74. (C) The important flame colors are:

Na^+	yellow
K^+	violet
Li^+	crimson red
Sr^{2+}	bright red

75. (C) The important reagents used for confirming the presence of cations are as follows:

Species	Reagent	Color
Fe^{2+} or Fe^{3+}	$K_3Fe(CN)_6$	dark blue precipitate
Cu^{2+}	NH_3	dark blue solution
Ni^{2+}	dimethlyglyoxime	red precipitate
Pb^{2+}	$CrO_4{}^{2-}$	orange precipitate
Zn^{2+}	H_2S	white precipitate
$NH_4{}^+$	NaOH	ammonia odor

Section II: Free-Response Questions

Scoring Guidelines

One point deduction for mathematical error (maximum once per question)

One point deduction for error in significant figures (maximum once per question and the number of significant figures must be correct within +/− one digit)

Part A:

Question 1

1. Acetic acid, $HC_2H_3O_2$, which is represented as HA, has an acid ionization constant K_a of 1.74×10^{-5}.

(a) Calculate the hydrogen ion concentration, $[H^+]$, in a 0.50 molar solution of acetic acid.

$HA_{(aq)} \longleftrightarrow H^+_{(aq)} + A^-_{(aq)}$ $K_a = \dfrac{[H^+][A^-]}{[HA]}$	1 point for properly setting up K_a.
Let x equal the amount of H^+ that ionizes from HA. Because the molar ratio of $[H^+] : [A^-]$ is 1:1, $[A^-]$ also equals x, and we can approximate $0.50 - x$ as 0.50 (5% rule). $1.74 \times 10^{-5} = \dfrac{x^2}{0.50}$ Solve for x: $x^2 = (1.74 \times 10^{-5})(0.50)$ $x^2 = 8.7 \times 10^{-6}$ $x = 2.9 \times 10^{-3}\ M = [H^+]$	1 point for correct $[H^+]$.

(b) Calculate the pH and pOH of the 0.50 molar solution.

$pH = -\log[H^+] = -\log(2.9 \times 10^{-3}) = 2.54$ $pH + pOH = 14$ $pOH = 14.0 - 2.47 = 11.46$	1 point for correct pH and 1 point for correct pOH.

(c) What percent of the acetic acid molecules do NOT ionize?

$\% = \dfrac{part}{whole} \times 100\% = \dfrac{[H^+]}{[HA]} \times 100\%$ $= \dfrac{2.9 \times 10^{-3}}{0.50} \times 100\% = 0.58\%$ $= 100\% - 0.58\% = 99.42\%$	1 point for correct percentage.

(d) A buffer solution is designed to have a pH of 6.50. What is the [HA] : [A⁻] ratio in this system?

$pH = pK_a + \log \dfrac{[\text{base}]}{[\text{acid}]}$	1 point for use of the Henderson-Hasselbalch equation.
$-\log(1.74 \times 10^{-5}) = 4.76$ $pK_a = -\log K_a = 4.76$ $6.50 = 4.76 + \log \dfrac{[A^-]}{[HA]}$ $\log \dfrac{[A^-]}{[HA]} = 6.50 - 4.76 = 1.74$ $\dfrac{[A^-]}{[HA]} = 5.5 \times 10^1$ [HA] / [A⁻] = 0.018	1 point for correct [HA] : [A⁻] ratio.

(e) 0.500 liter of a new buffer is made using sodium acetate. The concentration of sodium acetate in this new buffer is 0.35 M. The acetic acid concentration is 0.50 M. Finally, 1.5 grams of LiOH is added to the solution. Calculate the pH of this new buffer.

$0.35\ M = [NaC_2H_3O_2] \rightarrow Na^+ + C_2H_3O_2^-$ [HA] = 0.50 M	
1.5 g LiOH added to solution. $\dfrac{1.5\ \text{g LiOH}}{1} \times \dfrac{1\ \text{mole LiOH}}{23.95\ \text{g LiOH}} = 0.063\ \text{mole LiOH}$	1 point for determining the correct number of moles of LiOH.
pH = ? $HA + OH^- \rightarrow A^- + H_2O$	

Species	Initial Concentration	Final Concentration	
HA	0.50 M	$0.50 - \dfrac{0.063}{0.500} = 0.374\ M$	1 point for correctly setting up initial and final concentrations of HA and A⁻.
A⁻	0.35 M	$0.35 + \dfrac{0.063}{0.500} = 0.476\ M$	

$K_a = \dfrac{[H^+][A^-]}{HA} = 1.74 \times 10^{-5} = \dfrac{[H^+][0.476]}{[0.374]}$ $[H^+] = 1.37 \times 10^{-5}\ M$ $pH = -\log [H^+] = -\log (1.37 \times 10^{-5}) = 4.86$	1 point for correctly setting up the expression for K_a. 1 point for correct pH.

Question 2

2. Methyl alcohol oxidizes to produce methanoic (formic) acid and water according to the following reaction and structural diagram:

$$CH_3OH_{(aq)} + O_{2(g)} \rightarrow HCOOH_{(aq)} + H_2O_{(l)}$$

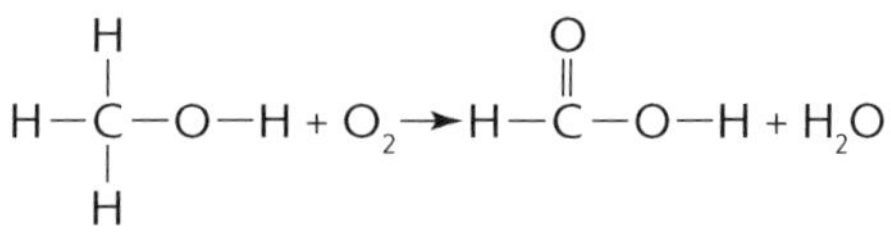

Given the following data:

Substance	$\triangle H_f^\circ$ (kJ/mol)	$S^\circ (J \cdot K^{-1} \cdot mole^{-1})$
$CH_3OH_{(aq)}$	−238.6	129
$O_{2(g)}$	0	205.0
$HCOOH_{(aq)}$	−409	127.0
$H_2O_{(l)}$	−285.84	69.94

(a) Calculate $\triangle H^\circ$ for the oxidation of methyl alcohol.

$\triangle H^\circ = \Sigma \triangle H_f^\circ{}_{products} - \Sigma \triangle H_f^\circ{}_{reactants}$ $= (\triangle H_f^\circ HCOOH + \triangle H_f^\circ H_2O) - (\triangle H_f^\circ CH_3OH)$ $= [(-409 \text{ kJ/mole}) + (-285.84 \text{ kJ/mole})] - (-238.6 \text{ kJ/mole})$ $= -456 \text{ kJ/mole}$	1 point for correct setup and answer.

(b) Calculate $\triangle S^\circ$ for the oxidation of methyl alcohol.

$\triangle S^\circ = \Sigma S^\circ{}_{products} - \Sigma S^\circ{}_{reactants}$ $= (S^\circ HCOOH + S^\circ H_2O) - (S^\circ CH_3OH + S^\circ O_2)$ $= (127.0 \text{ J/(K} \cdot \text{mole)} + 69.94 \text{ J/(K} \cdot \text{mole)}) -$ $\quad (129 \text{ J/(K} \cdot \text{mole)} + 205.0 \text{ J/(K} \cdot \text{mole)})$ $= -137 \text{ J} \cdot K^{-1} \cdot \text{mole}^{-1}$	1 point for correct setup and answer.

(c) Is the reaction spontaneous at 25°C? Explain your reasoning.

The reaction is spontaneous. Spontaneity can be confirmed by calculating the value of $\triangle G^\circ$. (If $\triangle G^\circ$ is negative, the reaction is spontaneous.) $\triangle G^\circ = \triangle H^\circ - T\triangle S^\circ$ $= -456 \text{ kJ/mole} - 298 \text{ K} (-0.137 \text{ kJ/mole} \cdot \text{K})$ $= -415 \text{ kJ/mole}$	1 point for correct setup and answer.

    (i)   If the temperature were increased to 100°C, would the reaction be spontaneous?

$\triangle G° = \triangle H° - T\triangle S°$ $T = 100°C + 273 = 373K$ $= -456$ kJ/mole $- 373\cancel{K}$ $(-0.137$ kJ/mole $\cdot \cancel{K})$ $= -405$ kJ/mole	1 point for supporting evidence to base conclusion on.
Because $\triangle G°$ is still negative, the reaction remains spontaneous.	1 point for correct conclusion.

    (d)   The heat of fusion of methanoic acid is 12.71 kJ/mole, and its freezing point is 8.3°C. Calculate $\triangle S°$ for the reaction.

$$HCOOH_{(l)} \rightarrow HCOOH_{(s)}$$

Because the freezing point and melting point of HCOOH are the same temperature, a state of equilibrium exists. Therefore, $\triangle G = 0$. $\triangle G = \triangle H - T\triangle S$ $T = 8.3°C + 273 = 281.3K$ Melting is an exothermic process . . . so $\triangle H$ is negative. $0 = -12.71$ kJ/mole $- 281.3K$ $(\triangle S)$ $\triangle S = \dfrac{-12.71\,kJ\,/\,mole}{281.3\,K}$ $= -0.04518$ kJ/(mole $\cdot$ K) $= -45.18$ J/(mole $\cdot$ K)	1 point for correct setup and calculation of $\triangle S°$.

    (e)   Calculate the standard molar entropy of $HCOOH_{(s)}$.

        (i)   Is the magnitude of $S°$ for $HCOOH_{(s)}$ in agreement with the magnitude of $S°$ for $HCOOH_{(l)}$? ($S°$ for $HCOOH_{(l)} = 109.1$ J $\cdot$ mole$^{-1} \cdot$ K^{-1}). Explain your reasoning.

$HCOOH_{(l)} \longleftrightarrow HCOOH_{(s)}$ $\triangle S° = \triangle S°_{products} - \triangle S°_{reactants}$ $= S°_{HCOOH_{(s)}} - S°_{HCOOH_{(l)}}$ -45.18 J/(mole $\cdot$ K) $= S°_{HCOOH_{(s)}} - 109.1$ J/(mole $\cdot$ K) $S°_{HCOOH_{(s)}} = 63.9$ J/(mole $\cdot$ K)	1 point for correct value for $S°$.
The magnitude of $S°_{HCOOH_{(s)}}$ is in agreement with the magnitude of $S°_{HCCO_{(l)}}$ because the greater the value of $S°$, the greater the disorder; the liquid phase has higher entropy than the solid phase.	1 point for correct conclusion.

(f) Calculate $\triangle G^\circ$ for the ionization of methanoic acid at 25°C. K_a of methanoic acid $= 1.9 \times 10^{-4}$.

$\triangle G^\circ = -2.303\ R \cdot T \log K_a$ $\log 1.9 \times 10^{-4} = -3.72$ $T = 25°C + 273 = 298K$ $\triangle G^\circ = -2.303\ (8.314\ J/K) \cdot 298K\ (-3.72)$ $\triangle G^\circ = 2.1 \times 10^4\ J = 21\ kJ$	1 point for correct setup and calculation of $\triangle G^\circ$.

Question 3

A student constructed a coffee cup calorimeter in the lab as shown in the following diagram:

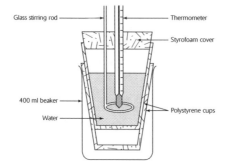

The student first determined the heat capacity of the calorimeter by placing 50.0 mL of room temperature distilled water in the calorimeter and determined the temperature of the water to be 23.0°C. He then added 50.0 mL of distilled water measured at 61.0°C to the calorimeter and recorded the temperature of the mixture every 30 seconds. A graph was drawn of the results and is shown below:

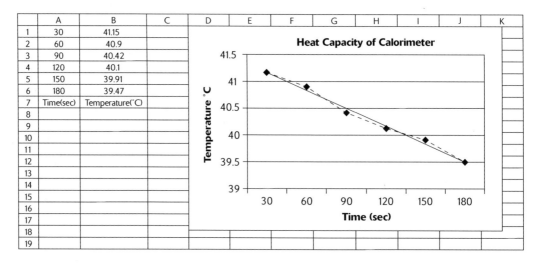

	A	B	C	D	E	F	G	H	I	J	K
1	30	41.15									
2	60	40.9									
3	90	40.42									
4	120	40.1									
5	150	39.91									
6	180	39.47									
7	Time(sec)	Temperature(°C)									
8											
9											
10											
11											
12											
13											
14											
15											
16											
17											
18											
19											

(a) Determine the heat lost by the water (q_{water}). The density of the water was determined to be $1.00 \text{ g} \cdot \text{mL}^{-1}$. The specific heat of water is $4.18 \text{ J/g} \cdot °C$.

Extrapolating the regression line to the Y axis (0 seconds) gives a temperature of 41.4°C at the moment the room temperature and warm water were mixed. Average temperature of room temperature and warm water = $\frac{23.0°C + 61.0°C}{2} = 42.0°C$ Vol. of H_2O_{total} = 50.0 mL + 50.0 mL = 100.0 mL total mass of $H_2O = \frac{100.0 \text{ mL } H_2O}{1} \times \frac{1.00 \text{ g}}{\text{mL}}$ = 100.0 grams q_{H_2O} = (mass H_2O) · (specific heat of H_2O) · ($T_{mix} - T_{avg}$) = (100.0 g) · (4.18 J/g · °C) · (41.4°C − 42.0°C)	1 point for proper setup.
= $-2.5 \times 10_2$ J (extra significant figure carried)	1 point for correct answer.

(b) Determine the heat gained by the calorimeter ($q_{calorimeter}$).

Heat gained by calorimeter = $-q_{water}$ = 2.5×10^2 J (extra significant figure carried)	1 point for correct answer.

(c) Determine the calorimeter constant (heat capacity) of the coffee cup calorimeter ($C_{calorimter}$).

$C_{calorimeter} = \dfrac{q_{calorimeter}}{(T_{mix} - T_{initial})}$ $= \dfrac{2.5 \times 10^2 \text{ J}}{(41.4°C - 23.0°C)} = 14 \text{ J} \cdot °C^{-1}$	1 point for correct answer.

The student then measured temperature changes that occurred when 50.0 mL of 2.00 M HCl at 23.0°C was added to 50.0 mL of 2.00 M NaOH at 23.0°C using the same calorimeter. The highest temperature obtained after mixing the two solutions was 35.6°C. The final density of the solution was $1.00 \text{ g} \cdot \text{mL}^{-1}$.

(d) Write the net ionic equation for the reaction that occurred.

$H^+_{(aq)} + OH^-_{(aq)} \rightarrow H_2O_{(l)}$	1 point for correct reaction.

(e) Determine the molar heat of reaction (q_{rxn}).

$q_{rxn} = \dfrac{-\left[(mass_{sol'n}) \times (specific\ heat_{sol'n}) \times (\Delta T_{sol'n}) + (C_{calorimeter} \times \Delta T_{sol'n})\right]}{volume_{sol'n} \times molarity}$	
(50.0mL + 50.0mL) = 100.0 mL total solution volume. 100.0 mL × (1.00 g/mL) = 100.0 g total solution mass.	
$\triangle T_{sol'n}$ = 35.6°C − 23.0°C = 12.6°C	1 point for proper setup with answer.
$= \dfrac{-\left[100.0 \text{ g sol'n} \times 4.18 \text{ J/g} \cdot °C \times (35.6°C - 23.0°C)\right] + (14 \text{ J/}°C \times 12.6°C)}{0.0500 \text{ L} \times 2.0 \text{ mole/L}}$	
$= \dfrac{-5.4 \times 10^3 \text{ J}}{0.0500 \text{ L} \times 2.0 \text{ mol/L}} = -5.4 \times 10^4 \text{ J/mol} = -54 \text{ kJ/mol}$	

The student then measured temperature changes that occurred when 50.0 mL of 2.00 M NH_4Cl at 22.9°C was added to 50.0 mL of 2.00 M NaOH at 22.9°C using the same calorimeter. The highest temperature obtained after mixing the two solutions was 24.1°C. The final density of the solution was $1.00 \text{ g} \cdot \text{mL}^{-1}$.

(f) Write the net ionic equation for the reaction that occurred.

$NH_4^+{}_{(aq)} + OH^-{}_{(aq)} \rightarrow NH_{3(aq)} + H_2O_{(l)}$	1 point for correct reaction.

(g) Determine the molar heat of reaction (q_{rxn}).

$q_{rxn} = \dfrac{-\left[(mass_{sol'n}) \times (specific\ heat_{sol'n}) \times (\Delta T_{sol'n}) + (C_{calorimeter} \times \Delta T_{sol'n})\right]}{volume_{sol'n} \times molarity}$ (50.0mL + 50.0mL) = 100.0 mL total solution volume. 100.0 mL · (1.00 g/mL) = 100.0 g total solution mass. $\Delta T_{sol'n} = 24.1°C - 22.9°C = 1.2°C$ $q_{rxn} = \dfrac{-\left[100 \text{ g sol'n} \times 4.18 \text{ J}/(g \cdot °C) \times (24.1°C - 22.9°C)\right] + (14 \text{ J}/°C \times 1.2°C)}{0.0500 \text{ L} \times 2.0 \text{ mole}/\text{L}}$ $= \dfrac{-5.2 \times 10^2 \text{ J}}{0.0500 \times 2.0 \text{ mol}} = -5.2 \times 10^3 \text{ J}/\text{mol} = -5.2 \text{ kJ}/\text{mol}$	1 point for proper setup with correct answer.

(h) Calculate the enthalpy change per mole for the reaction that would occur using the same calorimeter if one were to mix ammonia with hydrochloric acid.

$H^+{}_{(aq)} + OH^-{}_{(aq)} \rightarrow H_2O_{(l)}$ $\Delta H = -54 \text{ kJ} \cdot \text{mol}^{-1}$ $NH_{3(aq)} + H_2O_{(l)} \rightarrow NH_4^+{}_{(aq)} + OH^-{}_{(aq)}$ $\Delta H = +5.2 \text{ kJ} \cdot \text{mol}^{-1}$ $\overline{NH_{(aq)} + H^+{}_{(aq)} \rightarrow NH_4^+{}_{(aq)}}$ $\Delta H = -49 \text{ kJ} \cdot \text{mol}^{-1}$	1 point for proper setup.
*Note the change in sign for enthalpy in the second equation since the reaction was reversed.	1 point for correct answer.

Part B:

Question 4

(For a complete list of reaction types that you will encounter, refer to *CliffsAP Chemistry,* 3rd Edition.)

(a) A piece of solid magnesium, which is ignited, is added to water.

$Mg + H_2O \rightarrow MgO + H_2$	1 point for reactant(s), 2 points for product(s).
	Single displacement reaction where magnesium is displacing hydrogen in the water molecule.

(b) Methanol is burned completely in air.

$CH_3OH + O_2 \rightarrow CO_2 + H_2O$	1 point for reactant(s), 2 points for product(s).
	The products of complete combustion of hydrocarbons are carbon dioxide and water.

(c) Sulfur trioxide gas is bubbled through water.

$SO_3 + H_2O \rightarrow H^+ + SO_4^{2-}$	1 point for reactant(s), 2 points for product(s).
	Nonmetallic oxide + H_2O → acid.

(d) Iron(III) oxide is added to hydrochloric acid.

$Fe_2O_3 + H^+ \rightarrow Fe^{3+} + H_2O$	1 point for reactant(s), 2 points for product(s).
	Metallic oxide + acid → salt + water
	Cl^- is a spectator ion.

(e) Equal volumes of 0.5 M sulfuric acid and 0.5 M sodium hydroxide are mixed.

$H^+ + OH^- \rightarrow H_2O$	1 point for reactant(s), 2 points for product(s).
	Neutralization.
	Na^+ and SO_4^{2-} are spectator ions.

(f) Acetic acid is added to a solution of ammonia.

$HC_2H_3O_2 + NH_3 \rightarrow C_2H_3O_2^- + NH_4^+$	1 point for reactant(s), 2 points for product(s).
	Weak acid + weak base → conjugate base + conjugate acid

(g) Nitrous acid is added to sodium hydroxide.

$HNO_2 + OH^- \rightarrow H_2O + NO_2^-$	1 point for reactant(s), 2 points for product(s).
	Weak acid + strong base $\rightarrow$ water + conjugate base

(h) Ethanol is heated in the presence of sulfuric acid.

$C_2H_5OH \xrightarrow{\;H^+\;} C_2H_5-O-C_2H_5$	1 point for reactant(s), 2 points for product(s).
	Organic elimination (formation of an ether from an alcohol in the presence of an acid).

Question 5

5. As one moves down the halogen column, one notices that the boiling point increases. However, when examining the alkali metal family, one discovers that the melting point decreases as one moves down the column.

(a) Account for the increase in boiling point of the halogens as one moves down the column.

Bonding found within halogen molecule is covalent—formed as a result of sharing electrons.	
Forces found between halogen molecules are van der Waals forces, which are due to temporarily induced dipoles caused by polarization of electron clouds.	
Moving down the column, one would expect larger electron clouds due to higher energy levels being filled as well as greater atomic numbers and hence a greater number of electrons.	1 point for each item. Two items are required.
Moving down the halogen family, shielding effect and greater distance from nucleus would cause easier polarization of electron cloud.	
Therefore, greater polarization of electron cloud would cause greater attractive force (van der Waals force), resulting in higher boiling points.	
Furthermore, one must consider the effect of the molecular weight on the B.P. As the individual molecules become more and more massive, they need higher and higher temperatures to give them enough kinetic energy and velocity to escape from the surface.	

(b) Account for the decrease in melting point of the alkali metals as one moves down the column.

Alkali metal family are all metals. Metals have low electronegativity. and low ionization energy.	
Metals exist in definite crystal arrangements—cations surrounded by a 'sea of electrons'.	
As one moves down the alkali metal column, the electron cloud would be expected to get larger due to higher energy levels being filled.	
As one moves down the alkali metal family, the charge density would be expected to decrease due to significantly larger volume and more shielding.	1 point for each item. 2 items are required.
As a result, as one moves down the alkali metal family, one would expect the attractive forces holding the crystal structure together to decrease.	
Trends in boiling and melting points would be expected to be comparable because they both are functions of the strength of intermolecular attractive forces.	

(c) Rank Cs, Li, KCl, I_2, and F_2 in order of decreasing melting point, and explain your reasoning.

#1 KCl—highest melting point. Ionic bond present—formed by the transfer of electrons.	1 point for correct order of all 5 items.
#2 Li—alkali metal. Metallic bonds present (cations, mobile electrons). Low-density metal.	
#3 I_2—solid at room temperature. Covalent bond present. Nonpolar.	1 point for each item if reasoning is correct regardless if order was wrong.
#4 Cs—liquid at near room temperature. Metallic bonds present; however, due to low charge density as explained above, attractive forces are weak.	
#5 F_2—gas at room temperature. Covalent bonds present. One would expect a smaller electron cloud than in I_2 due to reasons stated above.	

Question 6

6. (a) Write the ground-state electron configuration for the phosphorus atom.

$1s^2 2s^2 2p^6 3s^2 3p^3$	1 point for correct answer.

(b) Write the four quantum numbers that describe all the valence electrons in the phosphorus atom.

Electron #	n	l	m_l	m_s
11	3	0	0	$+\frac{1}{2}$
12	3	0	0	$-\frac{1}{2}$
13	3	1	+1	$+\frac{1}{2}$
14	3	1	0	$+\frac{1}{2}$
15	3	1	−1	$+\frac{1}{2}$

1 point if only one set of quantum numbers are correct.

2 points if only two sets of quantum numbers are totally correct.

3 points if only three sets of quantum numbers are correct.

4 points if all quantum numbers are correct.

4 points maximum.

(c) Explain whether phosphorus atom, in its ground state, is paramagnetic or diamagnetic.

Phosphorus is paramagnetic because a paramagnetic atom is defined as having magnetic properties caused by unpaired electrons. The unpaired electrons are found in the $3p$ orbitals, each of which is half-filled.	1 point for answer that includes the concept of unpaired electrons.

(d) Phosphorus can be found in such diverse compounds as PCl_3, PCl_5, PCl_4^-, PCl_6^-, and P_4. How can phosphorus, in its ground state, bond in so many different arrangements? Be specific in terms of hybridization, type of bonding, and geometry.

	PCl_3	**PCl_5**	**PCl_4^-**	**PCl_6^-**	**P_4**
Type of Bond	covalent	covalent	covalent	covalent	covalent
Lewis Structure					
Geometry	triangular pyramidal	triangular bipyramidal	see-saw (distorted tetrahedral)	octahedral	tetrahedral
Hybridization	sp^3	$sp^3 d$	$sp^3 d$	$sp^3 d^2$	sp^3

1 point if only one of the species is totally correct. 2 points if only two of the species are totally correct. 3 points if only three of the species are totally correct. 4 points if all species are totally correct. 4 points maximum.

Question 7

7. (a) Draw Lewis structures for

(i) BF_3

	1 point for correct diagram.

(ii) $TiCl_3$

:Ċl—Ṫi—Ċl: :Ċl:	1 point for correct diagram.

(b) Determine the molecular geometries including all idealized bond angles for ClNO where the N atom is in the center of the molecule.

Because the central N atom is surrounded by three electron pairs, two bond pairs and one lone pair, the geometry is bent or V-shaped with the Cl–N–O angle approximately 120°.	1 point for correct geometry. 1 point for correct bond angle.

(c) Classify XeF_4 as polar or nonpolar and explain why.

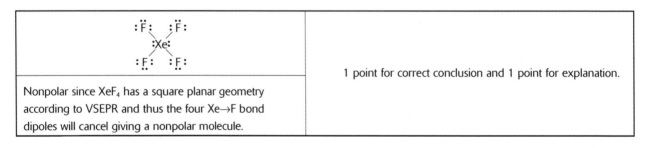 Nonpolar since XeF_4 has a square planar geometry according to VSEPR and thus the four Xe→F bond dipoles will cancel giving a nonpolar molecule.	1 point for correct conclusion and 1 point for explanation.

(d) Describe the orbital hybridization scheme used by the central atom in its sigma bonding for the following molecules. How many pi bonds are contained in each molecule?

(i) XeF_4

sp^3d^2 hybrid orbitals, 0 pi bonds F-••-F Xe F-••-F	1 point for correct hybridization. 1 point for correct number of pi bonds.

(ii) XeF_2

sp^3d hybrid orbitals, 0 pi bonds 	1 point for correct hybridization. 1 point for correct number of pi bonds.

Question 8

8. (a) Explain the Arrhenius theory of acids and bases.

Arrhenius acid—any substance that ionizes when it dissolves in water to give the H^+ ion. Arrhenius base—any substance that ionizes when it dissolves in water to give the OH^- ion.	1 point for correct answer.

(i) Give an example of either an Arrhenius acid or base dissociating in water.

$HCl_{(aq)} \rightarrow H^+_{(aq)} + Cl^-_{(aq)}$	1 point for an appropriate example.

(b) Explain the Brønsted-Lowry theory of acids and bases.

Brønsted acid—any substance that can donate a proton or H^+ ion to a base. Brønsted base—any substance that can accept a proton or H^+ ion from an acid.	1 point for correct answer.

(i) Give an example of either a Brønsted-Lowry acid or base dissociating in water.

$HCl + H_2O \longleftrightarrow H_3O^+ + Cl^-$ HCl is acting as the acid. Cl^- is the conjugate base. H_2O is acting as the base. H_3O^+ is the conjugate acid.	1 point for an appropriate example.

(c) Describe two advantages of the Brønsted-Lowry theory over the Arrhenius theory.

■ Acids and bases can be ions or neutral molecules. ■ Acids and bases can be any molecule with at least one pair of nonbonding electrons. ■ It explains the role of water in acid-base reactions; H_2O accepts H^+ ions from acids to form H_3O^+ ions. ■ It can be applied to solutions with solvents other than water and even in reactions that occur in the gas or solid phases. ■ It relates acids and bases to each other with conjugate acid-base pairs and can explain their relative strengths. ■ It can explain the relative strengths of pairs of acids or pairs of bases.	1 point for each advantage. Maximum 2 points.

(d) Explain the Lewis theory of acids and bases.

Lewis acid—any substance that can accept a pair of nonbonding electrons. Lewis base—any substance that can donate a pair of nonbonding electrons.	1 point for correct answer.

  (i) Give an example of either a Lewis acid or Lewis base.

$Al^{3+} + 6H_2O \longrightarrow Al(H_2O)_6^{3+}$ Al^{3+} acts as an acid, accepting an electron pair from water which acts as the base (electron pair donor).	1 point for an appropriate example.

(e) Discuss how indicators are used in the titration of acids and bases. What factors are used in selecting an appropriate indicator?

Chemical indicators indicate the end point of a titration by changing color. Indicators are either weak acids or weak bases. Indicators change color when the pH of the solution is equal to the pK_a of the indicator. To select the proper indicator, the pH at which the indicator changes color should be equal to the pH of the solution being tested at its equivalence point.	1 point for correct answer on how indicators are used in titration. 1 point for a correct factor in selecting an appropriate indicator.

Free-Response Answer Sheet

Free-Response Answer Sheet

Free-Response Answer Sheet

Free-Response Answer Sheet

Free-Response Answer Sheet

Free-Response Answer Sheet

Free-Response Answer Sheet

Free-Response Answer Sheet

CUT HERE

Free-Response Answer Sheet

Free-Response Answer Sheet

Free-Response Answer Sheet

Free-Response Answer Sheet

Free-Response Answer Sheet

Free-Response Answer Sheet

Free-Response Answer Sheet

Free-Response Answer Sheet

Free-Response Answer Sheet

Free-Response Answer Sheet